THE PHOTOGRAPHER'S TRAVEL GUIDE

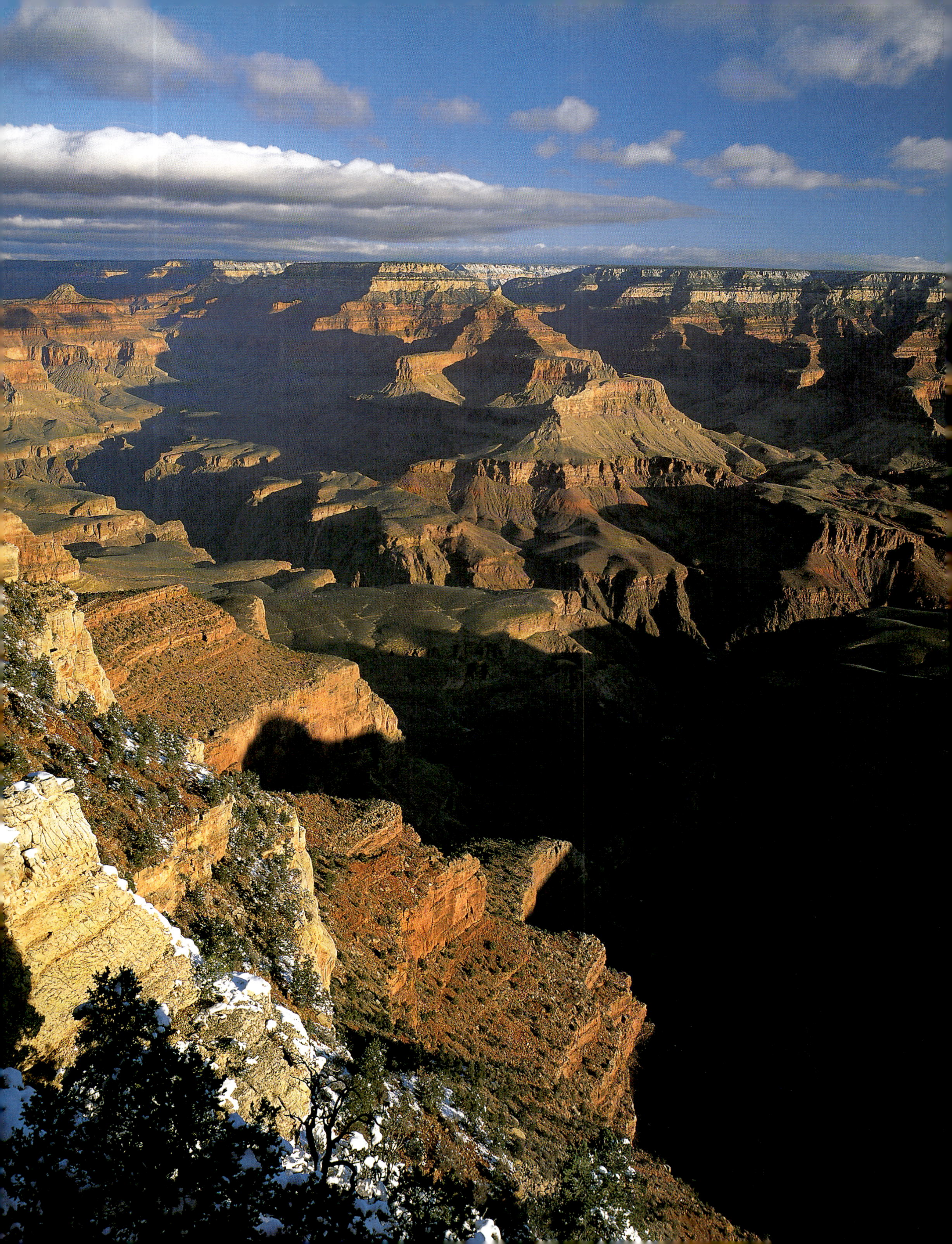

THE PHOTOGRAPHER'S travel guide

WILLIAM MANNING

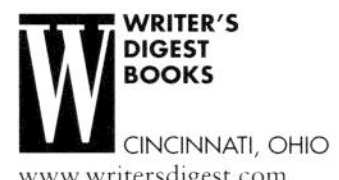

CINCINNATI, OHIO
www.writersdigest.com

DEDICATION

Carla, Luke and Matthew, at home and on the road, you make me smile.

 Published by Writer's Digest Books, an imprint of F&W Publications, Inc., 4700 East Galbraith Road, Cincinnati, Ohio, 45236. First edition.

Visit our Web site at www.writersdigest.com for more information and resources for writers.

Other fine Writer's Digest Books are available from your local bookstore or direct from the publisher.

07 06 05 04 03 5 4 3 2 1

Cataloging-in-Publication data is available from the Library of Congress at <http://catalog.loc.gov>.

Edited by Brad Crawford
Designed by Brian Roeth
Interior layout by Cheryl VanDeMotter
Production coordinated by Sara Dumford

ABOUT THE AUTHOR

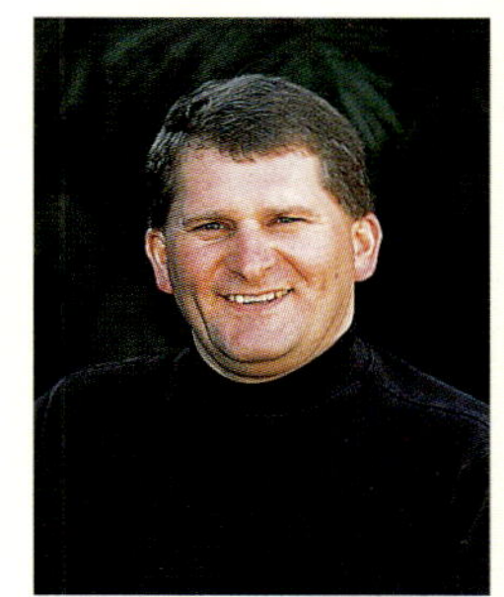

William Manning is a photographer, writer, lecturer and a photographic tour and workshop leader. William's career began in 1992 when he started Nature's Light, a photographic tour and workshop company. The early years of Nature's Light focused on journeys into America's natural landscape and later stretched beyond those borders into historic and unique travel destinations around the globe. William's photography has been published by numerous national publications and advertising clients, including *National Geographic*, *Readers's Digest*, American Airlines, Rand McNally & Co., *ESPN Magazine*, *Newsweek*, *Time*, *Outdoor Photographer*, Avon Cosmetics, Coldwater Creek and many others. William lives in Cincinnati, Ohio, with his wife, Carla, and their two sons, Luke and Matthew. Anyone interested in traveling with William or organizations wishing to schedule a photographic workshop or speaking engagement can obtain information from his Web site at www.natureslight.com or e-mail him at william@natureslight.com.

ACKNOWLEDGMENTS

Along any path of success, there are obstacles and people who help defeat those obstacles. No person succeeds without the helping hand of others. Like many others, I had my share of friends who helped me along my journey, both in the beginning and today. The following are a few of the many I owe thanks for their helping hands and words of encouragement. My best friend and wife, Carla, is my guiding light. No part of my career would have been possible without her. My very good friend Dave Vermette was one of the few people in those early years who always had a positive word of encouragement and, in ways he has no idea, kept me focused. Many of the photography friends I met over the years have been instrumental in helping me succeed in the photography business and in writing this book. To my very good friend Tony Sweet, I owe many thanks as we began our journeys together with foggy glasses photographing a dismal display of flowers at a local garden and still continue our growth together today. Adam Jones, one of the most talented photographers I know and my very good traveling partner and special friend, has helped me enormously with everything I know about photography. Ian Adams, who is one of the best-prepared photographers I know, has helped me over the years see the importance of knowing everything I can about the locations I shoot. His words to me, "Don't focus on what you can't shoot, but rather on what you can shoot," speak volumes about preparation. Brad Crawford, who was assigned the monstrous task of editing my writing, simplified my lengthy explanations into coherent sentences. I owe you many thanks for helping me to make sense of all those written words. And to the many folks who have traveled with me over the years, without you I don't know if I would ever had the many opportunities to photograph the great places we have traveled together. I have and always will enjoy your company. Many of you have become not only my friends but also my inspiration.

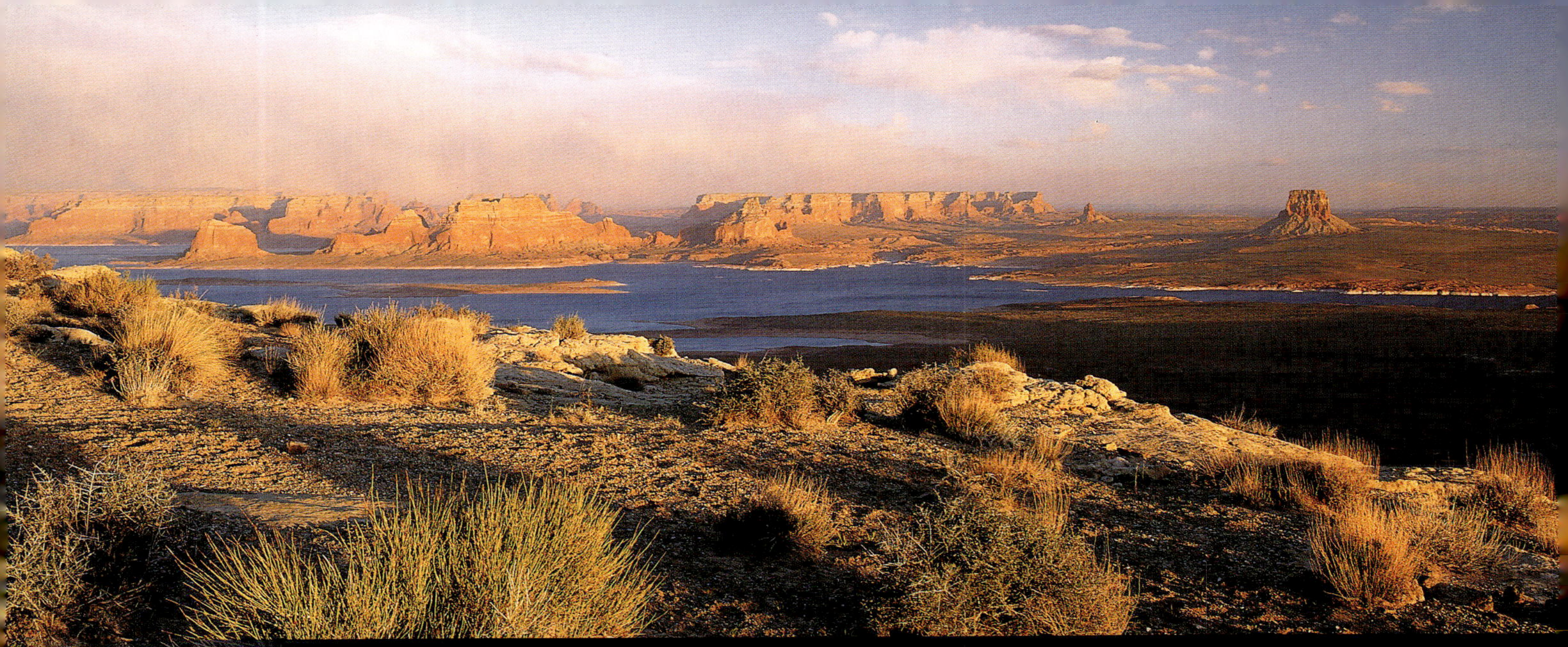

TABLE OF CONTENTS

INTRODUCTION
where to go?
page 10

CHAPTER 1
Planning and Equipment . . . *12*

Don't rely only on published photos to determine where you shoot. Scout locations through networking, bookstores, Web searches and on-location research. Plus, find tools to improve your photography and ways to make it more creative.

CHAPTER 2
Washington, DC . . . *26*

Our nation's capital is probably the last place you'd consider setting up a tripod, but it's also one of the most requested cities for stock sales. With a wide array of architectural styles and monuments at every turn, you'll come away with fantastic photos even as you shoot around the teeming masses.

CHAPTER 3
Acadia National Park & Nova Scotia . . . *34*

You can still explore the centuries-old interplay between man and nature in the old harbor towns of the Northeast coast. As much of the Maine coast gets developed, Acadia reveals it as it once was, and Nova Sotia offers additional respite. Come for both the coast and the interior—foggy forests, lichen-covered rocks and craggy hillsides.

CHAPTER 4
Great Smoky Mountains National Park . . . *46*

If you can brave the crowds to get into the park, the Smokies offer some of the best and most challenging photography on the continent. The forests here hold more than 1,500 species of flowering plants, sixty-five species of mammals and one hundred species of birds, as well as rushing streams and the best fall color around.

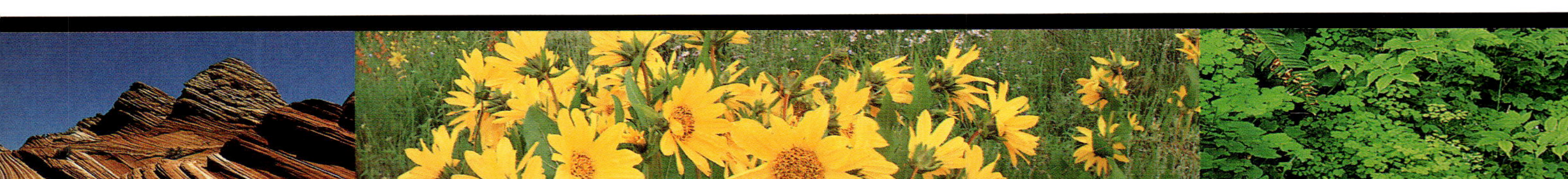

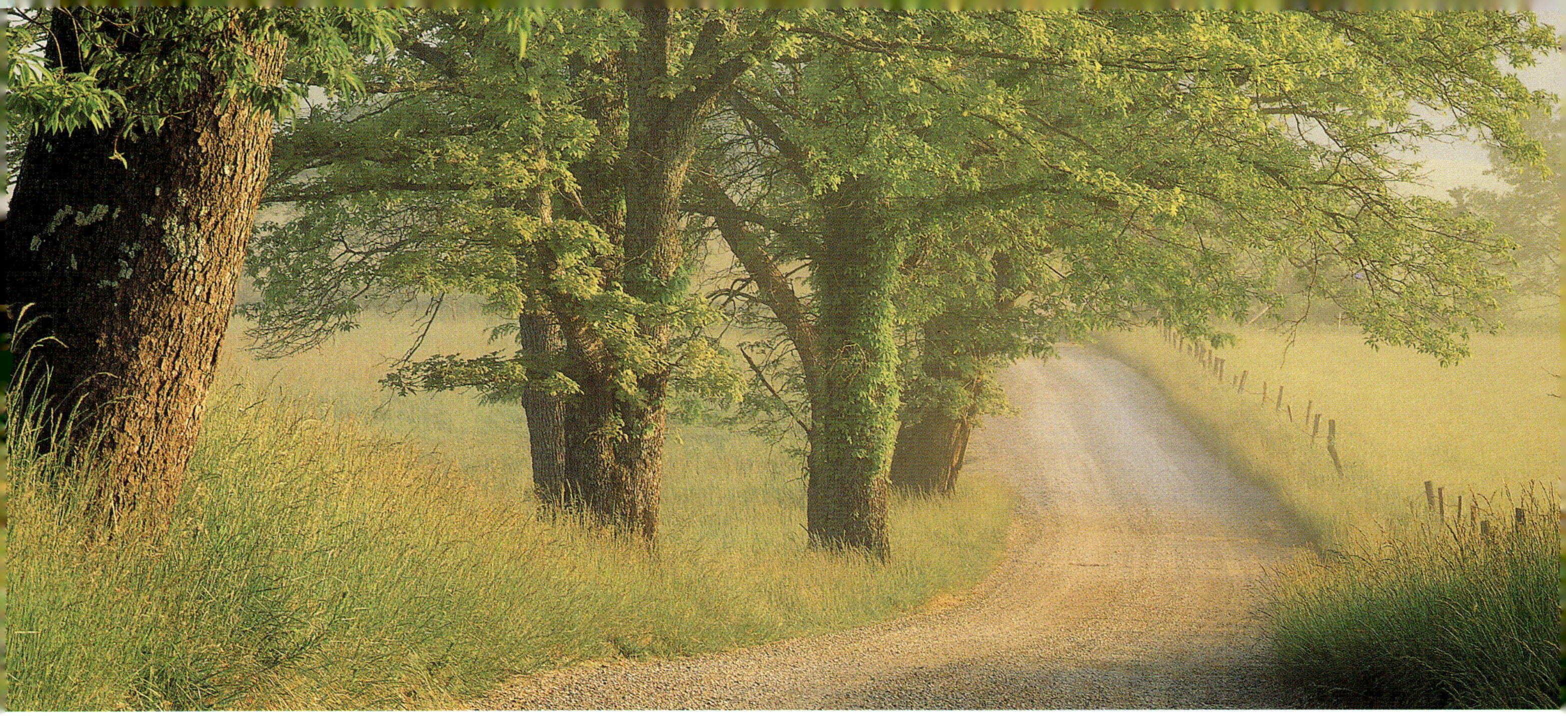

CHAPTER 5

Canaan Valley, West Virginia . . . 55

The Canaan Valley's wildness belies its proximity to civilization. You won't find vast unspoiled forests, but you will find breathtaking scenery, rugged topography and blazing fall color, all with few people. Highlights include Blackwater Falls State Park, the Cheat River and the Monongahela National Forest.

CHAPTER 6

Kentucky Horse Country . . . 62

Like the Maine coast, Nova Scotia and the Canaan Valley, photography in the horse country around Lexington documents people's coexistence with the land rather than their exclusion from it. Like one giant country club, the Kentucky countryside unfolds with beautiful rolling hills, miles of wood-plank fences, stables both imposing and rustic and, of course, graceful thoroughbreds.

CHAPTER 7

Tallgrass Prairies of Illinois . . . 69

Not far from the bustle of Chicago, tallgrass prairies still hold an intricate ecosystem of wildflowers, butterflies and grasses taller than you. (Bring a stepladder.) Try Iroquois County Conservation Area, Goose Lake Prairie Nature Preserve and the Indian Boundary Prairies.

CHAPTER 8

Wildflowers of the Texas Hill Country . . . 76

Credit Lady Bird Johnson and the Texas Highway Department for what is arguably the best wildflower display in America each spring. Indian paintbrush and lupine dominate the rolling hills north of Austin in April. Marble Falls should be your main stop, but you can also cruise the back roads around Granite Shoals, Kingsland and Burnet to round out your trip.

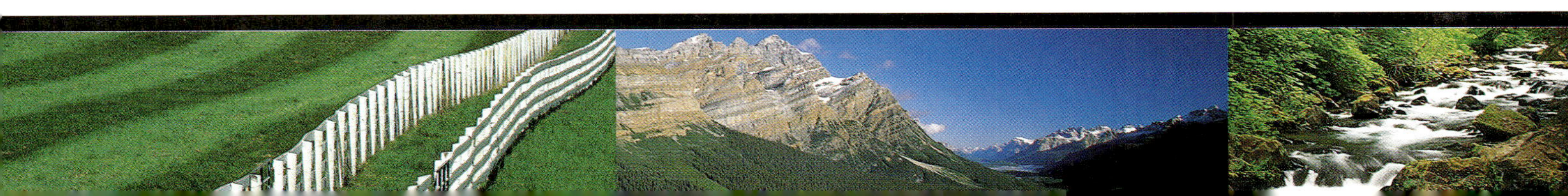

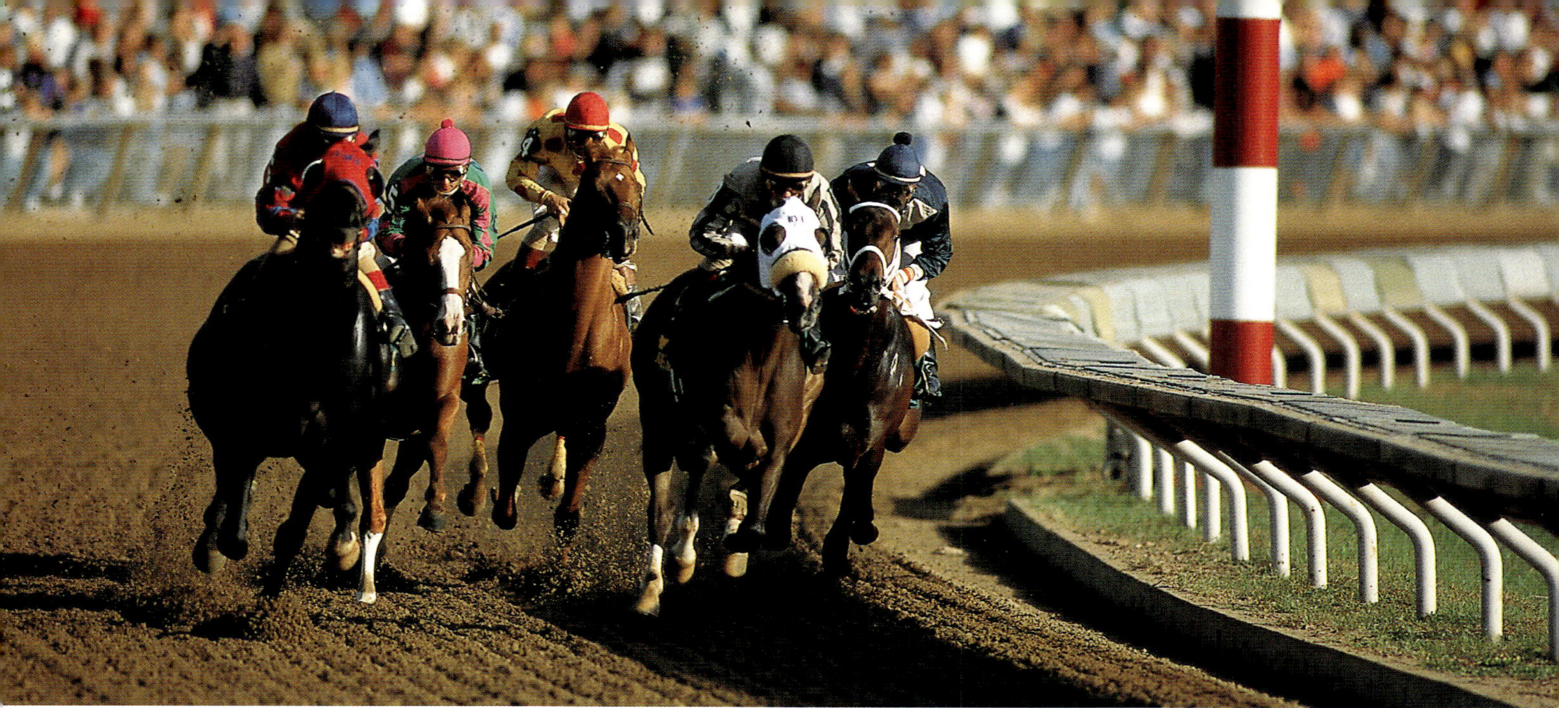

CHAPTER 9

San Juan Mountains, Colorado . . . *83*

Frenzied resort towns aside, the southwestern corner of Colorado ranks as the most isolated and attractive in the state. The Crested Butte/Ouray area is your go-to destination for wildflowers and wildlife and offers plenty of dramatic vistas and mountain lakes. Check out Yankee Boy Basin, Imogene Pass and American Basin, among many others.

CHAPTER 10

The Canadian Rockies . . . *92*

In most people's minds, Banff, Jasper, Yoho and Kootenay national parks *are* the Canadian Rockies—and with good reason. The four combined are the Canadian Rockies' greatest hits. You can shoot the area at any time of year and come up with fantastic images. Sweeping glacier-carved lakes and valleys, thickly forested slopes and breathtaking waterfalls all make this experience worthwhile.

CHAPTER 11

Utah's Color Country . . . *104*

"Color country" smacks of tourism bureau spin, but in this case it doesn't do the area justice. In addition to its dead heat with the Sonoran Desert for Most Iconic Southwestern Landscape, southern Utah is unlike any other landscape in the world. Zion and Bryce national parks anchor an all-star lineup that includes slot canyons and Arches and Canyonlands national parks.

CHAPTER 12

Arizona Canyon Country . . . *119*

As much a national symbol as the bald eagle, the Grand Canyon is one of the seven wonders of the natural world. Photographers can go for the sweeping panoramic or find countless intimate shots below the rim on one of the canyon's precipitous trails. Combine the trip with a foray to Coyote Buttes in the Paria Canyon/Vermilion Cliffs Wilderness, a wild land with the photographer's ultimate—the Wave.

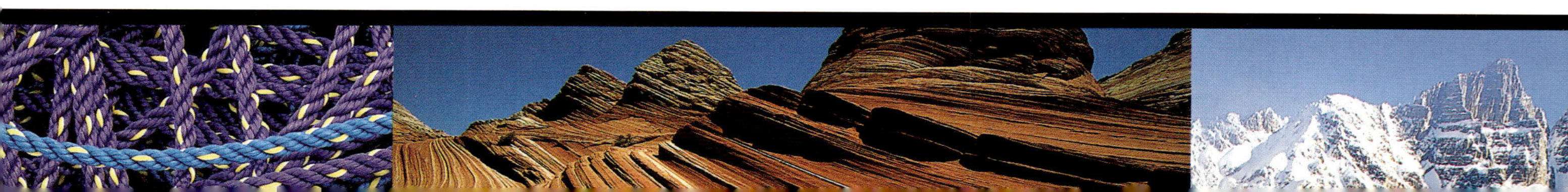

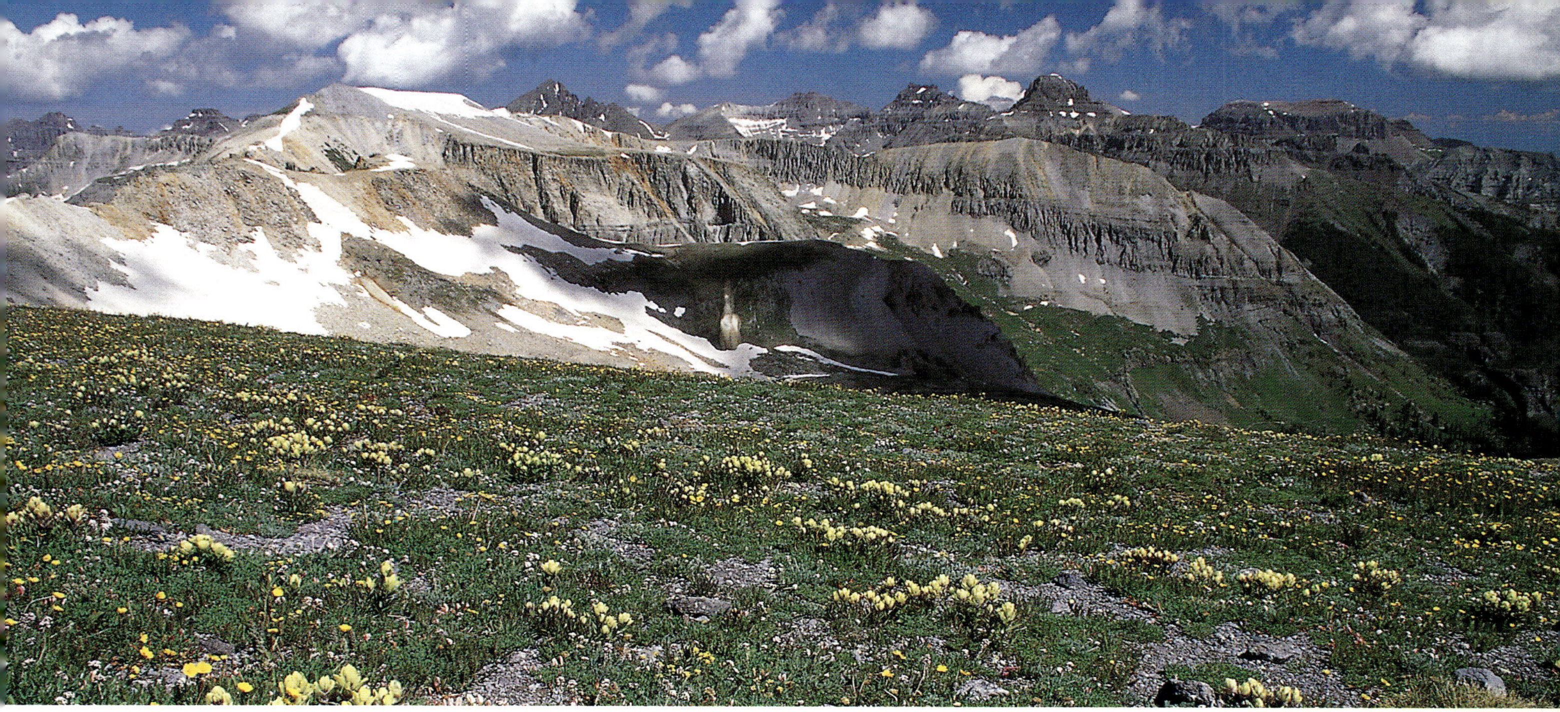

CHAPTER 13

Olympic National Park . . . *129*

If I had to label one location as my favorite, Olympic would probably get the nod. Capped by Mount Olympus, the park boasts incredible geographic diversity and is 95 percent designated wilderness. Where else can you photograph four types of forest—including temperate rain forest—mountains and wild coastline?

CHAPTER 14

Mt. Rainier National Park . . . *136*

Glacier lillies, plumed bear grass, magenta paintbrush, purple lupine and other flowers all dot the valleys and mountain shoulders in Mt. Rainier National Park, named for the highest peak in the Cascades. Photographers will find numerous opportunities for versatile landscape and wildflower shots, as well as icon shots of this famous mountain.

CHAPTER 15

Columbia River Gorge, Oregon . . . *143*

A short drive from Portland, the gorge attracts photographers for its abundance of waterfalls and pristine rain forests. Wahclella Falls, Eagle Creek, Ponytail Falls and Multnomah Falls will get you started, and with extra time you can check out Silver Falls State Park, Crown Point State Park and the Tom McCall Preserve.

CHAPTER 16

Coup de 'graph: Editing, Organizing and Marketing Your Photos . . . *150*

Editing and organizing the images you've spent so much time taking will put you in position to sell them when the time comes. Some advice on storage systems, breaking into the commercial market with photographic prints, and submitting to the calendar market.

APPENDIX

reference calendar
page 157

index
page 158

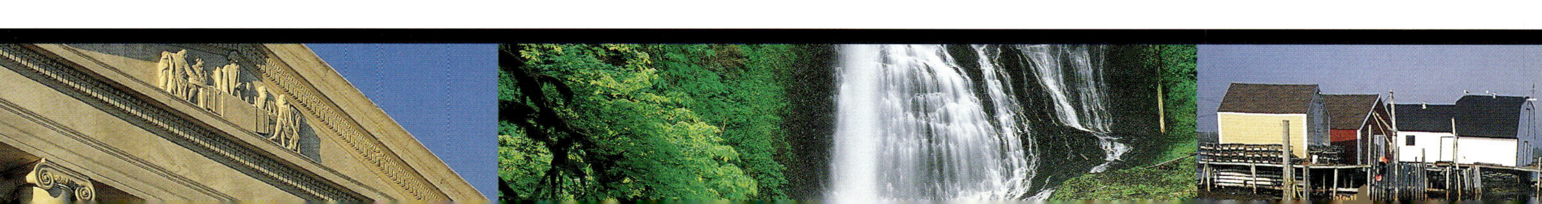

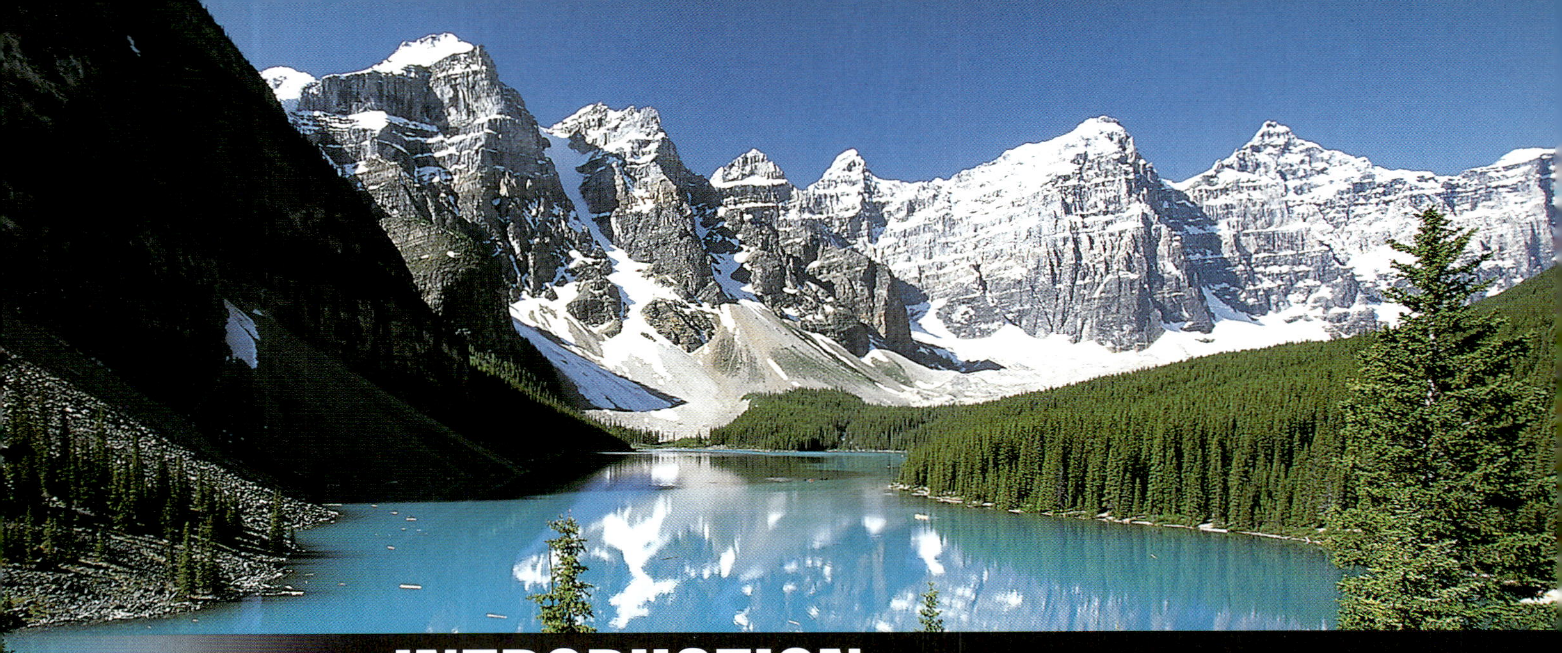

INTRODUCTION

where to go?

WHAT IS IT THAT INSPIRES PEOPLE TO VISIT A PARTICULAR location? It might be the history, the architecture, the culture, the unique geographical features, the wildlife or simply the excitement of travel. Whatever the reason, there is a preconceived image that we hold in our minds of that particular place. As photographers, we often decide where to go from images we've seen in advertising, calendars, books or posters. Because of these visual references, our expectations are high. We hope to return with a similar experience.

Early in my career I selected my travels based on images I had seen elsewhere and mostly ended up wandering aimlessly on location. My research techniques were as simple as buying a plane ticket, renting a car, and filling a folder with a few postcards or pictures plucked from a book or magazine. Occasionally I would return with a better image than that which I used as my resource, but too often I ended up disappointed. It took awhile before I realized luck was more of a factor than knowledge when I returned home from a trip I considered productive. My productive trips consisted of images that had been done over and over.

I have since learned that duplicating other photographers' images is not a satisfying creative outlet for me. There comes a point when you need to ask yourself, "What separates my photography from others'?" The content of your images depends on two variables: the locations you choose and the creative prism through which you capture them. Throughout the book, I will prepare you for a successful journey and also help you to think independently—manipulate that creative prism—so you can better define yourself as a photographer. (See "Creative Considerations" on page 21.)

The United States and Canada have no shortage of stunning locations to shoot. There are so many great places that sometimes just choosing is the hardest part. The other problem is when to go. This book will help there too. I can hardly tell you everything you need to know about each location, but the chapters on locations will save you time in choosing and researching a place and will give you a tremendous advantage by knowing what to take and how to approach each site to get your best shots. Because you can't get all your information from one source, I will also share with you my strategies for thoroughly scouting a location. You'll be well rewarded for your efforts.

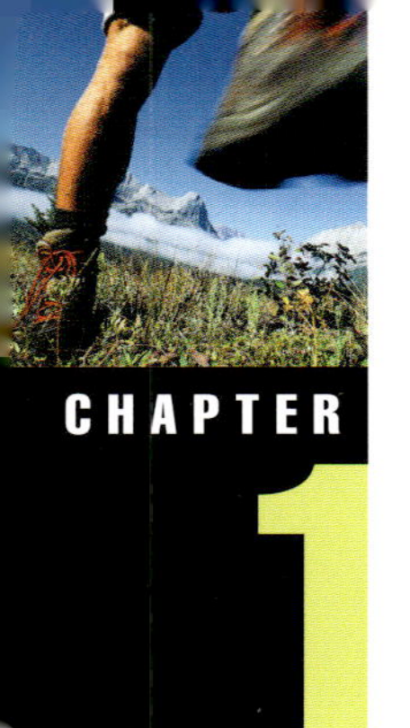

CHAPTER 1

Planning and Equipment

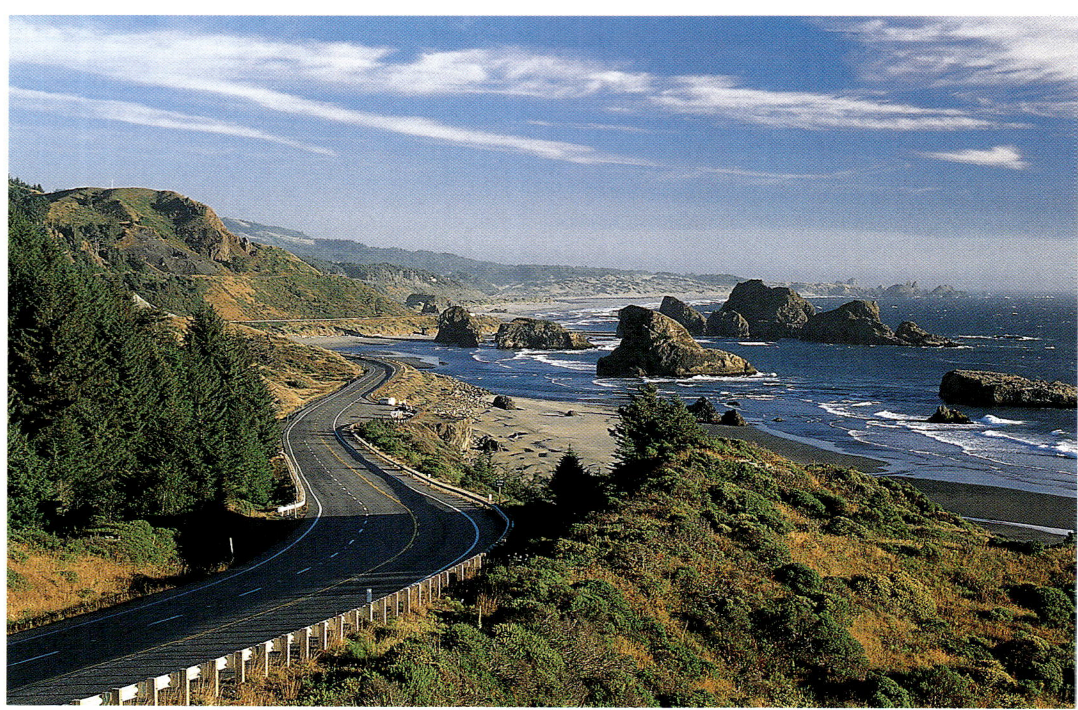

If someone asked to choose between the Canadian Rockies and the agricultural fields of eastern Washington for a photo trip, and you knew very little about either location, which would you pick? Most photographers would choose the Canadian Rockies because the first image that comes to mind when we think of agriculture is endless fields of corn and soybeans. When we think of the Rockies, we think of majestic mountain peaks. Your choice might become more difficult if someone handed you pictures of both locations. The eastern Washington agricultural region, better known as the Palouse, has striking colors, endless skies and beautiful rolling hills dotted with old, picturesque barns.

Most photographers rely on pictures to select photo locations. Even snapshots can reveal photographic potential, but we have better resources available. Relying solely on visual information can be deceiving and lead to major disappointments. Tourists travel loaded with guidebooks, maps and other information,

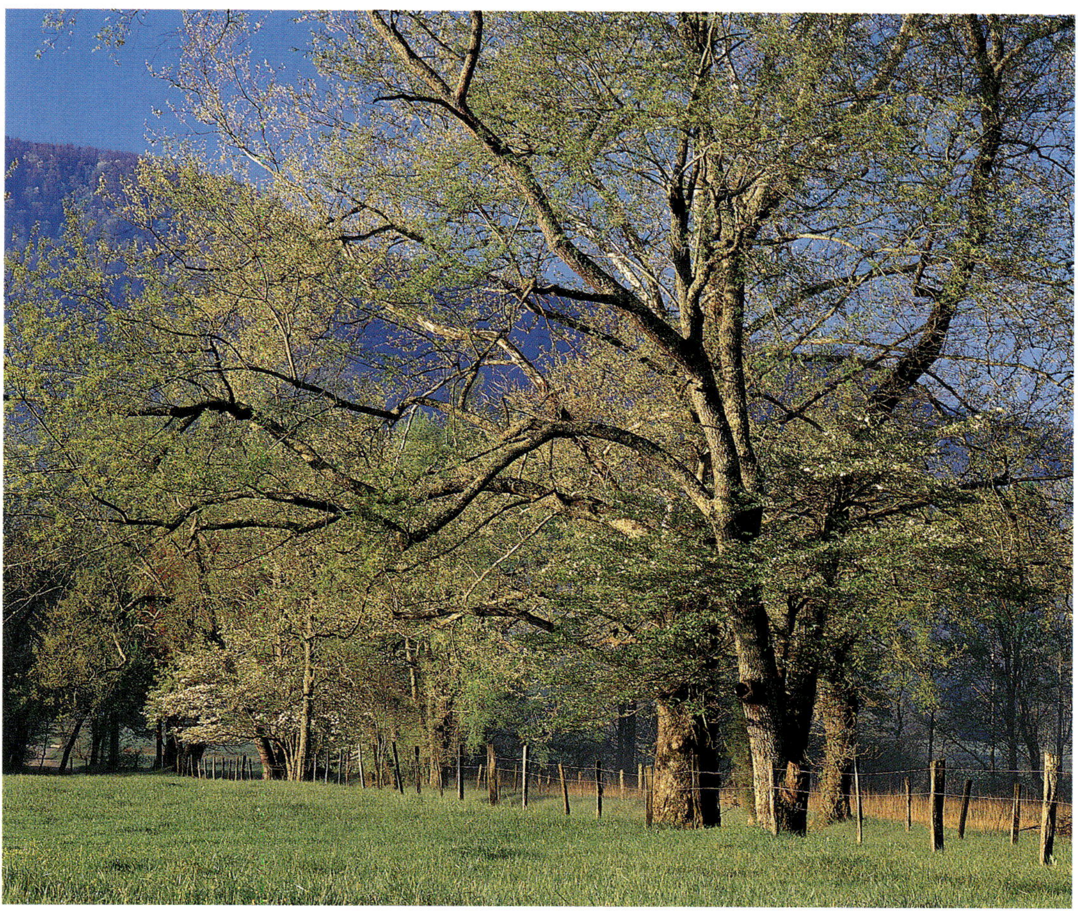

Cades Cove in Great Smoky Mountains National Park can either be magical or a complete bust. I shot this after waiting three days for lower temperatures and hoping for light fog and clear skies. What fog there was didn't last long, but I did get beautiful light and a wonderful spring sky to work.

but I am surprised by how few materials photographers think to bring. It seems to me that we should be as well prepared, or even better prepared, than these other travelers. Networking is one good source. Most camera clubs have several well-traveled members who have a wealth of information and are eager to share (see "Networking" on page 14). Obvious sources for visual reference are calendars, photo magazines, photography books, guidebooks, travel brochures and some advertisements. Photography travel company itineraries are one of the most reliable sources of information (see "Alternative Travel" on page 16).

One general rule here: If I have never heard of or seen another image from a location, I look into it much more carefully. It is risky to take on a location only a few photographers have explored and of which few images have been published. Good news travels fast in the photo community, and if there are good photo ops in a certain location, you can bet others will know about it. Regardless of where you travel, you usually need more than just one or two subjects to work in order to justify the time and expense. Find as much information about your locations as you possibly can.

PRE-TRIP PLANNING

Before you begin planning, make a list of everything about the destination that has photographic potential:

1. cities
2. towns
3. zoos
4. city parks
5. public gardens
6. architectural landmarks
7. natural landmarks

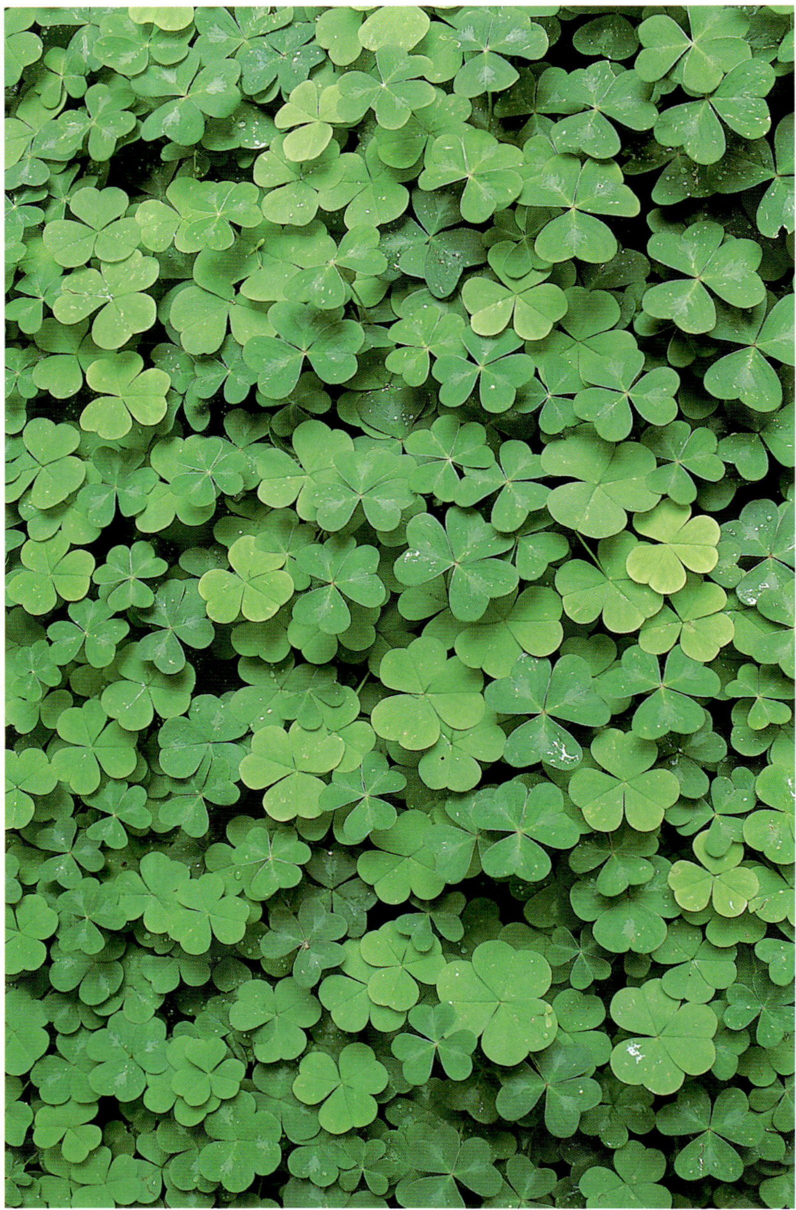

Generic images—those that could have been taken anywhere—are versatile and have great sales potential. The clover's lush growth and its positive connotation qualify it for a number of markets.

8. lakes
9. rivers
10. wildflowers
11. wildlife
12. historic landmarks

Add anything else that you can think of. The more you know, the better your chances of a productive photo shoot. Locations don't need to be major landmarks. In fact, shots that could have been taken almost anywhere (what I call generic shots) can be as beautiful and powerful as icon shots and, I might add, sell quite well. You probably won't shoot everything on your list in one trip, but these other possibilities can be part of your back-up plan when you prioritize later.

Bookstores are the best place to begin gathering information. I personally find libraries time consuming and often outdated for photography research. I love DK's (Dorling Kindersley) travel guides. Others I've found useful are Fodor's (formerly Compass American Guides), Falcon Guides, Moon Handbooks and National Geographic Guidebooks. There are also numerous regional publishers with wonderful books, although these are sometimes difficult to find outside the region. For these and other specialty books, such as field guides and hiking guides, you can also check one of the comprehensive online bookstores.

Networking

Networking with other photographers and well-traveled friends is one of your most valuable resources. Camera clubs and supply-store owners are wonderful resources for networking with others who share your passion for photography. These folks are incredibly creative and helpful. Many of them are well traveled regionally, if not nationally. They often know of secret spots tucked away in well-known places. Ask, listen and take notes—and not mental notes! I always make a habit of letting others know where I am going. I guarantee that if someone has been there, he will let you know. Your traveling friends, regardless of whether they take photographs on their trips, are full of useful information. Listen to what they have to say, but check it out. Remember, these friends' journeys might not be planned around photography.

Online photography and travel discussion groups such as <http://groups.yahoo.com/group/phototravel/> can provide useful information, but again, check out any information shared by these groups. (Also, see the sidebar at right on Internet searches.) Two very nice photography newsletters with valuable information are *Photo Traveler* [(800) 417-4680, <www.phototravel.com/index.html>] and *Photograph America Newsletter* [(415) 898-3736, <www.photographamerica.com/index.htm>]. These give detailed information on various locations across America. Use the information as a guide, but don't base your entire trip on it.

If you are fortunate enough to have stock photography agency representation or another source to market your work, talk with your agent to see if she needs stock from the areas you are considering. Your agent can be a valuable resource for your information gathering.

Other Essential Resources

AAA (AMERICAN AUTOMOBILE ASSOCIATION). If you travel just a couple times a year, you more than get your money's worth for the dues you pay. I love its State Tourbooks and maps. The AAA Tourbooks <www.aaa.com> are wonderful sources for hotel and motel information, and the AAA maps are more than detailed enough for an overview of where you are going. If you like to camp, AAA's camping guides are helpful for finding developed campgrounds. AAA will also make airline and car rental reservations if you don't want to make these arrangements yourself.

DELORME ATLAS AND GAZETTEER. This is as important to me as my camera bag. I have one for every state I have ever traveled in. The DeLorme maps <www.delorme.com> show interstates and state highways, as well as unmarked dirt and gravel roads that other atlases don't include. These maps have helped me get to places I never would have found on my own—at least not without asking directions!

On-Location Research

My research isn't complete until I spend a few minutes at a visitors center, a bookstore or gift store, or any other outlet where I might be able to get some last-minute information. I've found casual conversation at a coffee shop or other gathering place is sometimes helpful to pick up information on wildflower blooms, best color, wildlife sightings or anything that might be useful. A friendly smile and a kind word can yield the best research you produce for your entire trip. If time permits, I spend a couple hours driving the roads or taking short hikes to get acquainted with the area. This helps me decide whether morning or evening light is best at a given location, allows me to check stages of wildflowers or fall color, and

internet searches

Internet searches based on your bookstore findings and networking will help you flesh out your core information as you put together a shooting plan You'll be amazed at what you find in a couple of hours of surfing the Internet. National parks, state parks, most cities and towns, chambers of commerce, public gardens and zoos nearly always have an online presence. It's usually worth verifying the information with a second source, but I've found a wealth of information from my Web searches and even hidden or lesser-known places that I never would have found in a guidebook. A few helpful Web sites for trip planning:

- www.nps.gov *(U.S. national parks)*
- www.national-parks.net *(U.S. national parks)*
- http://parkscanada.pch.gc.ca/ *(Canadian national parks and world heritage sites)*
- www.wildernet.com *(trip planning and maps)*
- www.usparks.about.com *(U.S. national and state parks)*
- http://gorp.com/index.adp *(outdoor recreation and travel)*
- www.iloveplants.com/ *(public gardens)*
- www.e-ztown.com/zoos.htm *(U.S. zoos)*

Also, use search engines such as Dogpile, Google or AlltheWeb to search for other sites. Some information you should get from your Internet searches is traditional peak periods for wildflower blooms; peak autumn color; wildlife viewing opportunities; and information on entry fees, opening and closing hours, and entrance permits or permits for photography. I try to contact tourism offices, chambers of commerce, wildflower hotlines, fall color hotlines and weather services at least one to two weeks before I leave. Use this information to help you make any necessary last-minute changes to your shooting plans.

airline and lodging reservations

There really is no secret to getting a plane ticket. I do recommend booking online to get the best prices. The travel agents who have survived are usually squeezed by ever-leaner commissions. Book reservations several months in advance for peak-season travel or one month for other seasons. Don't forget that AAA can make airline reservations for you.

Depending on season and location, hotels can fill quickly. I sometimes travel without reservations if I'm covering a very large area and want to see what type of weather or other factors I'll encounter, but I always have a sleeping bag with me. Most hotels give you a forty-eight-hour cancellation period. If you are traveling during peak season, the cancellation policy might not be this generous. AAA Tourbooks are a great resource for finding lodging. You can also try one of the online reservation sites such as Travelocity or Onetravel for both airline and hotel reservations.

helps me calculate drive time from my campsite or hotel. Take notes, and use them.

Once your research is complete, take what you learned, and put it to use. If something on your list doesn't work out, move on. A good friend and colleague once shared with me a bit of helpful advice: "Don't dwell on what you can't shoot, but rather on what you can shoot." Enjoy what you can shoot, and your journey will result in many rewarding images.

Packing

I can sum packing up in one word: simplify. The truth is we don't need a whole lot to survive or to be comfortable. If I am carrying more than one piece of luggage for personal belongings and one camera bag (in my case, a backpack), I consider myself overpacked. For easy reference, I have included the packing list I use for every trip I take (see page 17). This list is generous and can be trimmed or customized as necessary. Pack smart, and be prepared for the weather conditions you are likely to encounter. It might sound silly at first, but I suggest you pack twice. First, pack what you think you might need. The second time, go through one item at a time and ask, "Do I really need this, or do I just want it?" You'll be amazed at what you can get by without.

The luggage you choose to carry is as important as the items in it. I have used a lot of different luggage over the years, and very little stood up to the abuse it went through at airlines. Look for durable products that have user-friendly features such as wheels and retractable pull handles. Remember that others won't treat it with the same care you do. One manufacturer I have found that does a great job with its designs and manufacturing is Eagle Creek [(800) 874-9925, <www.eaglecreek.com>].

Alternative Travel

Now that you've had the chance to think about what goes into a successful photo shoot, you may decide it is more work than fun. Consider a photography tour for your travels. There are a number of good tour companies that specialize in photography travel. Typically professional photographers who enjoy sharing their passion for photography run these tours. This is a great way to meet other photographers, learn and work side by side with a professional. I've been leading tours at Nature's Light for ten years and watched many participants develop friendships. The best way to find a photography tour is through one of several photography magazines on the newsstand, such as *Outdoor Photographer*, *Nature and Outdoor Photographer* or *Petersen's Photographic*. You can check my domestic and international tour schedule at <www.natureslight.com> or e-mail me at <william@natureslight.com>. My schedule, as with many other outfitters', changes from year to year.

CAMERA GEAR

The equipment you need can change from location to location and depends greatly on the subjects you plan on photographing. If you are an entry-level photographer, follow the list I

packing lists

SPRING/SUMMER PACKING LIST

3 T-shirts

Underwear

2 pair of lightweight field pants

2 pair of lightweight field shirts

3 or 4 pair of lightweight wool socks

2 or 3 pair of cotton socks

Sweatshirt or lightweight fleece jacket

Windbreaker or wet-weather jacket

Sleepwear

1 pair of tennis shoes or other comfortable shoes

1 pair of hiking boots

Ball cap or other sun protection for head

Sunglasses

- **This packing list is for a 7- to 10-day trip. If you'll be gone longer, consider adding extra T-shirts and socks.**
- **Field pants and shirts should be handwashable and quick-drying, such as 100% nylon.**
- **Wear one pair of the shoes on this packing list to help minimize bulk.**

AUTUMN/WINTER PACKING LIST

2 pair of poly-pro long-sleeved shirts

Underwear

1 or 2 wool shirts

1 medium- or heavyweight wool sweater

1 poly-pro long underwear

2 pair of heavyweight wool socks

2 pair of poly-pro sock liners

Sleepwear

1 pair of tennis shoes or other comfortable shoes

1 pair of snow boots or hiking boots

Fleece or wool cap

1 pair gloves

1 pair mittens

Sunglasses

Fleece jacket

Outer parka or cold-weather coat

- **This packing list is for a 7- to 10-day trip.**
- **Think layers when packing for cold-weather photography.**

TOILETRIES

Toothbrush

Toothpaste/floss

Shampoo

Comb/brush

Razor

Shaving creme

Pain reliever (aspirin, Aleve, Tylenol, etc.)

Anti-diarrhea medication

Sunscreen

Lip balm

Other medications or prescriptions if needed

Contact wearers (cleaning solution, eyeglasses)

FOR WINTER, ADD

Cold medication

Throat lozenges

- **Women's toiletries list may differ to some degree.**

CAMERA BAG

Basic camera setup

Two camera bodies (bring manuals for camera bodies)

Wide-angle zoom (or fixed focal length of 28–80mm)

Telephoto zoom (or fixed focal lenth of 80–200mm)

Extension tubes and close-up diopter (these work best with a telephoto zoom for macro photography)

Diffuser and reflector (these are optional and used for macro photography)

Polarizer and warming filters

Film (this will vary for every photographer; entry-level photographers allow at least 3 to 5 rolls per day)

Extra batteries for camera bodies

Flash (optional)

Tripod

ADVANCED CAMERA SETUP

All equipment listed above

Split neutral density filters (optional)

Ultra-wide-angle zoom (17–35mm)

Telephoto lens between 300 and 400mm

Macro Lens

1.4 and/or 2x teleconverters

- **As your knowledge grows, so will your camera bag. This is a suggested list; you will better be able to determine your needs with experience.**

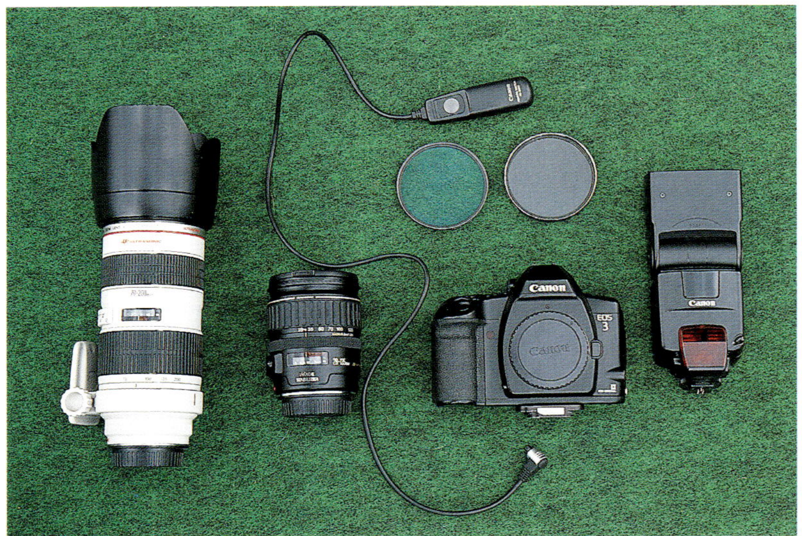

A basic camera setup: 35mm SLR body, 28–135mm zoom lens (or 28–80mm zoom lens), 70–200mm zoom lens, warming filter, polarizing filter, flash unit and cable release.

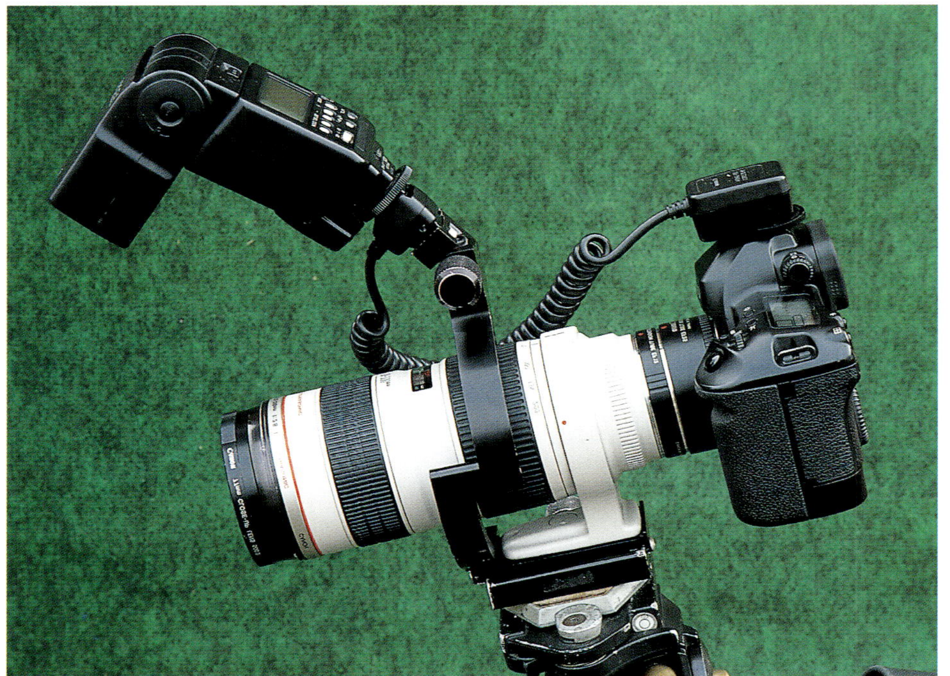

Macro setup with all pieces attached as shown above with flash bracket.

have on the following page for a basic setup. As your knowledge and experience grow, your needs will change, and over time you will better know what to pack for different circumstances. Camera gear becomes very personal after a while. My bag and your bag might be very different for the same locations and subjects based on our shooting styles. The most important advice I can give about your gear is 1) know how to use it and 2) know each item's capabilities and limitations. Don't ever take a new camera body on a trip without having run a few rolls of film through it.

Canon, Nikon, Pentax and Minolta are the most recognized names in 35mm SLR camera systems. All of these manufacturers produce good products. If you are in the market for camera equipment, I suggest you look at all the different systems to see what is available and how they feel to you. Don't let a few dollars be your deciding factor. Most equipment will be comparably priced. Buy into a system you feel good about and one with a history in keeping up with the times. Keep in mind that your needs will change over time and that this should play a role in your decision. Photography is addictive; I promise you'll want to expand your equipment at some point. I use Canon because it was my first system and offers an unbeatable variety of equipment, and I have never felt a need to change.

Accessories

Accessory equipment, such as filters and tripods, runs the gamut from really bad to extremely good. I suggest buying the best you can afford. Accessories will make a difference in your work. Filters are the most basic accessory. These are glass or plastic (resin) elements placed in front of the lens to alter tonality. Of the many filter manufacturers, I use both Hoya and Singh Ray filters. Singh Ray is an innovative company offering a limited number of filters that open doors to creativity. These filters are more expensive but of very high quality and many times are not available elsewhere.

The right tripod and tripod accessories

can save you a lot of frustration. Buy one that extends at least to eye level, preferably higher. Two of the better manufacturers are Bogen and Gitzo. Bogen offers several types of tripod heads, from ball heads to three-way pan tilt heads. In my opinion, the best ball head makers are (in order) Arca-Swiss, Linhof, Studioball and Foba. The best mounting plates and flash brackets for these ball heads are developed by Really Right Stuff. Really Right Stuff's flash brackets are by far the best tools you can have when using a flash.

Equipment on the Road

Traveling with camera gear and film has always been a concern for photographers, but with changes in airport security and tighter carry-on restrictions; this is becoming more of an issue. The best alternative I have found to traveling with equipment is to place my camera bag in a hard Pelican case. Once I arrive on location, I take my camera bag out of the Pelican case and put my other luggage (my personal items) in it. This eliminates the burden of carrying around three pieces of luggage and taking up valuable space in my vehicle. Film is the other major concern. Do not put your film in your checked luggage—it might get fried by high-powered X-ray machines. Carry all your film on the airplane with you. It is currently okay to have your film go through the X-ray machine for carry-on luggage. This X-ray will not harm your film. Professional photographers have had film X-rayed this way for years and never had a problem.

One last note on film: I have been asked countless times about protecting film from heat while on location. My answer is, don't worry about it. I don't put my film in a cooler when in the desert or other hot climates. I don't suggest having it sit in a car window with direct sun for two weeks, but as long as it's in a camera bag or another bag, it's protected well enough. Don't sweat the little things.

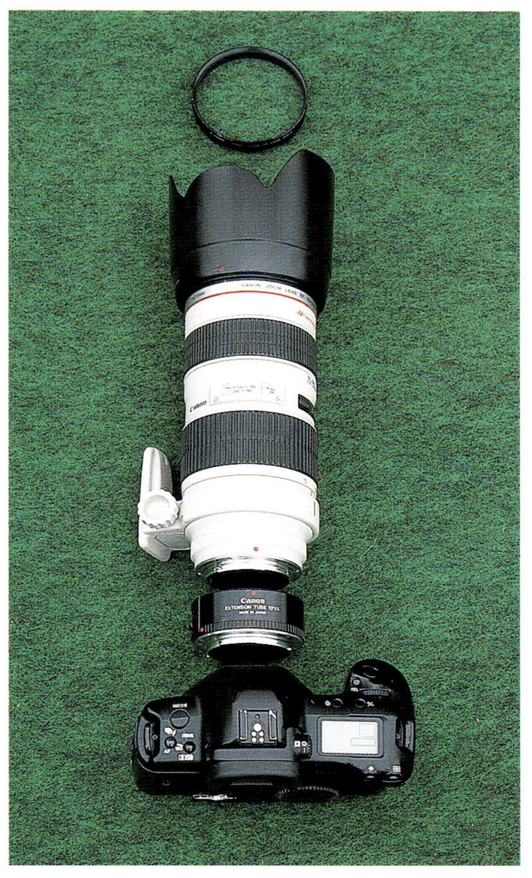

Inexpensive macro setup (shown detached): 35mm SLR body, extension tube, 80–200mm zoom lens, two-element close-up filter.

TOOLS FOR IMPROVING YOUR PHOTOGRAPHY

Throughout this book, I talk about using tools to improve your images. Following are some basic outlines of when and why you might consider using certain tools I mention. Keep in mind that as with any photographic equipment, practice makes perfect and my simply explaining their use won't improve your work. Use this as a jumping-off point to refine your own technique.

WIDE-ANGLE LENSES make it possible to photograph a wide angle of coverage and give great depth of field. They help convey the full sweep of an open landscape and enable us to include both immediate foreground and distant background. The standard wide-angle lens that outdoor photographers use is the 28mm lens. The 28–70mm wide-angle zoom is common and very popular among photographers today. The Canon 28–135 image-

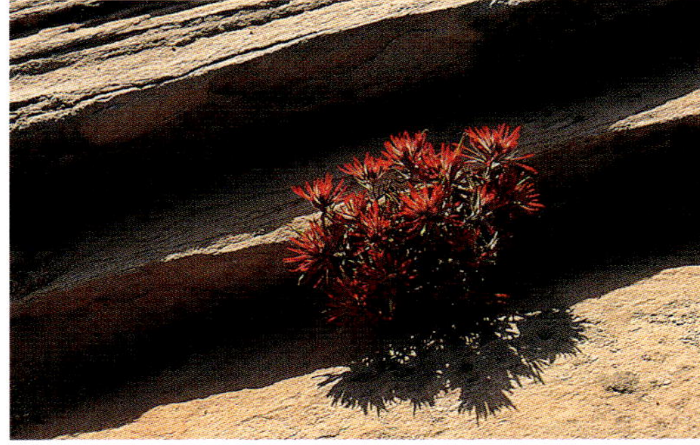

The bright afternoon sun created what I consider unfavorable lighting for this desert paintbrush.

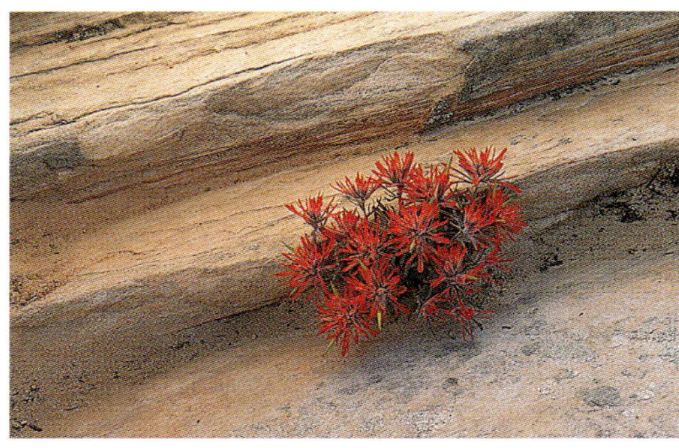

To mitigate the harsh shadows, I used a diffuser, which provided soft, even lighting.

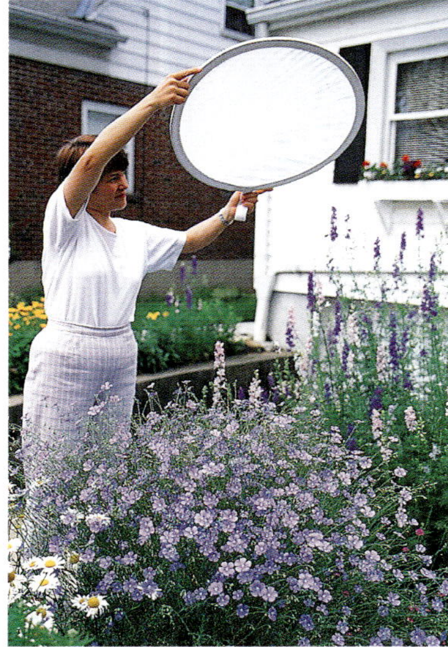

The position of the diffuser here creates a shadow. If you are photographing a large area, you might have no choice but to hold the diffuser away from your subject. The downside is that you cool the light, which could then require a warming filter.

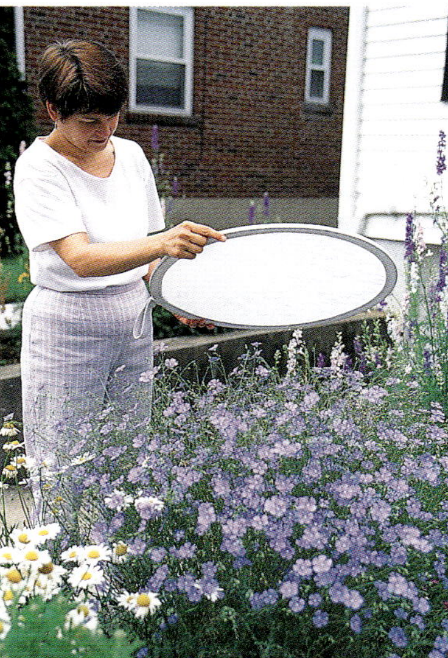

By holding the diffuser close to your subject, you create a soft, glowing light. In my opinion, this is much more appealing.

stabilization lens is becoming a popular choice. Wider lenses in the 17mm–24mm range are fun to use but are not as common as the 28mm.

TELEPHOTO LENSES make it possible to isolate elements and give your image a compressed perspective—elements in your composition appear closer to each other than they really are. Telephoto lenses come in fixed focal lengths and zoom ranges. The standard and most popular is the 70–200mm range, but manufacturers are producing a wider selection of telephoto lenses ranging from 100–300mm and 100–400mm. There is little need to own more than one of these. Research these before purchasing, and put quality before the focal length.

POLARIZERS are the most commonly used filters in a photographer's bag. Many think of them as the filter that makes blue skies bluer. This is sometimes true, but they're useful for other applications. I use polarizers a lot, and I don't restrict them to sunny days. They are very useful on overcast days too. Polarizers reduce glare on water, wet rocks, leaves and glass, and they improve the color saturation of almost anything that reflects light. The downside of polarizers is you lose two stops of light, which your in-camera meter will automatically compensate for.

WARMING FILTERS block blue light to provide a warm tone in otherwise cool light (shady and overcast conditions). The most commonly used warming filters are 81A and 81B. The 81B is the warmer of the two. You should experiment to see which one you like and when to use it. You may decide to own both of them for different situations and for different films—some films are warmer than others. I use another warming filter for extreme blue-light situations (open shade on a sunny day), the KR6 by B+W. Use this filter carefully as it is extremely warm.

SPECIALTY FILTERS include intensifying filters

and graduated neutral density filters. Intensifying filters deepen color saturation. Use graduated neutral density filters to reduce extreme contrast. This is where Singh Ray filters shine.

DIFFUSERS break up harsh light on small subjects, such as flowers. The examples on page 20 show what diffusers can do and also illustrate the best way to use them.

MACRO PHOTOGRAPHY is an enjoyable way to explore a world of patterns, details and all the little things that make up the world around us. True macro lenses are the best way to journey into this world, but cost and extra weight are sometimes a burden. The good news is there's a less expensive way to explore macro photography without losing quality. Extension tubes and close-up diopters are economical and add very little weight or bulk to your camera bag. You can use extension tubes and diopters by themselves or in combination to obtain different magnifications. (See the photos at right.)

LANDSCAPE PHOTOGRAPHY can be representational or abstract. Representational photography requires wide-angle lenses and depicts what one might see when standing in the same position as the camera. Abstract photography involves selecting strong graphic elements in the landscape using telephoto lenses. See the paragraph on telephotos on page 20.

CREATIVE CONSIDERATIONS

There is more than one way to photograph a subject. If I were to assign the same subject for six people to photograph, I would get six different results. Sometimes just a slight difference in positioning of a subject can make an average image successful. The following are a few tips to consider when photographing in the field. Experience will be your best teacher, but consider these suggestions, and you will be well on your way of improving your work.

• Make it your standard procedure to look at your subject several different ways.

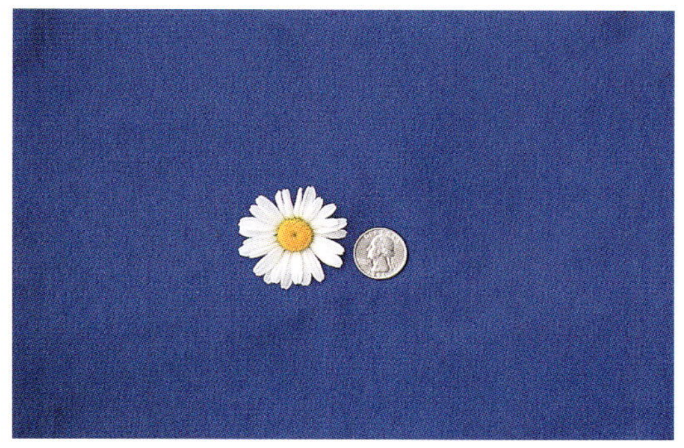

Maximum magnification for an 80–200mm lens with no attachments.

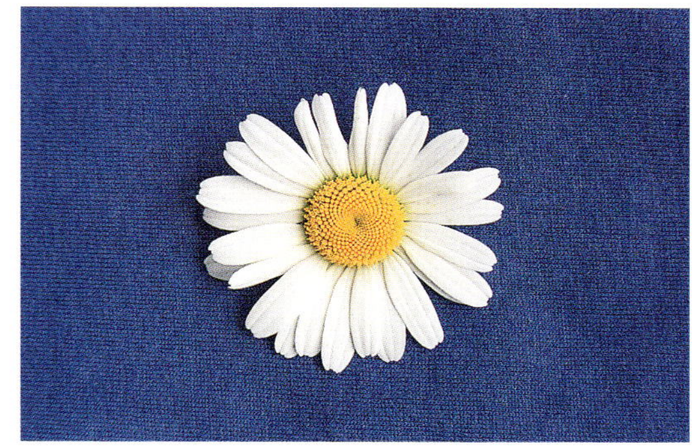

Maximum magnification for an 80–200mm lens with a Canon #25 extension tube.

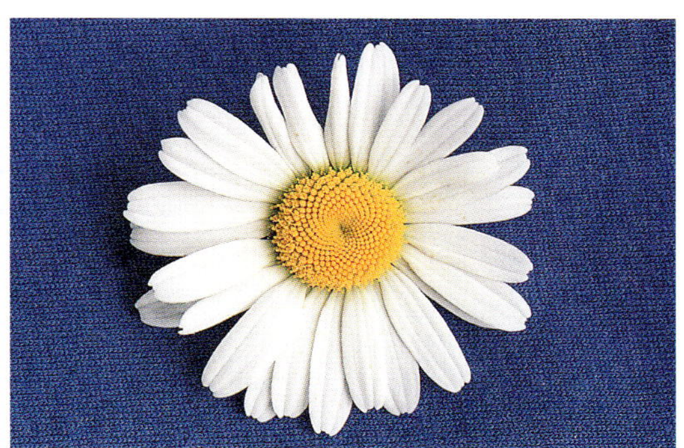

Maximum magnification for an 80–200mm lens with a Canon two-element close-up filter (also called a diopter).

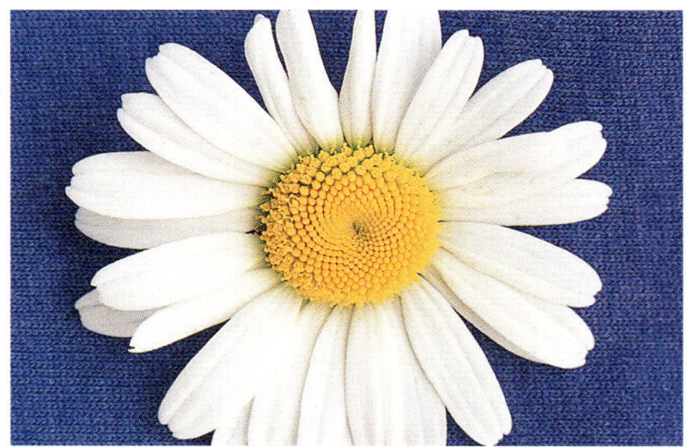

Maximum magnification for an 80–200mm lens with a Canon #25 and a #12 extension tube used in conjunction with a Canon two-element close-up filter.

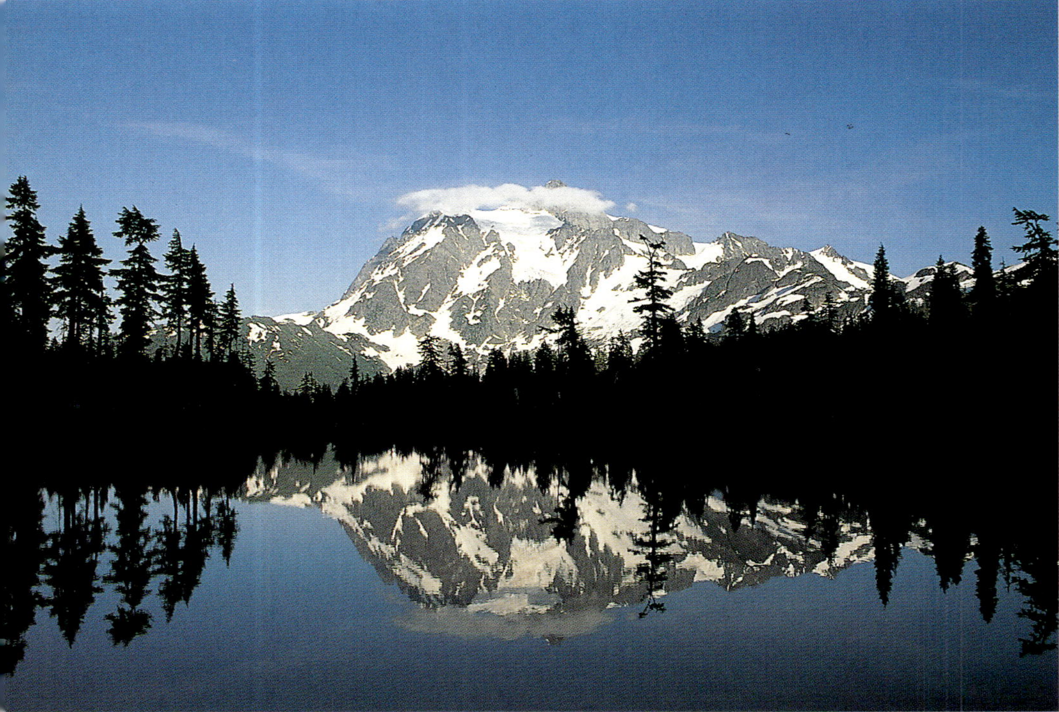

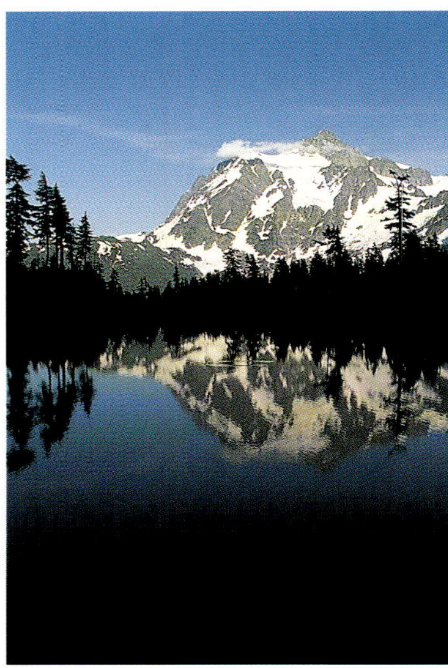

I switched from a horizontal to a vertical to create a different image.

These four photos illustrate the "explore and exploit" concept. The composition above was most obvious to me when I approached my subject. I took each photo from the same position using a tripod.

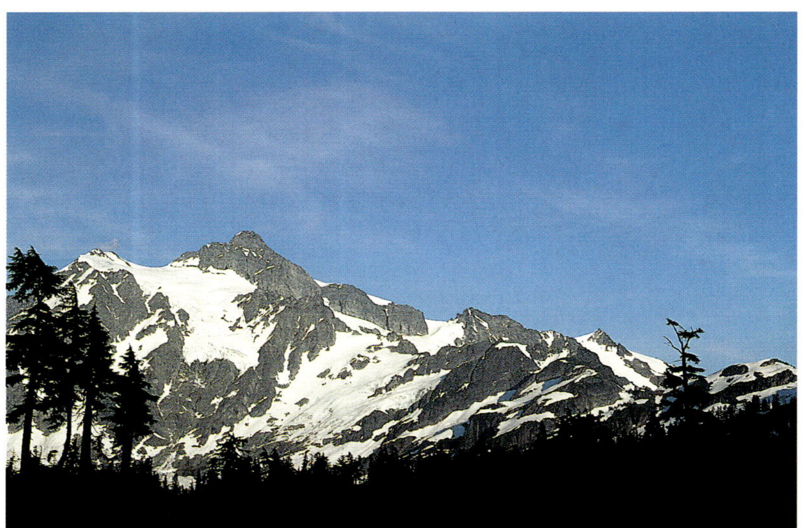

I used a telephoto to enlarge Mt. Shuksan and eliminated the lake.

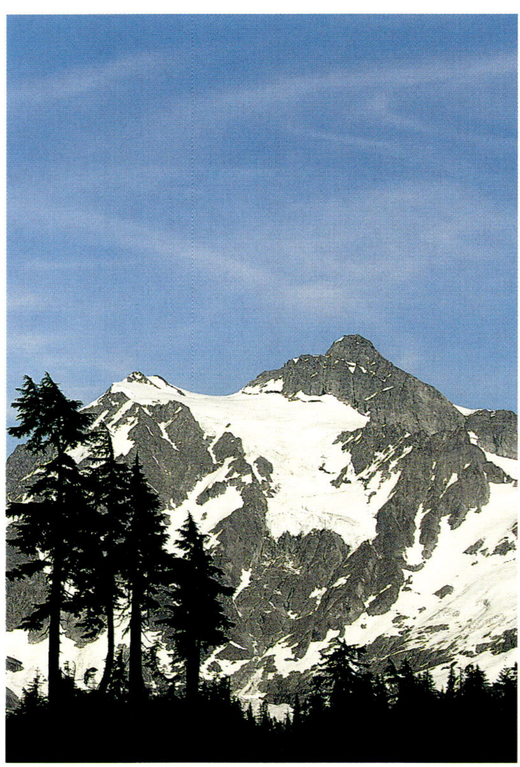

This is the same as the previous image but with a vertical orientation.

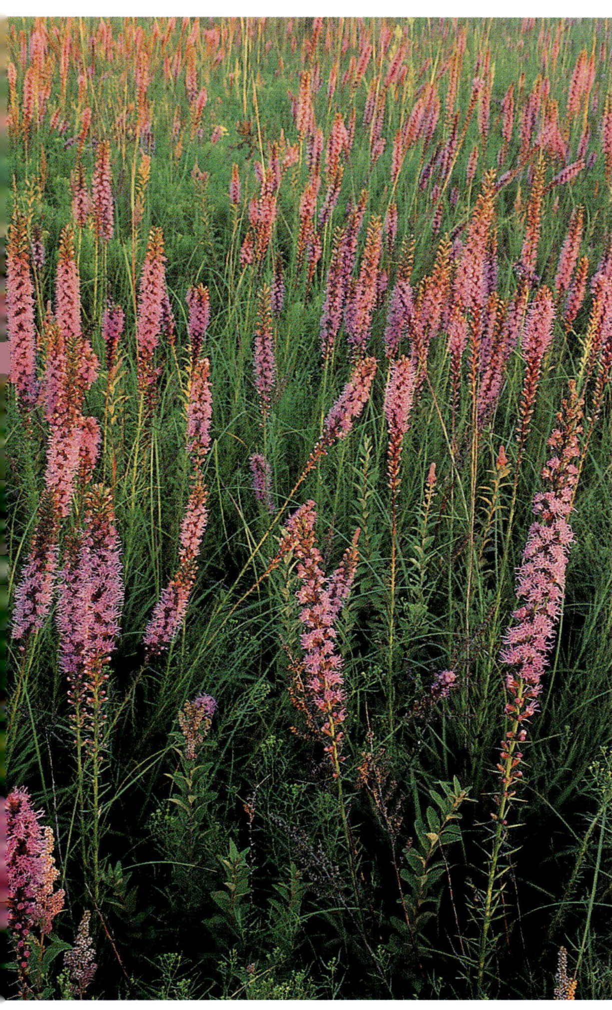

These two images illustrate the "explore and exploit" concept of finding one subject and moving into it to find another. This field of Prairie Blazing Star was the most obvious subject when I approached the area.

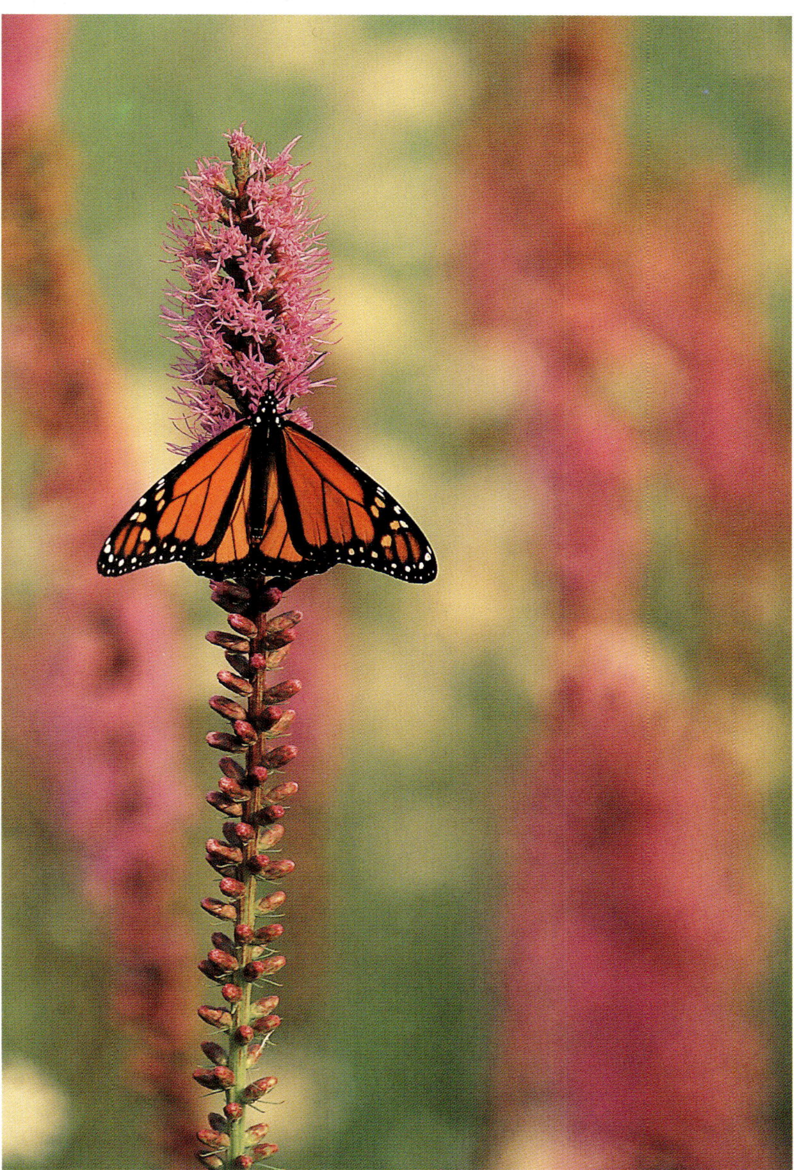

After getting the first image, I walked into the field to find another subject or angle. After exploring I came upon this monarch butterfly just as the sun struck the field.

With any subject I shoot, I use what I call "explore and exploit." I find as many different ways to shoot that one subject as I can possibly get. I will look at the subject horizontally, vertically, with a wide-angle lens and then a telephoto. I might move into the subject or simply raise or lower my tripod for different angles. The examples at left and above illustrate some elements of the explore and exploit concept.

• A pile of junk can be a photographer's treasure. Look for little design elements within your frame. (The picture on page 24 shows an example of an attractive subject found in an otherwise inconspicuous place.) There are opportunities everywhere if we just open our eyes.

• Consider using different f/stops. This will vary your depth of field and give a very different feel to your image. Changing f/stops will also change your shutter speeds, which in some situations will freeze or blur your subject if it's moving fast enough. Waterfalls are one good example. A fast shutter speed will freeze the water's movement, rendering it nearly as you see it, while a slow shutter speed will blur

Finding a subject within clutter: The lobster traps and old ropes lying around on this old pier intrigued me but weren't very attractive, even after I considered several angles.

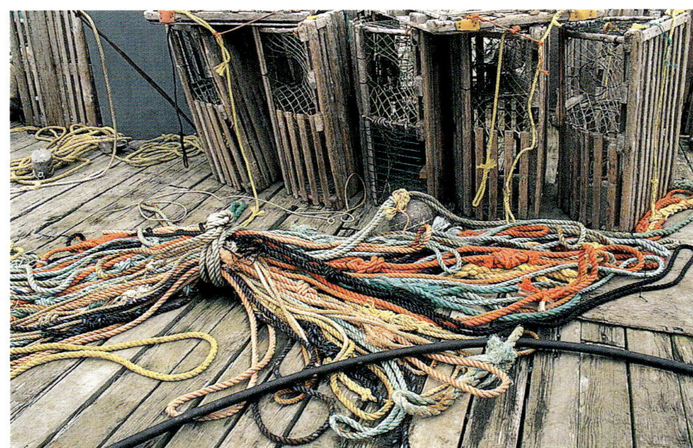

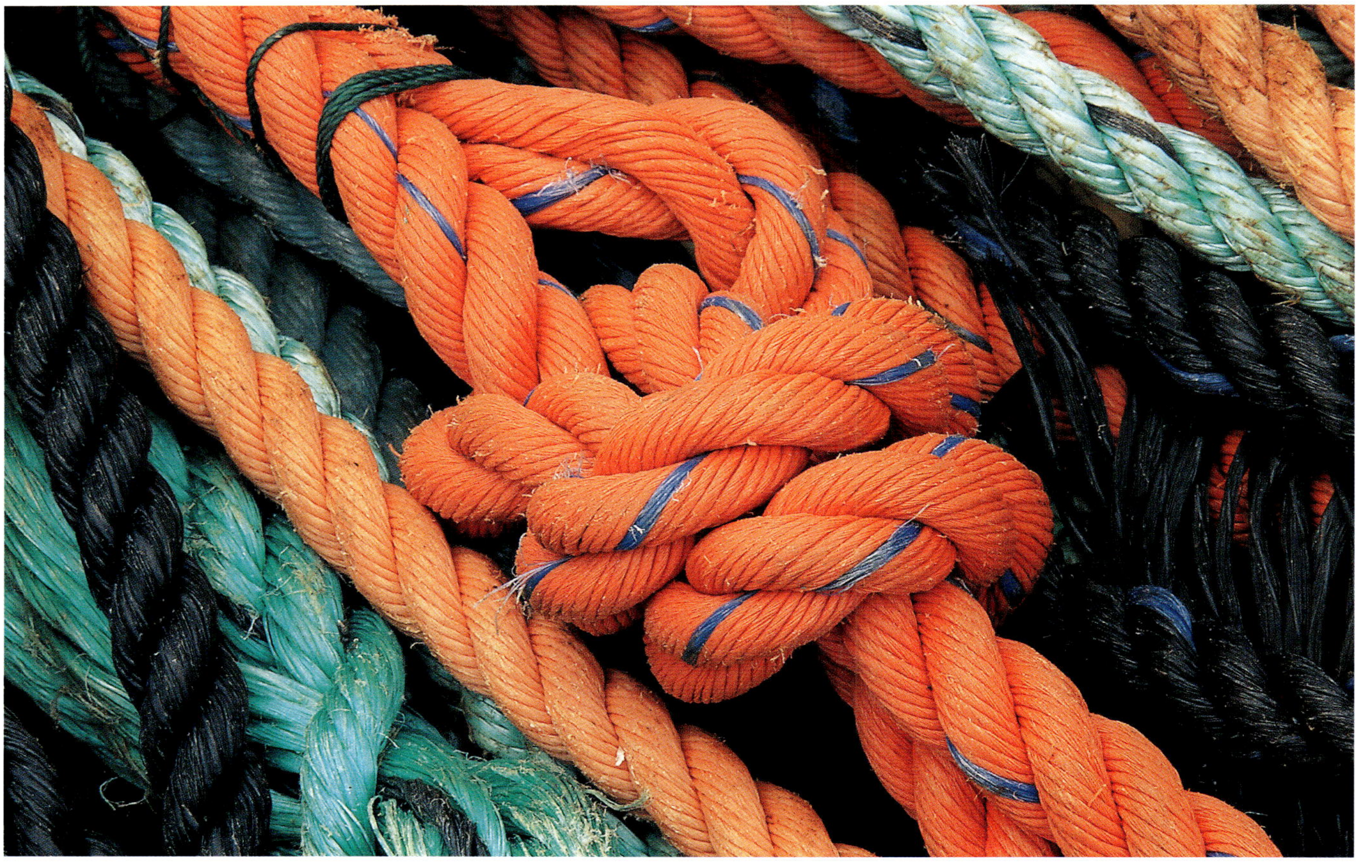

I decided to play with just the ropes because there was much more color and many interesting lines and shapes created by both old and new.

it, resulting in what we sometimes call a cotton candy look.

• Shoot with lenses of several different focal lengths. When you find a subject that can be photographed with everything from a wide-angle to a long telephoto, you can walk away with several different images.

• For a subject that isn't very exciting or is in a constant breeze, consider zooming in or out during a long exposure. You can also handhold and rotate your camera around in circles during a long exposure. (Two results appear on page 25.) You won't like the result every time, but you won't know unless you experiment.

• Sandwich two slides for an artsy look. Expose one frame at f/22, and overexpose two stops. Expose a second frame using an identi-

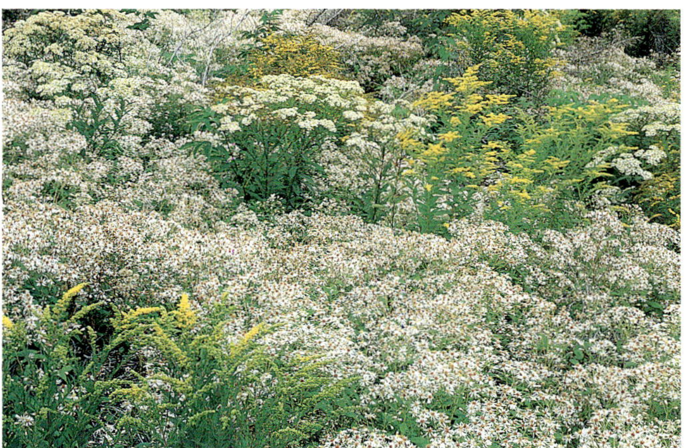

I didn't find the initial subject appealing and decided to experiment.

Using the same frame as in the previous illustration, I calculated the exposure for a small aperture, knowing that it would give me a slow shutter speed. During the exposure I moved the lens around in a circular motion to get this abstract pattern.

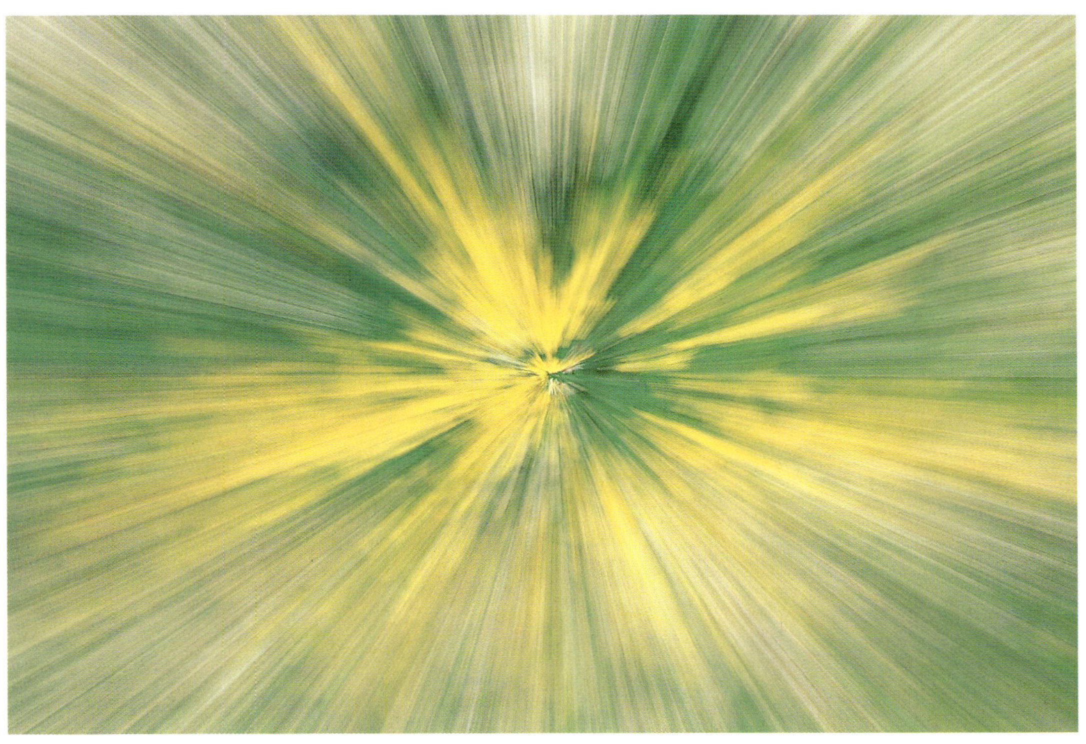

My subject is the same area of flowers. The only difference here is that I zoomed out with an 80–200mm lens during the exposure to create this abstract pattern.

cal composition, and shoot wide open at f/4 or f/5.6 (your widest aperture). Throw it slightly out of focus, and overexpose one stop. After you get your film back, put the slides in a slide mount to create a sandwich. The technique isn't foolproof, but it will get you thinking creatively.

Look at the work of other photographers, and ask yourself what you like or dislike about a particular image. Try to figure out how they accomplished a certain task, and experiment with it on your own. Spend time at your local bookstore browsing the photography books. Purchase the books you feel might be helpful in learning new ways of looking at subjects. These can be some of the best investments you spend in time and money. Have fun, and enjoy every frame you shoot.

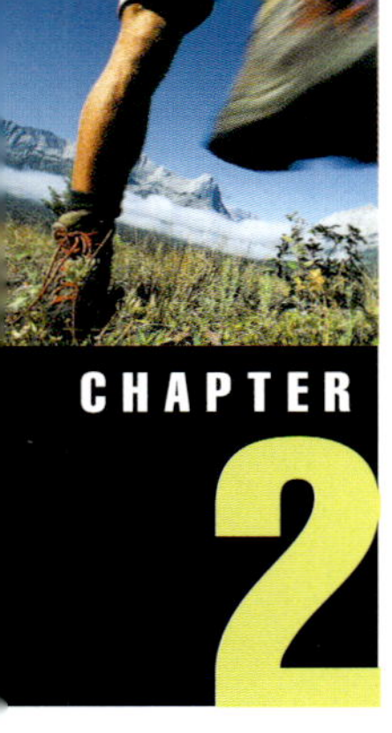

CHAPTER

2

Washington, DC

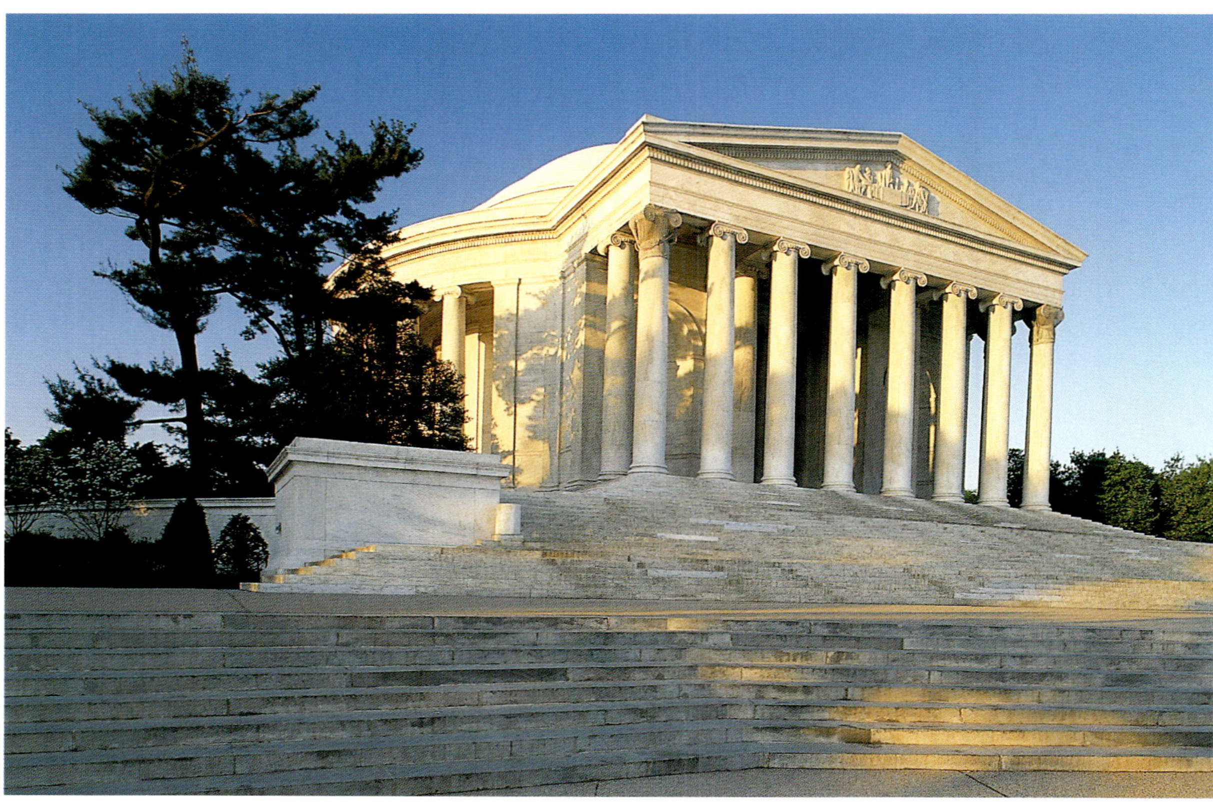

Aside from making it possible to include many of the locations that follow, Washington, DC offers myriad photographic opportunities. This site of historic battles, groundbreaking legislation, civil rights demonstrations, and revered monuments and memorials draws millions of visitors a year and appears regularly in textbooks, newspapers, magazines and stock photo collections of all kinds, making it among the most salable of locations. The city has few, if any, natural settings other than an occasional shade tree. Instead, Washington, DC is made up of granite, concrete and history. There is little doubt where you are when you step into this city. I encourage every photographer to take the challenge and photograph our nation's capital. A worthy experience? You bet.

PHOTOGRAPHER'S VIEW

If you're an avid outdoor photographer, Washington, DC is probably the last place you would consider setting up a tripod. I understand—you'll be hard pressed to find so much as an unclaimed shade tree on a hot afternoon.

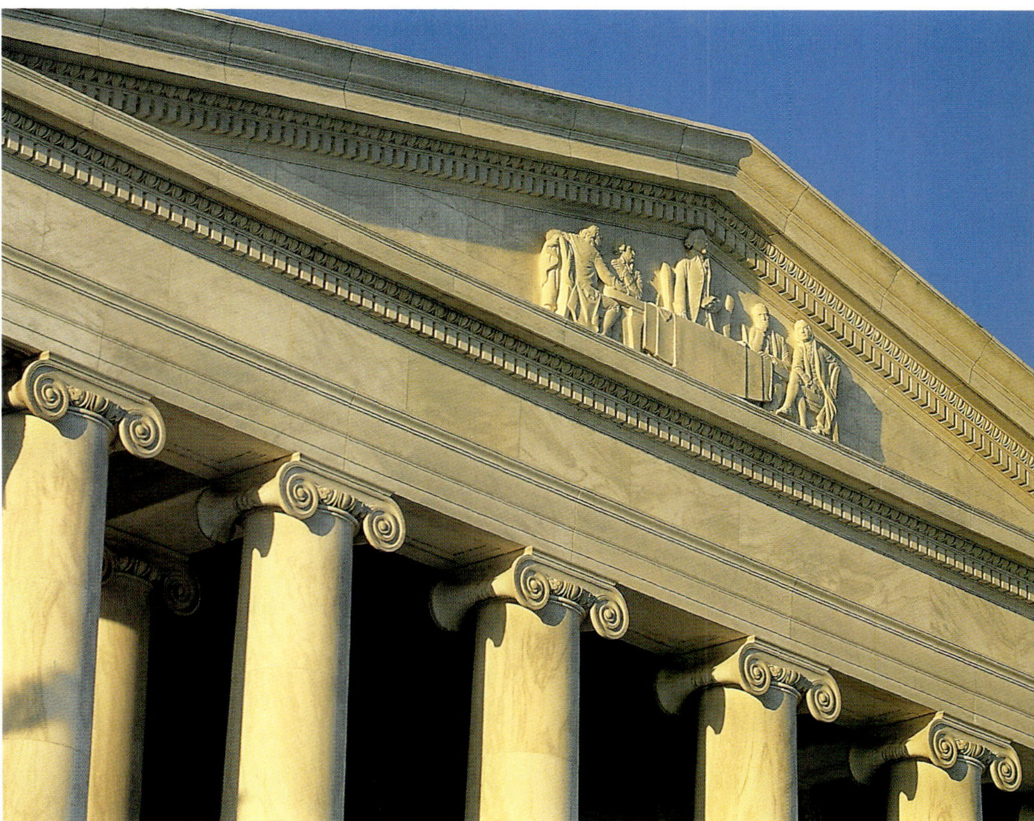

But keep an open mind. Aside from the potential for repeat sales with DC images (it's one of the most requested U.S. cities for stock sales), the city boasts a wonderful array of architectural styles and unusual shapes in its buildings and monuments. Those options, and the masses of people who will inevitably float into your frame, will push you to find new angles and shapes to photograph. Even if you're shooting for fun, the educational experience itself is worth it.

PARKING. With icons at every turn, Washington, DC is esthetically easy to photograph but more difficult physically. Parking can be difficult, but following my advice can save you a little time and a lot of frustration. You'll need to tackle most of DC on your feet, and parking won't be as bad as you might think if you look for parking in the areas I list below. The majority of subjects you'll want to photograph sit between Arlington National Cemetery and the Capitol from east to west and between the White House and the Jefferson Memorial from north to south.

1. THE TIDAL BASIN: You'll spend a lot of time here, and there is plenty of free parking on Ohio Drive along the Potomac River and in the parking lot at the Thomas Jefferson Memorial. You will need to arrive in the morning before the large tour groups, but you ought to be here early for the good light anyway.

2. THE U.S. CAPITOL: Another area where you'll spend a lot of time. You'll find plenty of parking at Union Station. The Union Station lots charge a fee, but it's very reasonable.

3. ARLINGTON NATIONAL CEMETERY: Parking is available here for a minimal fee.

4. THE MARINE CORPS WAR MEMORIAL: This is the last of the major landmarks that require driving, and parking can be an issue here. There *is* a small parking lot at the memorial. If there are no spaces, drive around for about five to ten minutes, and something should open up.

These are really the only places you need to drive; the rest is on your feet. The exceptions are attractions or landmarks that sit outside the metro area, such as the National Zoo or the Washington National Cathedral.

PEOPLE. The second issue you'll have to deal with is people. I don't think there is ever a time during the year where you won't encounter large numbers of people. You'll need to hit the Tidal Basin early and work the monuments hard before the crowds arrive. The U.S. Capitol, Supreme Court Building, Library of Congress and other important architectural landmarks won't be a problem for the most part as people tend to spread out and typically

I look for details (in this case the columns of the Jefferson Memorial) on my return trip around the basin when more people are out. Tourists are less likely to interfere with these types of shots.

don't hang out for long periods of time in these areas. You'll be confined to the hours of Arlington National Cemetery for photographing that area, but there are plenty of locations within the grounds where you can escape the crowds.

EQUIPMENT. The equipment you need is pretty simple. A wide-angle zoom or fixed focal length from 28 to 35mm will be used more than any other. If you have the ability to work with Canon's tilt/shift lenses, these will help tremendously. Tilt/shift lenses allow you to correct converging verticals (the leaning of buildings) that occur when you photograph architecture with a regular lens. These lenses can be expensive but aren't necessary. You can use the converging effect as a creative technique. If the leaning disturbs you, move farther away and use a long telephoto to eliminate the problem. If you're selling your work or if you shoot a lot of architecture, the expense of a tilt/shift lens can be justified. Telephoto lenses between 100 and 300mm can be useful for photographing the city from afar and for working details of the monuments. The key to success in Washington is to work fast. Hauling equipment from place to place is going to slow you down and eventually wear you out. Travel light whenever possible.

The Tidal Basin

The Tidal Basin is probably the area most people associate with when they think of Washington DC. (I'm including the Mall in this area.) The basin is where the major monuments are: the Jefferson, Lincoln, FDR, Washington, Vietnam War and Korean War memorials. This is also where you will encounter the most people.

The Tidal Basin has so much to photograph you'll have no choice but to deal with the crowds. The best way to successfully approach the Tidal Basin is to be on location before sunrise. This will give you a couple hours to work the monuments at first light and beat the crowd. My strategy has been to tackle the monuments starting at the Jefferson Memorial and make my way toward the Vietnam War Memorial. I make this route twice, the second time working in reverse order. My first trip

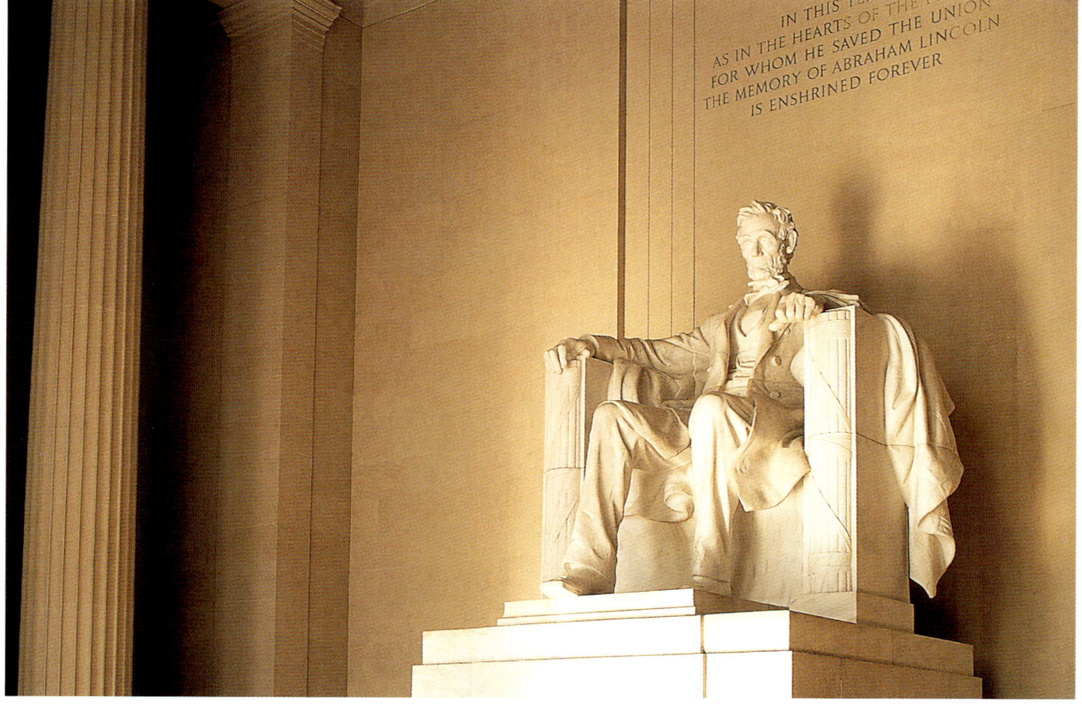

The Lincoln Memorial is white, but the warm morning light and the artificial light from within the monument gave the walls this pinkish color. I metered the walls and opened up one stop from that reading.

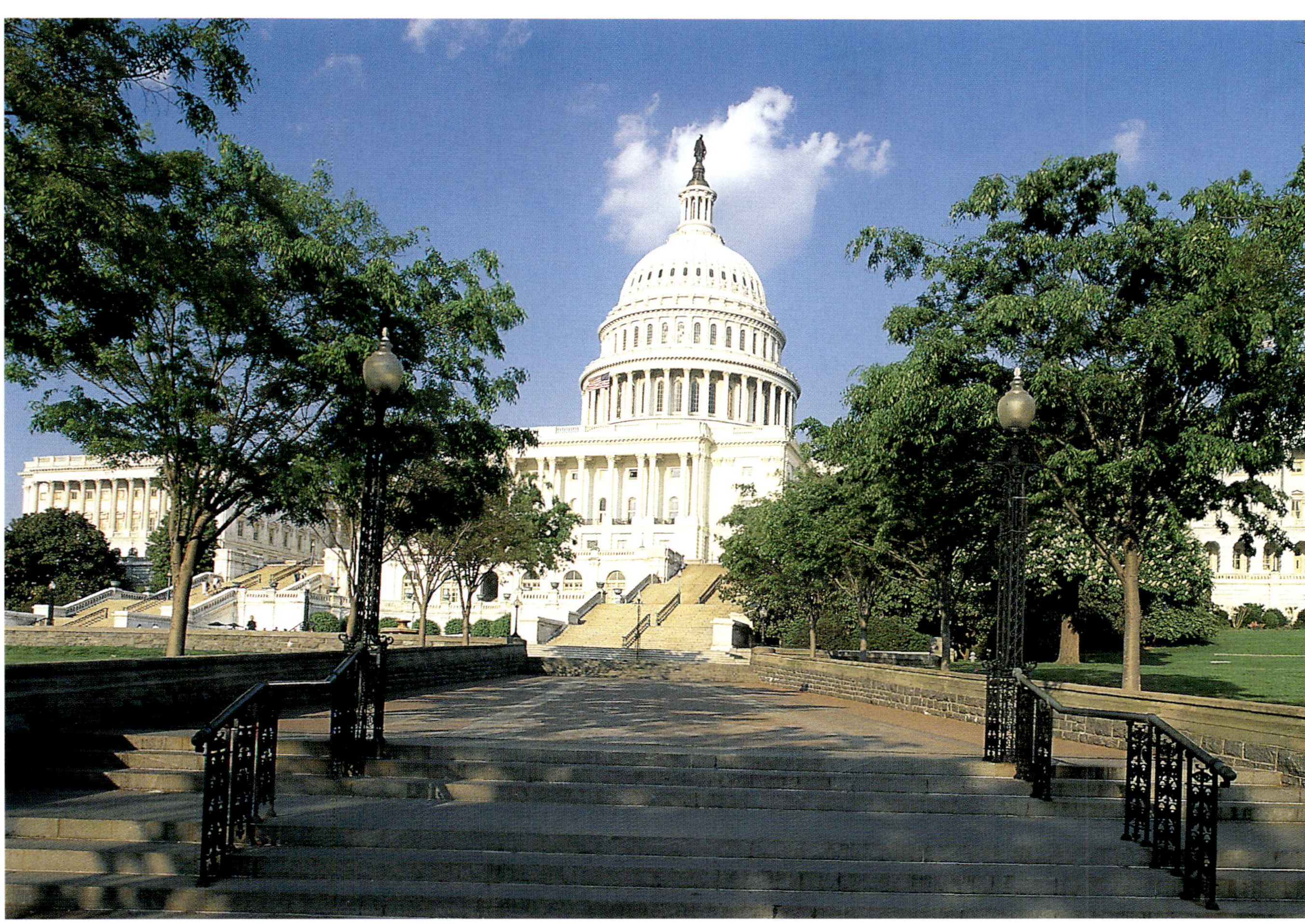

starting at the Jefferson Memorial is to compose images containing the entire monument or any other images I can't get when crowds are present. You might have only one chance to work the monuments without people unless you return on another early morning. I try to get at least a couple different compositions at each monument, and then I walk briskly or even jog to the next monument. After I have gotten all the monuments, I make another visit to each and shoot details or portions of the monuments where people are not a factor or maybe try to get some good stock images with tourists. I should mention the walk to the Washington Monument is a long hike from the others in the area, but the best way to photograph this monument is from a distance in other areas around the basin. You will have no problem finding available parking on Ohio Drive or at the Jefferson Memorial if you arrive early.

When photographing light-colored architecture on a sunny day, I take my meter reading off the grass, which I usually consider to be middle toned, then close down a half stop. This will render some detail in the building, as it did with the U.S. Capitol here, and keep it from being washed out.

The U.S. Capitol and Surrounding Area

The U.S. Capitol has so many angles to work, you'll want to be in the area both in the morning and in the late afternoon. I try to make an entire day in the area. There is unfortunately one problem when photographing the Capitol from the Capitol grounds: You can't set up a tripod without a tripod permit. Security guards will ask you to leave if you don't have a permit, which isn't difficult to get. You'll need to go to the Capitol Police Office inside the Capitol to register and sign a release.

While you're near the Capitol, there are several other important architectural subjects you might consider: the U.S. Supreme Court, the Library of Congress, Union Station and the White House. All of these are within easy walking distance of the Capitol, with the exception of the White House. The White House will require a good hike. Consider leaving your tripod behind if you want to lighten your load because you cannot photograph the White House with a tripod. Security will be all over you within minutes. I find some of these policies a little ridiculous but bite my tongue. If you want a close-up shot of the Washington Monument, this is the time and place to do it. The Washington Monument is only a block away from the White House.

Pick up a map of the city (AAA has a user-friendly map; also see the map on page 33) and highlight other landmarks that interest you in this area. Sure enough, as you get caught up in capturing the major landmarks, you'll forget something. This is also the area where many of the museums and galleries are. If you have a bad weather day or just an extra day to spend in the city, I recommend at least one museum or gallery. When you need a break, Union Station has many eateries and is a great place to sit back and relax for a while. Union Station is also the place you'll want to park. There are several long-term parking lots in the area. You can park for the entire day at a reasonable price. Street parking is difficult to find and limited to a couple hours.

Arlington National Cemetery and the Marine Corps War Memorial

I can't imagine going to Washington, DC and not going to Arlington National Cemetery. To walk the paths in Arlington is to walk among heroes. This is their final resting place, and Arlington exists to honor these men and women.

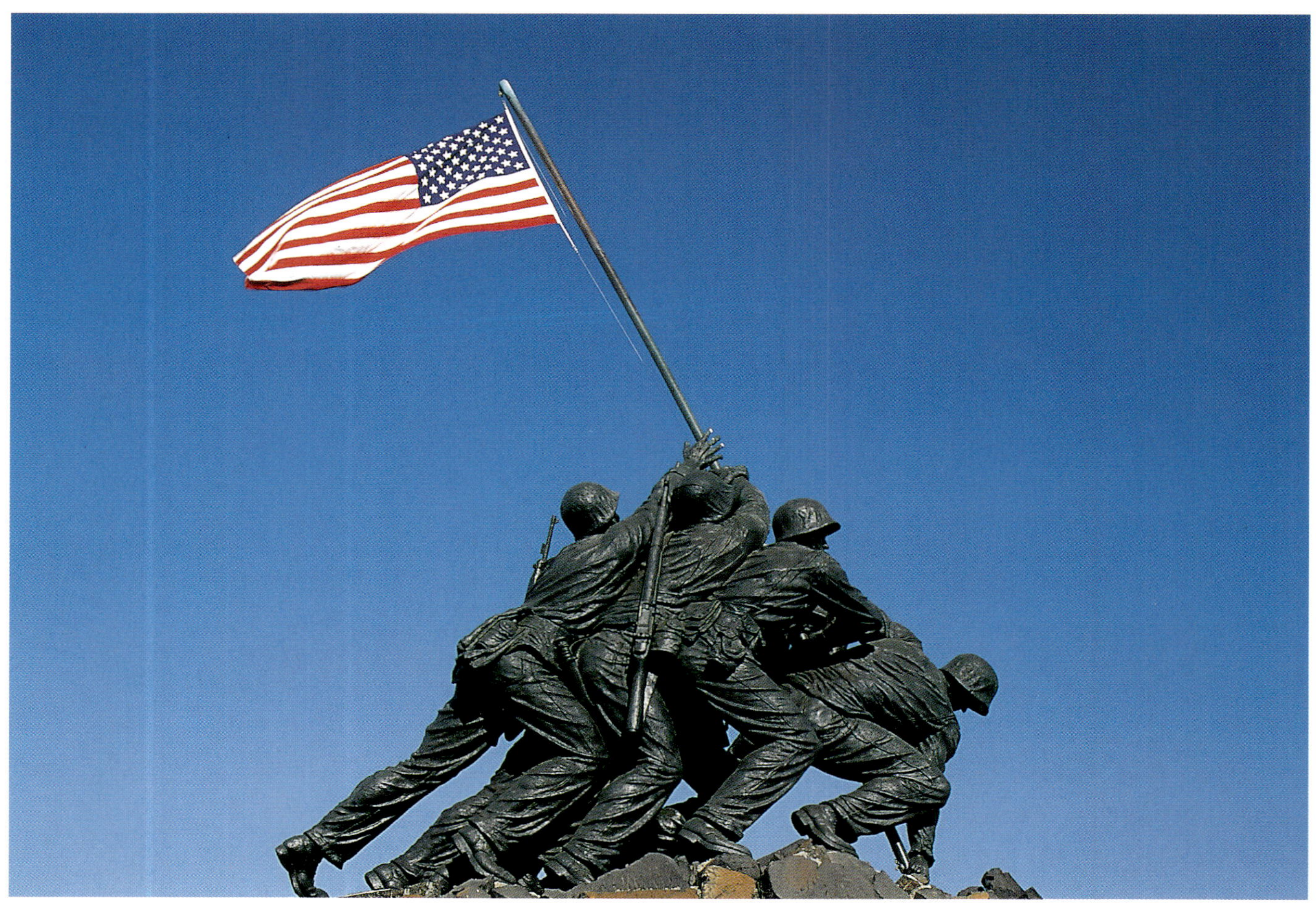

The Marine Corps War Memorial is the most famous military and war memorial in Washington, DC. I can't imagine not photographing this famous landmark. I cut out the base of the memorial, where busloads of tourists flocked, and used the beautiful sky I had.

Veterans from every war that involved America can be found here. As a visitor, it is a privilege to be a part of Arlington even just for a moment. It doesn't matter if you ever pull your camera from the bag. Go for the experience. This is one you'll remember for a long time.

The photograph most photographers want from Arlington National Cemetery is the rows of white stones marking our fallen heroes. There are many places to capture this image, and you'll know it when you see it. The Tomb of the Unknown Soldier sits atop a hill in Arlington National Cemetery and is very much worth the visit. This is not a photo opportunity as much as it is an experience. The changing of the guard takes place throughout the day and is a must-see. There is no picture taking allowed during the ceremony. A couple hours in Arlington is all you will need but might be the best two hours you spend in the city.

The Marine Corps War Memorial, also known as Iwo Jima Memorial, is just a short drive from Arlington National Cemetery. Of all the military and war memorials, this is probably the most recognized, with the Vietnam War Memorial not far behind. This memorial sits atop a hill overlooking the Lincoln Memorial and the city of Washington, DC. This is a beautiful setting and offers several angles from which to capture the monument as well as the city across the Potomac. There's not much here other than the memorial. I suggest visiting this area before or after Arlington National Cemetery. It's just a five-minute drive from Arlington.

Other Attractions

There is so much to see and photograph in Washington, DC that I'm sure much will be passed up. A productive photo shoot in DC depends on a good sky, but if you do get an overcast day and you want to spend it photographing, I suggest visiting the National Zoological Park. The National Zoo is a photo-friendly zoo with several wonderful exhibits for photographing. One of the most notable is the panda exhibit. The Washington National Cathedral is another beautiful landmark and a worthy photo stop. Nearby Georgetown offers some good opportunities for street scenes or maybe just to sit in a street café for lunch or a cup of coffee.

A photo shoot in Washington, DC requires a well-thought-out game plan. Don't expect to accomplish a lot photographically if you don't have a game plan and a good contingency plan. It might also be a good idea to check to see about any rallies planned during your visit. I would put plans off if some major rally or other event were going on. I remember visiting once not knowing of a rally and ended up turning around and going home. Fighting tens of thousands of people rallying in the Mall is a photographer's nightmare. Plan before going.

WHEN TO GO

Spring, summer and fall can all be good times in Washington, DC for photography, but the most productive are spring and autumn. The summer months are hot and humid. Mid April to mid May is my first choice and October my second choice. These two seasons are also the best chances to get the blue skies you'll need to be successful. The sky in the summer months is good at times, but you have a greater chance of finding white, smeary skies, a hot, humid climate and, of course, too many people.

Many people think of the cherry blossoms as the time to be in Washington. The blossoms are pretty but limiting. You will be hard pressed to try to include the blossoms with many of the monuments. Without blossoms all of the other trees will be bare and hardly attractive for photography. The cherry blossom

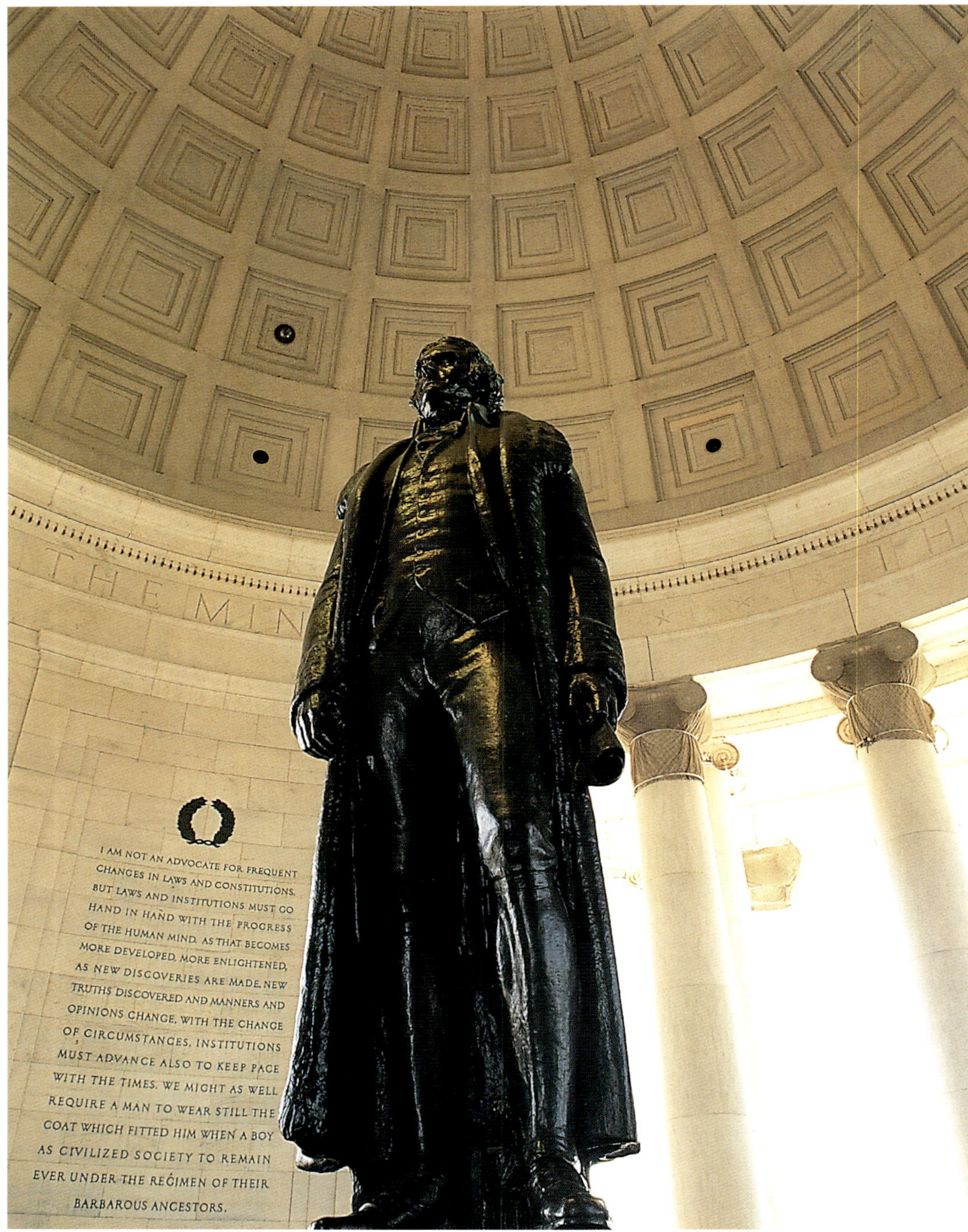

Standing at the base of Thomas Jefferson's statue looking skyward seemed the most appropriate way to compose this American leader. Notice one of his speeches inscribed on the distant wall. These details are important, and I recommend looking for and including them when appropriate.

blooms also bring big crowds, adding another frustration to your shooting. If you insist on photographing the blossoms, you need to be in town in late March. These blooms can be unpredictable. Therefore, I recommend calling the chamber of commerce to get an update or networking with other photographers who might have information to share.

TIME REQUIREMENTS

You can shoot Washington, DC in a long weekend, or you can allow a whole week and have no problem keeping yourself busy. I recommend a minimum of four full days of shooting. This should give you time to get acquainted with the city and provide enough time to photograph most of the major attractions. If you get a day with a bad sky, you probably won't get everything you want. I always like to give myself at least one extra day just in case I have bad weather or something else gets in the way.

NEED TO KNOW

There are many places for lodging with a wide variety of prices. I like easy access to my early-morning shoots, so I prefer Alexandria. Lodging in this area can be more than you want to spend, and if so, you'll need to stray from the beltway. The problem with this is the traffic getting into the city. Traffic is heavy regardless of when you leave your hotel in the morning. I prefer to spend the extra money and save a lot of headaches and nail biting while driving with people who know these roads better than I do. For more about the city and help on trip planning, head to <www.dcvisit.com> and <www.dcchamber.org>.

photographer's choice

SAVANNAH, GA., AND CHARLESTON, S.C., offer unique alternatives to Washington, DC with a fraction of the crowds. You won't find mega-monuments here, but the historic homes framed by azaleas and moss-draped oaks make for a wonderful urban photographic experience. [Savannah, www.savannah-online.com; Charleston, www.charlestoncvb.com]

directions

Regardless of where you're coming from, you'll need to get on Interstate 495. I-495 circles the entire Washington, DC area. From I-495 I recommend getting on I-395 north toward Alexandria and Arlington. From Arlington you'll go across the Potomac River into Washington, DC on I-395 or Route 1. On Route 1 you can take the first exit after crossing the bridge to get to the Tidal Basin, or you can follow I-395 and take the U.S. Capitol exit.

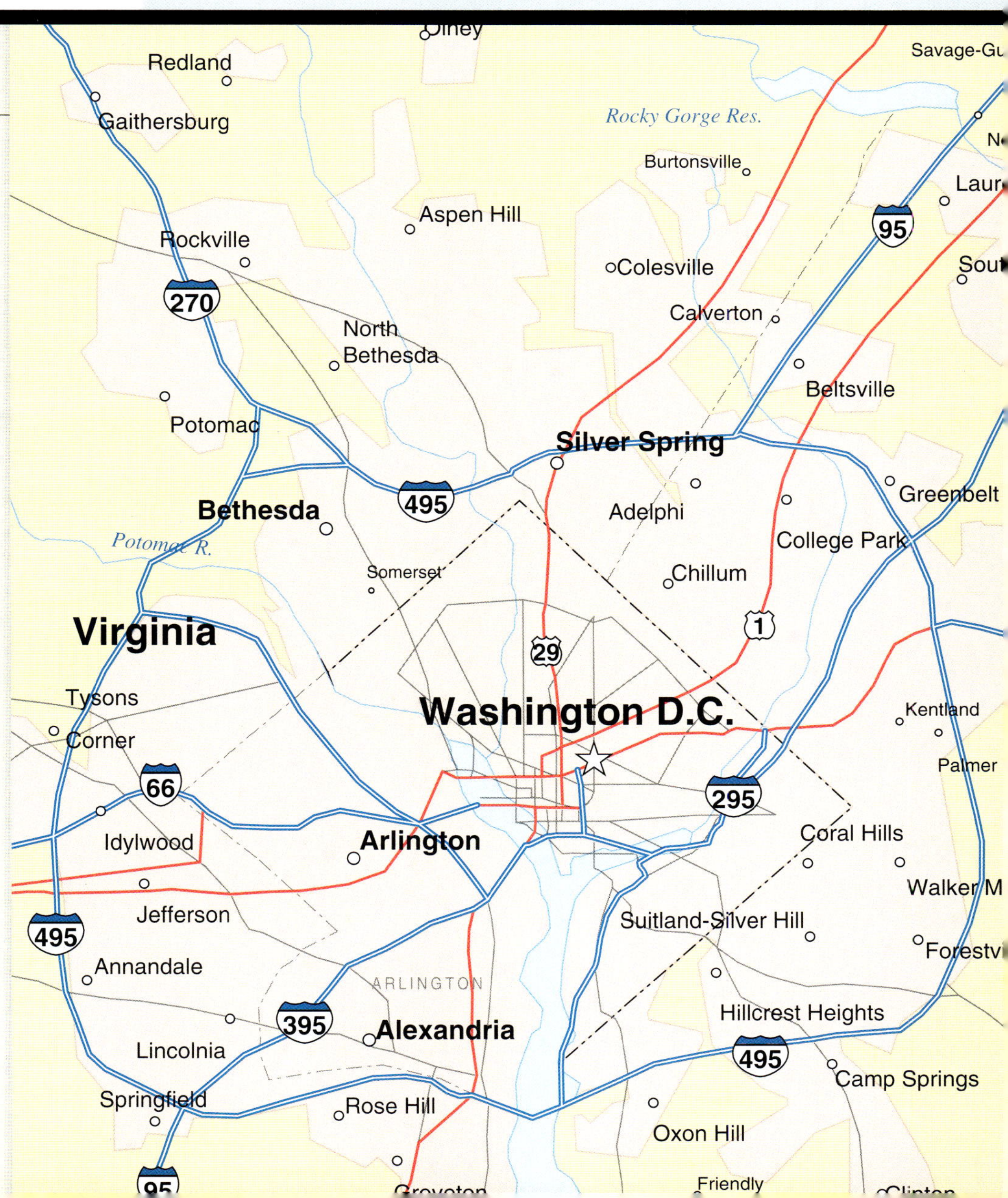

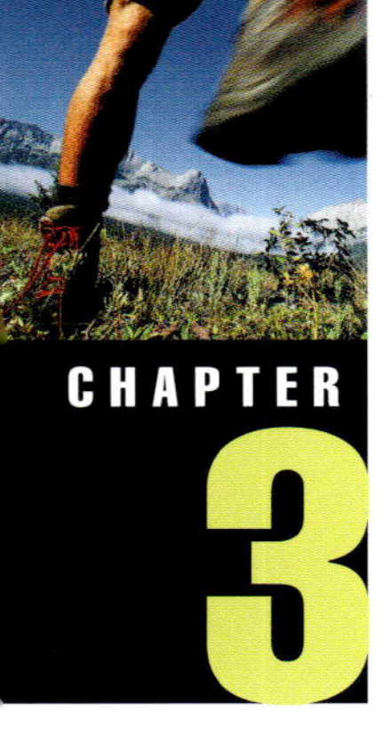

CHAPTER 3

Acadia National Park & Nova Scotia

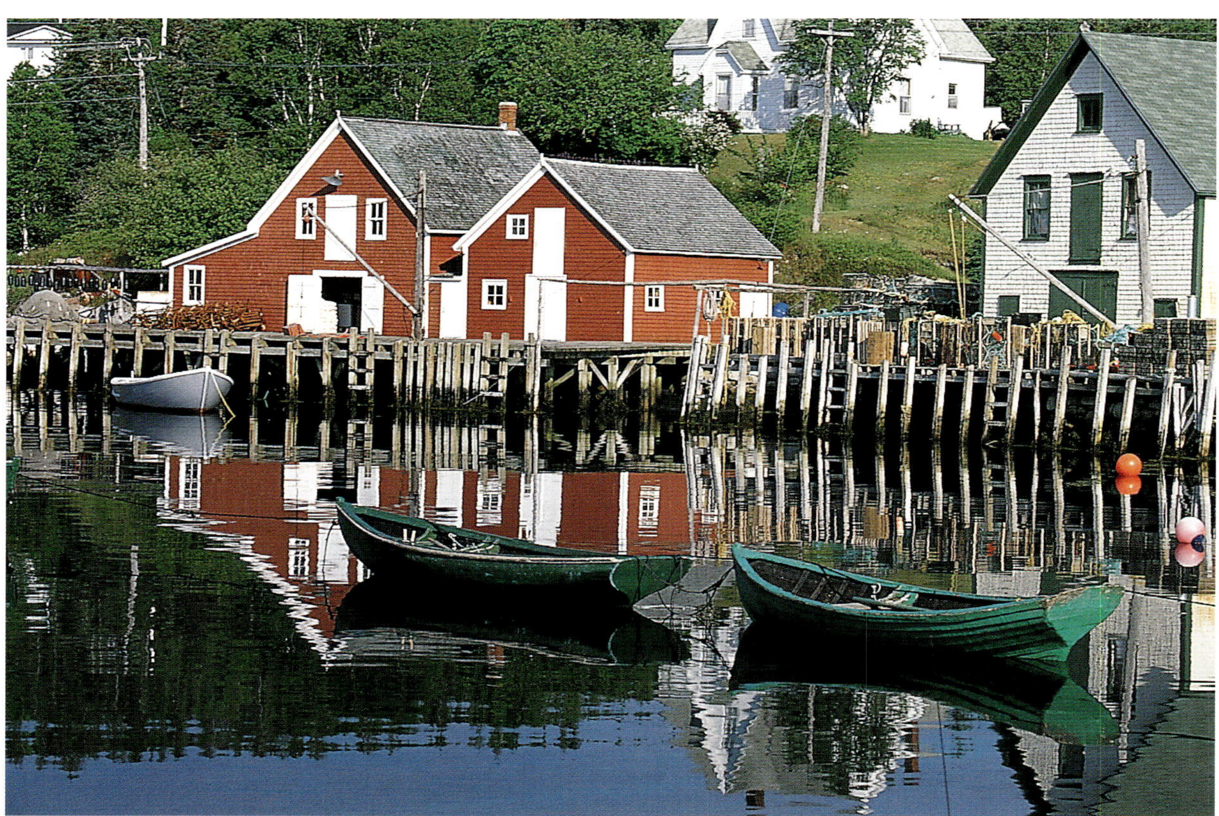

The New England coast and that of its northern Canadian neighbor, Nova Scotia, is a quiet, rocky coastline known for quaint fishing villages and secluded coves. This stretch of coast is hardly typical of more southerly shores, where sandy beaches and sunbathers are the norm. The Northeast coast attracts the explorer or the traveler looking to experience the wonders of the sea, hike in a wooded cove or spend time on a squeaky wood-planked dock watching local fishermen bring in their day's labor. A day might end over a lobster dinner or next to a cozy fire, but it always ends with tired feet and a refreshed spirit.

The New England coast is slowly losing its quaintness and old rustic fishing towns to

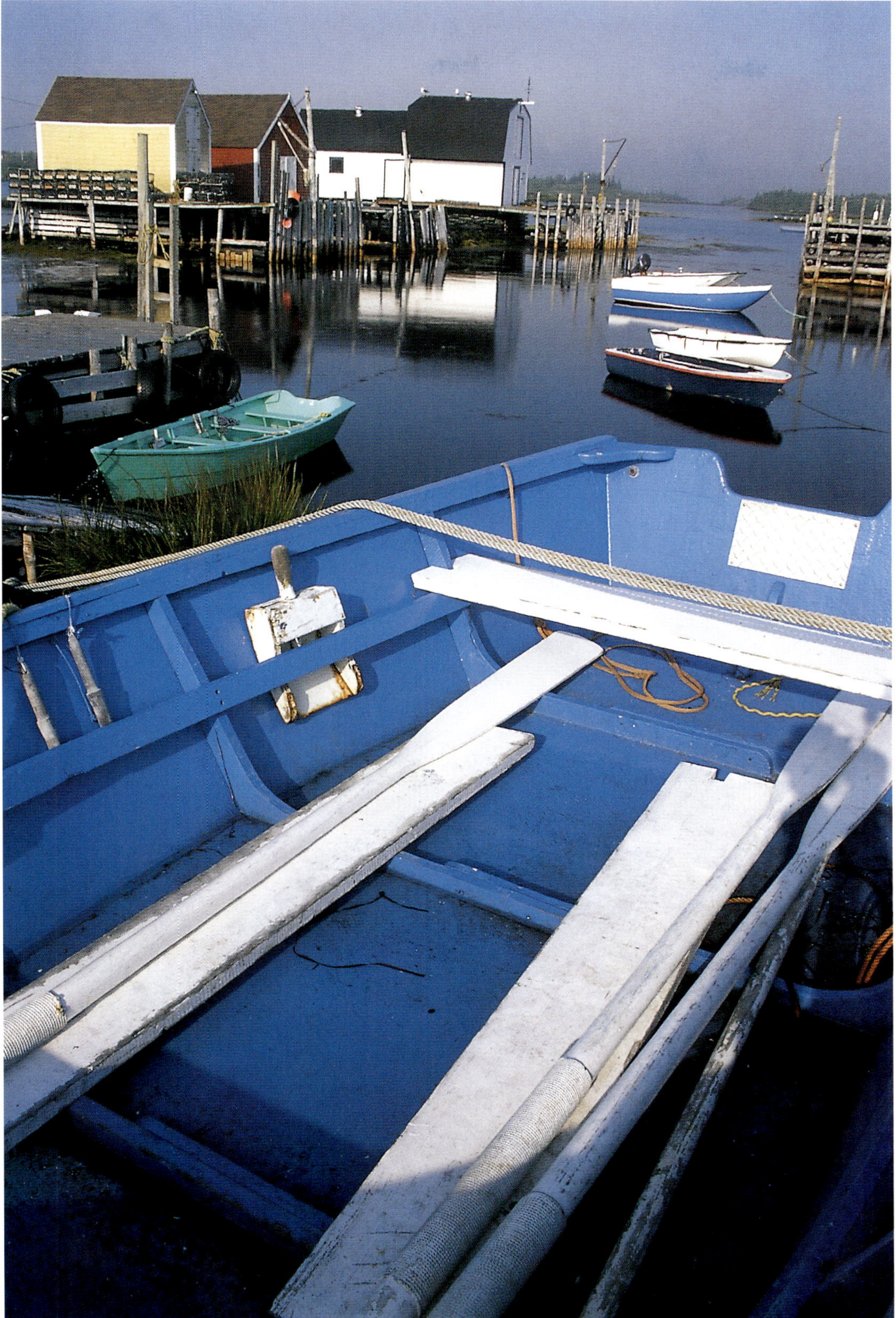

Boat docks are often loaded with clutter. I saw potential in this scene as soon as I walked up to it, but it took me forty-five minutes to find a composition that eliminated old tires and other distracting elements.

upscale developments. I spent a recent spring exploring most of the Maine coast and found only a few fishing towns untouched by development and increasing pressures to change with the times. It's only a matter of time before many of these hidden fishing towns see mortar drying on new condominiums. The old harbor towns now share their fishing docks with recreational craft. Acadia National Park is the only place along this stretch of coast protected from future developments. You still can experience the old-coast charm to some degree, but Acadia ensures seclusion that other towns just can't guarantee.

The Nova Scotia coast has fallen on hard times in recent years as the seas are being depleted of fish, the staple of this economy. The timeless fishing villages you envision for New England are still common here. You can witness fishermen hard at work making their daily rounds to check lobster traps and bringing in the sea's offerings. The friendly faces of Nova Scotia welcome travelers alongside their docks and are making strides to accommodate and attract more tourists. It should be many years, if ever, before they face the issues that the New England states are facing with development, but for now Nova Scotians warmly welcomes all who visit their docks.

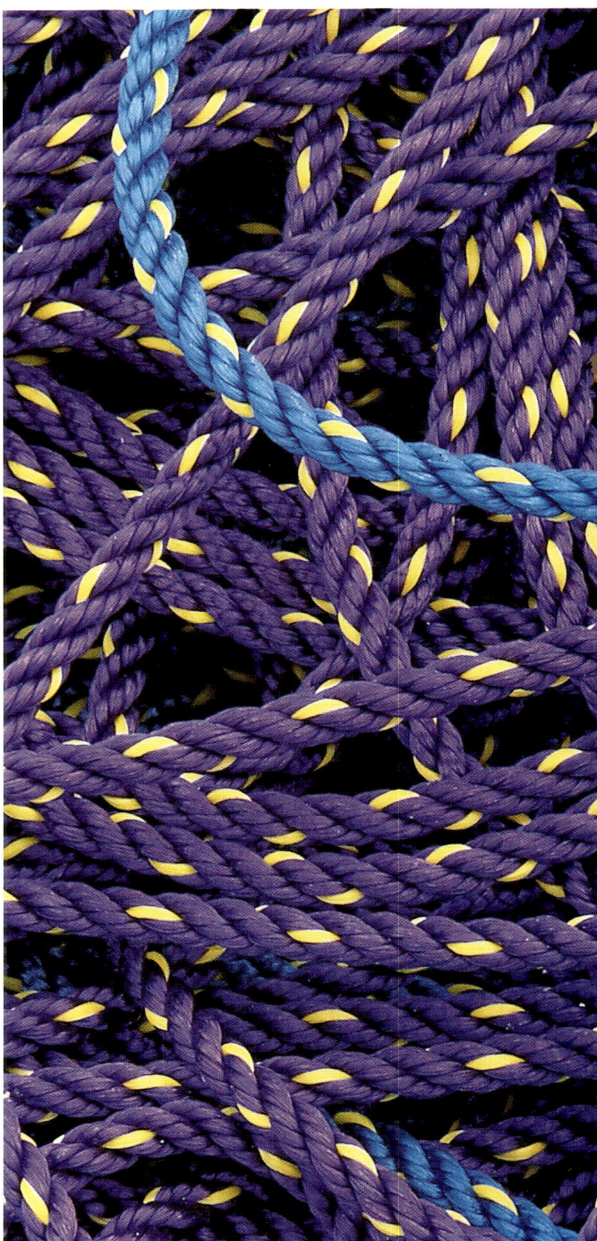

PHOTOGRAPHER'S VIEW

Photography along the northern coast of Maine in Acadia National Park and across the Gulf of Maine in Nova Scotia is as fun as it is rewarding. You won't find complete isolation, but you'll have no problem escaping from other tourists. I have lost interest in exploring the lower Maine coast (with the exception of lighthouses) because of the burgeoning development I already mentioned. During the high travel season, you spend more time in traffic than you do on the coast. Acadia offers the opportunity to enjoy the beauty of the rugged coast and northern forests. The National Park Service continues to purchase land and place restrictions on developments, with the help of residents and others interested in protecting the region. This is good news for everyone. Future photographers will have the same great opportunities we do today to capture this iconic coastline and the forests surrounding Mt. Desert Island that make up Acadia National Park.

Nova Scotia's coast is as wild as Acadia's. Many of Nova Scotia's coastal communities

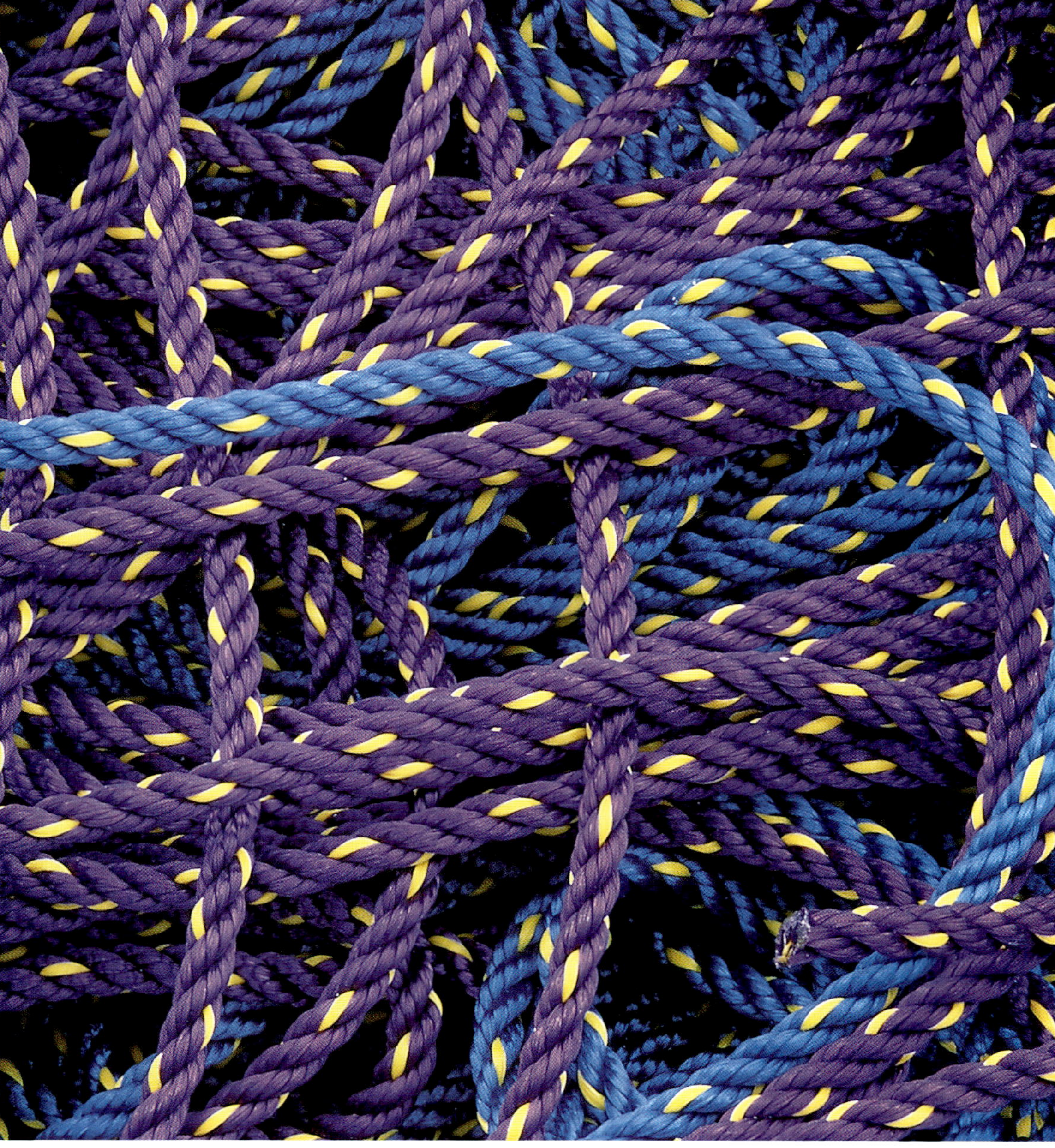

Colorful subjects such as these ropes are common around the old boat docks. I spent two hours on a cold, ugly, overcast day shooting several compositions of these ropes. I could have given up for the day but instead made it as productive as possible. This shot has sold a couple times, so it turned out to be profitable as well.

are still working harbor towns. Subjects here include wooden shacks, weathered docks and sea-beaten fishing boats. Fog can roll in and out of Nova Scotia as quickly as a gull can swoop down on a crab, or it can linger for the entire day. Much of inland Nova Scotia isn't very interesting and can make for a boring drive. But once you make your way along the coast, you will see why I like this North Atlantic coast for photography.

I recommend combining Acadia and Nova Scotia into one trip because the subjects you will work differ. In Acadia I prefer to focus on natural landmarks, such as the rocky coastline and hidden inland lakes. In Nova Scotia I focus on the old fishing communities, although there are a few areas where you can work natural landscapes. You could make an entire trip out of one of these locations if you prefer, but weigh your options carefully. Whichever way you choose, you will have no problem finding enough to shoot.

Provided the weather holds, most of your photography in both Acadia and Nova Scotia will be landscapes. Be prepared to shoot other subjects, though, because the weather can turn bad quickly and stay bad for days—eliminating any chance of shooting landscapes. I have encountered bad weather on several trips, one of which involved gray skies and rain for five straight days. These are days where you will need to focus on architectural details or experiment with set-up shots of maritime subjects (lobster traps and colorful ropes) or tide pools.

Your camera bag should include everything from wide angles to long telephotos and macro equipment. Make sure you have a diffuser and polarizing and warming filters. You may never see a single day of clouds, but don't be caught without plastic or an umbrella to protect your gear in misty rain and a cloth to dry both your lenses and camera body. Regardless of the weather, I always carry an extra cleaning cloth for the front glass element of my lenses, especially in New England.

Acadia Sea Coast

Bar Harbor, a small seaside community where lobster is as common at lunch as a hot dog is at a picnic, is the gateway to beautiful Acadia National Park. Acadia has a long history of settlement, established first for farming and lumbering and later for fishing and shipbuilding. These communities coexisting with the austere natural environment are what will make your journey to this North Atlantic region unique.

Photographers take in both the mild summers and the colorful autumns in Acadia. The first and most obvious attraction is the park loop road, which is an ideal way to get a quick introduction to the park. The road begins just outside Bar Harbor and makes its way along the breathtaking granite coastline. The sea can be as gentle as a reflection pond or as ravaging as a twister. Both situations lend themselves to dramatic photo opportunities, the gentleness to beautiful sunrises and sunsets and the pounding surf to impressive shots of ocean spray spurting into the air.

Walking the coast from around Thunder Hole to Otter Point isn't difficult and is the best way to exploit every opportunity. This is the best stretch and example of the Acadia coast you'll see with little effort. Every day is different, and I recommend making this walk at least a couple times during your stay. Consider a morning and an evening shoot along this stretch of coast. First light is the best time to shoot the area. On days with good weather, it's nearly impossible to photograph without people, so sunrise is your best chance. Otter Point is popular with photographers and offers a chance to see the coast from a different vantage point. The western side of Otter Cove also provides a unique perspective of the coastline. The terrain here sits high above the sea and is a bit more rugged and dangerous, but with few people.

Acadia has four lighthouses, but only one, Bass Harbor Head, is easily accessible. This is a popular spot for photographers, but few available vantage points means that almost every shot you see of this lighthouse looks the same. Most of the fishing communities on Mt. Desert Island, Seal Harbor, Northeast Harbor, Southwest Harbor, Bass Harbor and Bernard, are not the old rustic harbor towns you might envision when you think of Maine. Like others in Maine, they are losing their historic charm. You might find a few photo opportunities around these towns, but I recommend waiting till Nova Scotia if you're making this part of your journey. If you're not planning to visit Nova Scotia, take a day and head down the coast to Stonington, about an hour's drive from Bar Harbor south of Mt. Desert Island. Stonington is photogenic and still very much a working harbor.

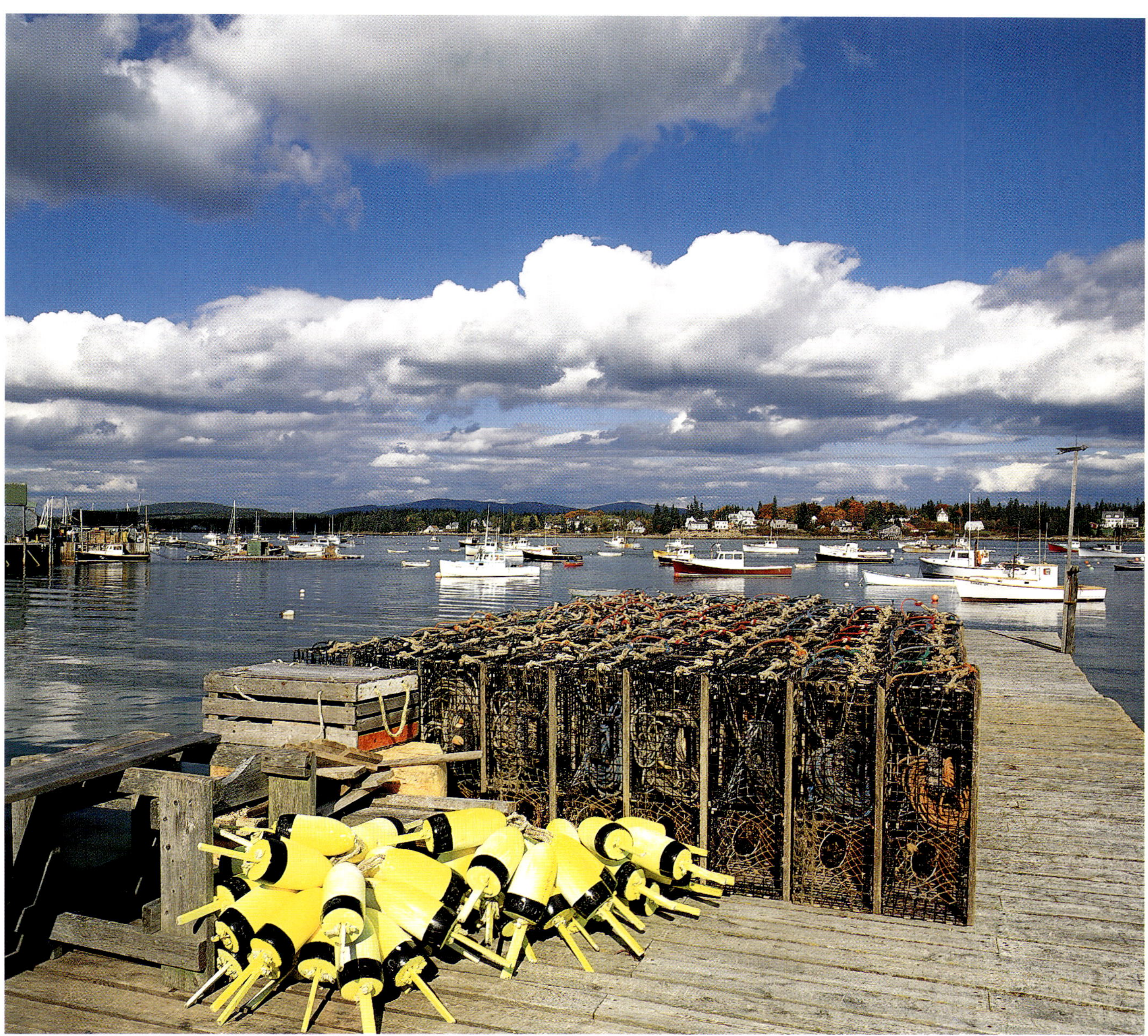

A typical harbor on Mt. Desert Island. Look for colorful foregrounds when photographing an otherwise uninteresting scene.

Acadia's Interior

When one thinks of Acadia National Park, the first thing that comes to mind is the coast, but Acadia is much more than the sea. Many photographers find the interior as good and at times better than the coast. This wooded island has many getaways connected by old carriage roads built by John D. Rockefeller Jr., who donated more than eleven thousand acres, one-third of the national park. These wooded areas hide secluded lakes and ponds that reflect their forested surroundings. Several are within a short walk of a parking lot, while others require a hike along a carriage path.

The three most popular are Bubble Pond, Jordan Pond and Long Pond. (Although maps label them ponds, they're really lakes.) Bubble Pond is my favorite because it has an intimate setting with grasses growing from the shallow waters near the shore. Spring is calm and fragrant with the new season's growth. In autumn the colors reflect in calm water and complement the golden-toned grasses growing near the pond's edge. Jordan Pond is probably

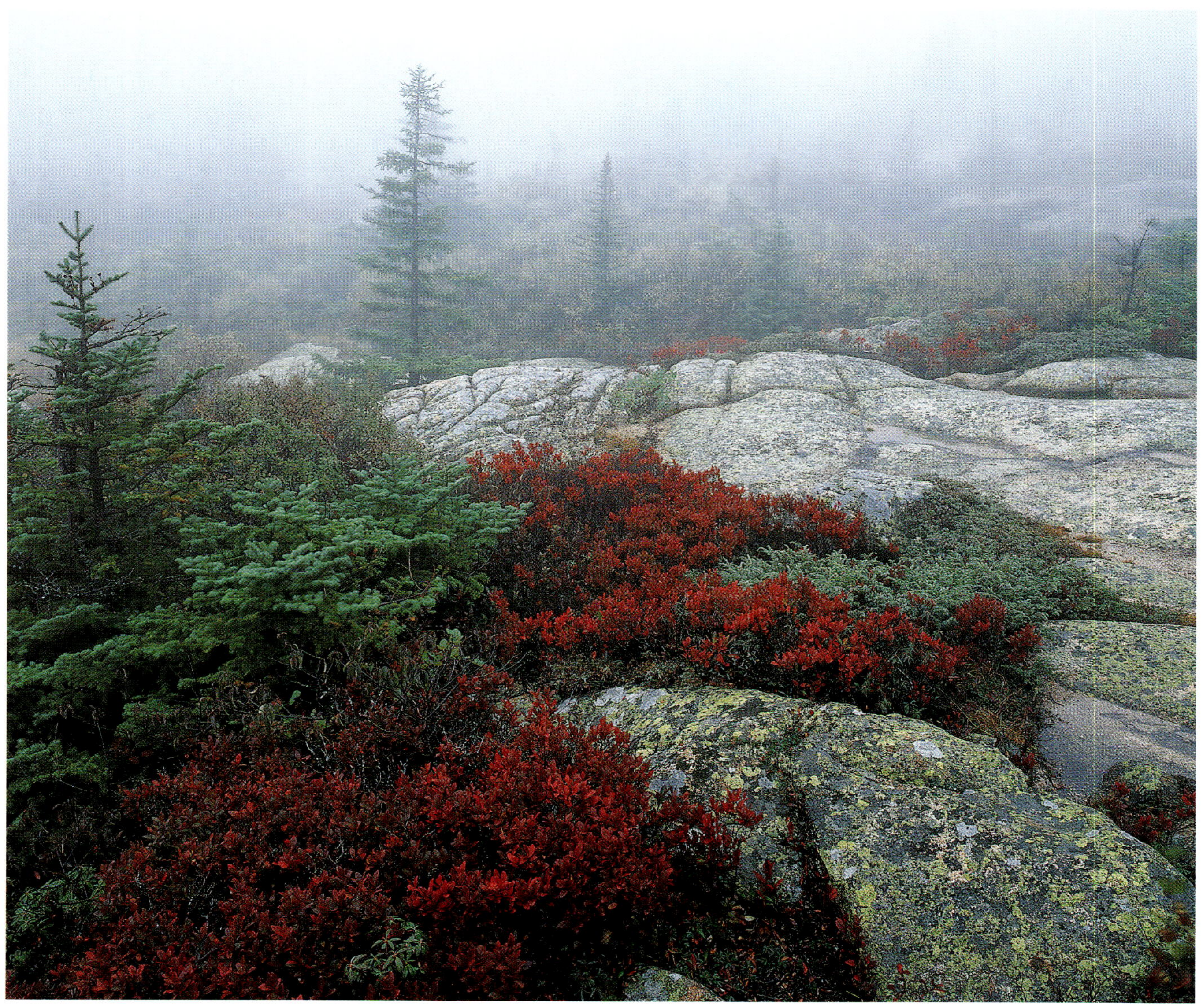

I don't care much for photographing the sunrise atop Cadillac Mountain. I typically head up the mountain on mornings when most photographers pass it up—when heavy cloud cover socks it in. I was the only person on the mountain on this morning.

the most popular among visitors. Jordan is not as intimate as Bubble Pond but is still a peaceful retreat with many good photo opportunities. The shoreline has some large boulders to use as foreground subjects with the distant landscape mirrored in its crystal-clear waters. Long Pond is unique and sits at the bottom of a hill surrounded by open fields. Spring here is quiet, and autumn brings a smattering of color that reflects from the few trees on its banks. Long Pond is visible from the road and therefore attracts many people. (Acadia has two Long Ponds. I am describing the one on Route 3 just beyond Seal Harbor.) There are some nice images to be taken in the area.

Cadillac Mountain rises 1,530 feet southwest of Bar Harbor. This is a popular spot for tourists and photographers to catch the sunrise, and between October 7 and March 6, it's the first place in the United States the sun touches each morning. The view from atop Cadillac Mountain is stunning, giving an overall view of the distant islands out in Frenchman Bay. As the sun breaks the horizon, the sea turns golden as it reflects the first rays of light. Any time of year is beautiful on Cadillac Mountain, but autumn fog adds a special touch to the landscape when mixed with reds and golds in the grasses and scrubs that dot the landscape. The fog can get pretty thick as you climb the steep road, and you might be discouraging if you intended to catch the sunrise. Don't worry. You still will have subjects to work on the mountain itself.

You won't just set up a tripod in Acadia and have a great shoot waiting for you. This park requires an observant eye and a little creativity. The coastline is pretty, but you'll need to look at a lot of angles and have good light. So many images I have seen of the Acadia coast look the same. You really need a strong element—boulders, a tree, great light—to catch and hold the viewer's attention. The interior of the park is no different. Walk around, and explore the surroundings. The lakes can be incredible under the right conditions, but if you don't have great light, a little fog or something interesting happening, it's just another shot. View the lakes away from where the average tourist is going to wander. Being a lazy photographer in Acadia is going to show in your images.

Nova Scotia

Nova Scotia is very different from Acadia. This is where you'll come for the old fishing towns. Here you'll find the weather-beaten boat houses and squeaky wood-planked docks piled with lobster traps and faded ropes. (Wire traps are replacing wooden lobster traps, but Nova Scotia still has some wooden ones.) Getting to Nova Scotia from Acadia is easy. From Bar Harbor you can catch the ferry ("The Cat") to Yarmouth. The Cat hydroplanes across the gulf to Nova Scotia in about three hours and carries both you and your car (reservations online at <www.catferry.com>). The cost is reasonable and beats driving. I recommend getting a reservation a month in advance if you're traveling during the peak summer season. Peggy's Cove is a three-hour drive from Yarmouth and is where I recommend you begin working south along the coast. If you have an entire week in Nova Scotia, consider starting even farther north and making your way south. (Check out <www.explore.gov.ns.ca> as you plan your trip.)

Peggy's Cove is as close as you'll come to finding the rustic fishing villages that you might have expected before your trip. Peggy's Cove is well adapted to tourists and I'm sure maintains some of its old charm for that reason. You can spend an entire day here and never run out of subjects to work. If you get a foggy morning, you'll be even more inclined to stay the day. Besides the old wooden boat houses and the sea-beaten fishing boats tied to the docks, Peggy's Cove has a picturesque lighthouse atop its rocky shore. Today it's a post office mainly used by tourists, but it's very photogenic, with several angles to work in both the morning and evening light.

Indian Harbor is a hop and a skip from Peggy's Cove and has many old boathouses and dilapidated docks. From Indian Harbor I suggest traveling at a leisurely pace and stopping in as many little towns along the coast as you have time for. If you are pressed for time, make your way to a tiny community called Blue Rocks. I have found lots of compelling and colorful subjects to work in this area. Even if you are limited on time, you should still stop in a few communities on your way from Peggy's Cove to Blue Rocks. Most of these have something interesting to photograph. Lunenburg is much more tourist oriented but has some colorful subjects along the docks and on the outskirts of the town. If you're out of time, from Blue Rocks you should get back onto Route 103 and head to Yarmouth. If you still have time to explore, continue south along the coast and make stops along the way. The farther south you travel, the less photogenic many of these towns become. I suggest making a stop in Kejimkujik National Park on the sea (not the inland Kejimkujik National Park).

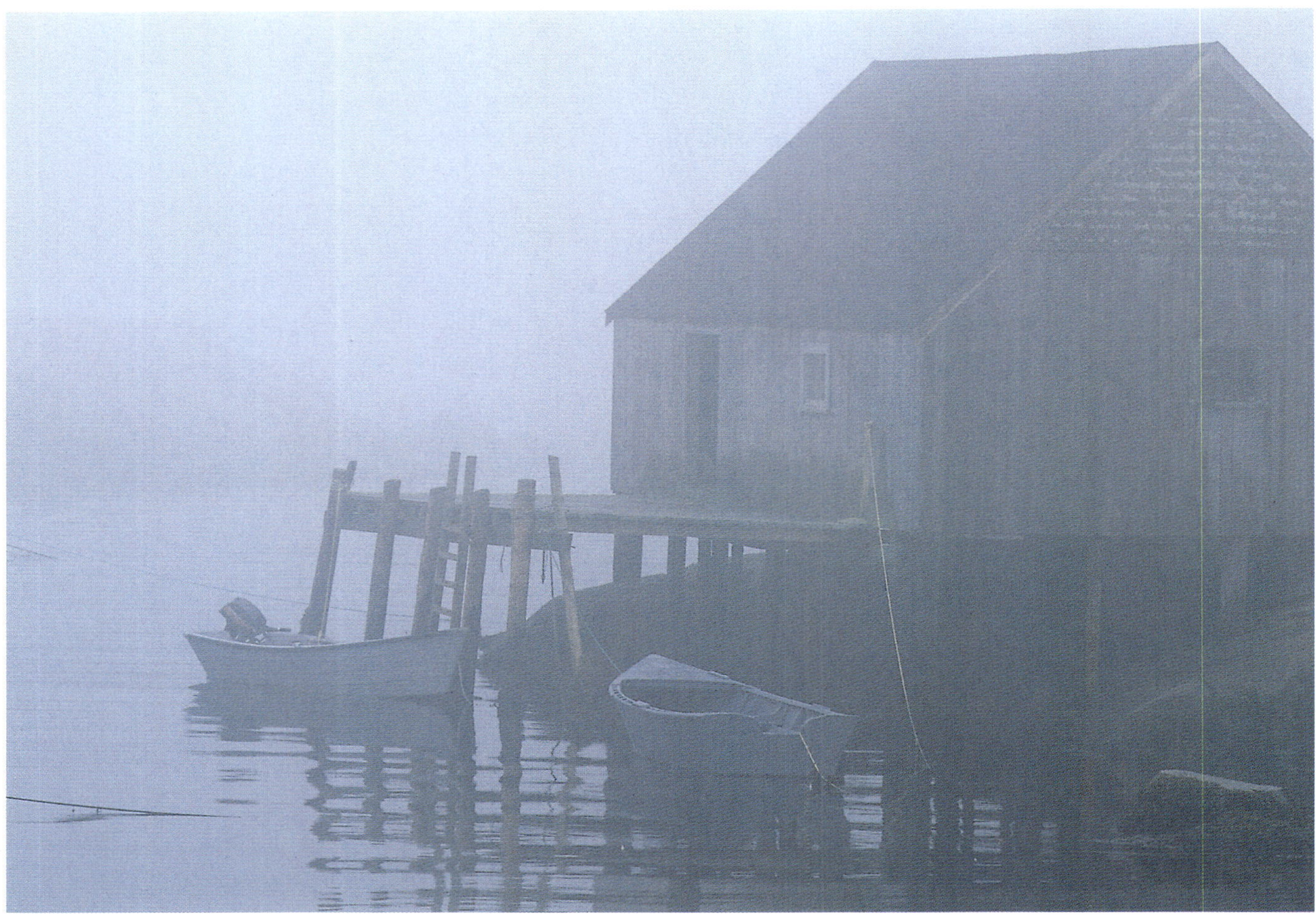

I spent three days around Peggy's Cove in Nova Scotia on this particular trip and was hoping for fog, but saw none until the morning of my departure. Flexibility is crucial in these situations.

Nova Scotia continues much farther north than Peggy's Cove, which is only about a third of the way up the coast. You can travel as far north as Cape Breton Island. Cape Breton Highlands National Park sits in the northernmost part of the island. The park has some pretty coastal areas made up of beautiful, rugged red-rock coastline and sandy, brownish-red beaches. The drive from Yarmouth to Cape Breton takes an entire day. The coastal towns on Cape Breton Island are as authentic as it gets to real working fishing harbors.

The early summer months (June is best) in Nova Scotia are especially pretty because the lupine is blooming in many different colors around the small coastal communities. Lupine in Nova Scotia can grow more than three feet high and typically grows in large open areas. Late September to early October is also pretty as the ground cover turns to beautiful reds and oranges. Weather can be unpredictable any time of the year on the island. Allow for at least one bad weather day, but even on bad weather days photographers might set up smaller shots around the docks. If you decide to spend more time exploring Nova Scotia, pick up *Discover Nova Scotia: Beaches, Parks, & Natural Sites*, by Patty Mintz.

Lighthouses on the Maine Coast

Those historic structures responsible for guiding sailors and fishermen safely into harbor are an integral part of the New England photographic experience. Maine has sixty-three lighthouses. Many are not very photogenic, and some are impossible to reach without a boat. I have been to every one that offers access by road and can save you a lot of time.

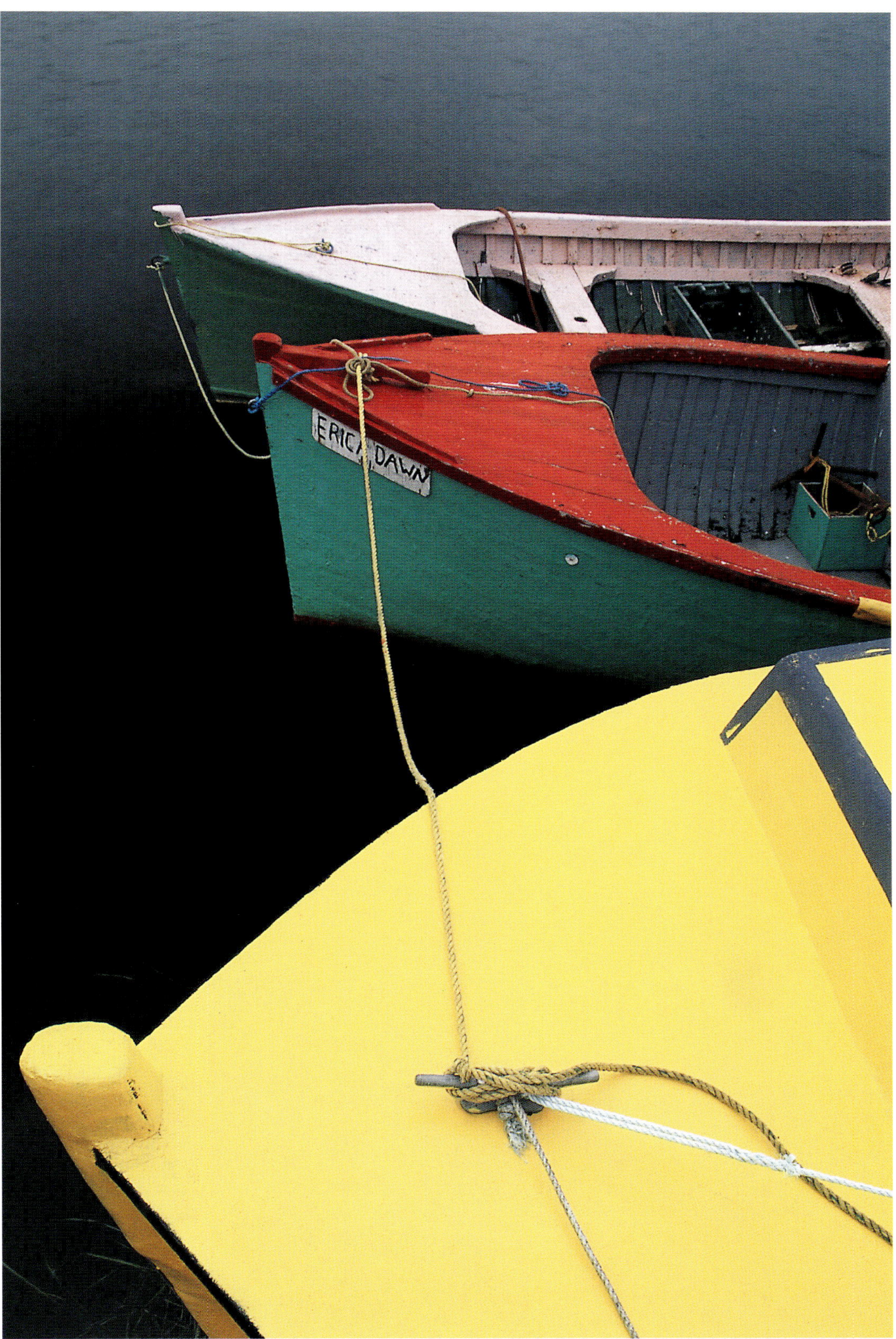

Colorful boats are common in the northern reaches of Nova Scotia. I discovered these boats in a fishing harbor cluttered with equipment. It's okay to crop an element in your composition as long as it's still easily identifiable.

The nine listed below are the most popular and what I deem to be the most photogenic. From south to north:

1. Cape Neddick (York)
2. Portland Head Light (Cape Elizabeth)
3. Cape Elizabeth (Cape Elizabeth)
4. Pemaquid Point (Bristol)
5. Marshall Point (St. George)
6. Rockland Breakwater (Rockland)
7. Bass Harbor (Southwest Harbor, Acadia)
8. Prospect Harbor (Gouldsboro)
9. West Quoddy (Lubec)

If you're interested in lighthouses beyond photography, try visiting others not on this list. As always, your DeLorme Atlas and Gazetteer will be your best guide in getting to these lighthouses.

photographer's choice

For more picturesque coastline, check out the OREGON COAST—the most beautiful stretch of natural coast anywhere, dotted with sea stacks and graced with old-growth forests and sand dunes. It's also one of the best-protected coastlines in the United States. The isolated BIG SUR COAST just south of San Francisco is much smaller but also offers great opportunities. [Oregon coast, www.visittheoregoncoast.com; Big Sur coast, www.bigsurcalifornia.org]

WHEN TO GO

Mid to late June is when the weather becomes predictably better for photography in both locations and the beautiful lupine in Nova Scotia is at its best. July, August and September are not only tourist season but also tourist weather—endless days of cloudless skies. This is not what you want for photography. My favorite time in Acadia is the first and second week of October. I time my arrival in Acadia around Columbus Day, the most predictable time for good fall color. If you're planning to visit Nova Scotia on the same trip, travel to Nova Scotia first, then finish up in Acadia.

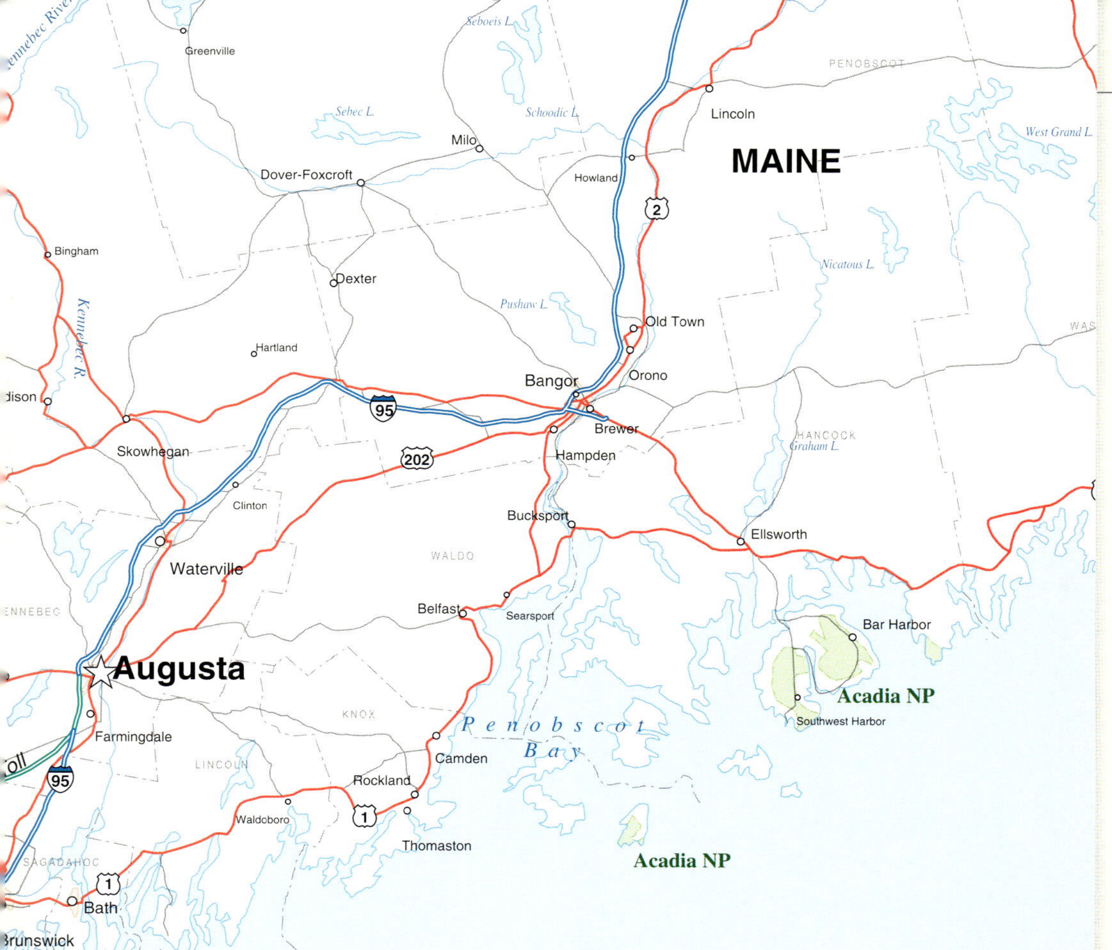

directions

From Bangor, Maine, take I-95 to Route 1A toward Ellsworth. In Ellsworth pick up Route 3, and follow it into Bar Harbor. In Bar Harbor there are several ways to enter Acadia. Road signs will guide you from Bar Harbor.

TIME REQUIREMENTS

The ideal itinerary: Arrive in Bar Harbor for three full days of shooting in Acadia National Park. Depart on the fourth day, travel by ferry to Yarmouth, and drive to Peggy's Cove. Take two full shooting days in Nova Scotia, working from Peggy's Cove down to Blue Rocks. Take another full day to return to Bar Harbor, and depart from there. I recommend at least a week if you want a nice introduction to both Acadia and Nova Scotia. You could easily spend one week in each location for exploration beyond the major areas.

If you do decide to photograph the lighthouses, give yourself a morning or late afternoon for each one. You will be hard pressed to shoot more than two per day. The drive from Cape Neddick to West Quoddy on the expressway takes most of a day, so the drive on the less expedient coastal route will take an extra day or two.

NEED TO KNOW

Lodging for Acadia is plentiful in Bar Harbor. Lodging in Nova Scotia is a little scarce along the coast. Halifax has plenty of lodging you can use while shooting around Peggy's Cove, but that will require a thirty- to forty-minute drive for your first shoot in the morning. Indian Cove has a small family-run motel called Clifty Cove [(902) 823-3178]. You need to make reservations well in advance if you want to stay here. This motel will put you right on the coast with a five-minute drive to Peggy's Cove. Most locations in the book have a decent number of accommodations, so I don't give hotel names, but I'm making an exception for Indian Cove because lodging is difficult to find. For more information on Acadia, you can reach the park at (207) 288-3338 or <www.nps.gov/acad/>. Also, take a look at *Acadia Revealed: The Complete Guide*, by Jay Kaiser.

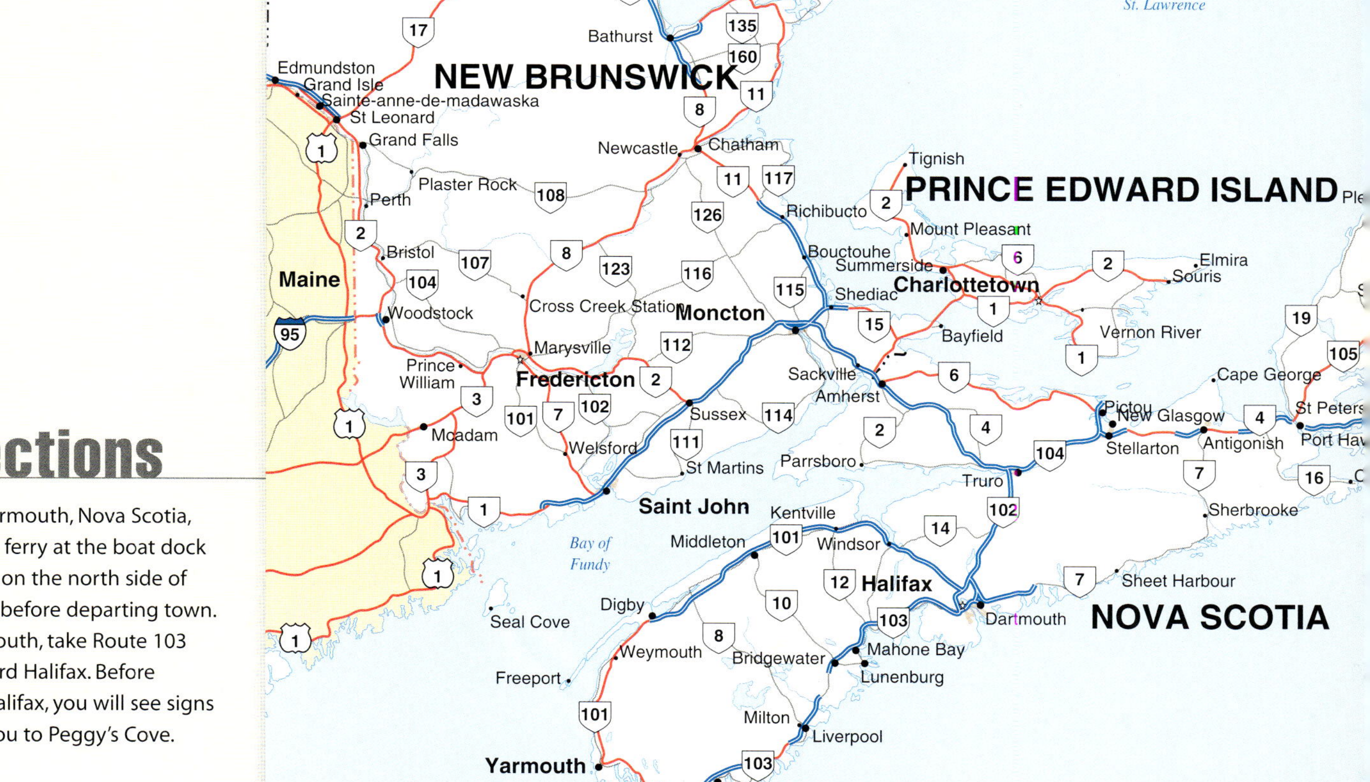

directions

To reach Yarmouth, Nova Scotia, pick up the ferry at the boat dock on Route 3 on the north side of Bar Harbor before departing town. From Yarmouth, take Route 103 north toward Halifax. Before reaching Halifax, you will see signs directing you to Peggy's Cove.

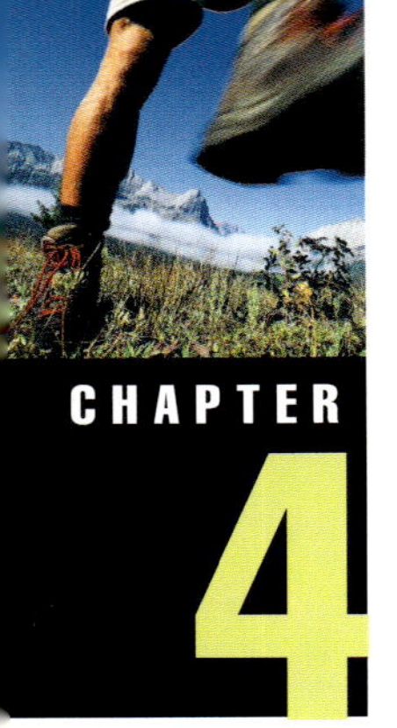

CHAPTER 4

Great Smoky Mountains National Park

TENNESSEE/NORTH CAROLINA

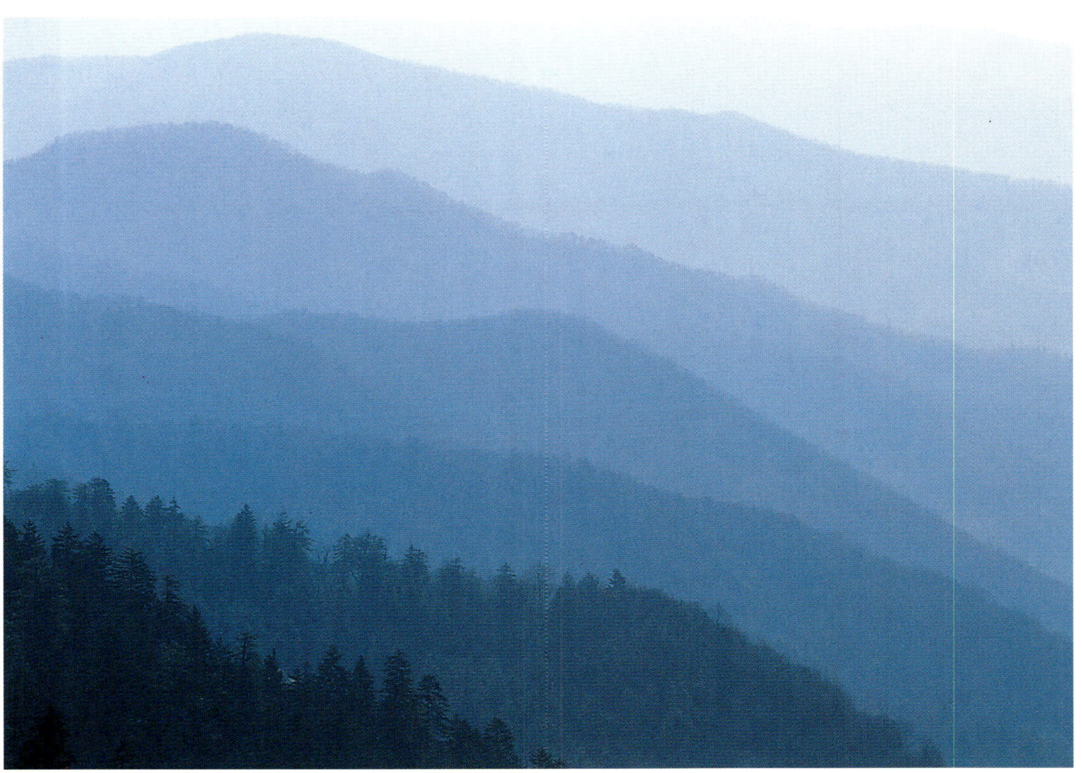

Great Smoky Mountains National Park, one of the few national parks in the East, warrants mention in the same breath as Yellowstone or Yosemite and is the heart of the entire Appalachian chain, which extends from northern Georgia to Maine. All of the Appalachians are beautiful, but their most spectacular scenery might lie here in America's most visited national park. At times the crowds pulled off at one of the many overlooks can make your jaw drop, but solitude awaits a feet hundred feet off the road.

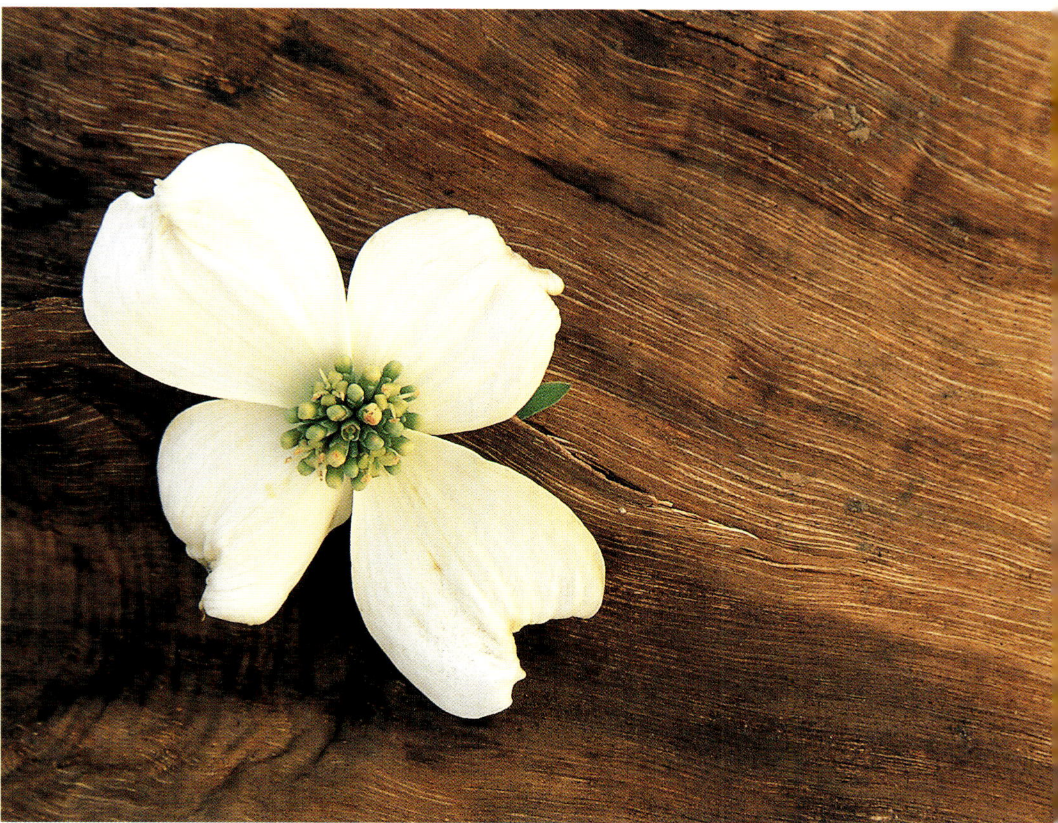

I used the back side of this piece of bark as a background for the dogwood flower. There is nothing wrong with setting up a composition in nature as long as nothing is damaged in the process.

The Smokies get their name from the thick haze that wraps itself around the mountains on the horizon, common throughout the year. The actual park is almost equally divided between Tennessee and North Carolina and consists mostly of mountains blanketed in five different types of forest (spruce-fir, northern hardwood, pine-oak, hemlock and cove hardwood) with more than one hundred varieties of trees. This diversity, notable even by Appalachian standards, is a result of abundant rainfall, high humidity and a wide range of elevations, from 875 feet to 6,643 feet, at Clingmans Dome.

The forests are home to more than fifteen hundred species of flowering plants, sixty-five mammal species, and more than one hundred species of birds that breed within park boundaries. They also boast the most beautiful mountain streams anywhere in the United States. The boulder-covered streams are rife with lush mosses that often lead to a cascade or waterfall. Park guides list eleven major waterfalls along developed trails. With the abundant rainfall and the number of streams in the park, one can find a hidden cascade or waterfall off the beaten path, and occasionally a seasonal stream converges with a trail to present you with an unexpectedly beautiful forest scene.

The Great Smoky Mountains are also part of Appalachian history. The Park Service has relocated and restored several historic homesteads, the most popular of which is at Cades Cove. Early settlers cleared flat valleys, which they called coves, and built their homes and raised families and crops. The cabins and barns are fine examples of early pioneer architecture. These pioneers tilled the land in the park for about one hundred years, until the Great Depression, when settlers sold their land to government agencies for the creation of Great Smoky Mountains National Park.

PHOTOGRAPHER'S VIEW

The Smokies are one of my favorite places to photograph. I have spent time photographing during all four seasons here and have always returned home with something special. A first-time visitor to the Smokies might find the park intimidating initially. As every good photographer knows, you have to warm up to new surroundings. Get your creative juices flowing by taking a short walk through the forest to get a feel for the environment. Those can't-miss landscapes that stand out in many of the western parks don't exist here. You'll have to work the land, but it is well worth the effort. I have always felt my images of the Smokies are some of the best in my library, and that may come

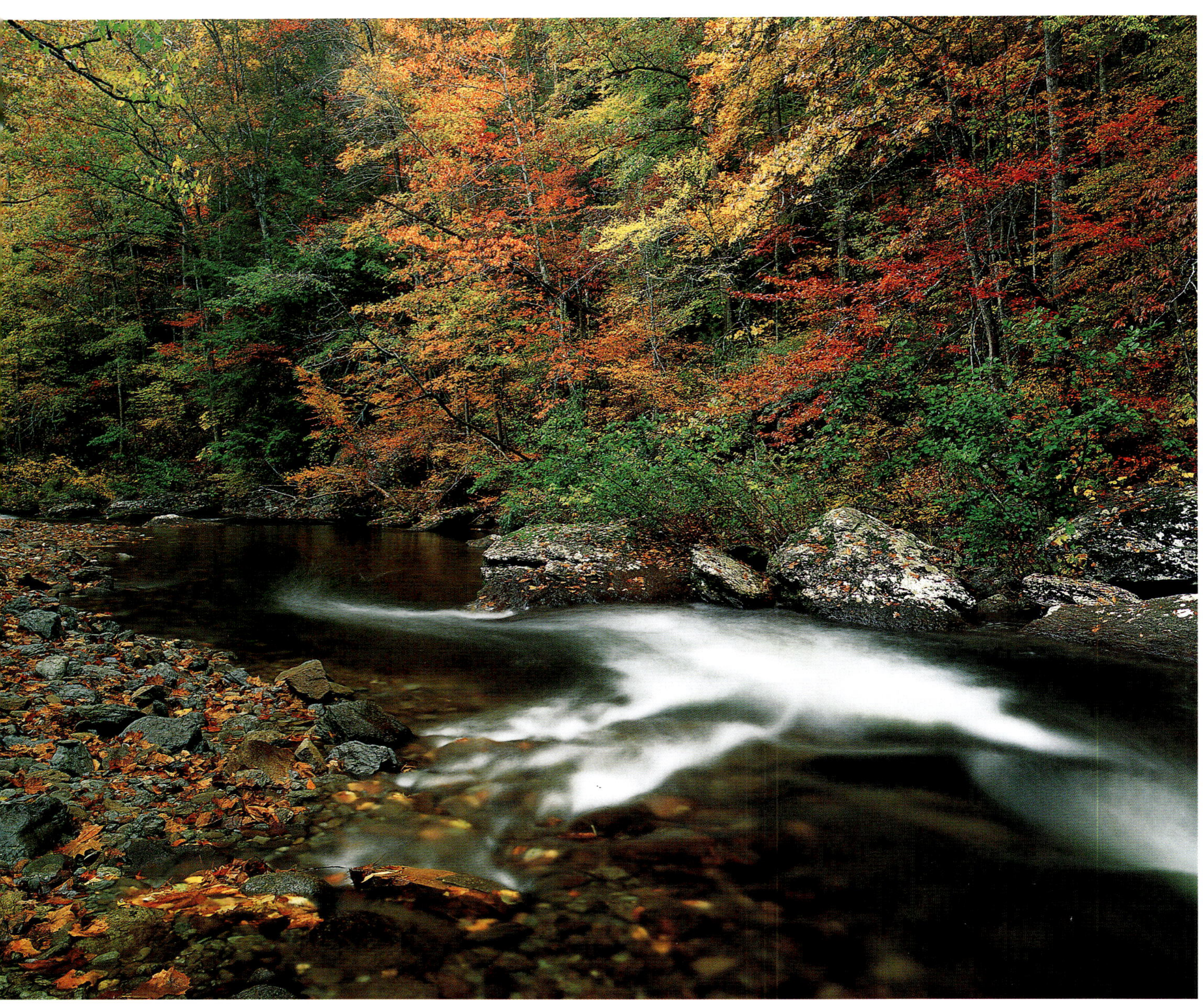

Autumn color in the Smokies can be excellent—if you can handle the traffic. Although the colors are beautiful, autumn scenes don't sell very well. Calendars are typically the best market for these images, and even that's limited.

from my having to work harder here than in many other areas.

Gatlinburg is the common park entrance; the other big entrance is in Cherokee, North Carolina. First-time visitors should stop at Sugarlands Visitor Center (near the Gatlinburg entrance) or Oconaluftee to get a good grasp on how the park is laid out. Both places have lots of great information. Park rangers are very helpful for pointing you in the right direction, but keep in mind that the ranger probably isn't a photographer. It's best to ask general questions about the park and then decide what you think is worth photographing.

Photographers come to the Great Smoky Mountains to shoot eastern forests. Few places rival the Smokies for eastern forest photography. Eastern forests are typically cluttered with fallen trees and lots of undergrowth. The Smokies are no different, but there is so much unbroken forest here that with a little work you'll find plenty to shoot. Mid April to early May is the best time for forest photography in the lower elevations, 2,500 to 4,000 feet. The higher elevations won't see any greening until the latter part of May. June thru September is typically not a good time to shoot the forest. The canopy is too thick. Mid to late October is the best time for autumn color. The color can be excellent but is unpredictable from year to year. It is best to make late travel plans if autumn color is your focus. Another downside of autumn is the crowds and traffic. One year I spent four hours in bumper-to-bumper traffic to drive seventeen miles from Newfound Gap to Gatlinburg. Other places rival the Smokies for autumn color photography with a fraction of the traffic.

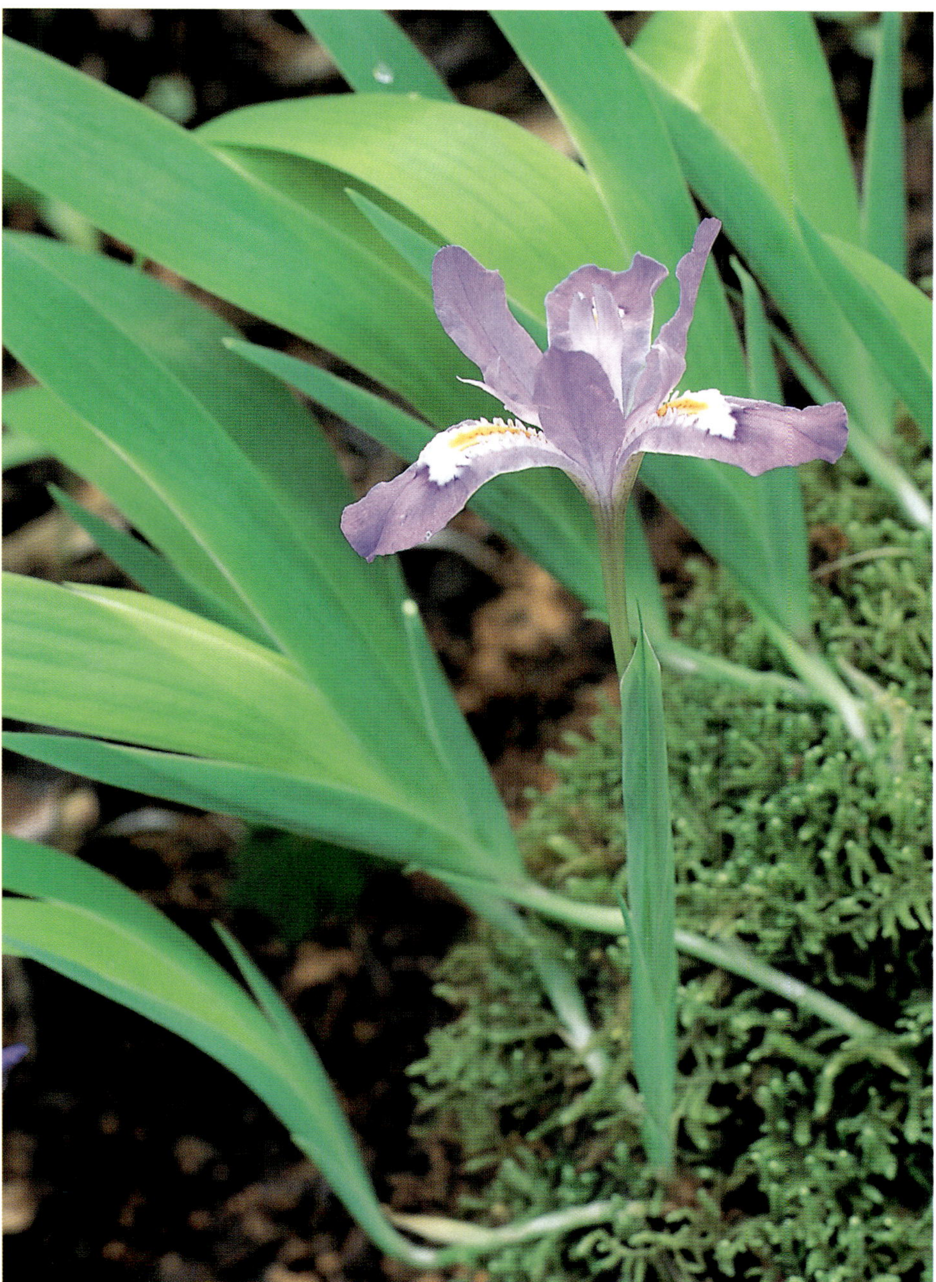

Dwarf crested iris is common during the spring season in the Great Smoky Mountains. There is nothing exceptionally creative about this image, but it might sell for a textbook or guidebook.

Spring wildflower photography is a good bet in most years. You won't find carpets of colorful flowers, but there are patches of trillium, dwarf crested iris, fringed phacelia and others scattered all over the park. With a little effort you can find yellow lady's slippers and showy orchids. The most predictable time for wildflowers in the Great Smoky Mountains is from the third week of April to about the first week of May. There are fewer crowds this time of year in the Smokies and, if you avoid the weekends, less need to worry about the traffic jams I mentioned for autumn.

Waterfalls and mountain streams are abundant and, I believe, the prettiest in North America. As I mentioned earlier, there are eleven waterfalls along established trails listed in park guidebooks, but you can find many beautiful cascades and small waterfalls along almost any stream in the park. The streams look good in early spring around wildflower time, but water levels might be high. Nevertheless, they are well worth photographing. The best time for the streams is mid May. The mosses are starting to get their vibrant green color, the water levels have tapered off and the forest canopy is still thin enough to let decent light reach the forest floor.

Snow cover in the Great Smoky Mountains is unpredictable. When there is snow cover, you can count on some great winter scenics, especially in the higher elevations. After a fresh snowfall, the road to Newfound Gap may be closed, but typically not for more than a day. Your best bet for good snow scenes will be the main road between Gatlinburg and Cherokee, North Carolina. I suggest not making long-term plans to visit the Smokies for winter shooting. It's best to call and get up-to-date reports on conditions [(865) 436-1200].

Forest Scenes

Good forest scenes for photography are anywhere and everywhere in the Smokies. The lower elevations are best from late April to mid May. At middle elevations, you can count on early May to late May, and for higher elevations from late May to mid June. As the growing season continues, it becomes increasingly difficult to photograph in the forest because of dim light under the thick canopy. I typically don't visit between June and September because of this and the summer tourist season.

Anywhere along Roaring Fork Motor Trail, the Elkmont area, Chimney Tops and Cosby, on the northeast edge, are good places to start with from spring to early summer. Your best results will come on overcast days or early in the morning before the sun hits the forest. When the sun is overhead, you'll get too much contrast for forest photography. Film cannot record the way your eye sees. The exposure difference between the sunlight and the shadow is more than the film can handle.

Mountain Ridges

The scene most often depicted in the Great Smoky Mountains is the overlapping distant mountains with its famous haze in the glow of evening light. This image illustrates the Smokies as well as any, and it isn't difficult to find these conditions whenever you choose to visit. The best places for sunrises, sunsets and that classic stacking of distant mountain ridges are at the higher elevations along Newfound Gap Road. Morton's Overlook, the Newfound Gap parking lot, and several pullouts along Newfound Gap Road on the North Carolina side all have great vistas. The road to Clingmans Dome is worthwhile but a little tougher to shoot. The trees along the ridge at the parking lot of Clingsmans Dome are dead and just don't look very good. You'll need a much longer telephoto lens to achieve the same results you would at the places I just mentioned. Shoot from Clingmans Dome after you have shot from the other locations if you want more chances to get that classic shot. Any time of year can be cold and windy, and you can still get freezing temperatures and snow in spring.

Streams and Waterfalls

It would be a mistake to photograph here and not spend any time exploring the countless miles of streams. The streams in the Smokies are probably the prettiest anywhere in North America. One of the best steams to work is at Greenbrier. The road into Greenbrier runs along the Little Pigeon River. There is something worth exploring everywhere along this river. The best part is at the end of the road, where you meet Porters Creek trailhead. Follow Porters Creek Trail for lots of great stream shots. The Little River is another wonder. Little River Road runs alongside the Little River between Elkmont and Cades Cove. There are numerous places to pull off and photograph along the road, or you can explore farther afield with little effort. The best part of the river runs between Elkmont and Townsend. The road into Tremont along the Middle Prong Little River is especially nice during the spring months. Another popular photo area is along the Roaring Fork Motor Trail. The creeks and streams along Roaring Fork Motor are a little more challenging but

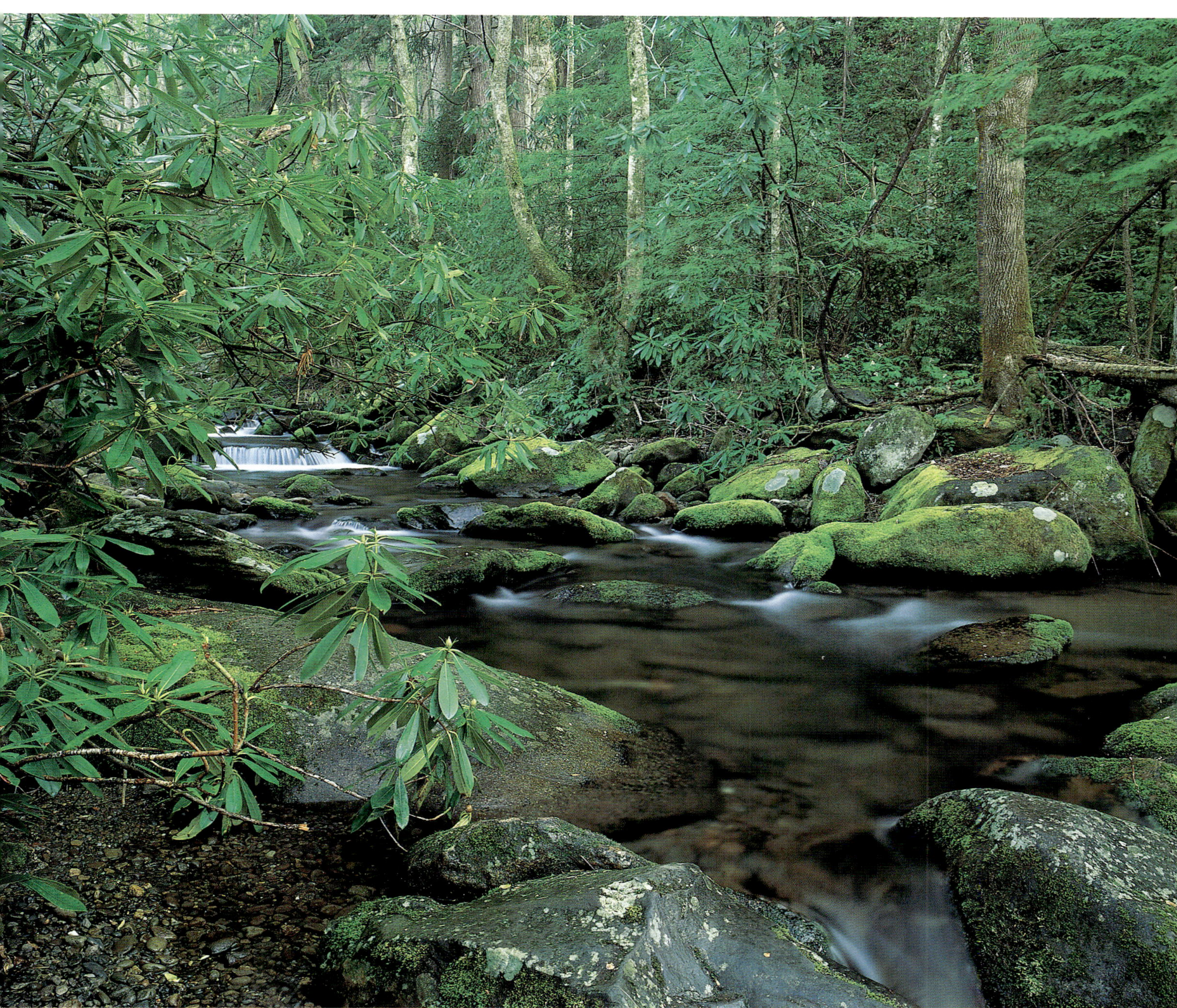

well worth exploring.

There are so many wonderful cascades and waterfalls throughout the park that you could spend an entire week just exploring these treasures. I recommend spending time around several of the falls listed in the park guides and then setting out to explore some not listed in park literature on your own. Almost any trail you find will have a stream somewhere along its route. Some streams are seasonal and make unique opportunities that not everyone will have in his library. Ramsay Cascades and Mouse Creek Falls are two of the more photogenic falls listed in the park's visitor guide, but both require long hikes. I enjoy exploring on my own when looking for cascades and waterfalls because so many of the ones listed by the Park Service attract

A typical Smoky Mountain stream. The rhododendron in the foreground is subtle, but I intentionally composed it as an invitation into the scene.

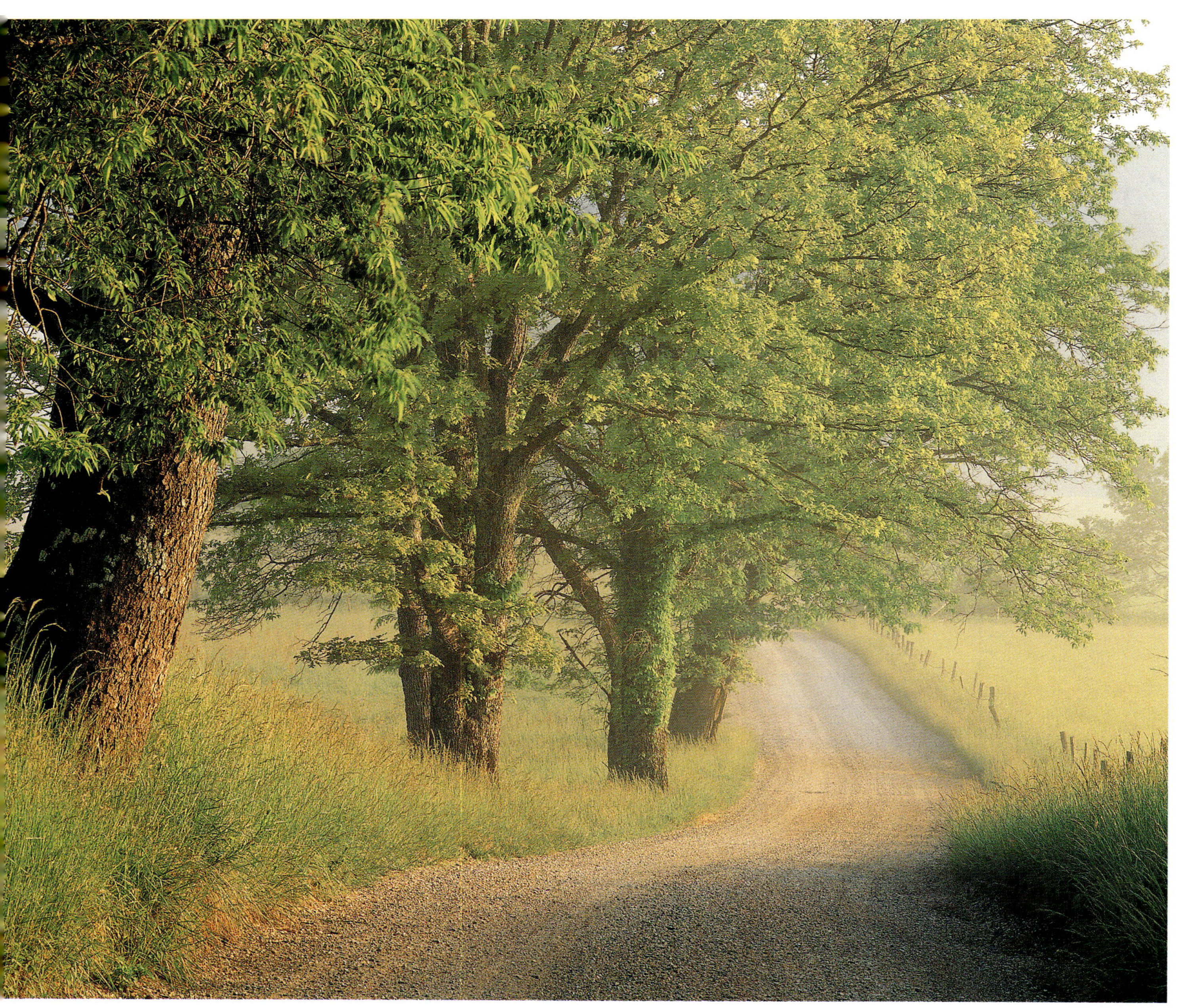

This was one of those magical moments in Cades Cove. The warm light and dissipating fog in the background make the shot. Road shots are very marketable. This image has sold many times.

crowds and become difficult to shoot. *North Carolina Waterfalls: Where to Find Them, How to Photograph Them*, by Kevin Adams, is an excellent book for finding lesser-known falls in and around the park.

Cades Cove

Cades Cove can be absolutely magical, or it can be a bust. More times than not, you'll be happy you made the effort. I highly recommend driving along the road in Cades Cove on an early morning as soon as the gates open. Gates open up at 6 A.M. Don't be surprised if you see thirty to forty cars lined up when you arrive. Most of these people will never get out of their cars. After 9 A.M. it starts getting really crowded, plus you'll have lost the magical light. Morning fog during the spring and fall is common and opens up a lot of possibilities. Cades Cove is a must at least one morning. Allow one hour to reach Cades Cove if you're staying in Gatlinburg or Pigeon Forge.

I also suggest checking at the visitor center the night before to see if the road will be open [(865) 436-1200]. At certain times of year, the Park Service closes the road through Cades Cove once or twice a week in the morning for bicycles.

WHEN TO GO

The Smoky Mountains can be good anytime of year, but you will have obstacles in a few seasons. Winter is fabulous if you get a good snowfall. The problem is, snow is unpredictable in these southern highlands. If you do get good snow, the roads can be closed for the day or until the Park Service gets them cleared. Spring is the absolute best time to be in the Smokies, especially if you've never been before. From mid April through early May is the best time for wildflowers and new growth in the forest. Besides winter, this is the least crowded season. Summer is good too, but if the heat and humidity don't get you, the crowds will. The forest is thick and makes shooting difficult, and at times impossible. June to September is the height of tourist season in a national park with, if you stay in Gatlinburg, some of the most expensive lodging in the country. The autumn color from mid to late October is great in most years, but still uncertain, and precipitates awful traffic.

Snowfall is unpredictable in the Great Smoky Mountains. If you want to go in the winter to shoot snow, call before you leave. When metering snow like this, I spot meter somewhere within the composition and open up 2 stops. If I hadn't, I would have underexposed this scene.

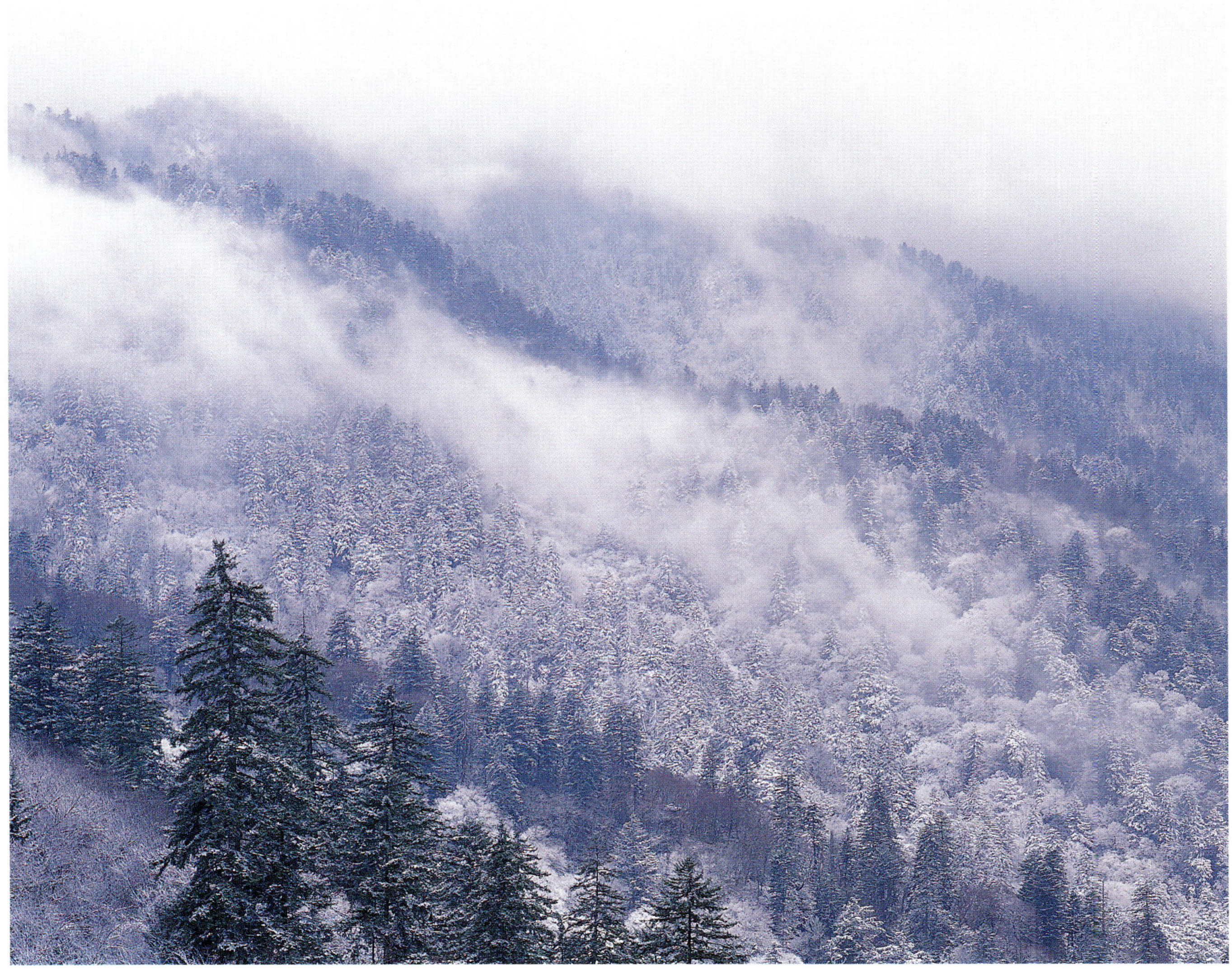

TIME REQUIREMENTS

The great thing about the Smokies is you can accomplish a lot in just a few days. You can make it a long weekend or an entire week, and still have plenty to do. I like at least four full shooting days in spring. Because of the heat and the long days, you might need five or six days in summer. For autumn, I recommend at least five days. If you're going for snow, watch the weather forecast, and call the Park Service [(865) 436-1200] before you leave home. Planning around the big snowfall can be risky, but you could end up with some wonderful shots.

photographer's choice

THE GREEN MOUNTAINS OF VERMONT have a great reputation for autumn color but shouldn't be passed up during the spring growing season. Wonderful forest scenes, waterfalls and mountain streams abound throughout the region. [www.greenmountains.worldweb.com/]

NEED TO KNOW

I recommend three towns for lodging and dining. Gatlinburg, the gateway to the park, is the most common name you'll hear for lodging. Hotels in Gatlinburg are expensive any time of year, and the extra cost won't save you time or much convenience. Pigeon Forge is a ten-minute drive from Gatlinburg and a better bet for more reasonable rates. This town offers plenty of lodging and dining facilities. You'll get much better hotel prices, especially weekdays in April and the first half of May. Townsend, a quieter town, gives easy access to the west end of the park but is limited on both lodging and dining facilities. Driving distances are much longer from Townsend to many of the parks great photo locations, with the exception of Cades Cove. For more information on the park, go to <www.nps.gov/grsm/>.

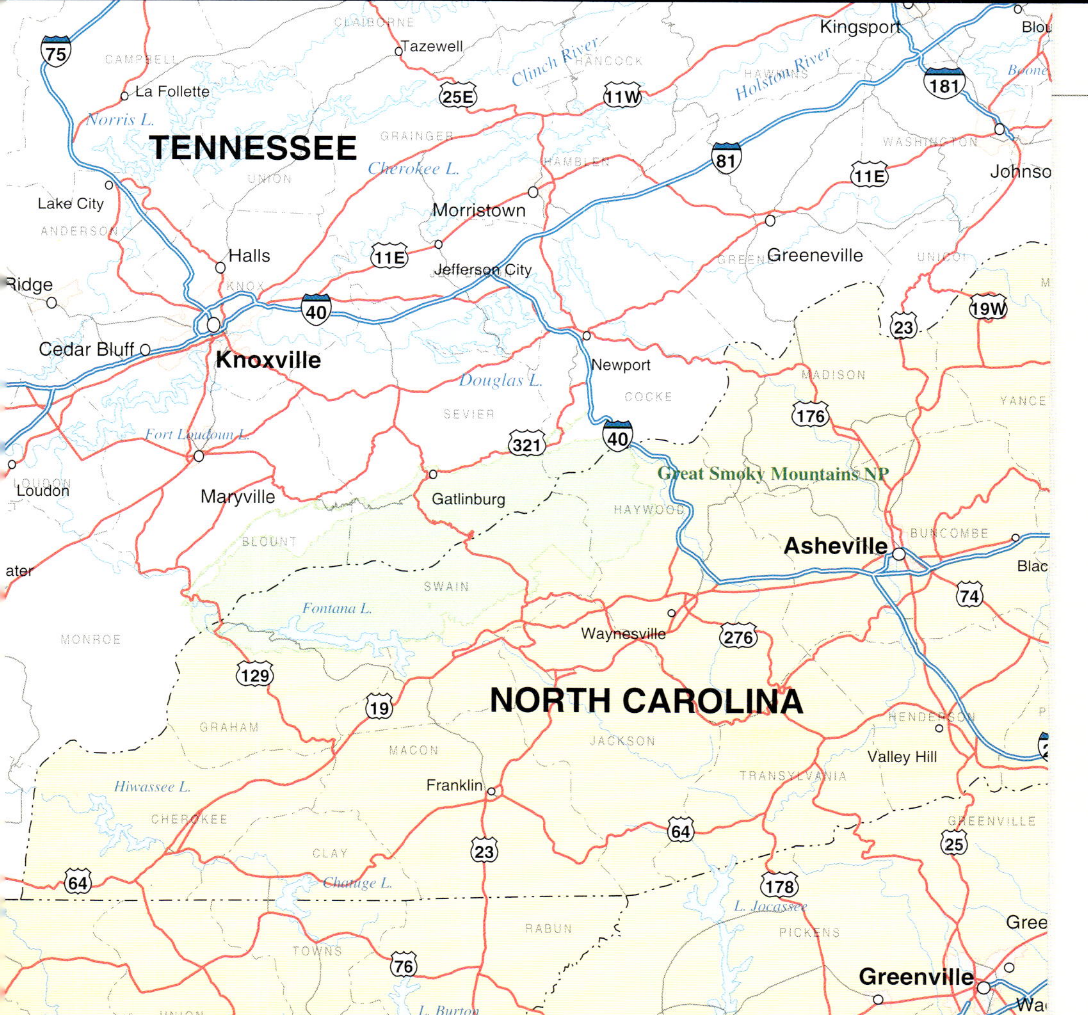

directions

The nearest major airport is McGhee-Tyson in Alcoa (Knoxville), Tennessee, 45 miles west of Gatlinburg.

IN TENNESSEE:

- From the east (I-81): take I-40 to exit 407 (Sevierville) to TN Route 66 South, and continue to U.S. 441 South. Follow U.S. 441 to the park.
- From I-40 in Knoxville: exit 386B U.S. Highway 129 South to Alcoa/Maryville. At Maryville proceed on U.S. 321 North through Townsend. Continue on TN Route 73 to the park.

IN NORTH CAROLINA:

- From I-40: take U.S. Route 19 West through Maggie Valley. Proceed to U.S. 441 North at Cherokee. Follow 441 North into the park.

FROM ATLANTA:

- Follow U.S. 441 and 23 North. U.S. 441 North leads to the park.

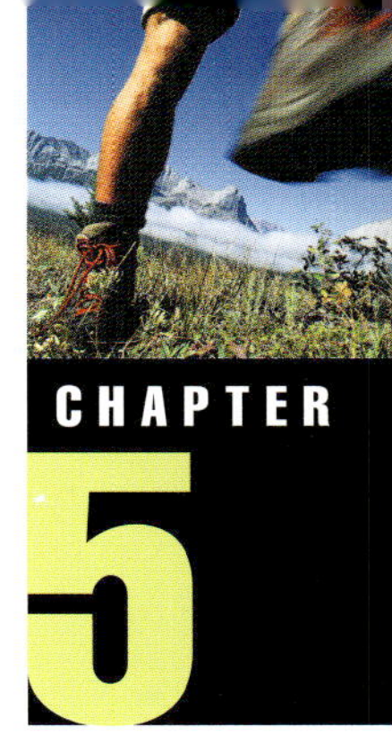

CHAPTER 5

Canaan Valley, West Virginia

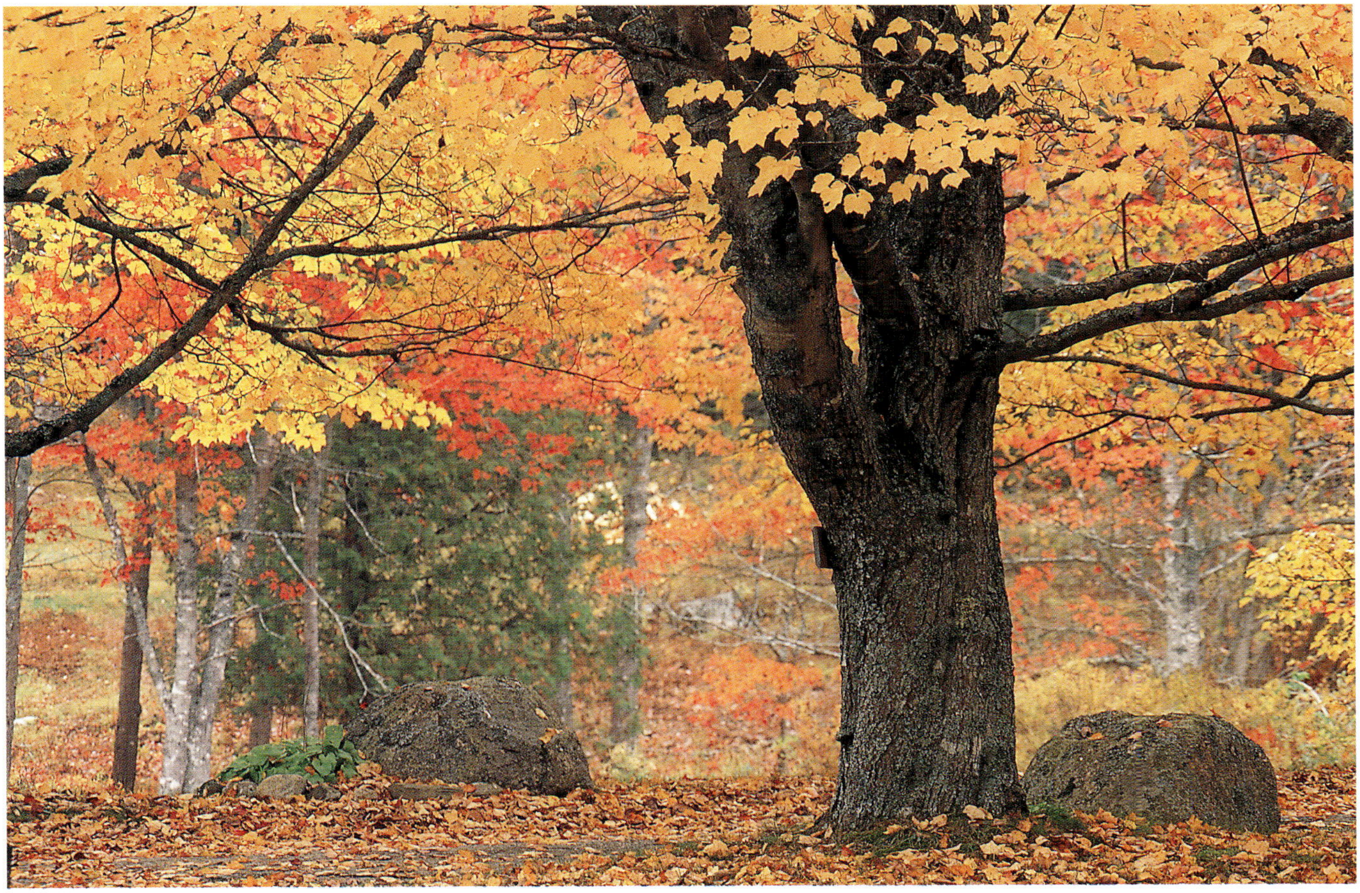

The Monongahela National Forest sits in the Allegheny Plateau of West Virginia and comprises craggy mountain terrain and fertile valleys. You can best experience the unforgiving mountain environment in Dolly Sods Wilderness Area, Blackwater Falls State Park and Spruce Knob, while Canaan Valley State Park is the place to be in the friendlier lowlands. Canaan Valley's gentle landscape consists of inviting forests and open meadows, allowing you to experience it on your terms. At higher elevations, Dolly Sods's rugged landscape can be bitterly cold with an accompanying wind that puts you at the mercy of the elements. The entire region was clear cut at one point and provides an isolated natural experience just this side of wild.

Monongahela National Forest is not as dramatic as Great Smoky Mountains National Park. You won't find beautiful moss-covered streams or endless unbroken forests, but you will find incredible autumn color and a less-traveled countryside. I recommend the Canaan Valley as an alternative to the Smokies because it's free of the nightmarish traffic problems in that park yet offers a similar southern Appalachian experience. Autumn here rivals the Smokies but is more predictable for good color.

PHOTOGRAPHER'S VIEW

The Canaan Valley region is a quiet, rural area filled with deciduous forests, rolling hills, rugged mountain terrain, old farms and solitude, but not necessarily breathtaking scenery. You won't endure overcrowding to see a wonderful display of autumn color. Each mile you drive can change dramatically in elevation, which makes this region unique. The climate here is more northern than southern; therefore autumn comes earlier than in neighboring areas and spring later, with more snowfall in between.

The photography opportunities are going to depend on your ability to create something out of what appears to be nothing. This is not a pull-off-the-road-and-set-up-your-tripod kind

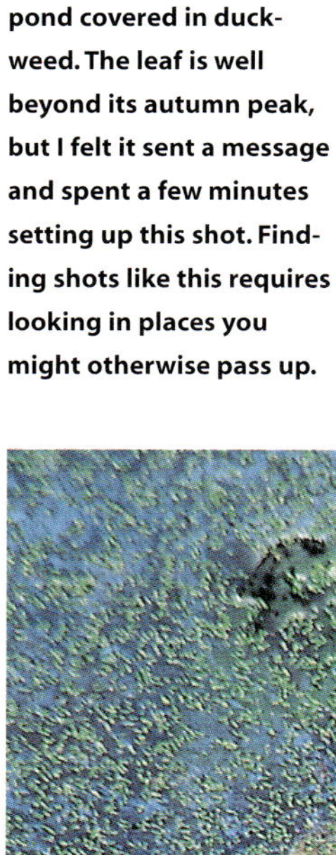

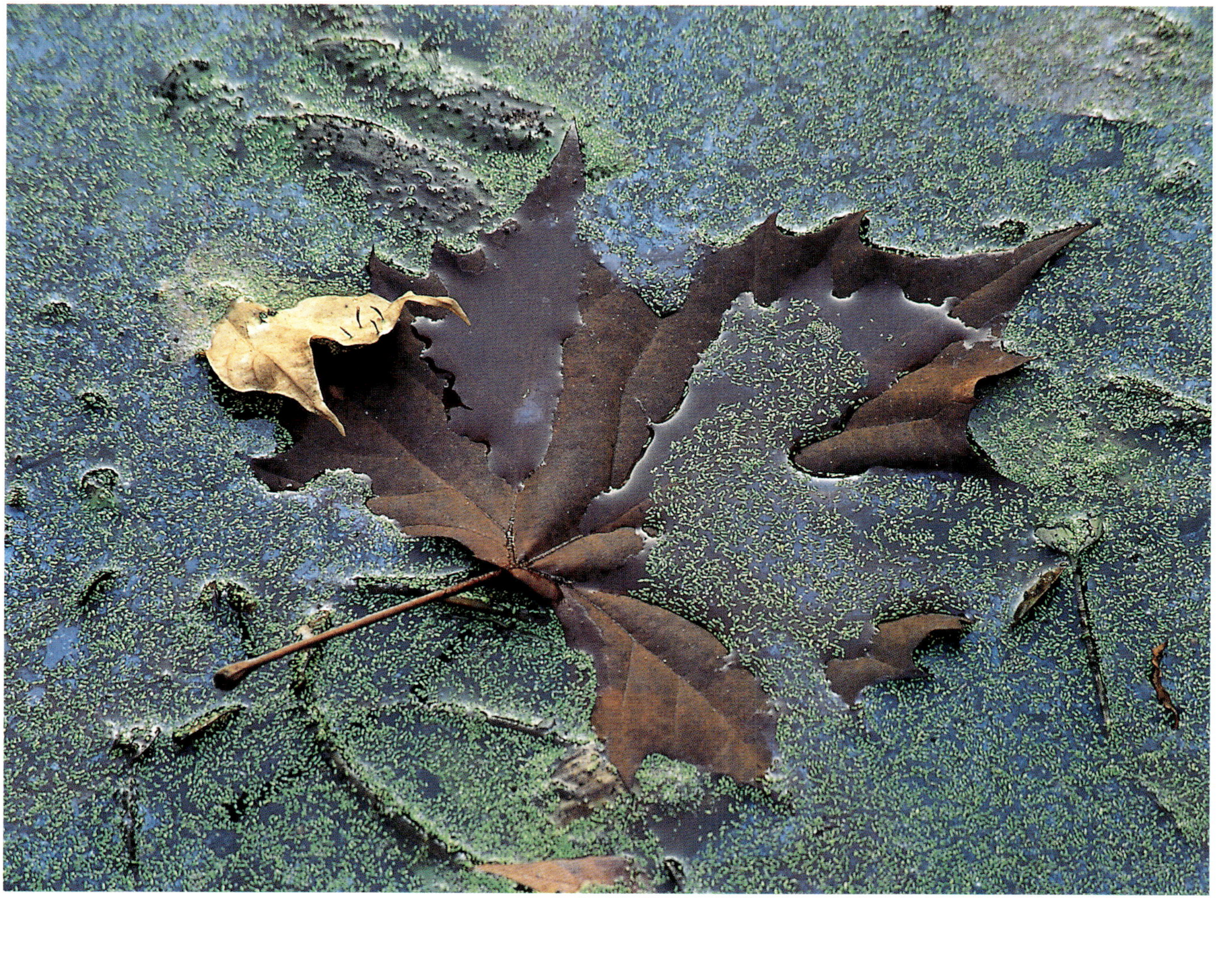

I found this maple leaf floating in an old farm pond covered in duckweed. The leaf is well beyond its autumn peak, but I felt it sent a message and spent a few minutes setting up this shot. Finding shots like this requires looking in places you might otherwise pass up.

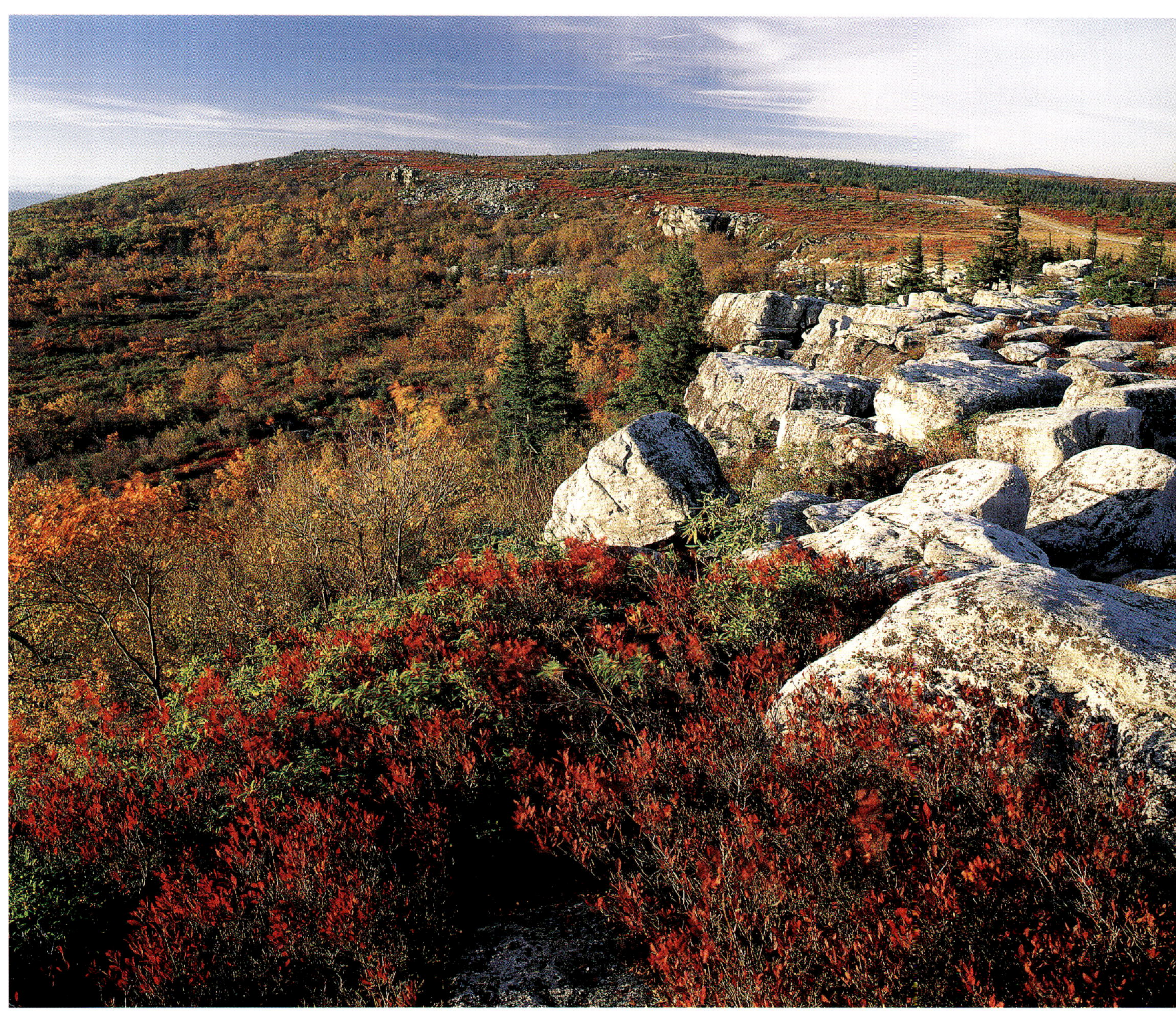

The Dolly Sods Wilderness is a favorite among photographers for early-morning shooting. Next to the freezing temps, jet trails will be your biggest obstacle here.

of location. You will fare far better by walking along the forest edge and observing your surroundings carefully. Be creative, and keep an open mind. Small patterns and little set-up shots on the forest floor will open more avenues than simply pointing your camera into the forest and capturing the changing color. Morning frost, common in autumn, can create opportunities otherwise lost during the later hours of the day. You will be challenged from time to time, but as with any location, surveying the landscape with a critical eye will key you into the possibilities. After all, this is what separates the good photographers from the other photographers.

True to its essence, the area has few major attractions or landmarks to focus on. Canaan Valley State Park is a good starting point because you will likely use this as your base to work from day to day. Canaan Valley scenery is very generic. Set-up shots and general forest shots of changing colors will probably be your main focus. Many photographers have told me that this state park is also great for photographing white-tailed deer.

Dolly Sods Wilderness Area

Dolly Sods Wilderness Area is usually photographers' favorite in this region. Dolly Sods sits on a high plateau overlooking distant mountains and valleys and is made up of an extensive rocky plain scattered with boulders among sphagnum bogs, heath barrens, grassy sods, rhododendron and laurel thickets. The reds and deep greens of the blueberry and heath shrubs dominate Dolly Sods's autumn display. This windswept landscape can be unfriendly during the early-morning hours when you're on location for sunrise photography. The one-sided red spruce (nicknamed "flag-

I took this photograph in Blackwater Falls State Park and thought it might be useful as a background for a client at some point.

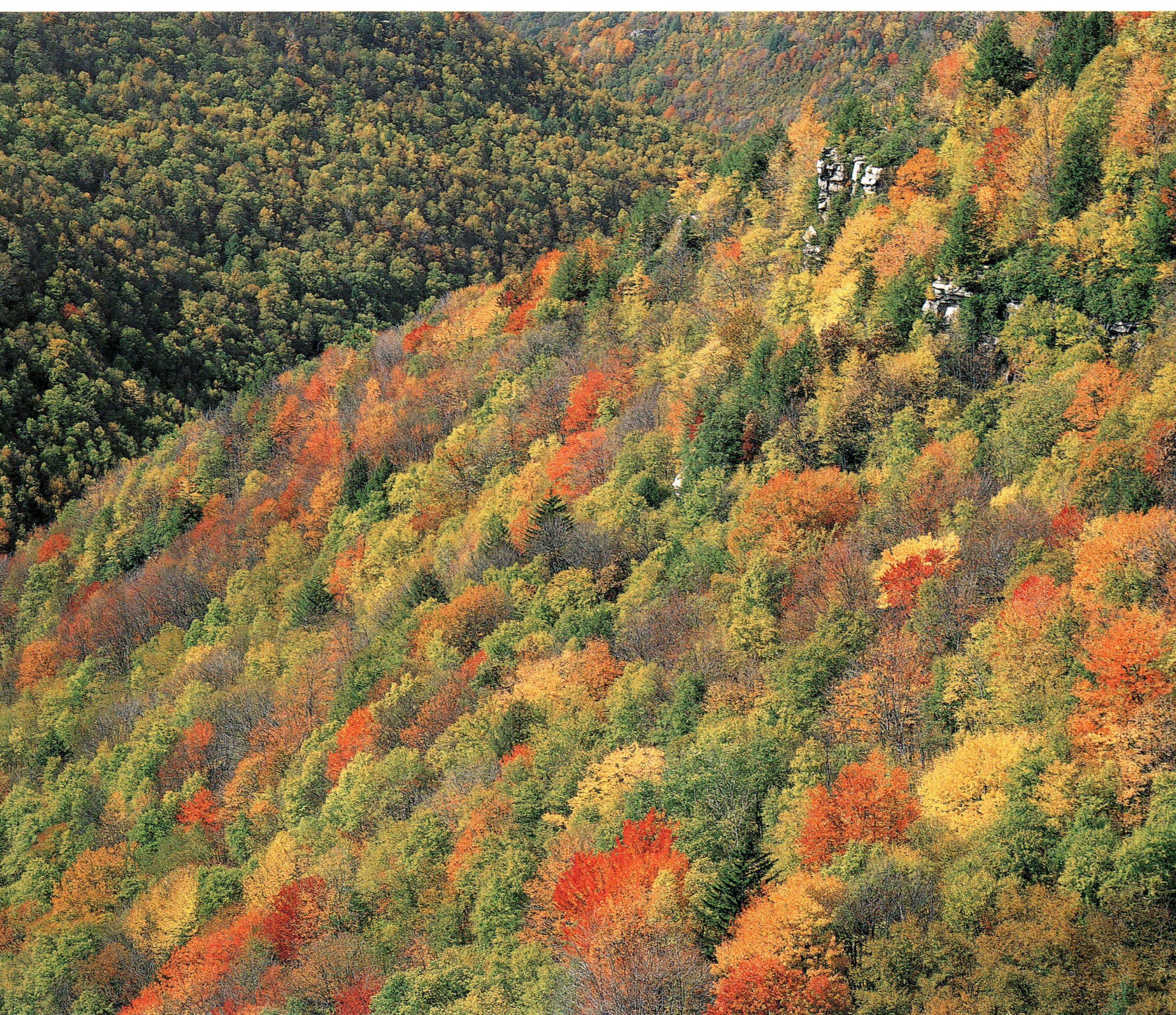

pole spruce" because of its wind-shaped form) is an excellent example of how unrelenting winds whip over the plateau and shape the vegetation. Be prepared for gale-force gusts, and dress accordingly.

Dolly Sods has several areas for good views of the surrounding landscape. Forest Road 19 has a couple signs posted as viewpoints, but one of the better vistas is at the end of Forest Road 19. There are a few nice opportunities here for photographing the landscape with the distant mountains and valleys, but most of your work will be the autumn color of the heath barrens, frosted leaves, small intimate scenes or set-up shots of elements you find within the landscape. I prefer Dolly Sods over Blackwater Falls State Park for early-morning light (see below). You'll have the sun to your back here so that the landscape catches the warm morning light. You can continue on farther into the wilderness area on Forest Road 75 for another ten miles. This takes you to Bear Rocks viewpoint, the best area for sunrise photography looking toward the sun. If you are set on photographing the sunrise over the distant mountains, beware of jet contrails. Dolly Sods sits in the flyway of Washington, DC, so contrails are a constant battle. Your best chance of avoiding them is on Sunday, when fewer flights depart in the early-morning hours.

Blackwater Falls State Park

Blackwater Falls State Park has some of the best color in the area, and the best vistas for photographing these colors. Looking into Blackwater Canyon from Pendleton Point, you'll find an entire wall of incredible color broken only by the sky and the Blackwater River below. Lindy Point has become one of my favorite overlooks in recent years. The blacktop extension of Forest Road 13 has permitted easier access to the area. To get to Lindy Point, simply follow the road beyond the State Park Lodge through the campground, and follow Forest Road 13 until the blacktop ends. Don't go beyond the blacktop part of this road unless you have a 4x4 vehicle. From here you will hike about a half mile to Lindy Point. Blackwater Falls State Park has a lot of trails and nature walks less than a mile long. These are probably your best bet for finding small intimate scenes using the changing color and detail shots of fallen leaves, pine cones or other elements from the forest.

The Cheat River

There are few areas in the Monongahela National Forest where you can drive for any length of time along a scenic river. The best river I know of is the Dry Fork of the Cheat River. The road runs along the river for several miles and has many nice areas for photography. This pretty river runs swiftly over boulders and through large pools reflecting color from the nearby hillsides. Autumn color is spotty along the river, but you should have no problem finding several pockets along the route. Dry Fork runs along County Road 43-12. To get here from Canaan Valley State Park, follow State Route 32 south to State Route 72 (Jenningston Road) to County Road 43-12. County Road 43-12 is not easy to find. Look for a very steep road on your left going downhill from State Route 72. The turn is extremely sharp and may take a little effort. County Road 43-12 eventually ends up back on State Route 72.

Other Locations

Several other locations in Monongahela National Forest beyond the Canaan Valley are worth mentioning. A couple of these will require relocating your lodging or campsite. Seneca Rocks is an hour drive south of Canaan Valley and sits on the eastern edge of the Monongahela National Forest. This incredible rock formation, the best you'll find in

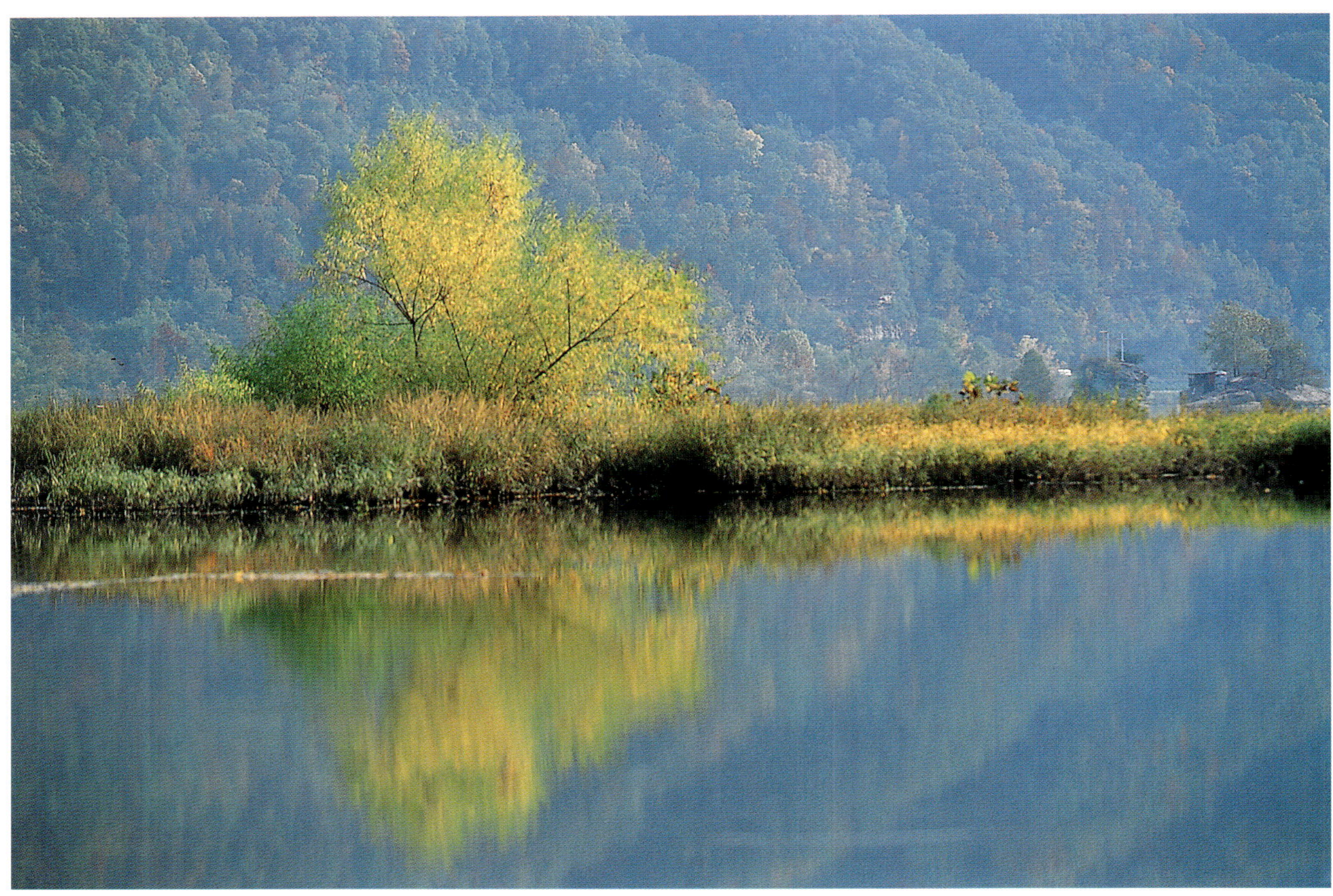

If I traveled around looking only for breathtaking scenics, I would go broke. As long as an image is technically correct—properly exposed, focused and composed—there is a potential market for that image.

the entire state, can provide a couple opportunities for something a little different from the typical West Virginia landscape you have already spent time photographing. Seneca Rocks is best known as an eastern U.S. climbing mecca. Just southwest of Seneca Rocks is the highest point in West Virginia, Spruce Knob, at 4,861 feet. Spruce Knob has some incredible vistas overlooking the surrounding mountains and is one of the best locations for sunsets in the Monongahela. The observation tower at the peak gives you an excellent view of the surrounding landscape. A short hike from here will put you in position to shoot the distant mountains with the setting sun directly behind the mountains. Cranberry Glades Botanical Area on the southern edges of the Monongahela National Forest is another unique opportunity to photograph something a little different. The landscape turns a brilliant red at the end of the season.

Navigating the roads of the West Virginia highlands is like riding a roller coaster. Roads twist and turn with constant elevation changes. This is also an easy place to get lost. I highly recommend spending a little time at the tourism office in Davis [(304) 622-4121]. These people can help you get started. Your DeLorme Atlas and Gazetteer will be your friend to get from location to location—don't leave home without it.

WHEN TO GO

Autumn comes early to this part of the Allegheny Mountains. The climate here is more like Canada than the continental United States. Your best bet for catching peak fall color is the first week of October. Sometimes the color will hang on through the second week. It takes only one deep freeze to wipe everything out, and this can happen any time in early October. The interesting thing about this region is that rapid elevation changes create micro-climates with their own seasons. Don't expect to leave here and see great color in other parts. A common mistake photographers make is to move on to the unknown after they get the photo they want. Keep working the areas where you're having luck.

TIME REQUIREMENTS

The Canaan Valley and the surrounding areas don't require a whole week. You can squeeze a lot of shooting into a long weekend because most of the good color is within a reasonable drive of Canaan Valley State Park. If you feel compelled to spend a week, consider moving up through the Blue Ridge Parkway or another location in the Appalachian highlands.

NEED TO KNOW

This location gives you only two choices: Canaan Valley State Park Lodge [(304) 866-4121] or the Village Inn [(304) 866-4166], which is two miles north of the state park. The State Park Lodge fills up early, and it's difficult to get last-minute reservations. I suggest calling several months in advance. The Village Inn is a better bet for getting reservations and a better price.

photographer's choice

THE KANCAMAGUS SCENIC HIGHWAY and White Mountain National Forest of New Hampshire is a great autumn color getaway with fewer crowds than its western neighbor, Vermont. If you don't mind driving quiet and seemingly endless logging roads, try MICHIGAN'S UPPER PENINSULA. There are countless opportunities along the paved routes as well. [Kancamagus Scenic Highway, www.visitnh.gov/scenicdrives.html; Michigan's Upper Peninsula, www.uptravel.com/uptravel]

directions

There is no direct route to Canaan Valley State Park. The following are only a few of many ways to get to Canaan Valley.

- From the east in Harrisonburg, Va., follow U.S. Route 33 west, then north, and pick up State Route 55 in Seneca Rocks. Follow 55 to Harman, and pick up State Route 32 to Canaan Valley State Park.
- From the west in Clarksburg, W.V., take Interstate 79 south to U.S. Route 33 east, and follow to Harman. Pick up State Route 32, and follow it north to Canaan Valley State Park.
- From the north in Pittsburgh, Pa., follow Interstate 79 south to Clarksburg, W.V., and follow the directions mentioned above.
- From the south in Charlotte, N.C., follow Interstate 77 north to U.S. Route 19 north (just north of Beckley, W.V.). Take U.S. Route 19 to Interstate 79 north, and follow that to U.S. Route 33 east to Harman. Pick up State Route 32 north to Canaan Valley State Park.

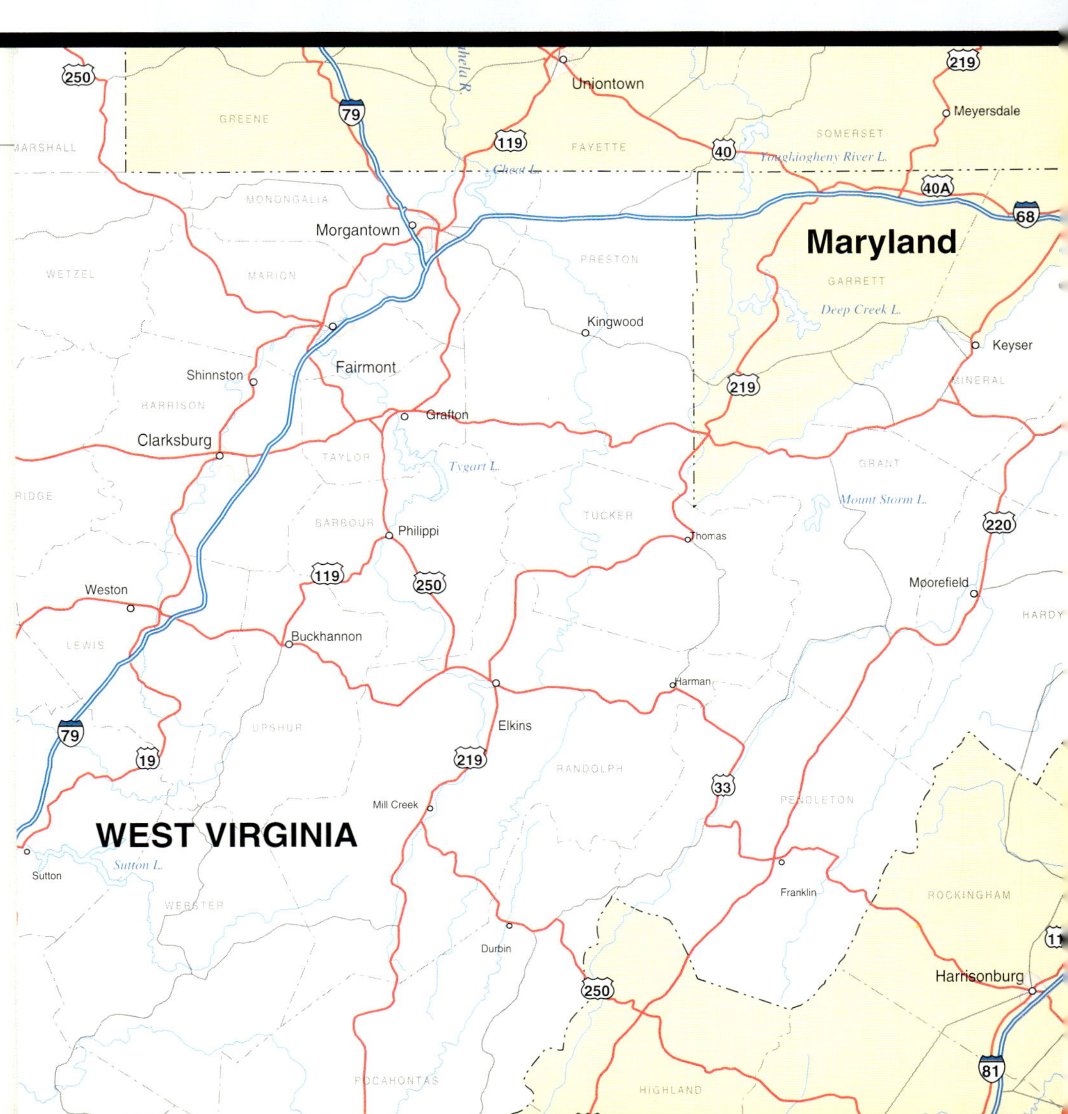

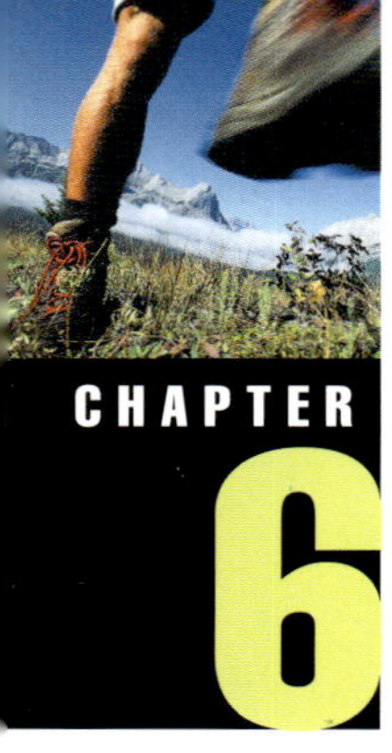

CHAPTER

6

Kentucky Horse Country

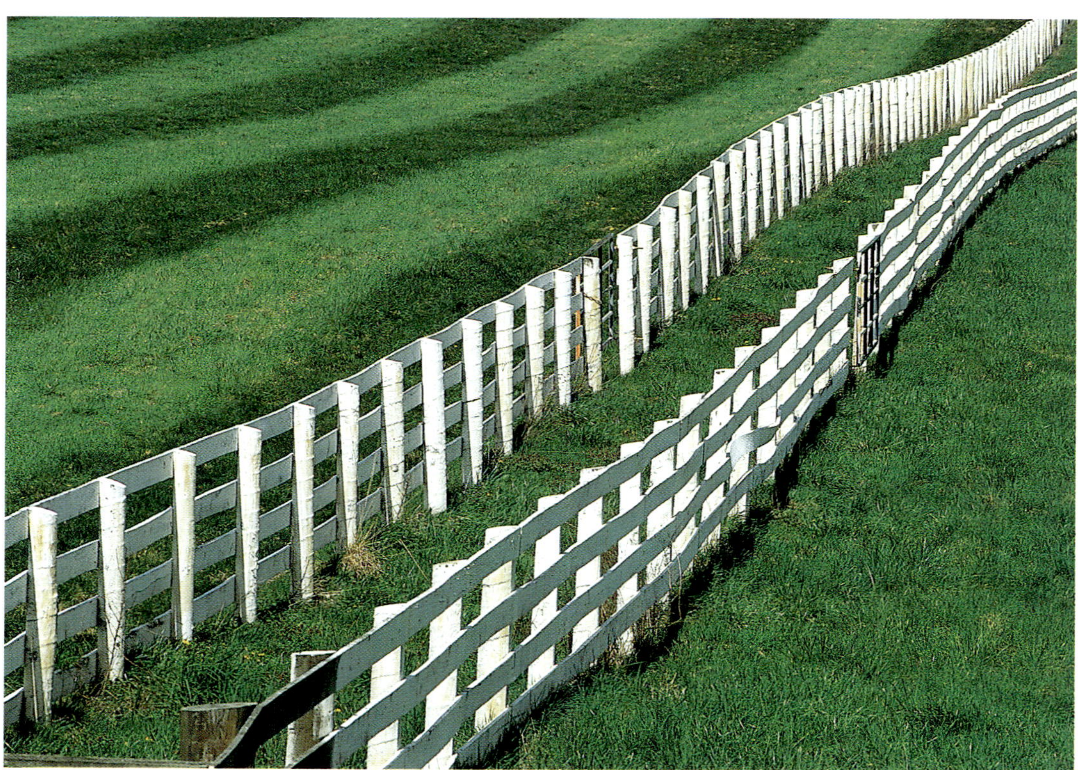

The "Horse Capitol of the World" and its rolling hills, beautiful horse farms and picturesque landscapes are special to me. The area boasts 460 thoroughbred and standardbred farms dedicated to breeding and training, and it's the center of thoroughbred horseracing in America. The horse country is a landscape of white and black wood-planked fences dividing grazing pastures for some of the country's finest thoroughbreds. These pastures are as common as the sky above. Mowing patterns and fence lines are typical in this pastoral landscape. Royalty and common folk come from around the world to admire and enjoy the land that celebrates the history and excitement of the graceful and elegant thoroughbred, whether it be grazing in a distant pasture or racing before a thunderous crowd.

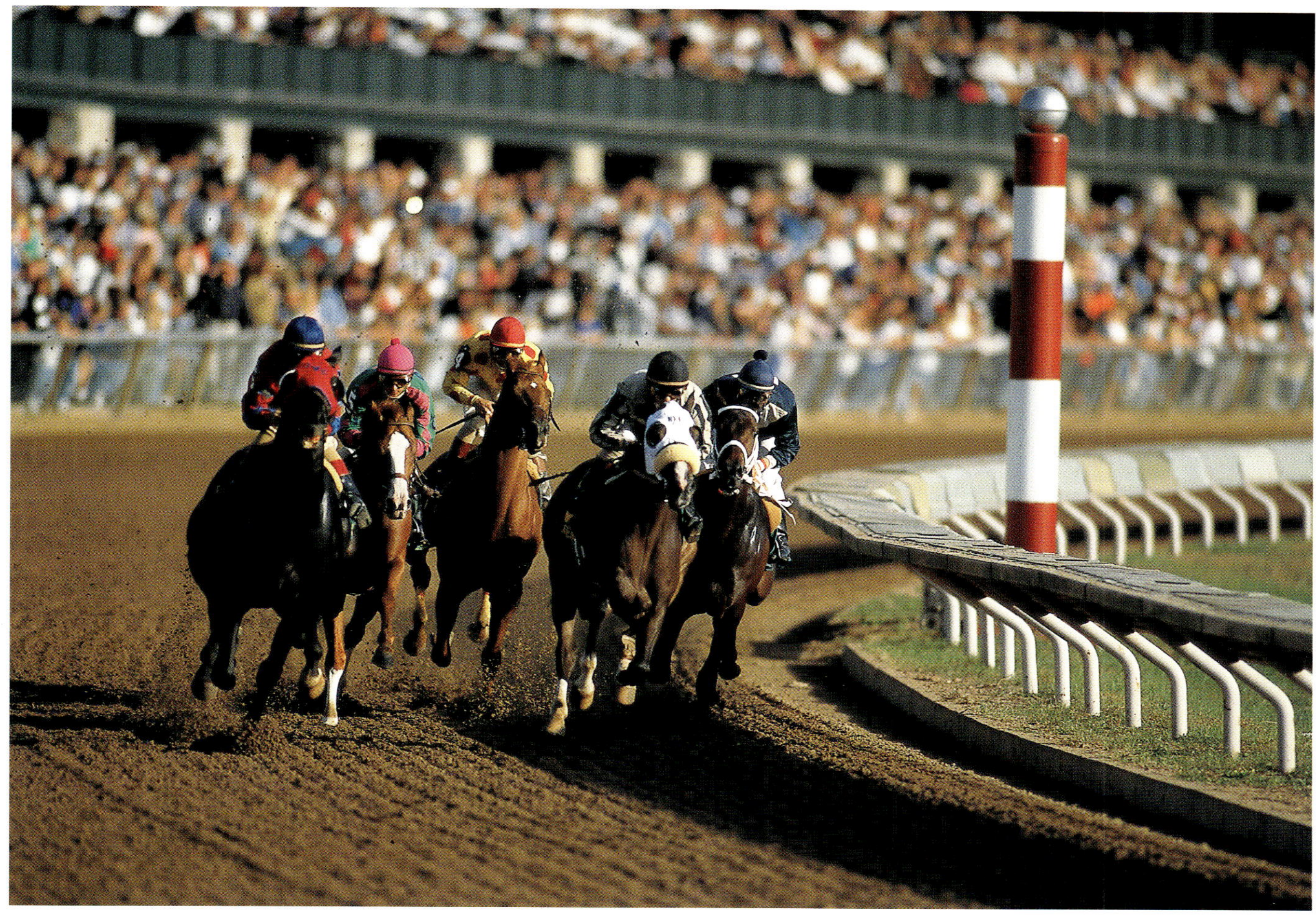

This is a classic shot of thoroughbreds rounding the bend at Keeneland with the grandstand in the background. The best thing about photographing at Keeneland is you don't need a long telephoto lens. You couldn't sell an image like this for advertising purposes unless you got a property and model release, but editorial use is okay.

The photographer can enjoy both the tranquil settings of the rural landscape and the high-energy crowds gathering around the meticulously manicured racetracks to witness the running of the horses. Kentucky horse country has plenty of history and open spaces and has horse-related events throughout the year. Spring and autumn are the better seasons for exploring, but summer has its share of offerings. Regardless of when you visit, there's something to shoot.

PHOTOGRAPHER'S VIEW

The beauty of photographing in Kentucky's horse country is that most of the time there is nothing between you and the open pastures except a gentle breeze. The quiet landscape is broken only by the roaring crowd rooting for horses at one of the historic racetracks, which I highly recommend for a unique photographic experience. Kentucky has three famous tracks in the heart of horse country: Churchill Downs in Louisville and Keeneland and The Red Mile in Lexington. You can forget about any productive shooting at Churchill Downs, but Keeneland and The Red Mile are photographer friendly.

The Kentucky horse country is physically easy shooting. For the most part, you'll drive the back roads and pull over when you see something you want to shoot. *The Insider's Guide to Greater Lexington & the Kentucky Bluegrass*, by Susan Miller and Jeff Walter, is a good travel reference for this. The driving isn't stressful at all; you can drive at a leisurely pace and encounter little traffic. The one point you must keep in mind at all times is that all of these farms are private property, and the owners have millions of dollars invested in the horses, not to mention the farm itself. They are very protective of their property and will stop and ask what you are doing. Don't touch the fences and especially the horses. They are rightfully concerned about the safety of their horses. Still, you are doing nothing illegal if you pull over and photograph. The roadsides are public domain, and there is nothing the owners can do about your pulling over.

The equipment you'll need is very basic. A wide-angle zoom or any wide-angle fixed focal

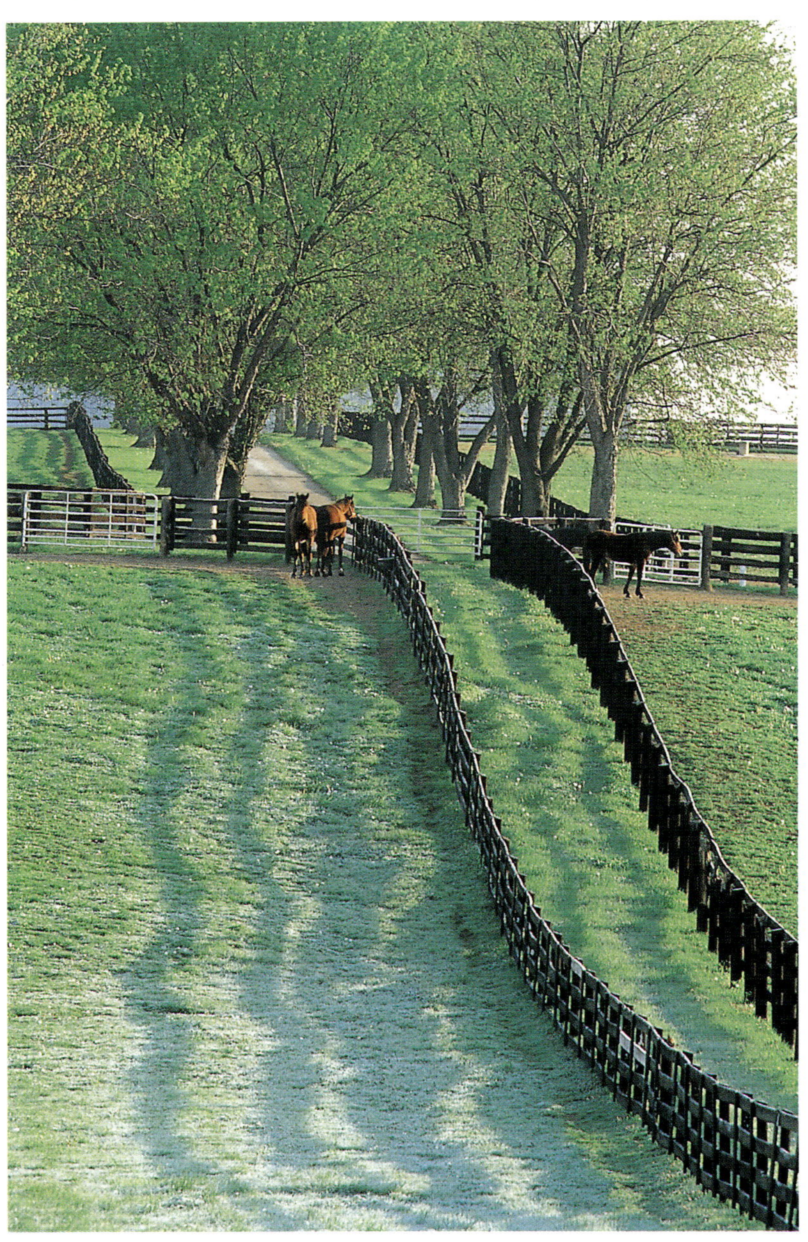

Photographing horse farms is an easy and enjoyable way to spend your time before heading to the afternoon races. This is a typical scene along the back roads of thoroughbred country.

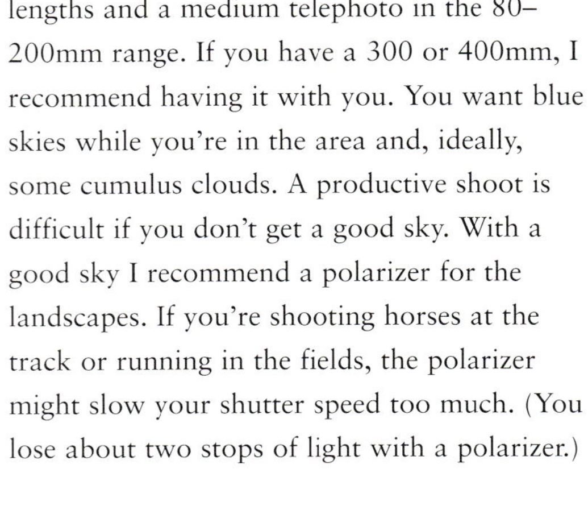

lengths and a medium telephoto in the 80–200mm range. If you have a 300 or 400mm, I recommend having it with you. You want blue skies while you're in the area and, ideally, some cumulus clouds. A productive shoot is difficult if you don't get a good sky. With a good sky I recommend a polarizer for the landscapes. If you're shooting horses at the track or running in the fields, the polarizer might slow your shutter speed too much. (You lose about two stops of light with a polarizer.)

Horse Country Back Roads

You can operate out of Lexington for all of your shooting. The prettiest time to be in the area is spring. The grasses are green, fences and roadsides are lined with blooming dogwoods, and best of all new colts are galloping alongside their mothers. Autumn is another good time to be in the area. The autumn color isn't wonderful, but it does bring beautiful light and another racing season (see page 65 for information on the racetracks).

Begin your backcountry forays by following the Bluegrass Country Driving Tour. You can always detour from this route to explore beyond. Check with the Lexington Visitors Center in downtown Lexington [(800) 845-3959] for a map of this driving tour. This map will direct you to many of the famous and most picturesque farms in the area. Your DeLorme map will become very handy when you stray from the main driving tour. Don't worry about getting lost as all roads eventually end up back on the tour route. I recommend highlighting areas of interest to return to if the light isn't right.

There are a couple things to keep in mind when photographing horse farms. You can photograph whatever you want for personal use; there are no limitations. If you are selling your work, you cannot sell a photograph with distinguishable property, such as buildings and horses, without a property release. The one exception is editorial use. I try to photograph horses from a distance galloping in the field; head shots might be questionable, so I stay away from these. The second item to keep in mind is the warning I already gave about touching horses and crossing over private property.

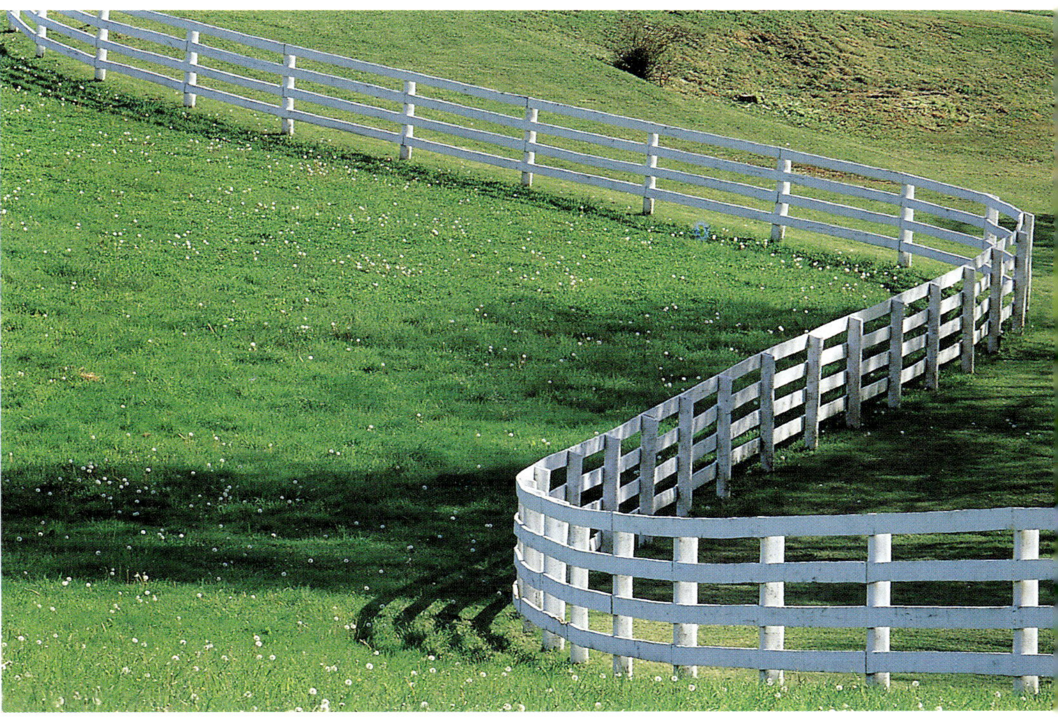

Central Kentucky has thousands of miles of beautiful wood-planked fences. Look for patterns and lines that flow across your frame. The beauty of these images is that you don't need a property release.

There are ways of entering a farm legally if you feel limited by roadside photography: The first is on a guided tour with a group, although that might not yield productive shooting. Other options are hiring a private guide or making an appointment with the farm. A few farms will allow this during certain times of the year. This provides the best opportunity. The same rules apply here as for property releases, even with permission to be on the farm. Contact the Lexington Convention and Visitors Bureau for details on farm tours before you arrive, and make arrangements well in advance.

I approach the Kentucky horse country with the idea of photographing fence lines and patterns of fences, small sections of the fence with a beautiful dogwood or a simple tree overhanging the fence. Horses from a distance, where no distinguishable marks or background property can be identified, make good, usable photos. Simple, clean images are the best and safest to shoot if you're selling. If you aren't selling your work, shoot whatever you want. You shouldn't pass up any good situation, even if you can't sell it; the resulting images might still be good for a slide show or for editorial use.

Begin each day before sunrise. If you're in Kentucky during the spring and autumn months, there are good chances to catch fog sweeping across a pasture. Horses are pretty active when they are released from their stables, so the chances are good of capturing a horse galloping or a young colt being playful. The afternoon is a good time to head off to the track if you're in the area during the racing season.

The Kentucky Horse Park <www.kyhorsepark.com/khp/> is unique in the sense that it's a working horse farm and an educational theme park dedicated to horses, the only one of its kind in the world. There are a lot of opportunities to photograph in this park. The park sponsors events throughout the year, which I recommend taking advantage of if you're in the area. Steeplechase races, polo events, equestrian events, horse shows and many more are often world-class events and showcase the best of the best. Most of these events are photographer friendly. For a schedule of events, call (800) 678-8813. The park also offers camping; see details in the "Need to Know" section on page 68.

Racetracks

Lexington is home to two beautiful racetracks, Keeneland (thoroughbred racing) and The Red

Mile (harness racing). After an easy, slow-paced morning enjoying the rural settings of central Kentucky, I recommend spending at least one afternoon at one of these tracks. The racing calendars for these tracks are different, so head to whichever track is open for racing. Keeneland's races are held for three weeks in April and three weeks in October. The Red Mile holds a spring meet from the last week of April through June and a fall meet from late September through the first week of October. For exact dates check with Keeneland [(859) 254-3412; <www.keeneland.com>] and The Red Mile [(859) 255-0752; www.tattersalls redmile.com/>].

Keeneland and The Red Mile are two of the most photography-friendly tracks in America. You can photograph on the rail next to the track and have nothing between you and the horses. The best news is you don't need super-long telephoto lenses. You can get very good images with a simple 200mm lens, and better yet, you can use a tripod. Both tracks allow visitors to walk the grounds around the stables, opening other possibilities for photography. You really can't go wrong spending an afternoon at the races.

I prefer the spring meet in Keeneland for a couple of reasons. First, the countryside is fresh with new foliage and beautiful white dogwood blooms, and the racetrack is exceptionally pretty with dogwoods and azaleas in full bloom. Second, the sun is positioned at its best for photographing the horses coming down the grandstand side of the track, a classic shot of Keeneland. Regardless of your timing, you'll have opportunities.

As soon as I arrive at the track, I purchase a racing program to see where the races start and end on the track. This allows me to make

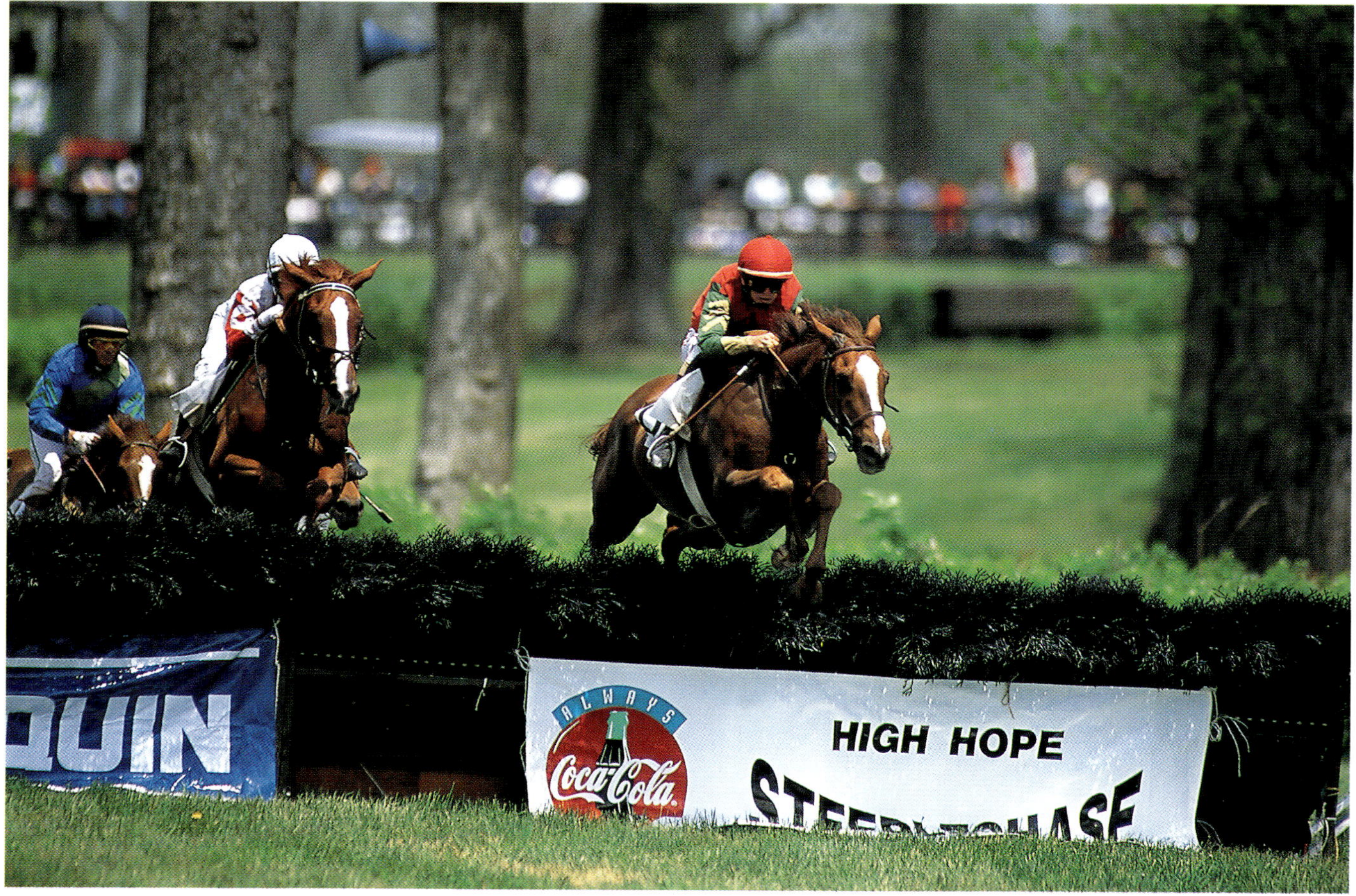

The Kentucky Horse Park has horse-related events year-round. The annual steeplechase race is a lot of fun to photograph. You don't need any special equipment to photograph the races; a basic 80–200mm zoom lens will take care of most of your needs.

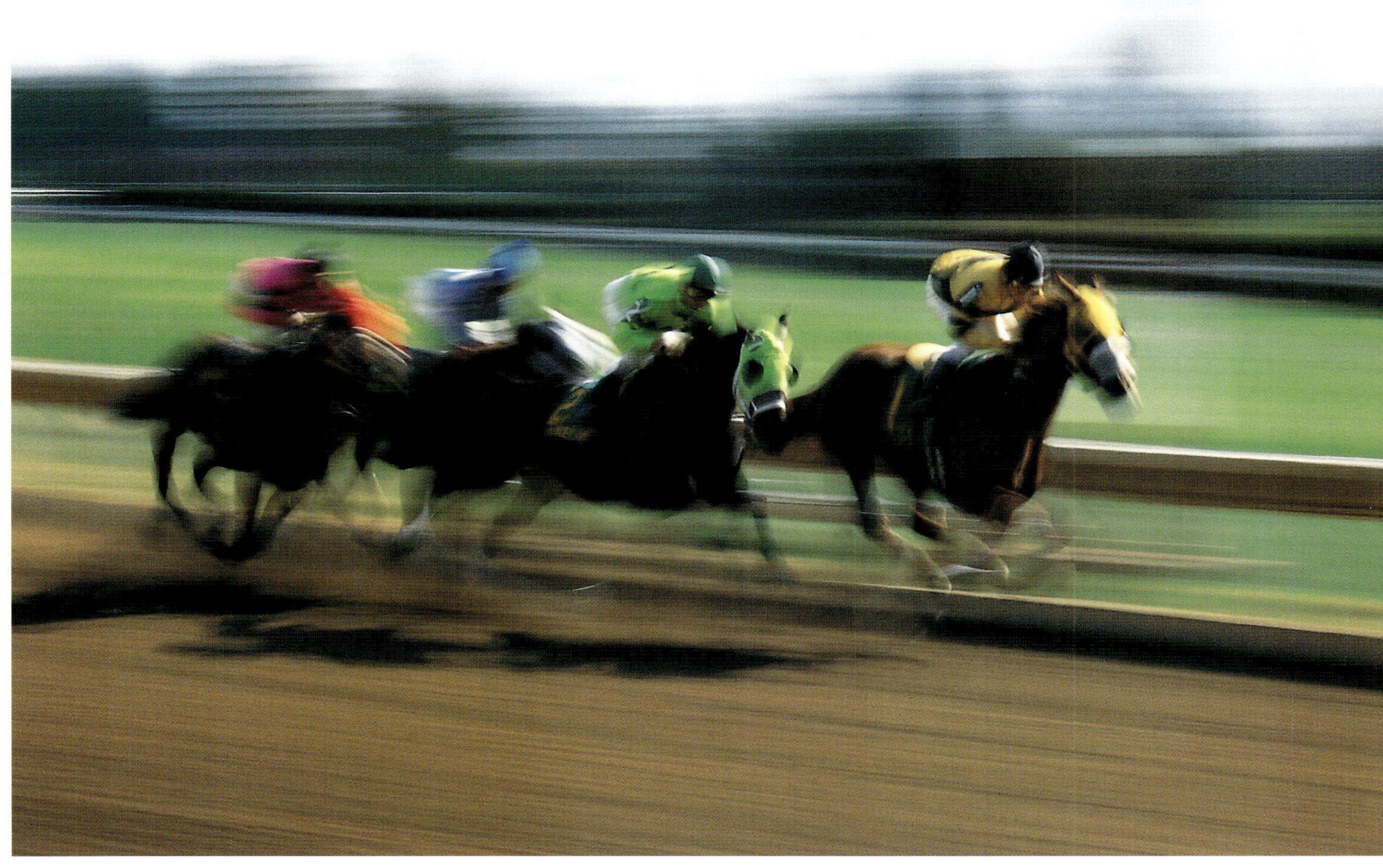

an informed decision about where to set up. (Starting points vary depending on the length of the race.) You get only one chance at each race, so make good choices based on the information you have. A typical race day will feature ten races. I also like to arrive early so I can walk around the stables and photograph trainers working with horses and other scenes associated with racing.

When photographing races, try to capture different aspects of the race, such as the horses breaking out of the starting gates or the horses making the turn with the grandstand in the background, or try panning a couple races to blur the image and show motion. Experiment with different angles and techniques, and come up with other ideas beyond what I just mentioned. Be creative. Every image will end up looking the same if you stick with one technique and one angle.

WHEN TO GO

I like the spring racing season at Keeneland, but May is also a good time to be in Kentucky. If you choose May, you will be visiting The Red Mile instead of Keeneland, but it's equally pretty and holds the same great opportunities except with harness racing. You could plan your timing to coincide with the end of Keeneland and the beginning of The Red Mile and get both locations. The surrounding landscapes in the farm regions are going to be good regardless of your timing in the spring. You might end up missing the dogwoods in bloom as you approach the middle of May. The autumn is nice, too, if you can't make it

Consider panning with long exposures in a few races. This image from Keeneland has wider market potential because the location and the horses aren't identifiable.

in the spring. There isn't a lot of brilliant color in central Kentucky, so don't set your heart on capturing beautiful fall color.

TIME REQUIREMENTS

I think the Kentucky horse country has many good photo opportunities, but a week might be overextending your stay unless you have permission to photograph on a couple farms and you take in two or three days at the race-tracks. An extended weekend of four days should allow plenty of time to catch the best of this region.

NEED TO KNOW

There are lots of hotels in the Lexington area. I suggest getting a hotel near Interstate 75. The cost will be much lower than in down-town, and you'll be closer to the rural areas to work the horse farms. Camping is available at the Kentucky Horse Park campground <www.kyhorsepark.com/khp/campground/>, a full-service facility with electrical and water hookups for trailers and RVs. Rates range from $15 to $23 per night from spring to fall. For more information, contact the Lexington Convention and Visitors Bureau [(800) 845-3959; <www.visitlex.com>], Kentucky's Blue-grass Region <www.bluegrasskentucky.com/> or the Kentucky Department of Travel [(800) 225-8747; <www.kytourism.com>].

photographer's choice

ASSATEAGUE AND CHINCOTEAGUE ISLANDS, VA., are home to the wild Chincoteague pony, a hybrid breed. On the last consecutive Wednesday, Thursday and Friday of July, the Chincoteague Fire Department conducts a roundup where the horses swim the Assateague Channel, a unique photographic experience. Combine this with a photo shoot in northern Baltimore County's horse country, where horse farms and horse-related activities are common. [Assateague and Chincoteague Islands, www.chincoteaguechamber.com, www.assateagueisland.com]

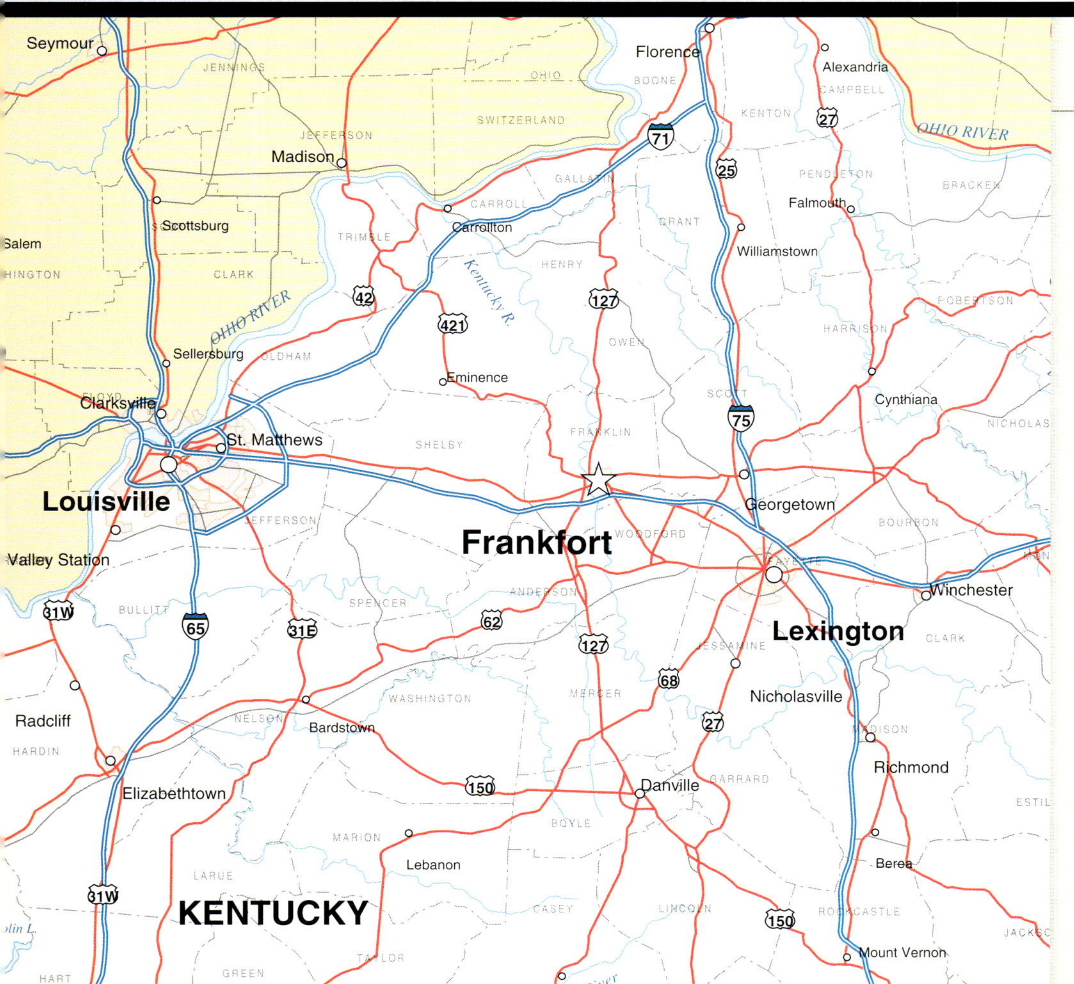

directions

Lexington sits right on interstates 75 and 64. The Lexington airport is across the road from Keeneland Racetrack and is only a ten-minute drive to down-town. Lexington is a small city and very easy to get around. The farm region is an extended area beyond Lexington, but with a map from the Lexington Convention and Visitors Bureau and a DeLorme Atlas, you should have no problem at all. All roads eventually end up back on the main tour route.

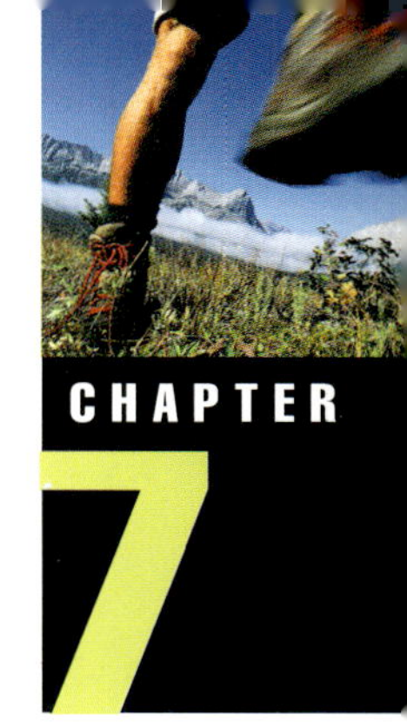

Tallgrass Prairies of Illinois

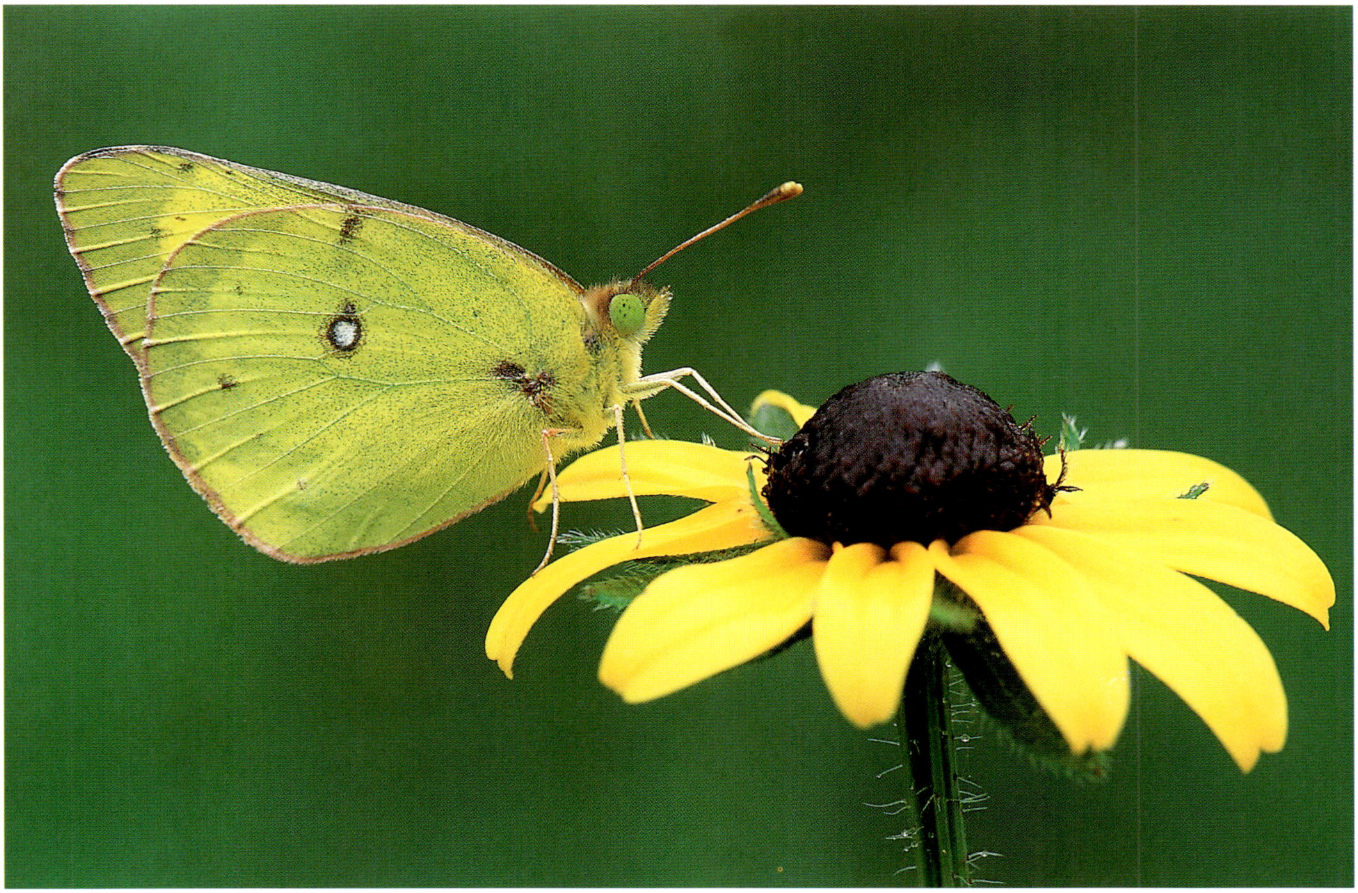

The Midwest, now America's agricultural belt, was once a vast prairie with grasses, wildflowers and North America's largest mammal, the American Bison. Tallgrass prairies covered eastern parts of North and South Dakota, half of Nebraska, eastern parts of Kansas, Oklahoma and Texas and stretched eastward into Minnesota, Iowa, Missouri and Illinois. Ohio, Kentucky and Tennessee had small pockets of tallgrass prairies as well. Today prairies are down to 1 percent of their natural expanse. The few areas that remain bring photographers every

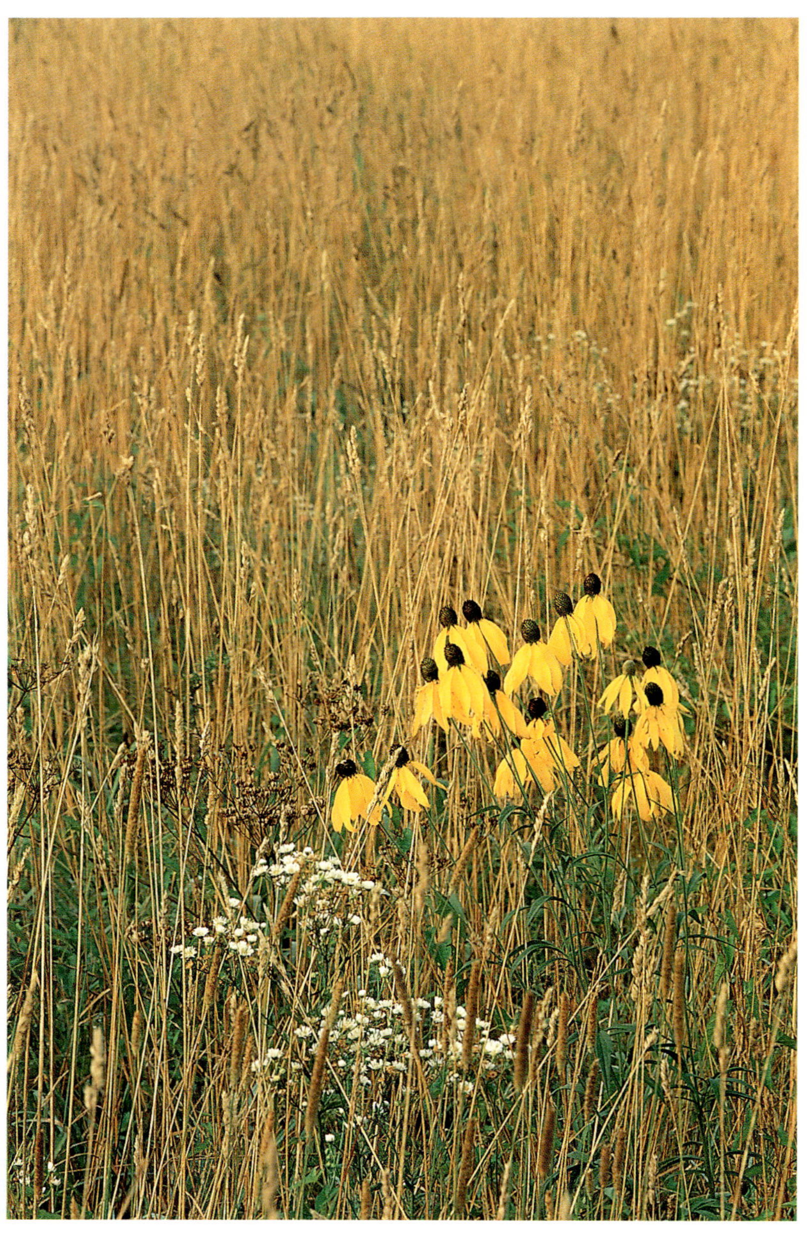

Coneflowers are one common plant visitors will see on the prairie. Clean, simple compositions are best.

year to work the colorful blooms. Paradoxically, several of the best-preserved examples of native tallgrass prairie lie in the shadows of sprawling Chicago.

Most people know very little about prairies and have never really visited one. Prairies fall into three categories: tallgrass prairie (in the eastern half of the Midwest), mixed-grass prairie (North Dakota, South Dakota, Nebraska, Kansas, Oklahoma, Texas) and shortgrass prairie (western North Dakota, South Dakota, Nebraska, Kansas, and into eastern Montana, Wyoming, Colorado and New Mexico). Prairies are dominated by herbaceous plants, mostly grasses.

The prairie ecosystem is complex, and much more could be discussed about this fascinating environment. I just wanted to give a few examples of the expanse of the prairie system and minimally show the importance the prairie ecosystem plays in the world today. Our focus is on the tallgrass prairie of Illinois, and this is where we'll go from here. If you'd like to learn more about tallgrass prairies, I recommend a book called *Tallgrass Prairie*, by John Madson.

PHOTOGRAPHER'S VIEW

If you're from the Midwest, you know all too well how much the weather can change from season to season and even within a season. If you aren't from the Midwest, let me forewarn you that July and August, the peak for wildflower blooms on the Illinois prairies, can be brutally hot and humid. The other downside is that some prairies are damp and therefore mosquito-friendly. Despite this, the prairies are very much worth the obstacles I just mentioned. Work in the cooler morning and early-evening hours, wear long-sleeved shirts, and cover your face with a safe repellant. I have also found rubber surgical gloves work wonderfully in mosquito-infested areas.

You will be amazed at how high the grasses can be. Several of the flower species are tall as well and can be difficult to frame. A lightweight two-foot stepladder will put you above the grasses and flowers. This also means, of course, that you'll need a tripod extendable to five or six feet with the camera mounted.

Don't expect to photograph breathtaking landscapes or endless expanses of flowers. Prairie wildflowers typically grow in pockets mixed with grasses. Anytime you're going to shoot flowers, I can't stress enough the importance of contacting locals before departing to check on peak bloom. Agriculture has divided prairies into small pockets scattered throughout the state, so plan on doing some driving in between locations.

Prairies start to look alike after a while. I don't believe it's necessary to visit more than two or three. Prairies also tend to be in the middle of nowhere with few or no amenities. A good sampling of prairies within a couple hours' drive of Chicago will give you plenty of photographic subjects. Take your time to explore and enjoy your experience. If you shoot with a keen eye and open mind, you should come home with plenty of beautiful and salable images—and enjoy an experience that measures well beyond your expectations.

Iroquois County Conservation Area

Iroquois County Conservation Area, once the largest wetland in Illinois, is near the Indiana border south of Chicago. This is a wonderful prairie with a mixture of dry to marshy conditions. Needless to say, you'll probably experience a lot of mosquitoes, but the flower blooms should be some of the best you see on your journey. Prairie blazing star is plentiful and one of the most common plants you'll find here, along with an assortment of rattlesnake master, goldenrod and big bluestem grasses.

Your best bet in this prairie is to look for clusters of plants and small intimate scenes. You'll be challenged and walk away disappointed if you're looking for a big overall prairie scene. August skies in the Midwest aren't very attractive. You will probably experience some white, hazy skies. Avoid using any sky in your composition under these conditions. White skies will render very bright and draw the viewer's eye away from your subject. Many of the plants at Iroquois County Conservation Area are tall plants mixed in with tall grasses. A stepladder or step stool will elevate you enough to shoot down into a cluster of flowers or little scene and avoid the sky. This can't solve all of your creative problems but will open more opportunities.

This image of prairie blazing star and rattlesnake master is an excellent example of selecting a flower grouping. They aren't as easy to compose as you might think. This image might be useful for editorial illustrating tallgrass prairie ecosystems.

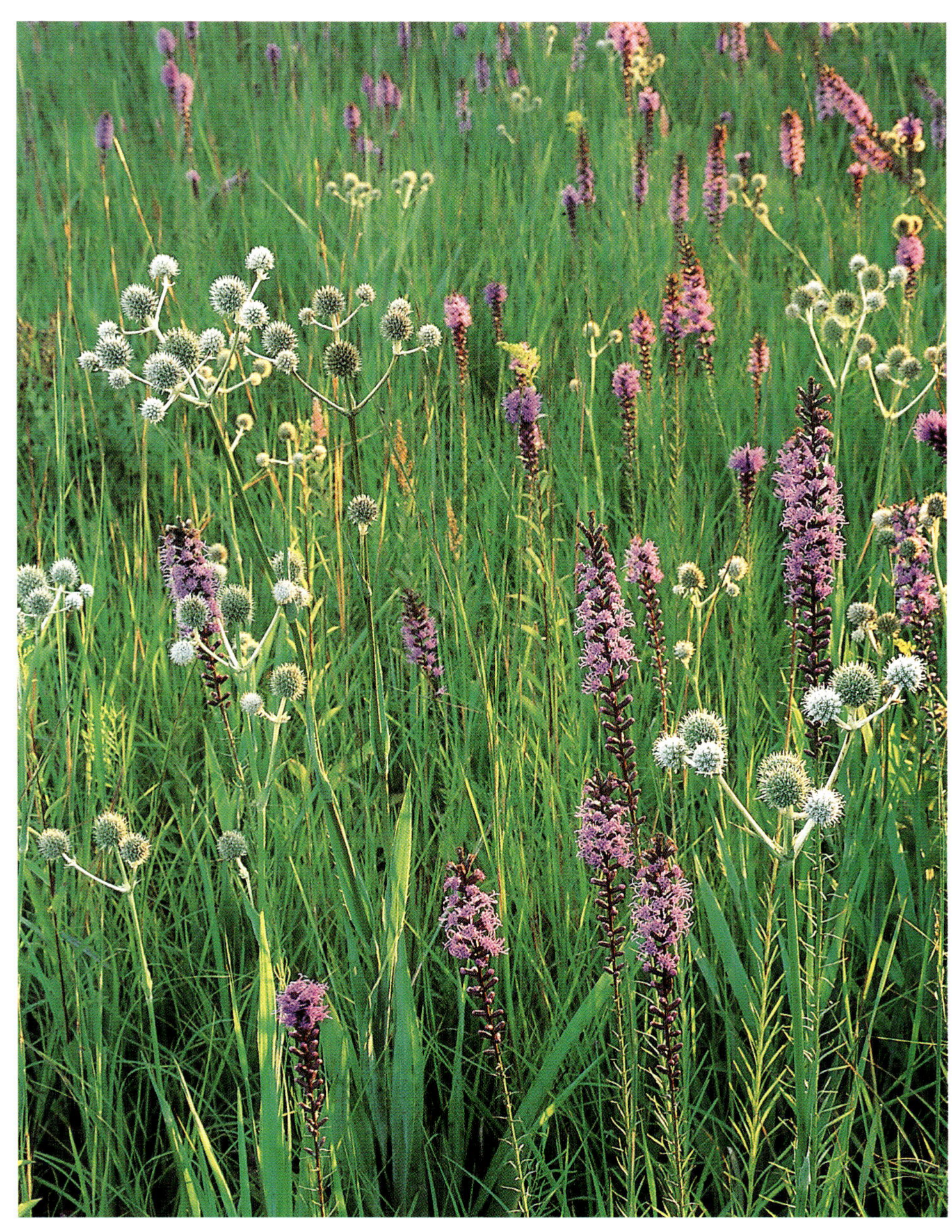

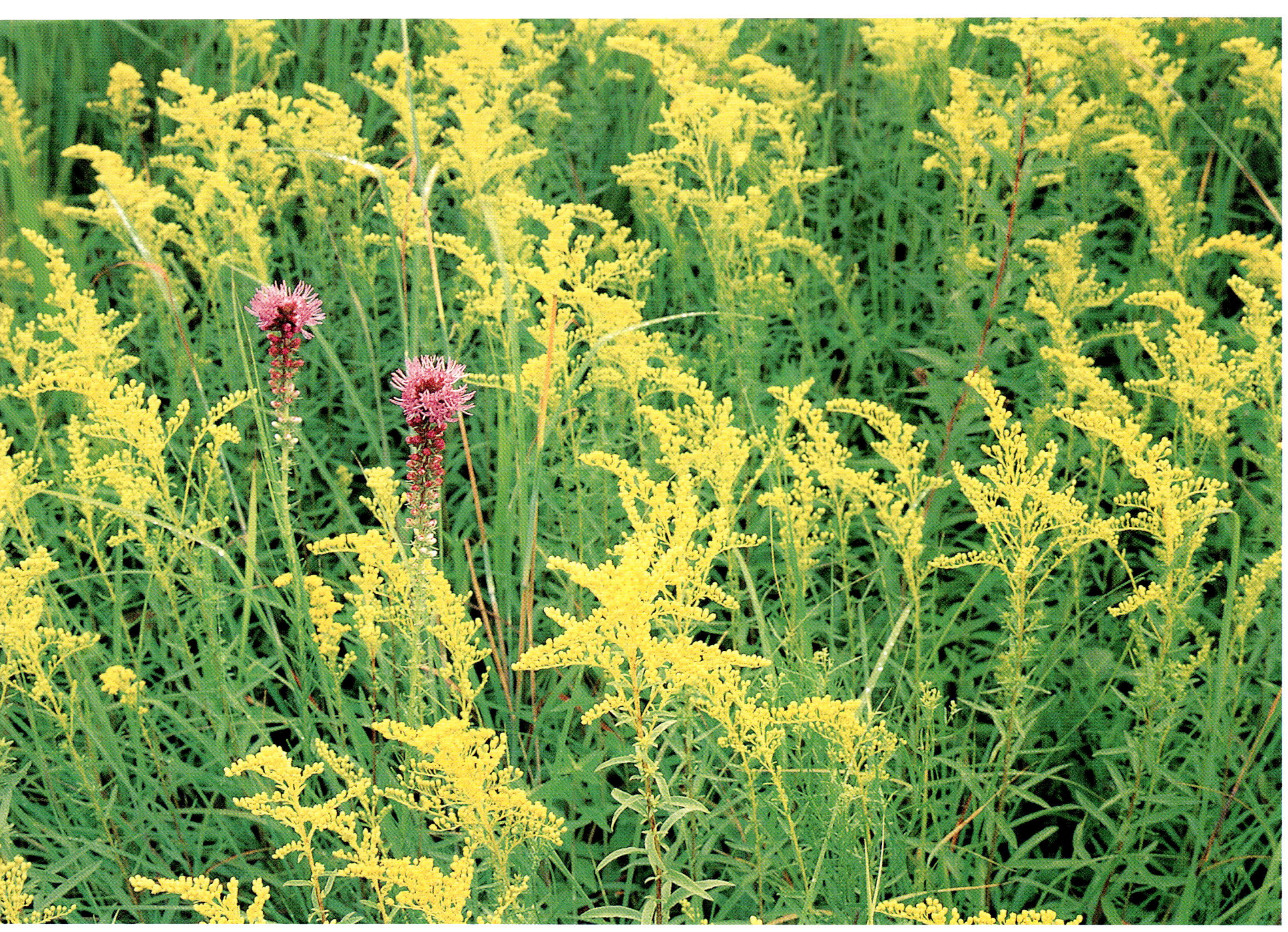

Look for an element that stands out from its surroundings. In this case it's prairie blazing star surrounded by goldenrod. Images like these can be interpreted in many positive ways and have good market potential for greeting cards and possibly advertising.

Goose Lake Prairie Nature Preserve

Goose Lake Prairie is the largest of the Illinois prairies, at 2,838 acres. Several trails within this preserve allow for in-depth exploration of the prairie ecosystem, but you won't need to hike very far from the road. There aren't really major land features to consider for photography, so let the flower blooms dictate where you photograph. Goose Lake Prairie should offer you the most predictable of flower blooms. Sixty percent of Goose Lake Prairie consists of grasses such as big bluestem, Indian grass, switchgrass and the tallest of the grasses, prairie cordgrass, which can reach heights of eight to twelve feet. The remaining 40 percent is flowering broad-leaved plants.

Goose Lake Prairie is commonly known in the photography community and is probably one of the more visited prairies among photographers. I have an easier time here than other places composing images with a wide variety of plant species in a single visit. Besides wildflowers, you should come prepared for early-morning butterfly photography. You won't want to miss butterflies sitting on colorful flower blooms covered in morning dew. Once the sun warms these little critters, you can forget photographing them.

Indian Boundary Prairies and Others

You could rack up a lot of miles in your car visiting prairie after prairie, but there's little

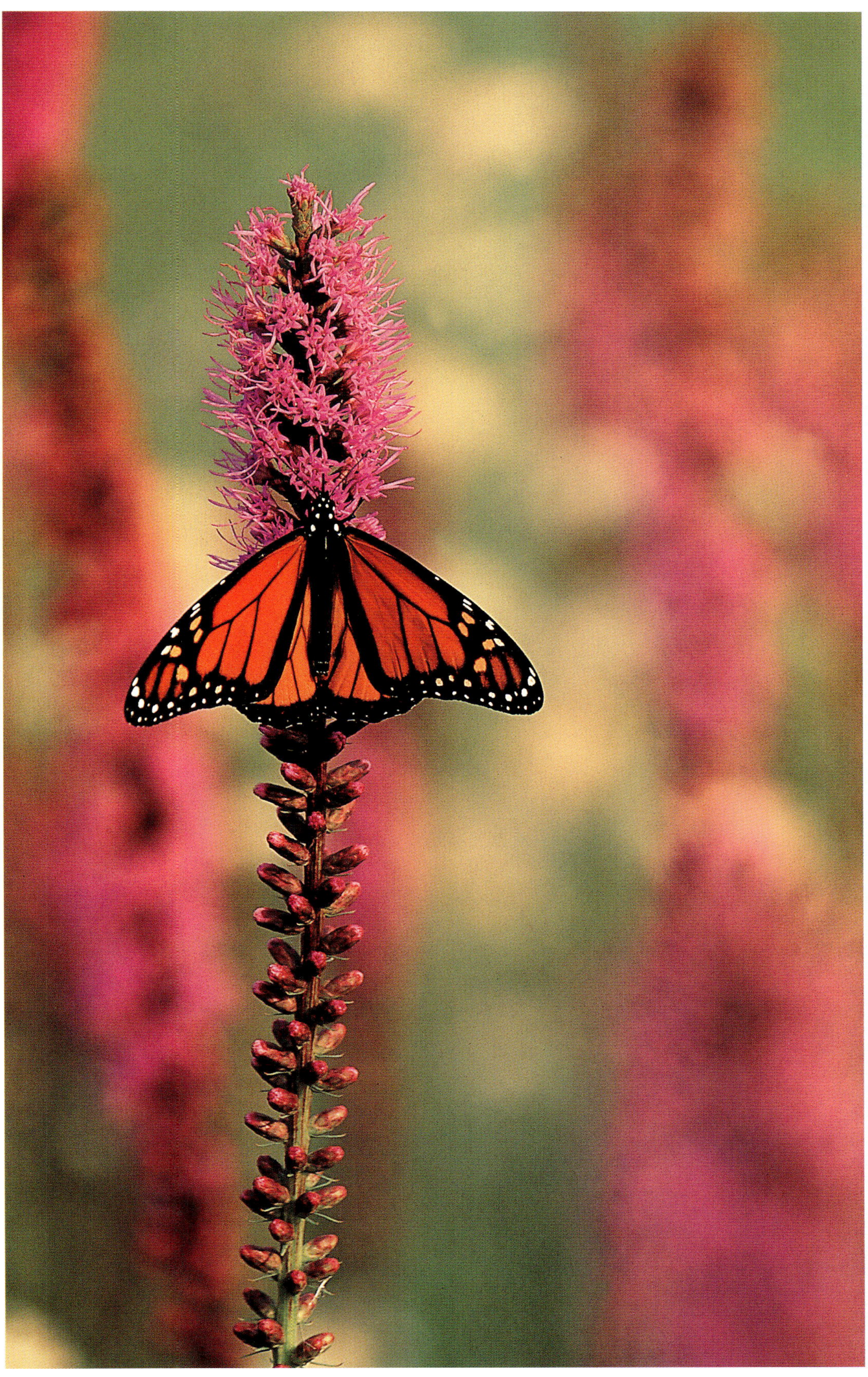

Monarch butterflies are common in the Illinois prairies. Start out early if shooting butterflies is your goal. They become much more active and difficult to photograph once the sun rises.

need to do so. Beyond Iroquois County and Goose Lake, consider Indian Boundary Prairies, which is a group of four prairies, Gensburg-Markham Prairie, Dropseed Prairie, Paintbrush Prairie and Sundrop Prairie. These four prairies combined take up three hundred acres known as the Indian Boundary Prairies and sit in the shadows of Chicago. Part of this group has been named a National Natural Landmark because of its plant and butterfly diversity and genetic resources. These prairies are quite small compared with the two I have already covered. You will be confined to macro photography or small intimate flower scenes.

If you want to see more prairies or want to skip the smaller sites for more secluded prairies, do an Internet search on tallgrass prairies of Illinois, or consult the Madson book I mentioned earlier in this chapter. He lists several prairies throughout the state, which are all very good, but much farther afield and more secluded than the ones I have covered here. Most important before you visit any of these prairies is to make contact with a naturalist or prairie manager to see what's in bloom at what stage the blooms are in. You will want to photograph around the peak of a wide variety of plant species. If only one or two plants are in bloom, the flower groupings you hope to capture could be all but impossible, and you'll end up disappointed. Two Web sites to consult for bloom status and other plant information are <www.prairiepages.com> and <www.prairies.org>.

photographer's choice

You'll find plenty of prairie reserves beyond Illinois. Check out FLINT HILLS DRIVE and KONZA PRAIRIE, Kans.; TALLGRASS PRAIRIE, Okla.; and PRAIRIE STATE PARK, Mo. When researching prairies, make sure the land is open to the public and is large enough to keep you busy for a couple days. [Flint Hills Drive and Konza Prairie, www.manhattan.org; Tallgrass Prairie, www.state.ok.us; Prairie State Park, www.mostateparks.com/prairie.htm.]

WHEN TO GO

Prairie wildflowers can bloom anytime from April through October. I consider the peak bloom for variety to be from early July through the middle of August. The July/August window has the most showy plants and best compositional variety. This is the time frame in which you should encounter a mixture of tall plants with smaller plants and variety of color. You should also see several species of butterflies.

TIME REQUIREMENTS

Three to four days will give you plenty of time. You might struggle to keep yourself busy for an entire week, and the heat and humidity take their toll. Contact each of the prairies you plan on visiting before you depart to see what is in bloom, and base your shooting schedule on this information. You can spend a lot of time traveling in between prairies. Make sure your decisions on what prairie at what time are well thought out.

NEED TO KNOW

Lodging near Iroquois County Conservation Reserve isn't available. Bourbonnais or Kankakee is your best bet for lodging. Both locations will only set you back thirty minutes at the most in the morning. Camping is an option if you want to be closer to your morning shoot. Morris has several motels if you'll be at Goose Lake Prairie. Tinley Park and Joliet are best for lodging near Indian Boundary Prairies. Tinley Park is closer but with fewer offerings. Joliet has many more hotels to choose from but will put you an additional fifteen to twenty minutes away. For additional resources on prairies and prairie ecosystems, see <www.prairiesource.com> and <www.npwrc.usgs.gov>.

directions

Getting to the Illinois prairies will entail the use of a good back seat driver. Keep your DeLorme Atlas and Gazetteer handy.

IROQUOIS COUNTY CONSERVATION AREA:

- Interstate 57 Southto U.S Highway 45 east. Follow 45 to State Highway 1. Turn north onto State Highway 1 to St. Anne, and follow signs to Iroquois County Conservation Area. There is an office on the premises, and you will probably need to speak to someone inside for additional guidance.

GOOSE LAKE PRAIRIE STATE NATURAL AREA:

- Interstate 80 west to Morris. Follow State Highway 47 south from Morris. Cross over the Illinois River Bridge, and take the first left onto Pine Bluff Road. Drive east on this road for 7.5 miles. Turn left onto Lorenzo Road, and the entrance is on the corner of Lorenzo and Jugtown Road.

GENSBURG-MARKHAM PRAIRIE:

- Keep in mind this is a series of four prairies south of Chicago. Near the junction of U.S Route 57 and Interstate 294 exit eastbound from U.S. Route 57 onto 159th Street (U.S. Route 6). Continue on 159th to Whipple Avenue. Turn north on Whipple until it ends in a small parking lot at Gensburg-Markham Prairie.

PAINTBRUSH PRAIRIE:

- Turn west on 159th Street from I-294 and Route 57. Turn north onto Pulaski/Crawford Avenue, and continue to 155th past Millard road. Parking is to the north.

SUNDROP PRAIRIE:

- Exit eastbound from Route 57 onto 159th street. Continue on 159th to Kedzie Avenue. Turn north onto Kedzie, and turn west onto 151st Street to the parking lot on the southwest corner of the preserve.

DROPSEED PRAIRIE:

- Exit eastbound from Route 57 onto 159th Street. Continue on 159th to Kedzie Avenue. Turn north on Kedzie, and turn west on 157th Street. Continue on 157th until Homan Avenue. Turn north on Homan, and continue to the parking north of the community center on the west.

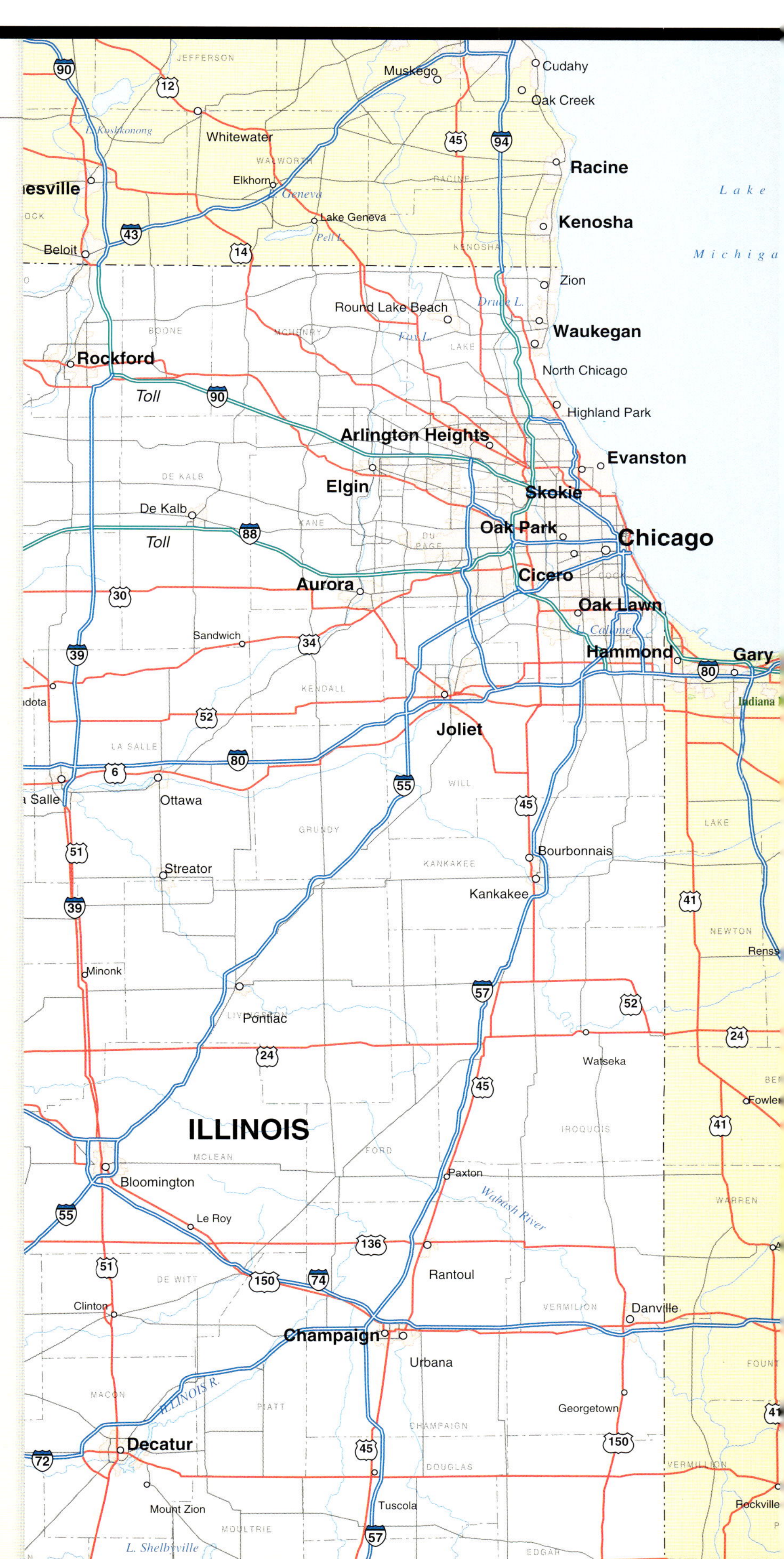

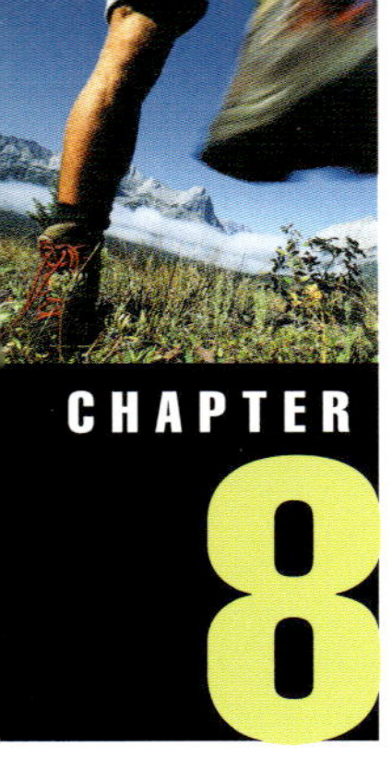

CHAPTER 8

Wildflowers of the Texas Hill Country

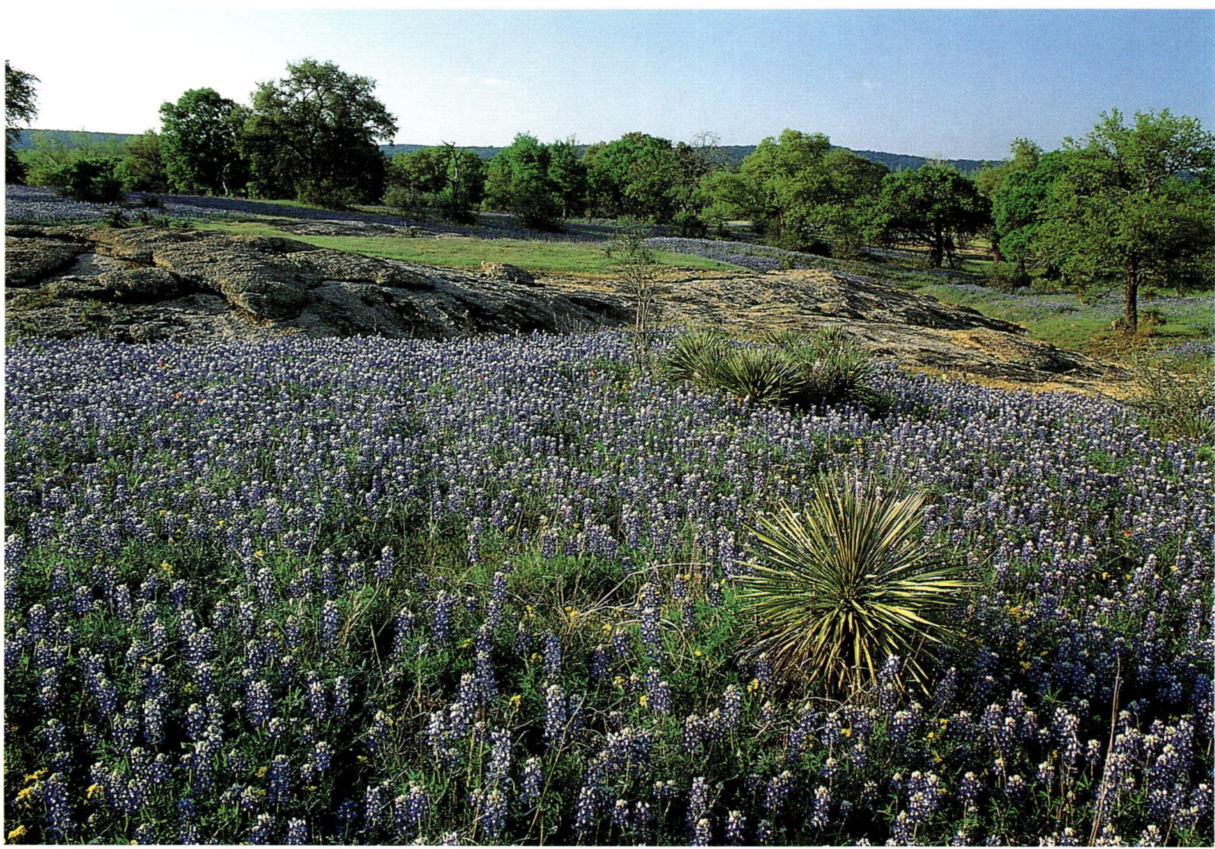

Beautiful, stunning and incredible are only a few of many words one could use to describe the spring wildflower bloom in the Texas hill country. Lupines, better known in Texas as the Texas bluebonnet, and Indian paintbrush dominate the landscape with an endless carpet of purple and red. The Texas hill country is situated at the southern end of the Midwestern prairies, the eastern side of the Chihuahuan desert, the western side of the Southeast woodlands and the northern edge of the Tamaulipan thorn scrub. This diversity of ecosystems is the reason for the proliferation of wildflower blooms.

The rolling hills of central Texas make

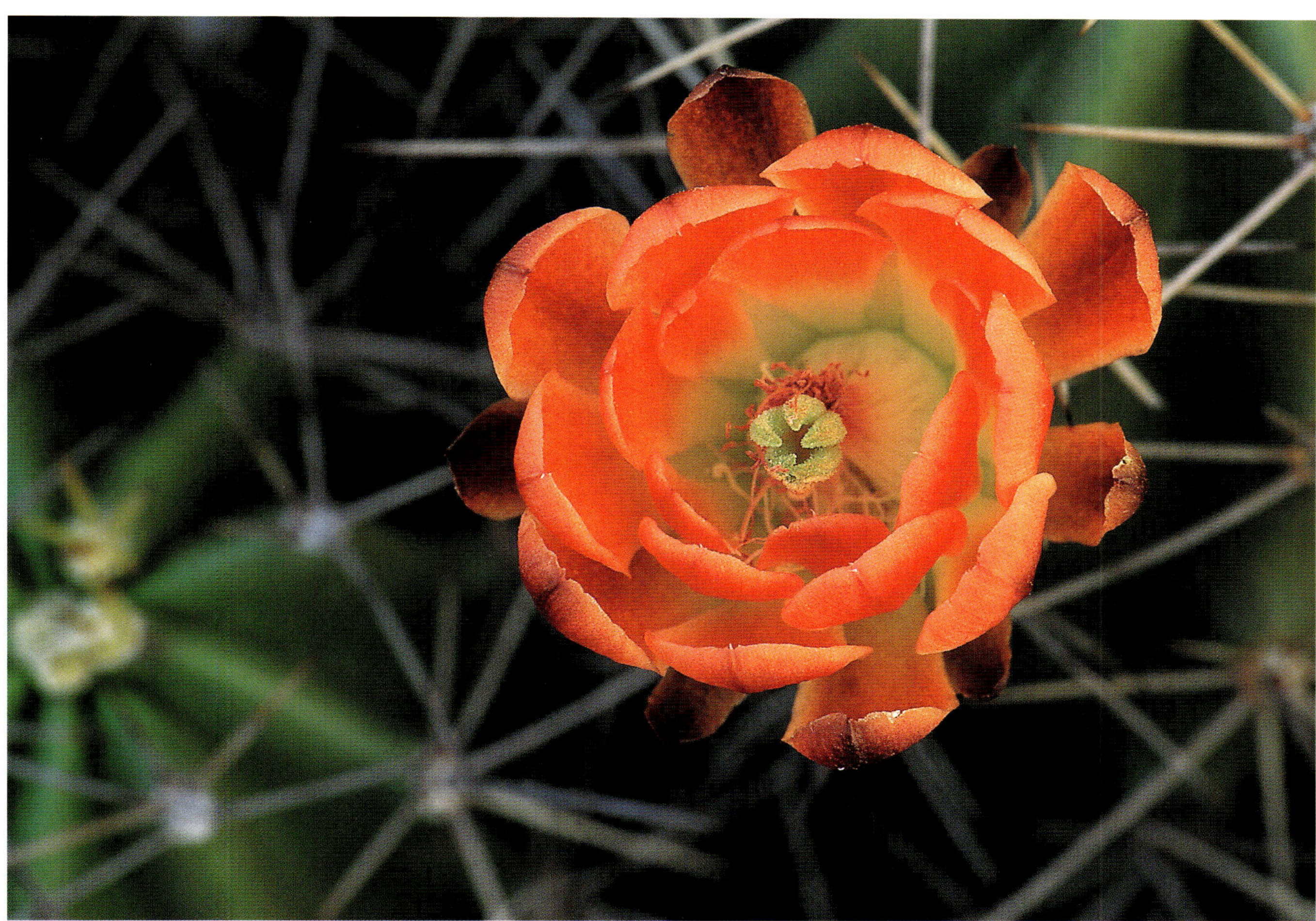

When I photograph the Texas hill country, it's hard to make myself shoot something other than landscapes, but I also recognize the importance of a diverse collection. Close-ups of individual plants, such as this claret cup cactus, are as important as the big scenic.

this the most attractive of Texas landscapes, arguably the best overall wildflower display in America. Texans take their wildflowers seriously and enjoy showing them off to visitors. The spring bloom in the hill country has become a major attraction for both tourists and photographers. Lady Bird Johnson and the Texas Highway department are credited in part for the profusion of wildflowers from their efforts of implementing a highway beautification program, which landscapes more than 800,000 acres.

PHOTOGRAPHER'S VIEW

A Texas wildflower journey can be one of the most rewarding photography opportunities you embark upon, and if you're selling your work, one with very good financial returns. As with the Illinois prairies, you need to communicate with a local naturalist or other authority to see how the blooms are doing. I have been in Texas many times and have had years when one could barely see a break in the endless carpet of flowers and others when flowers were meager and at times nonexistent. Botanists say that for a good spring bloom, the flowers need a dry summer (keeping the flowers from going to seed too early), a wet autumn, a cold winter and a wet spring. I have seen very good blooms when just a couple of these factors existed. The Texas Wildflower Hotline [(800) 452-9292] is a good starting point when deciding the right time to be on location. Another wonderful source of information is the Lady Bird Johnson Wildflower Center [(512) 292-4200; <www.wildflower.org>]. If the wildflower blooms are not good, pass up Texas until another year. You'll be

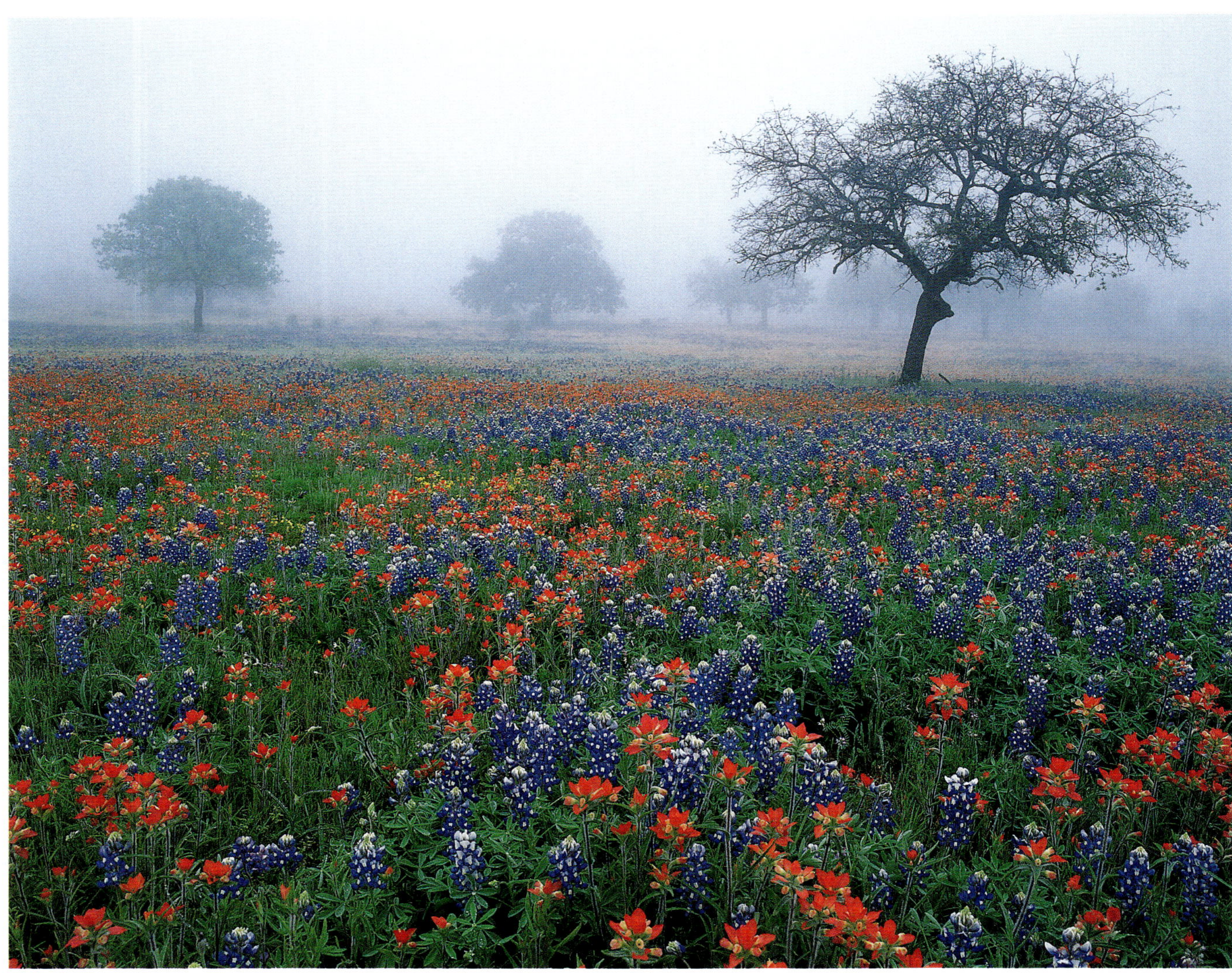

Strong foreground color makes this image. Fog generally doesn't sell well because it can be interpreted as eerie or uncertain, but this image has sold over and over.

hard pressed to find much to shoot if there aren't any flowers.

Prepare yourself for a variety of shooting opportunities from wide-open landscapes to intimate scenes to macro subjects. With a good season of wildflower blooms, you will have a wide range of shooting opportunities, so make sure you're prepared for it. I suggest having focal lengths between 28mm and 200mm. A wider lens might be helpful at times but isn't necessary. Bring a diffuser for those sunny days when a good macro subject pops up. Hope for sunny days along with a couple overcast days. Both lend themselves to various situations you will encounter. One persistent problem in the hill country is wind. If you get a day with no wind, take advantage of it. If you work the fields early in the morning, you'll have your best chance for little or no wind and quite possibly a light fog cover. I have experienced fog a couple of times and captured some beautiful, well-paying shots.

The Texas hill country is a large area within a very large state; you can put a lot of miles on your car. If the wildflower blooms are good, you won't need to cover the whole region anyway, but if they're sporadic, you'll cover a lot of ground. Austin is the gateway to the hill country, and this is where you'll start seeing your first signs of bluebonnets in large numbers. Marble Falls is fifty miles northwest of Austin—a great starting point and a good place to base your entire stay. There are many wonderful shooting locations within a reasonable drive from Marble Falls.

Marble Falls Region

If I can't find wildflowers blooming elsewhere in the hill country, I head to the area around Marble Falls. If anything is in bloom, you'll find it here. One of the biggest problems you'll find here, as well as other parts of the hill country, is lots of private property. It never fails; the best blooms seem to be on the other side of the fence. The good news is that Texas hospitality is some of the best you'll find anywhere. I have been given permission more times than not when I ask a landowner if I can come on her property to photograph. Always ask before you walk onto private property. If no one's home, or the owner refuses, simply find somewhere else to photograph.

There are dozens of scenic drives in the hill country and several beautiful roads within the Marble Falls region. With almost any road you choose, you have a good chance of finding beautiful fields of flowers. The blooms can change from year to year; therefore you'll need to drive along the routes yourself to see what is happening. A good source for route information is the visitors center in Marble Falls (801 Highway 281), run by the Marble Falls/ Lake LBJ Chamber of Commerce [(800) 759-8178; <www.marblefalls.org>]. These folks will have driving route maps of the area and can give you some idea of which routes have the good blooms. I also recommend picking up a DeLorme Atlas and Gazetteer of Texas and driving many of the old farm roads.

A beautiful picturesque drive I have found to be productive is Route 1431 along the north shore of Lake LBJ through the communities of Granite Shoals and Kingsland. Continue on Route 2241 (at Bluffton) on the west shore of Lake Buchanan to Tow. You'll need to backtrack to Route 29 and continue east toward Burnet and south on 281 back to Marble Falls. There are typically good flowers along this route and plenty of places to pull off. You can detour off Route 29 onto Farm Road 2341 along the eastern shore of Lake Buchanan. This is just before the town of Burnet.

Inks Lake and Longhorn Caverns State Parks might have some blooms, but if you're having luck elsewhere, pass these parks up. The landscapes are not as pretty here as in

I made the lupine and paintbrush appear denser than they actually were by shooting from a low angle (about waist high) when I set up my tripod.

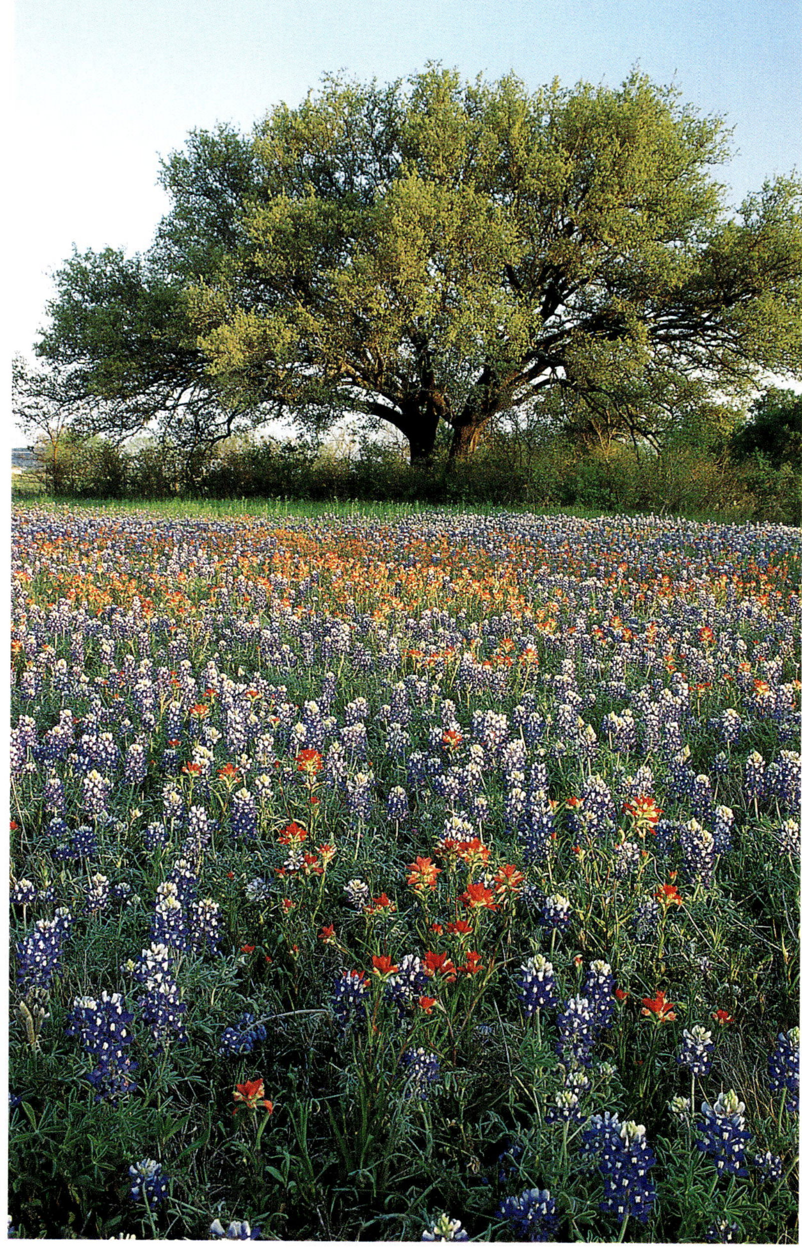

other places. I have had some success at Enchanted Rock State Natural Area and suggest trying this if you're running out of other options. The one point I really stress is to explore: Get off the main roads and drive the back roads. This is where your DeLorme Atlas will be helpful.

The out-of-focus stem on this spiderwort in the background makes this plain image interesting. If the stem were in sharp focus, it might steal attention away from the flower. This is where depth-of-field preview comes in handy.

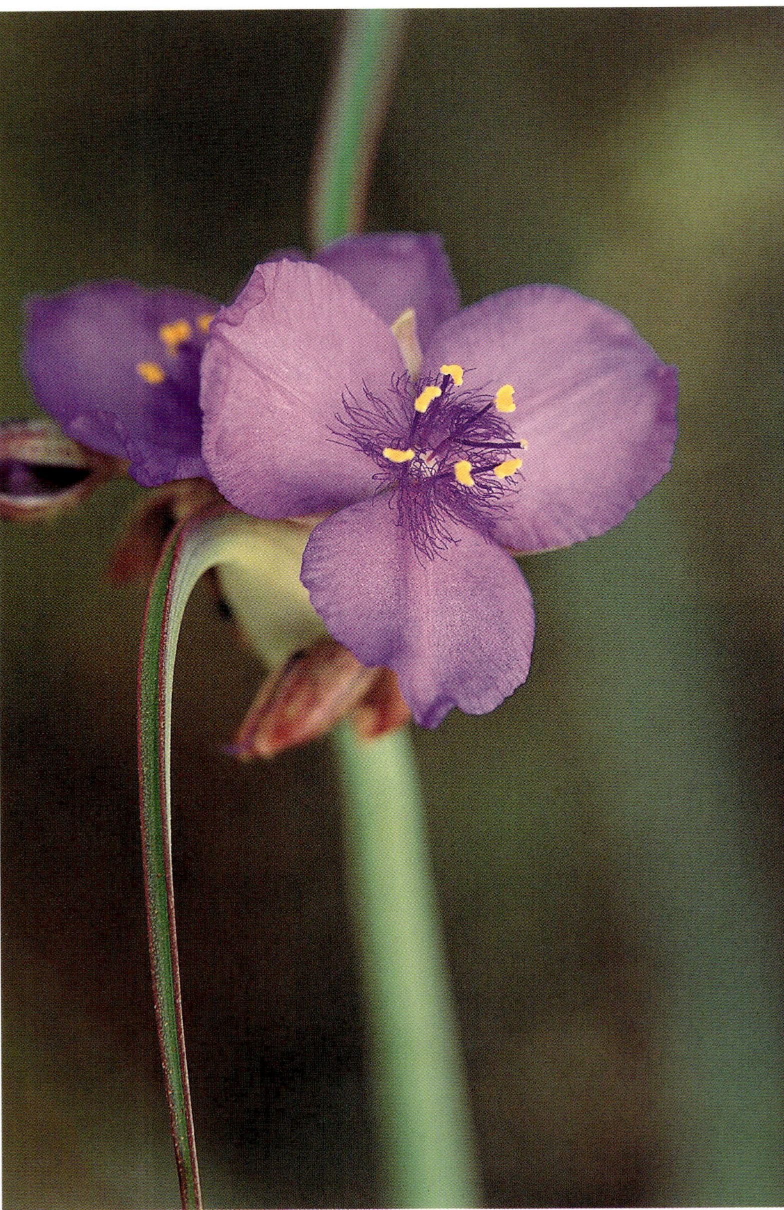

Other Hill Country Options

One of the best-known drives often talked about in photography circles is the Willow City Loop drive. I highly suggest giving it a try. The Willow City Loop sits in the middle of the scenic drive between Llano and Fredericksburg on Route 16. Willow City is on Farm Road 1323.

The drive between Fredricksburg and Johnson City on Route 290 can also be good. Along this route is the LBJ State and National Historic Parks. Many locals and tourists offices will direct you to these parks, but I would pass them up. They are very restrictive on where you can go and there will more than likely be busloads of people. There is one subject worth taking a look at if you need to stretch your legs: The working farm at the LBJ State Historic Park can be okay for a shot or two.

Mason County is known for its stone fences and stone houses. There can be good opportunities using these structures with flower fields. The best part of the drive is between the town of Mason and Fredonia on Route 386 and continue on Route 71. It's best to return the same route. There is little need to continue too far up Route 71. If you don't see much bloom or anything of interest within a few miles of Route 71, turn around.

If you're willing to relocate your base for a day or two, consider an area east of Austin. The hill country around Brenham, in Washington County along the Brazos River, is rated one of the state's best scenic drives. From Austin take Route 290 east to Brenham. From Brenham continue on Route 290 to Chappel Hill and Hempstead. Pick up Route 6 north to Navasota, then return on Route 105 to Brenham. Washington on the Brazos State Park is on this return route. Before heading out on this long drive, you should check the Texas Wildflower Hotline. Also, I highly recommend sharing what you have seen with other photographers and tourists during your visit; in turn they'll usually share what they're finding. This is just good networking and an incredible time-saver.

Photographing the Texas hill country de-

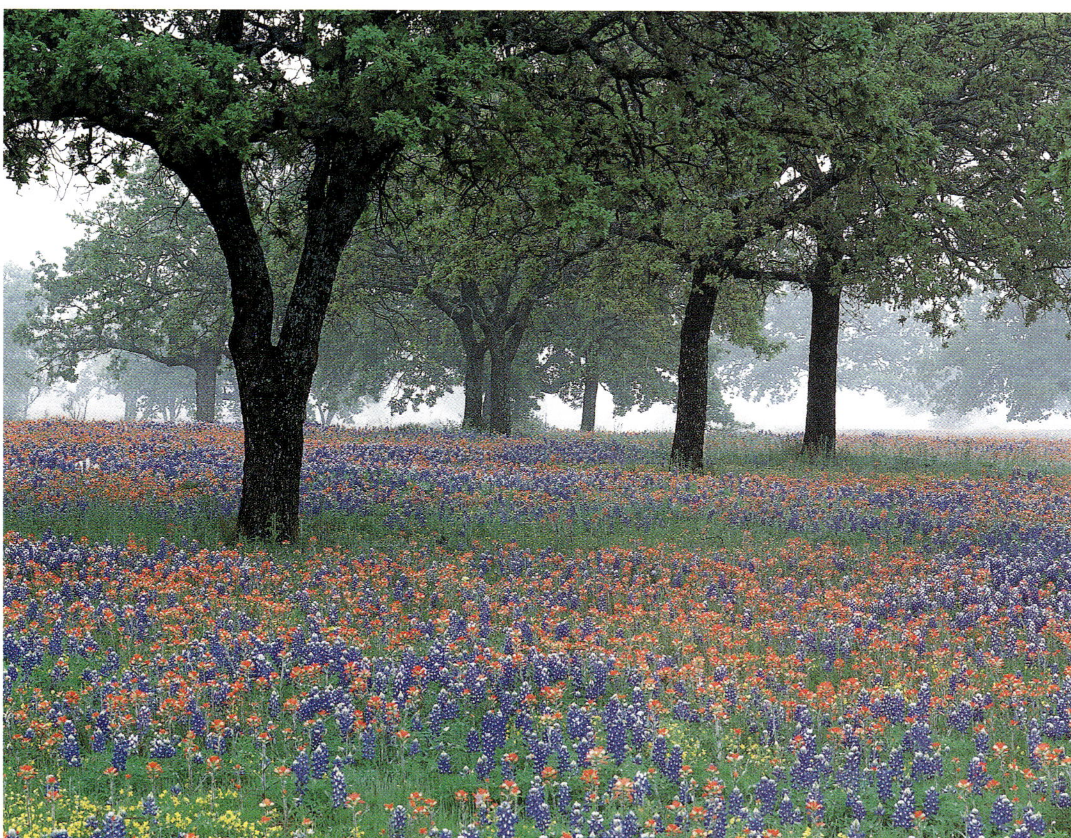

Texans take their wildflowers seriously. Take care not to trample any during your shoot.

pends on a good wildflower bloom; therefore it is difficult to be location-specific. Let the flowers dictate where you need to be. One year the bloom may be fantastic in one location and the next there may be nothing in that same location while other areas may be having a banner year. You really need to be willing to explore and put in your time driving and scouting the landscape. But most important, let the local tourist offices and wildflower hotline keep you informed about the wildflowers, and use their information as a guideline.

WHEN TO GO

Lots of literature says wildflower bloom is the last two weeks of March through April in the Texas hill country. There may be some truth to that, but I recommend the first two weeks of April. This is pretty predictable for peak bloom in most years. I would much rather be on the later side of the bloom than the early side. If you're too early, you'll have nothing to shoot. On the later side, you should have some bluebonnets and paintbrush hanging on and also some other wildflowers starting to show, such as Indian blankets, primrose, buttercups, coreopsis, spiderwort and verbena.

TIME REQUIREMENTS

The Texas hill country can be a great weekend getaway or a great week-long journey. Three full days of shooting would be the least amount of time I would spend here. If there's a great wildflower bloom, you will have no problem keeping yourself busy for an entire week. Keep in mind that you can spend a good deal of time driving in between places. Spend a day just scouting and deciding when and where you want to be during the best light. This will give you the opportunity to see where the flowers are in their blooming cycle in different locations.

NEED TO KNOW

Lodging in the hill country is sparse and unfortunately requires early reservations. Marble Falls does have several hotels, B&B's and RV campgrounds to choose from—see <www.marblefalls.org>—and plenty of other amenities. Plan ahead, and if the flower blooms aren't good, you can always cancel or just take a chance and see if something is available when you arrive. Camping is available at Inks Lake State Park [(512) 389-8900], Krause Springs [(830) 693-4181] and several other places throughout the Marble Falls area and the local state parks. Austin is another option for hotels but will require an extra hour or more before you get to any good shooting locations. If you plan on heading to Brenham, get hotel reservations in that area. Marble Falls is too far to drive. For more information on the Texas hill country, see the Texas Parks and Wildlife site <www.tpwd.state.tx.us/nature/plant/plant.htm>.

photographer's choice

Just as beautiful but more unpredictable are the desert blooms at ANTELOPE VALLEY CALIFORNIA POPPY RESERVE. If you're feeling lucky, you might try the desert blooms near TUCSON, ARIZONA, and in ANZA-BORREGO DESERT STATE PARK, California. Desert blooms are capricious, so keep a close eye on conditions before you depart. [Antelope Valley California Poppy Reserve, www.calparksmojave.com/poppy; Tucson, Arizona, www.ci.tucson.az.us/visitor.html; Anza-Borrego Desert State Park, www.anzaborrego.statepark.org]

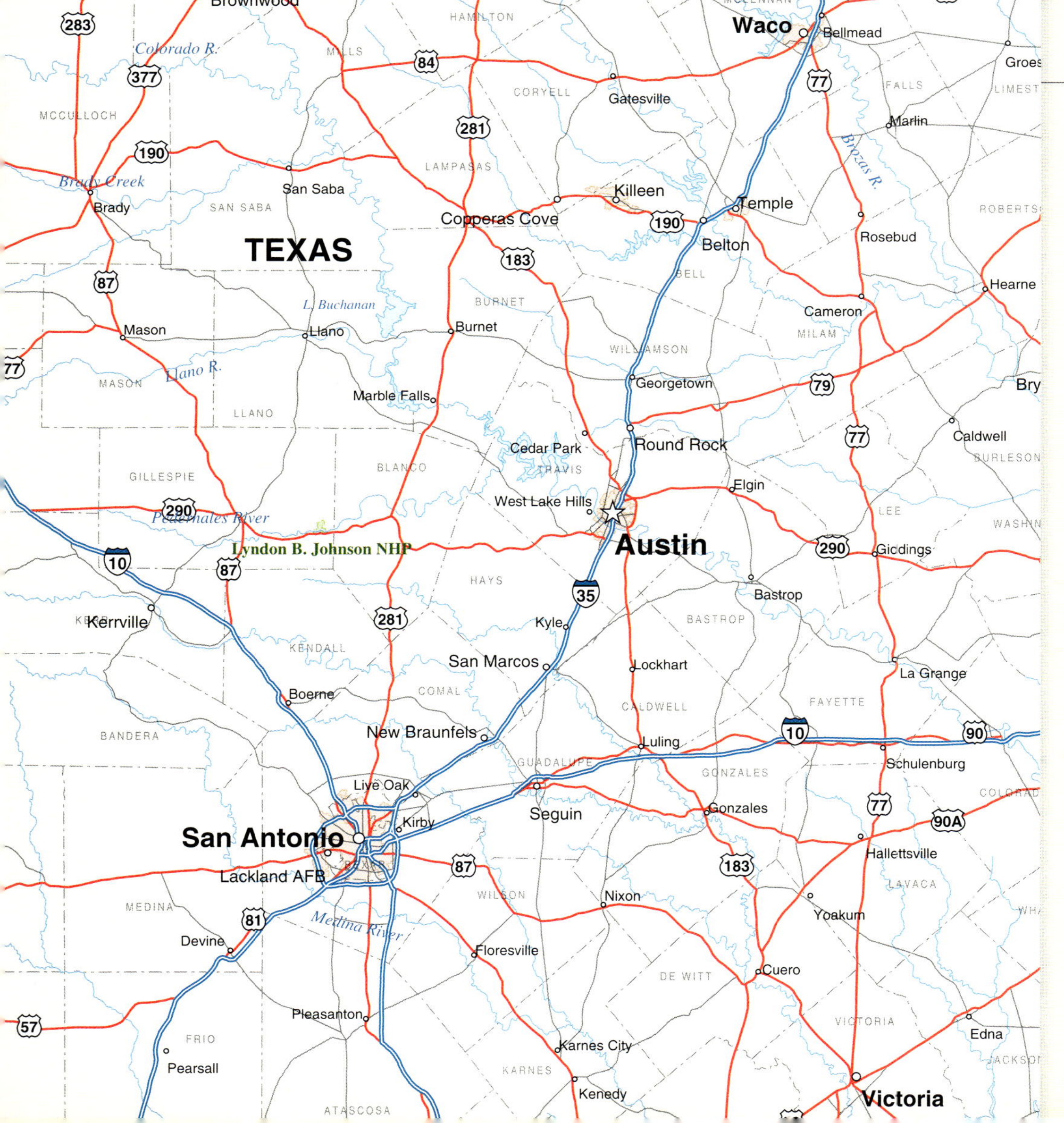

directions

From Austin drive west on Route 71 to Route 281. Turn north on 281. Marble Falls is about 50 miles northwest of Austin.

CHAPTER 9

San Juan Mountains, Colorado

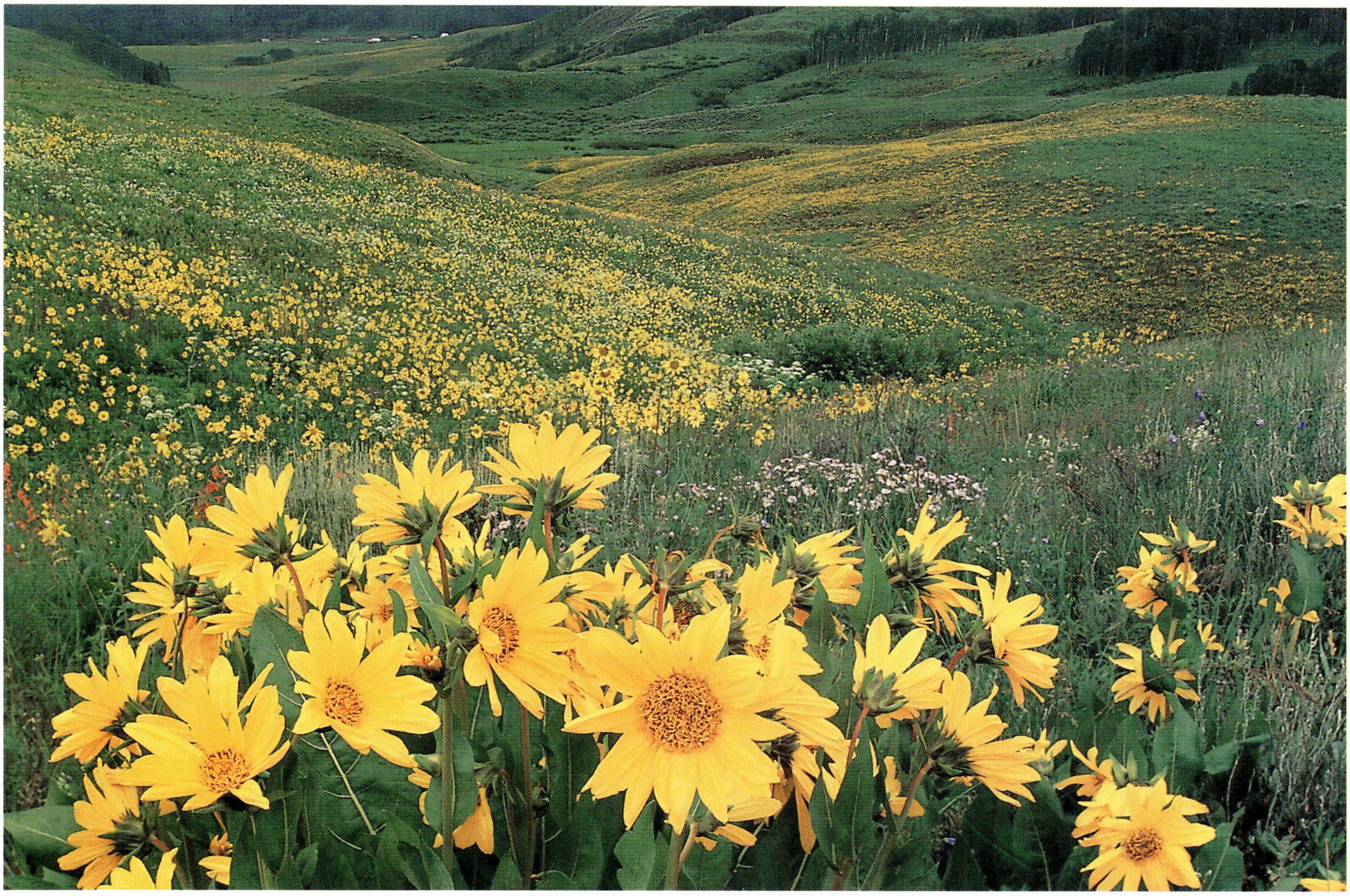

The San Juans, the Rocky Mountains of southwestern Colorado, are sparsely populated. The mining industry, once common throughout the region, provided the foundation for the booming tourism industry. Skiing and other mountain related sports have taken over many of the small towns that at one time served the mining industry. The southern and central Rockies were major mining areas for zinc, silver, iron ore, gold, copper, lead, molybdenum, petroleum, coal and natural gas.

Natural beauty intertwined with human

history can best describe the shaping of life in the San Juan Mountains today. The deserts to the west abruptly clash with the skyward-reaching peaks carved by glaciers, wind, water and volcanic flow. The ancient culture of the Anasazi people left behind a rich history in the San Juans, and the Navajo and Ute Indians have added to that. They have lived here for generations and still inhabit the foothills. The influences of these cultures and the ever-changing dramatic scenery tend to enchant those who visit.

The San Juan Mountains were at one time a booming region for mining, but only small remnants of these times remain. Ghost towns can still be found tucked away and hidden in the shadows of the San Juan Mountains. Fortunately, this mining era left behind a means for enjoying the interior of the mountains—mining roads. These old mining roads in no way make it possible to explore in the comfort of an RV or family car but rather confined to 4x4 vehicles. The dirt, rocky and pot-holed roads make for a roller coaster ride and add to the excitement of exploring in the heart of true wilderness where you face the elements on their terms. Sound like fun? It is.

Before I begin, I think it's important to talk about the commitment of venturing into the mountains in 4x4 country. Wildflower season is in height of summer thunderstorm season and you will encounter rain. Be prepared, and know what to do if you're in the mountains during one of these thunderstorms. Never take lightly a rain shower that could turn into a heavy thunder and lightning storm. Driving on mining roads requires a 4x4 vehicle. I suggest some experience driving in 4x4

Imogene Pass is an incredible drive. Afternoon rain showers during summer months are common, so try to reach the top before noon.

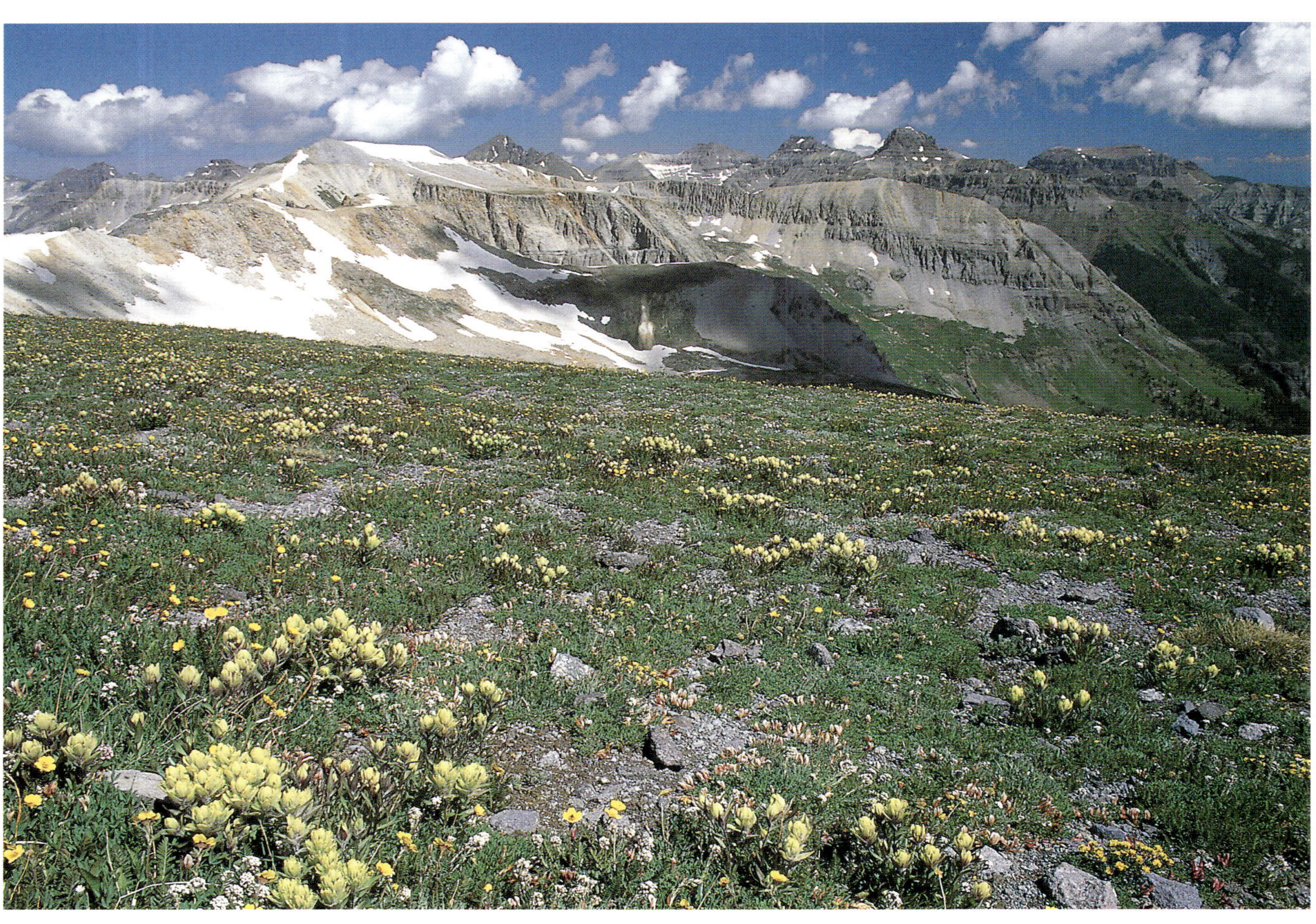

conditions, as you will be climbing rough roads regardless of their classification. 4x4 roads have five different classifications: Class 1, easy; Class 2, moderately difficult; Class 3, difficult; Class 4, very difficult; Class 5, use extreme caution. Literature is available in most local bookstores and tourists offices giving classifications of different roads, and I do suggest checking before driving the roads to make sure you're confident of your ability to drive in these conditions. You'll find route suggestions for your trip in *4WD Adventures Colorado*, by Peter Massey and Jeanne Wilson. I don't recommend attempting to drive these backcountry roads into the mountain passes before sunrise, and give yourself plenty of time to be off the roads before dark. There's really no need to be on location before sunrise or after sunset.

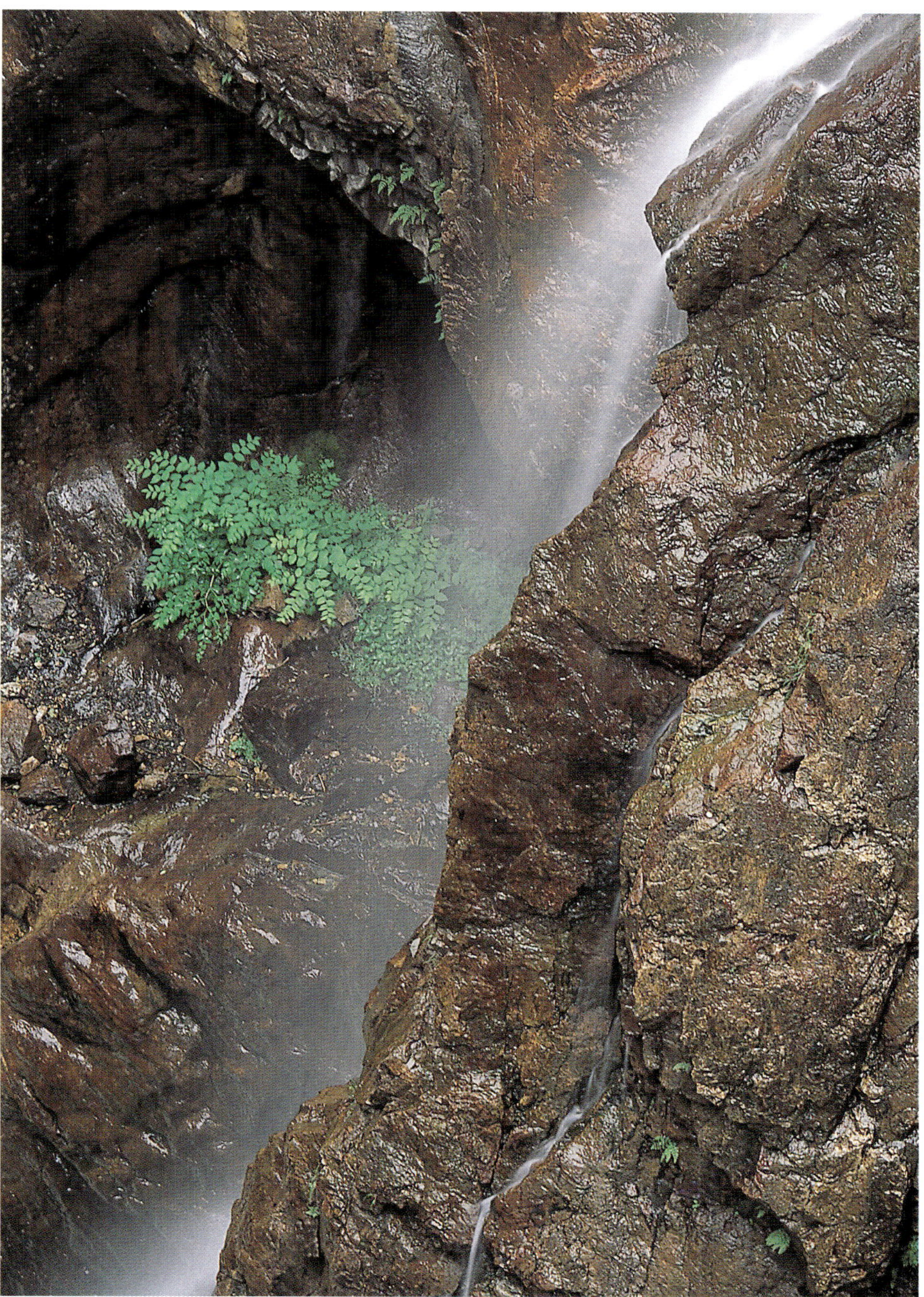

Lens selection is every bit as important as position. This waterfall got lost when I tried a wide-angle zoom, so I used an 80–200mm lens, zoomed out to 200mm, and eliminated all the distracting elements and simplified the composition.

PHOTOGRAPHER'S VIEW

Truly a wonderful experience, the wildflower meadows and mountain scenery of the San Juan Mountains are a memorable journey. I have conducted several photography workshops in these mountains, and participants walk away excited and energized, as much from the experience as they do the photography. I recommend the San Juans to all who enjoy the solitude and beauty of the mountains. My warning in the beginning of this section is to be taken seriously but not meant to frighten anyone away. If you aren't comfortable with driving in this environment, there are other options, such as photography workshops. Or one of several outfitters in the Ouray area can arrange quality time in the alpine meadows.

You will experience elevations your body may find challenging. Take your time and within a couple days your body should acclimate to the elevation change. Most of your photography will take place within eye contact of your vehicle. There is really little need to hold back on equipment. You can load up on your camera gear and take into the field what you need and leave the rest in your vehicle. Long telephotos aren't necessary unless you plan on photographing the little critters of the mountains, marmots and pikas. There are plenty, and you'll need at least a 400mm lens. It's not really worth the hassle of carrying these long lenses through the airports for what little use you will get from them. You'll be using wide-angle to medium telephotos (24mm–100mm) most of the time, but make sure you're covered to 200mm. As I mentioned before, be prepared for rain. You will encounter rain during the summer wildflower season. Bring rain gear for both you and your camera gear. I find people to be a little overprotective of their camera gear; a light drizzle will not destroy your camera. Take advantage of these light drizzles. You might find some nice water droplets reflecting surrounding colors or another creative opportunity. Downpours are a different story—wait these out in your vehicle. Overcast light is perfect for flower photography, and you'll probably experience more of this than you will bright sunlight. Always bring along a diffuser when your goal is flowers. You might never use it, but if you don't have one, you'll need it.

Crested Butte

Technically, Crested Butte isn't part of the San Juan Mountains but rather the western edge of the Sawatch Range in the Gunnison National Forest. I use Crested Butte for my first couple of days of shooting for three reasons. First, the wildflowers are predictable and in great abundance. Second, Crested Butte is at a good elevation to begin getting acclimated, and third,

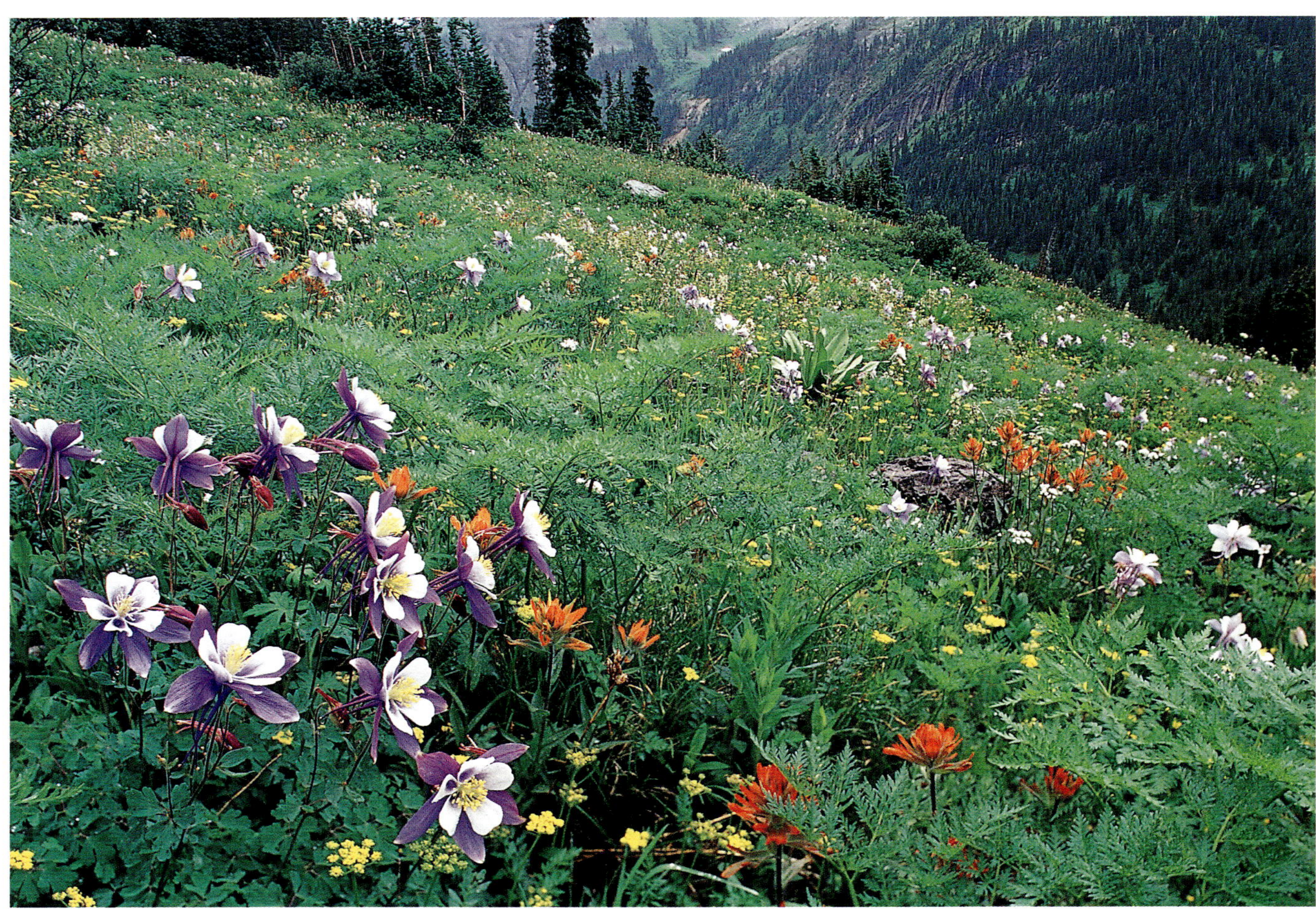

Yankee Boy Basin is a field of rainbows. These Colorado columbine work well as a foreground subject, but the constant breeze tried my patience.

it's a good location to get acquainted with off road driving as these roads are Class 1 and 2 and easy to drive.

Crested Butte is made up of rolling hills, valleys and meadows more than it is of rugged mountain terrain. The hillsides and valleys fill every summer with some of the most predictable wildflower blooms in all of Colorado. The window for good flowers is not long, but with a little planning you can catch the peak or near peak bloom. The second and third weeks of July have typically been the best times, but as with anything in the outdoors, Mother Nature has the final say. The best time of day for photographic opportunities in Crested Butte—or for that matter throughout the San Juans—is the morning. Don't pass up a nice overcast sky when the opportunity presents itself, usually when the afternoon showers move in.

I suggest finding a good topographic map with forest roads and highlight several routes that are an easy drive into Gunnison National Forest from Crested Butte. One of my favorite drives is a circle route beginning on Forest Road 317 (also called Gothic Road) from Mt. Crested Butte through the old town of Gothic and Schofield Pass to Paradise Divide, at 11,250 feet. I eventually make my way to Crested Butte. Forest Road 317 begins where the only road through Mt. Crested Butte ends. You can also do this route in the opposite direction. This gives you the opportunity to get early-morning light in both directions. The entry point for driving this route in the opposite direction begins on Washington Gulch Road (gravel road) on the west side of the main road connecting Crested Butte and Mt. Crested Butte. The drive between these two towns is a quick three to four minutes, and the turn is about halfway in between. There are two wonderful reflection lakes on this route: one called Emerald Lake just beyond the town of Gothic coming from Mt. Crested Butte, and the other at the crest of Paradise Divide. Both lakes sit next to the road. The lake at Paradise Divide has no known name but is the prettier of the two. This lake has three great angles to photograph; two of the three are mirror reflections of nearby mountains. One of these reflection shots is an evening shoot. Wildflowers can be found almost anywhere along this route. Two-grooved milk-vetch, lupine, magenta paintbrush, columbine, larkspur and cow parsnip are all very common throughout the region. One of the best locations for an abundance of Aspen sunflowers and arrowleaf balsamroot is the very beginning of Forest Road 317 just outside of Mt. Crested Butte looking back into the valley toward Crested Butte. These yellow flowers make great foreground subjects with the valley and mountains in the background.

Ouray

Ouray is the gateway community to many of the beautiful mountain passes in the San Juans. Ouray offers me everything I need to satisfy my thirst for backcountry mountain photography. From here I can begin one of several great backcountry drives each morning and fill an entire day with excellent photo opportunities and still make it back before dark. I will briefly discuss three locations I find predictable and reasonably safe out of Ouray. These are in no way the only backcountry roads you can reach out of Ouray. During your information gathering you will come across others that may sound inviting, but the ones I will discuss are proven to produce good results.

Yankee Boy Basin

Getting to Yankee Boy Basin is very easy. Follow Highway 550 out of Ouray southbound, and turn onto the gravel road leading to Box Canyon Falls. This road is called Camp Bird Road. Continue up this road into Yankee Boy

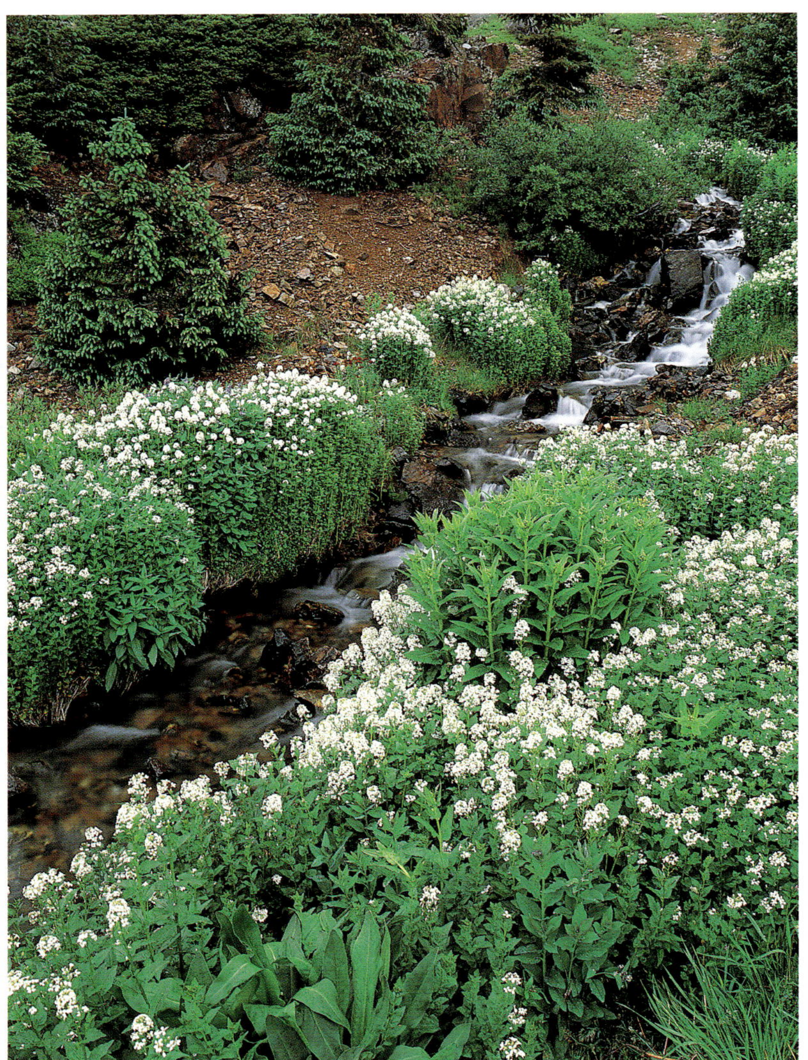

Intimate scenes like this are common throughout Yankee Boy Basin. This stream was no more than twelve to eighteen inches wide, proof that you don't need a grand subject to make an attractive image.

Basin, passing the old mining area of Camp Bird. The higher the climb into the Basin the more difficult the road becomes for driving. There is no need to follow the road to its end. You will know when you have come far enough; the flowers will tell you to stop.

Yankee Boy Basin is the most popular and maybe even the best location for all-around alpine photography with an abundance of wildflowers and incredible mountain vistas. The drive to Yankee Boy Basin is relatively easy (Class 1 road). Yankee Boy Basin is very popular, and you won't be alone. Many of the Ouray outfitters make this one of their featured destinations. There is plenty of room to spread out, so don't worry about crowding.

Wildflowers in Yankee Boy Basin are as colorful and in as great variety as any in Colorado. Columbine, magenta paintbrush, mountain bluebell, bittercress and many others cover the meadows in a delicate array of bright colors. Small cascades flow in many directions, and some are hidden in grasses with flowers hanging on in precarious positions along stream edges. Twin Falls is very noticeable as you enter into Yankee Boy Basin. This waterfall can be shot from several angles, and in a good year can be found with patches of flowers along the streambed.

Imogene Pass

Imogene Pass may prove to one of the most dramatic drives you choose in the San Juan Mountains. This is truly an exciting journey through the heart of the southern Rockies on a Class 4/5 route. You can choose your starting point of Imogene Pass in either Ouray or Telluride. If you're lodging in Ouray, it makes sense to begin your route here and end in Telluride, returning back to Ouray via developed roads. Or you can choose to return on another backcountry road over Opher Pass. To reach Opher Pass from Telluride, follow State Road 145 south for about eight miles. The junction for Opher Pass is on the east side of the road.

Imogene Pass has several steep climbs as you near the summit and begin your descent into Telluride or Ouray. The peak of Imogene will put you at a breathtaking 13,114 feet with incredible views of Mt. Sneffels and other surrounding peaks in the north and the colorful Red Mountain Pass to the southeast. I suggest you begin your journey early and enjoy it at a leisurely pace. There are several meadows and waterfalls along the route toward the summit. The Ouray side of Imogene Pass is the more photogenic and will require more time. Keep in mind the chances of afternoon thunderstorms. Your descent into Telluride might be slow as there are typically many vehicles sharing the narrow road.

Wildflowers along Imogene Pass are pretty much the same as those you find in Yankee Boy Basin. You will more than likely have some cloud cover providing overcast light, but I suggest having a diffuser just in case. With the exception of the summit, you won't have great vistas of distant mountains. You will find flower patterns and small intimate scenes are your better photo opportunities here. There are several streams, cascades and a couple waterfalls along the way but, unlike Yankee Boy Basin, few flowers surrounding water sources.

American Basin

American Basin rivals Yankee Boy when it comes to its wildflower display, but the surrounding peaks are not as dramatic. Driving to American Basin requires special attention to your map. The drive is not difficult if you follow your map carefully and look for signs at backcountry intersections. Follow Highway 550 south out of Ouray (approximately three

Although I took this shot atop Schofield Pass in Crested Butte, it really doesn't matter if it's from Colorado, Oregon or California. What is important is how it is interpreted—peaceful, pristine or wild. An advertising client would likely use an image like this to convey a positive message.

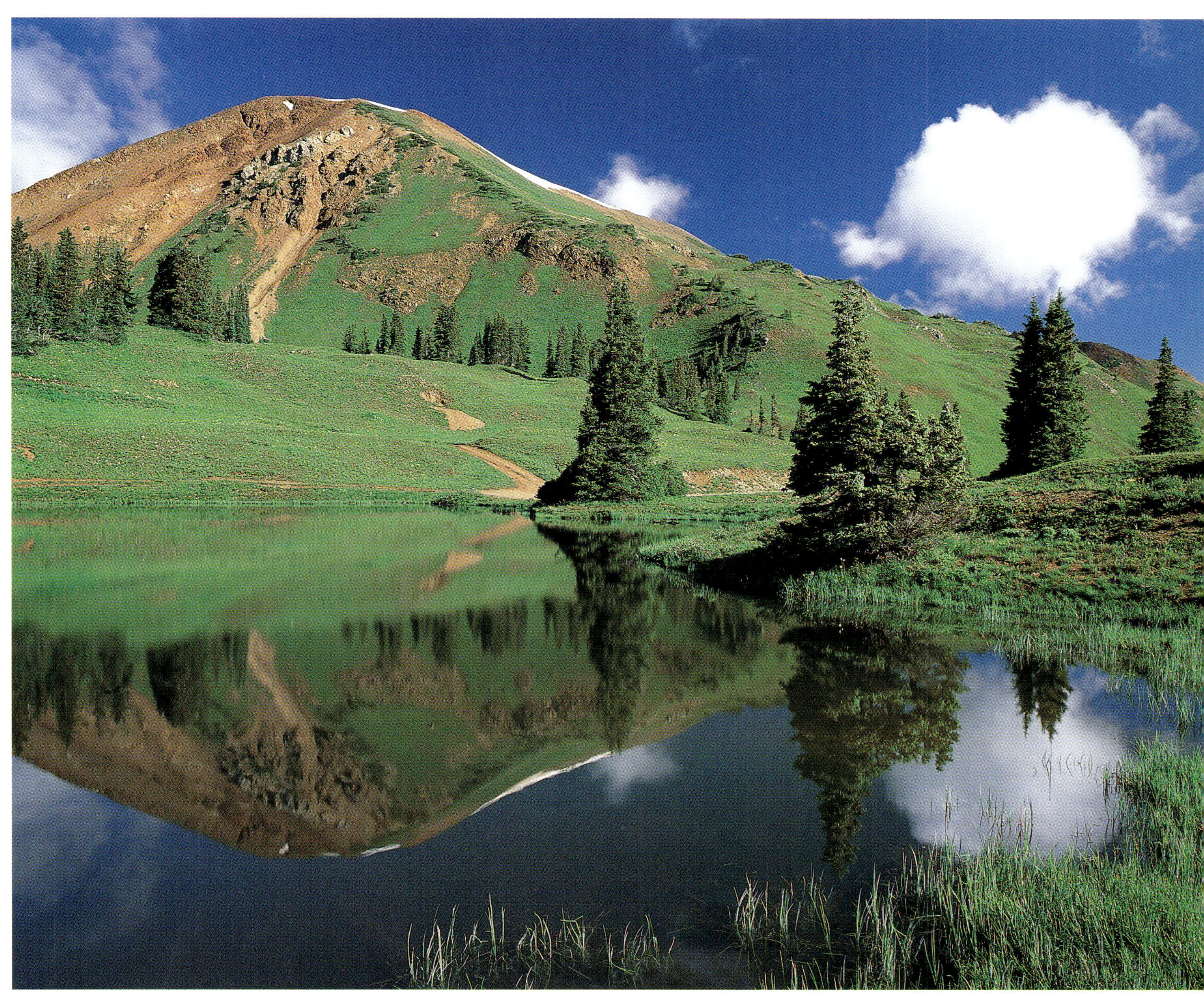

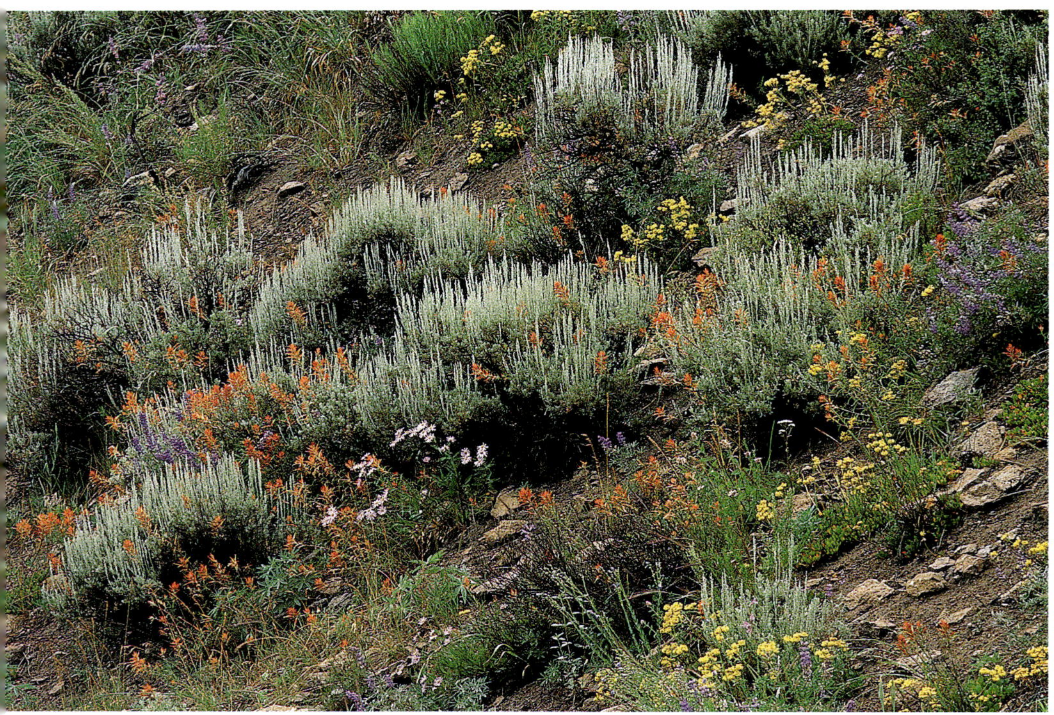

Yankee Boy Basin, Imogene Pass and American Basin have but a few of the many wonderful backcountry roads. If you have an extra day or two, you should have no problem finding additional mountain passes to explore. Local people are very helpful and knowledgeable of backcountry roads and wildflower conditions throughout the region. If you get a bad-weather day, consider exploring Owl Creek Pass or areas where you can travel in lower elevations. Owl Creek Pass is a very easy drive and doesn't require a 4x4 vehicle.

Position is everything. If you see something that catches your eye but it loses luster once you approach it, return to where you first saw it, or try another angle. I first saw this mixture of colors from a distance, but as I walked closer, the composition I liked disappeared. I backtracked and used my 80–200mm zoom lens to get what I wanted.

miles), and look for Alpine Loop trailhead. You will see a gravel parking area on the left-hand side of a hairpin turn on 550; this is the entrance onto the backcountry road of Alpine Loop. Follow this road toward Engineer Pass. *Do not* turn left at the first major road intersection. This will put you on the road to Poughkeepsie Gulch. This is an extremely difficult road to drive and can be dangerous for those not experienced in 4x4 conditions. Continue on toward Engineer Pass until you come to a second intersection, and turn right away from Engineer Pass toward Cinnamon Pass. The road to Cinnamon Pass will take you to American Basin.

American Basin is an incredible journey and very much worth the effort. For the spirit of adventure and for those who wish to hike beyond the roads into American Basin, there's the American Basin trail leading up to Sloan Lake with magnificent views of Handies Peak and the surrounding basin. If hiking interests you, consider American Basin as your final destination. This should allow your body plenty of time to acclimate.

WHEN TO GO

The wildflowers in the high elevations of the San Juan Mountains are at their peak from about the third week of July through the first week of August. This window varies, but for the most part it's predictable. The lower elevations throughout the San Juans can see wildflower blooms throughout the month of July. Crested Butte peaks a week or two before the higher elevations and makes a worthwhile trip before you head into the mountains. The best scenario based on my experience is to arrive in Crested Butte during the early part of the third week in July and move on to Ouray after a couple of days. I'd rather be in Crested Butte during the peak in that area and maybe a little on the front side of the peak in Yankee Boy Basin and other San Juan locations. You'll still be greeted by a wonderful display there, but Crested Butte loses its appeal when the flowers are beyond peak and begin to look wilted.

TIME REQUIREMENTS

Crested Butte is not a large area and can be explored and photographed in two full days.

This will also provide a period to get your body acclimated. You will lose the best part of your shooting day driving from Crested Butte to Ouray. The drive is only about three to four hours, but by the time you arrive, it will be too late to enter into the mountain passes. You might consider spending the afternoon in the Black Canyon of Gunnison National Forest for a couple of hours to break up the drive. This is a difficult photo shoot but is a nice area to see. Once you arrive in Ouray, you might consider gathering some last-minute information and scouting the trailhead to Yankee Boy Basin. Give yourself at least three full days to explore the area. Four days would be even better just in case you get a really bad day that keeps you out of the backcountry.

NEED TO KNOW

Crested Butte has several hotels. You should have no problem finding lodging in July. Crested Butte is a ski resort, and winter reservations are more difficult to obtain. The lodging in Crested Butte is on the higher side (around $100 per night). If you want less expensive lodging, Gunnison is twenty miles away and has several hotels ($69 to $89 per night). There are several smaller hotels in Ouray. Reservations are typically easy to get if you plan several months in advance. I don't recommend arriving without reservations, but there are always many great camping locations throughout the mountains and national forests.

photographer's choice

Wildlife in ROCKY MOUNTAIN NATIONAL PARK is much easier to spot than in the San Juans throughout the summer season. Access also is more convenient than for the Ouray area, and the park offers dramatic mountain scenery, lakes and streams. You'll find wildflowers here too, but not on the same scale as in the San Juans. [Rocky Mountain National Park, www.nps.gov/romo; www.rockymtntrav.com/estes]

directions

The Grand Junction airport is the best airport to fly into for your journey in the San Juan Mountains.

FROM GRAND JUNCTION:

- Drive south on Highway 50 south to Montrose and continue on 50 into Gunnison. Turn north on State Highway 135 into Crested Butte from Gunnison.

FROM CRESTED BUTTE TO OURAY:

- Follow State Highway 135 south to Gunnison and turn west onto Highway 50 and follow it into Montrose. From Montrose turn south on Highway 550 to Ouray.

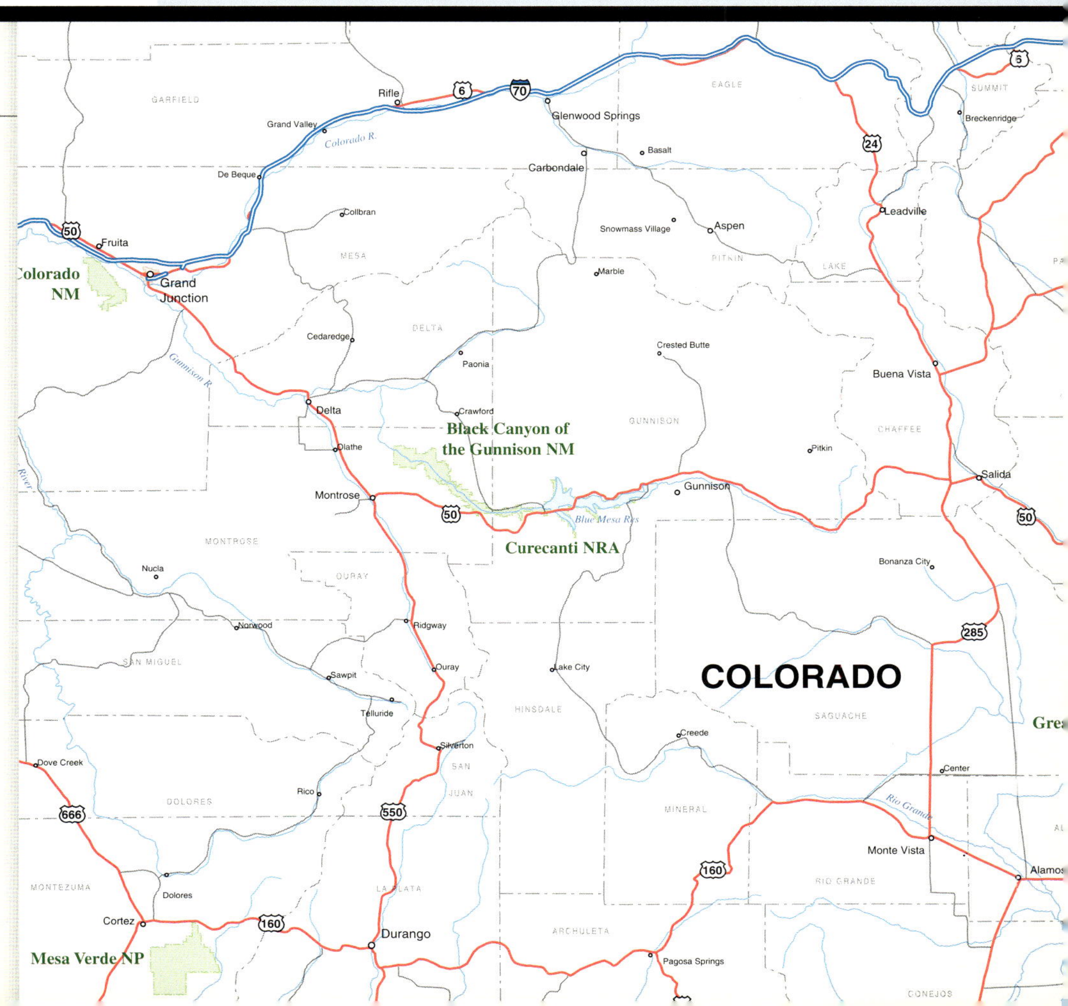

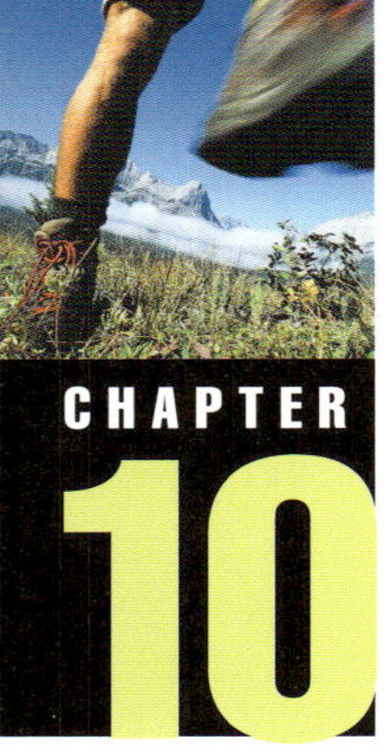

CHAPTER 10

The Canadian Rockies

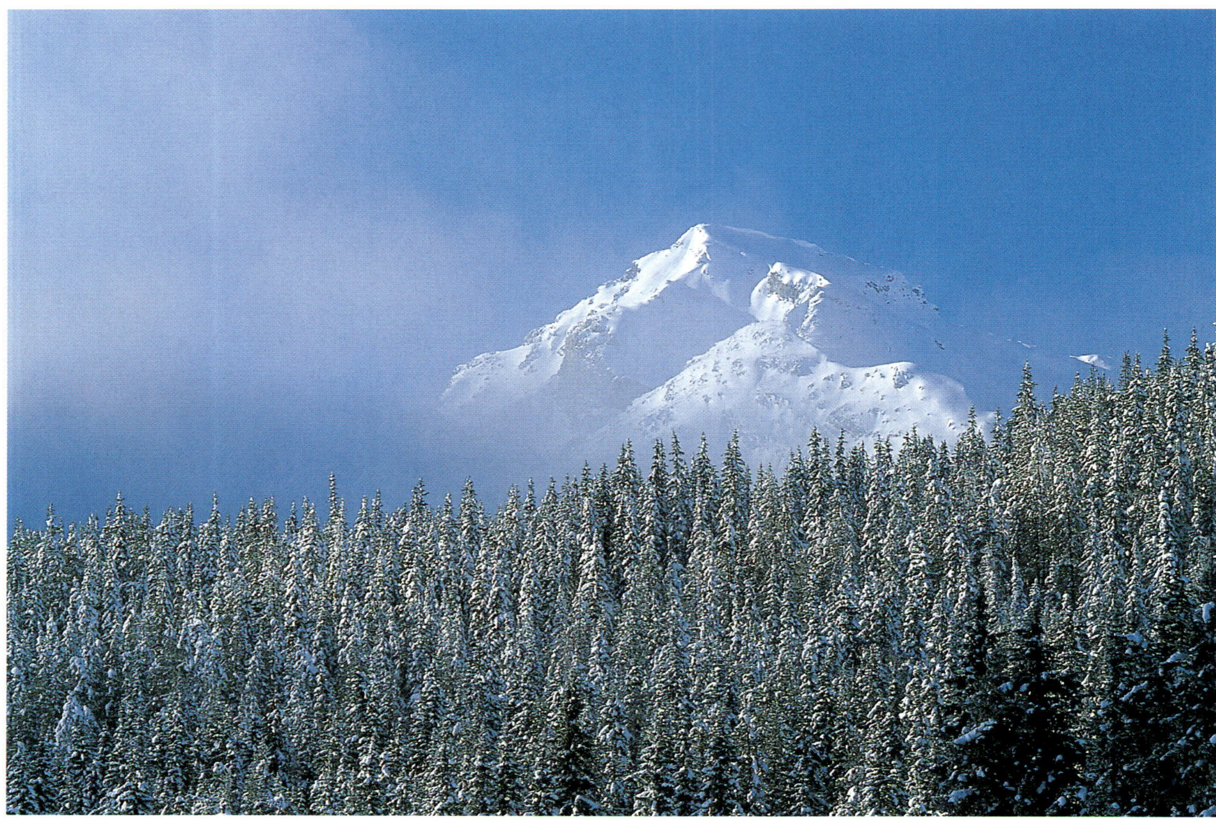

Banff, Jasper, Yoho and Kootenay national parks compose one of the world's largest—and arguably most beautiful—protected wilderness areas. Banff is the first and most famous of Canada's thirty-nine national parks. Yoho and Kootenay lie just west of Banff in British Columbia, with Jasper immediately to the north on the Alberta side. The parks offer access unmatched by others in the Rockies. Peaks rise suddenly from the valley floor, so you'll experience only gradual elevation gains on developed roads unlikely to induce vertigo.

Railroads brought wealthier visitors to this end of the Rockies in frontier days, and these transportation lines still play an important commercial role today. The towns of Banff, Jasper and Field, in Yoho National Park, still have railroad stations. In Yoho you still can see trains hard at work making their way through steep mountain passes, themselves engineering marvels. History likely will be as much a part of your visit as the wilderness. It is not impossible to experience these mountains as fur trappers and mountain men once did. The Canadian government has done a great job sharing this history with visitors. Road signs and literature are common throughout the park and visitors centers.

PHOTOGRAPHER'S VIEW

You can't go wrong in these four parks (known collectively, along with Waterton National Park to the south, as the Rocky Mountain Parks World Heritage Site) regardless of when you travel. Access in and around the parks is the best you will find anywhere—even the 130-mile-long Icefields Parkway between Banff and Jasper is open year-round. They also have the best winter landscapes for photography anywhere in North America. Spring holds another fine, uncrowded opportunity. As the height of tourist season, summer is best for exploring beyond the roads and short trails, when wildflowers are at their peak. Wildlife is most visible in autumn, during mating season, and the aspens turn a beautiful gold. This is

I visited Peyto Lake Viewpoint three days in a row: The first morning I arrived early and found the foreground forest in dark shadow; the second morning was overcast; and the third morning I arrived later, when the sun lit the tips of trees in the foreground. This was what I was hoping to capture. Sometimes it takes several visits to get what you want.

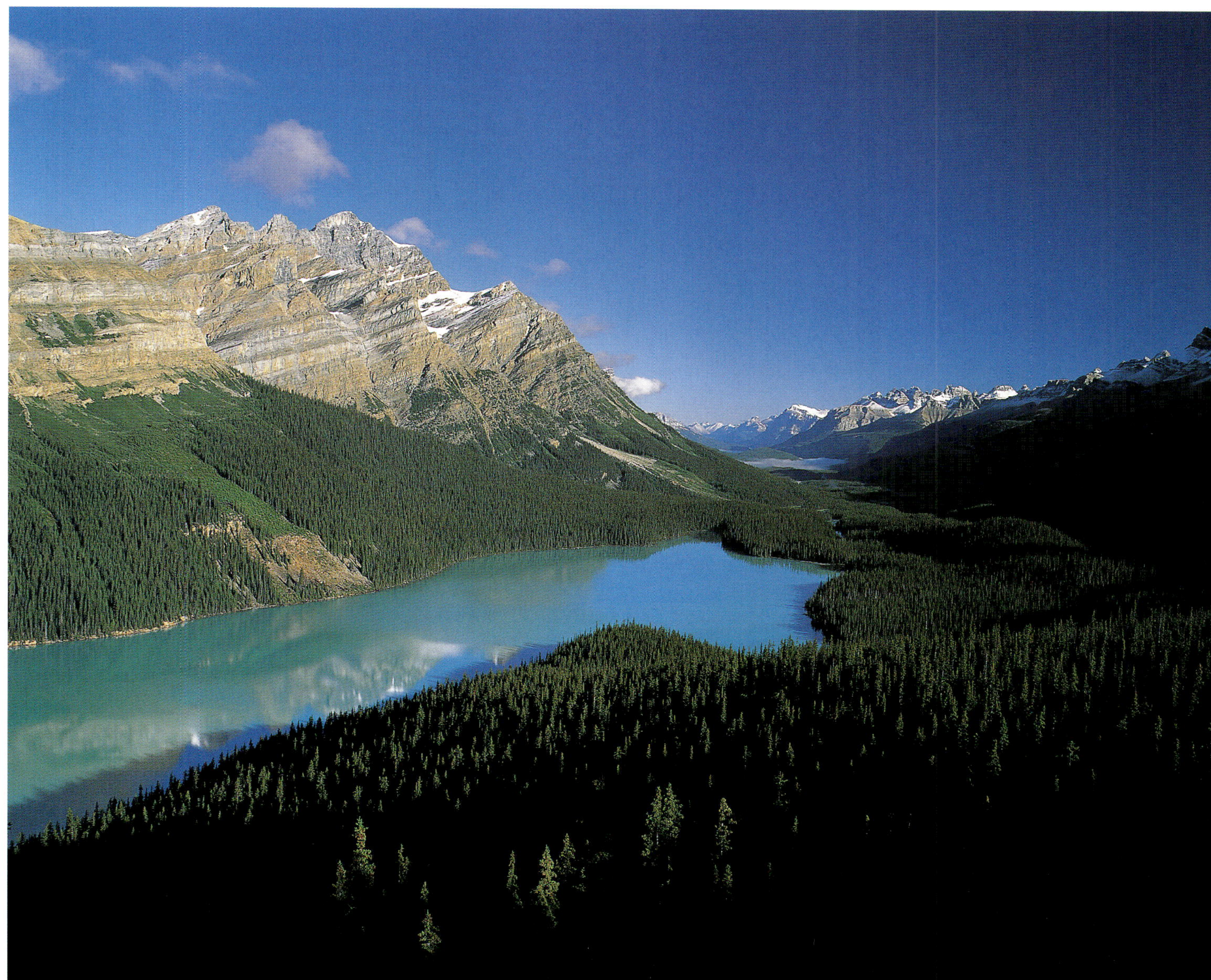

I woke up one morning and saw this mountain rising above a light fog from my campsite. The sky was so clear I decided to leave plenty of space for possible use with text. When this type of opportunity arises and doesn't detract from my subject, I'll leave part of my composition open for possible text use.

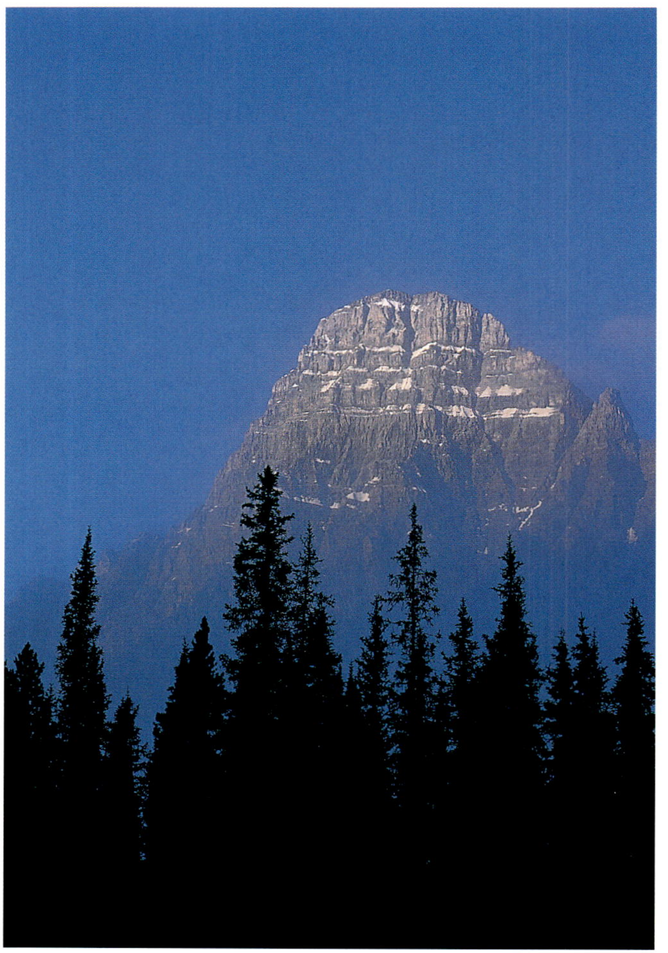

the best season for combining landscape and wildlife photography. Whenever you go, allow time to gather last-minute information on the parks, and spend time collecting information and asking questions at the ranger station in Lake Louise Village.

Banff National Park

Banff National Park is the Canadian Rockies in most visitors' minds, and for good reason. The region's major landmarks are all in Banff: Moraine Lake, Lake Louise, Peyto Lake, Vermilion Lakes, Mt. Rundle, and much of the scenic Icefields Parkway. As with most parts of the Rocky Mountains, morning is the best time to shoot. No need to be on location before sunrise unless you want to shoot silhouettes against the sky. The sun typically doesn't light up the peaks and valleys until it makes its way over distant mountains.

MORAINE LAKE. Probably the most sought-after shot in Banff, this beautiful turquoise lake sits amidst a ring of mountains in the Valley of the Ten Peaks. Climb atop a huge rock pile to the right of the parking lot, and take your pick of several great vantage points overlooking the lake. For shots from water level, a short hike to the east shore of the lake will yield still more opportunities. Mid to late morning is best.

LAKE LOUISE. Banff's most famous landmark has its share of challenges. Don't ignore Lake Louise, but don't expect it to be your most productive location. You will encounter a lot of people and difficult lighting situations in morning and late afternoon. The mountains to the east (right) are in dark shadow during the good morning light, and the mountains to the west (left) are in shadow during good afternoon light. Beautiful Victoria Glacier, at the end of Lake Louise, is your best bet for a morning reflection and good light. You'll need a couple hours and plenty of patience, but with a little effort, you should walk away with some good shots.

PEYTO LAKE. Surrounded by forest and stunning mountain peaks in the beautiful Mistaya Valley, Peyto is one of the three most popular lakes for visitors and photographers. The easy quarter-mile hike to the viewpoint offers several perspectives from which to photograph the lake with Peyto Peak, Mt. Mistaya, Mt. Barbette and Mt. Patterson rising high above the long Mistaya Valley. The light is best in mid morning; it takes awhile for the sun to reach the entire valley. You'll be hard pressed to find an original angle to shoot. Nevertheless, if you don't already have a shot of Peyto, you'll want one.

VERMILION LAKES. Vermilion Lakes sits just off Trans-Canada 1 at the Banff exit before you enter the town of Banff (signs will direct you) and represents your best chance to put your own stamp on Banff. The backdrop is not as dramatic as at other lakes in the park, but with good light and an observant eye, you can walk away with some great photos. A couple small islands and grassy pockets break up the lakes and give them personalities all their own. Photographers most frequently shoot Vermilion with Mt. Rundle in the background, but I suggest exploring in other directions and looking for more intimate, generic scenes. This is a good location for both morning and afternoon.

ICEFIELDS PARKWAY. This could be the most beautiful road in North America, and maybe the world. The parkway presents endless subjects to work: little ponds, mountain peaks,

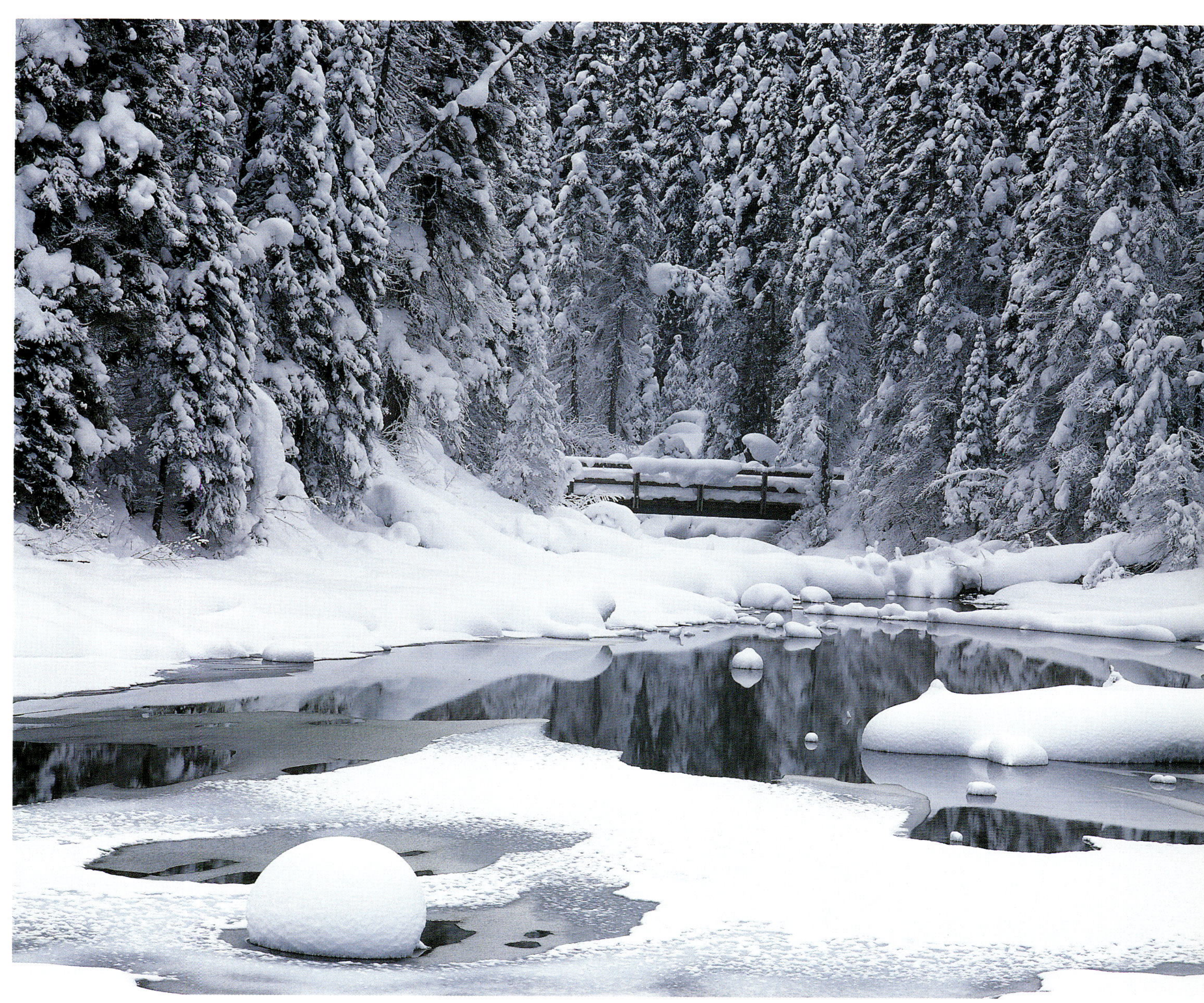

Snow cover in Yoho National Park is predictable. You could spend an entire day working the Emerald Lake area, where I took this shot.

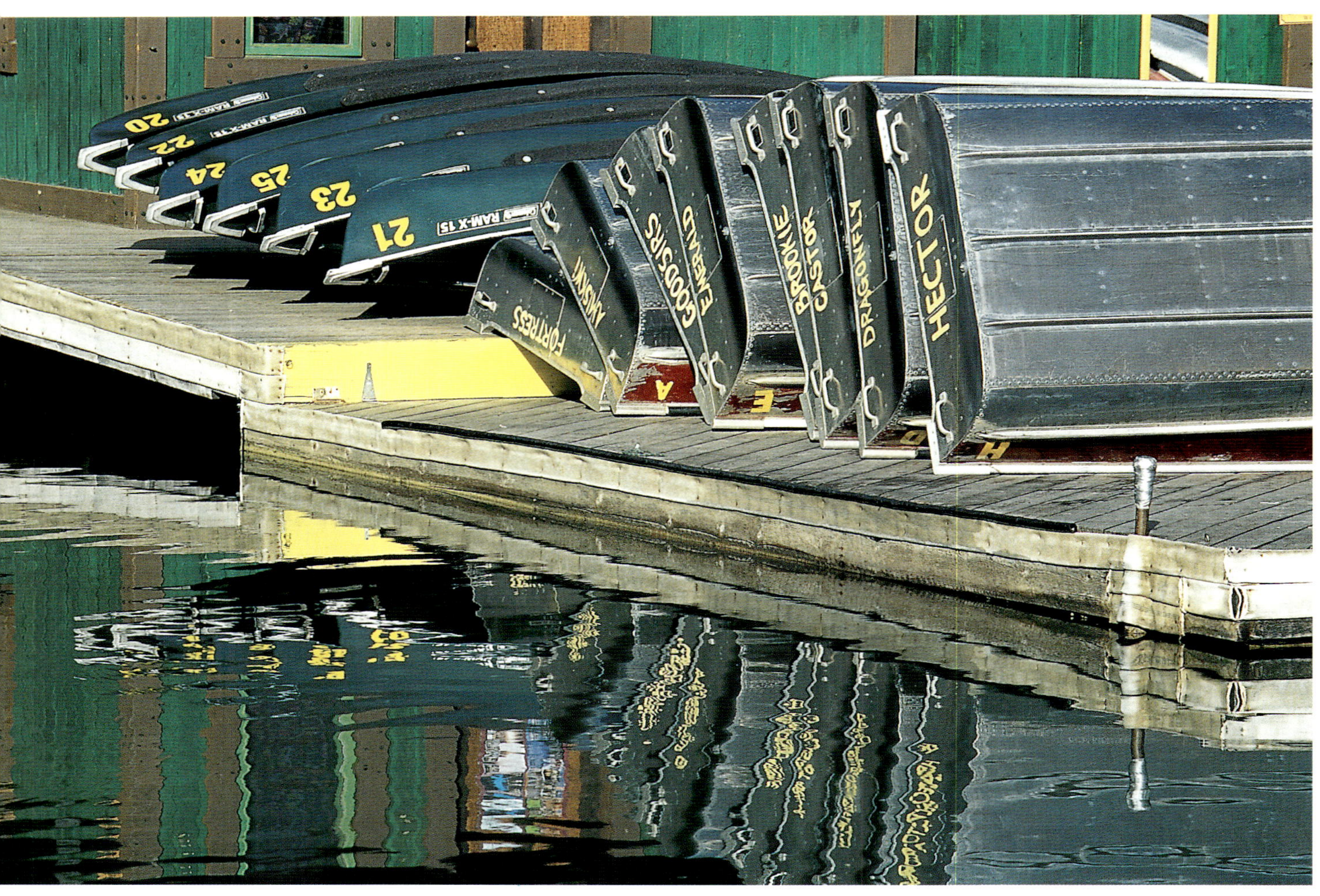

On an overcast day at Emerald Lake in Yoho National Park, when nothing seemed to click, I decided to survey the landscape with different lenses. By zooming in and out with an 80–200mm zoom lens, I found this composition, which I hadn't seen beforehand. Lenses can aid your visual exploration and expand your creativity.

meadows, flowers and on and on. This is a must-see spectacle. You'll need at least two mornings to work the road within the boundaries of Banff. As you get closer to Jasper, the scenery gets less dramatic, so you'll have to work harder to find good shots.

I have mentioned only Banff's most popular locations, and by all means if you have never been to the Canadian Rockies, you should see each of the above. Don't fall for the old theory that if you haven't seen pictures of it, it isn't worth photographing. The Canadian Rockies are surely an exception. Explore and exploit the endless opportunities beyond the beaten path. Hiking provides the best opportunity to create images that aren't over done. Roadside photography is so good in Banff, also redundant, that trails are all too often overlooked, therefore many other opportunities being passed over. Hiking doesn't necessarily mean taking on a strenuous ten-mile trail, it can be a simple half mile nature hike or a short one- or two-mile hike, regardless you'll end up in an environment many others never see. A little effort will separate your photos from many of the others taken in the Canadian Rockies. Create new tripod holes and let others try to find them.

There are hundreds of trails of various lengths throughout the Canadian Rockies National Parks. The best book I have found describing these trails is the *Canadian Rockies Access Guide*, by John Dodd and Gail Helgason. Trails range from gradual inclines to steep climbs. You will want to inquire at the ranger station before making your way on any backcountry trail for bear warnings or other possible hazards. Trails are rated easy to difficult. When you are carrying a heavy camera bag you might want to take the liberty and upgrade the trail one step to give you a realistic idea of the physical challenge that awaits you. You might also want to lighten your load to a basic camera system before departing on even the easiest of trails. My experience is a tired body makes for a lazy photographer, so why defeat the purpose of your hike.

Jasper National Park

Jasper National Park is popular but doesn't experience the same crowds as Banff. This might be because it's a five-hour drive from Calgary, where most visitors fly into, and the scenery isn't as dramatic. Don't pass up Jasper. It has some great photo opportunities and lends itself to a more intimate photo shoot. The mountains in Jasper National Park don't have the grandness of its neighbor to the south. You're not swallowed up in the shadows of towering peaks as most peaks are off in the distance but you will be welcomed by a multitude of lakes and beautiful forests.

The Icefields Parkway in Jasper isn't as dramatic as in Banff, but tucked away not far from the pavement are many nice waterfalls and secluded lakes. You will find many of these areas in Jasper all your own or maybe an occasional hiker experiencing the same solitude. The Columbia Icefield is the first (if you are traveling north from Banff), the most no-

Images can be found anywhere if you look. I found this image driving down a dirty, slushy road on a hillside where the snow was still untouched. I pulled over and explored with different focal length lenses and decided on this composition using the fence. I also shot a few compositions with just the shadows but didn't feel they were as effective.

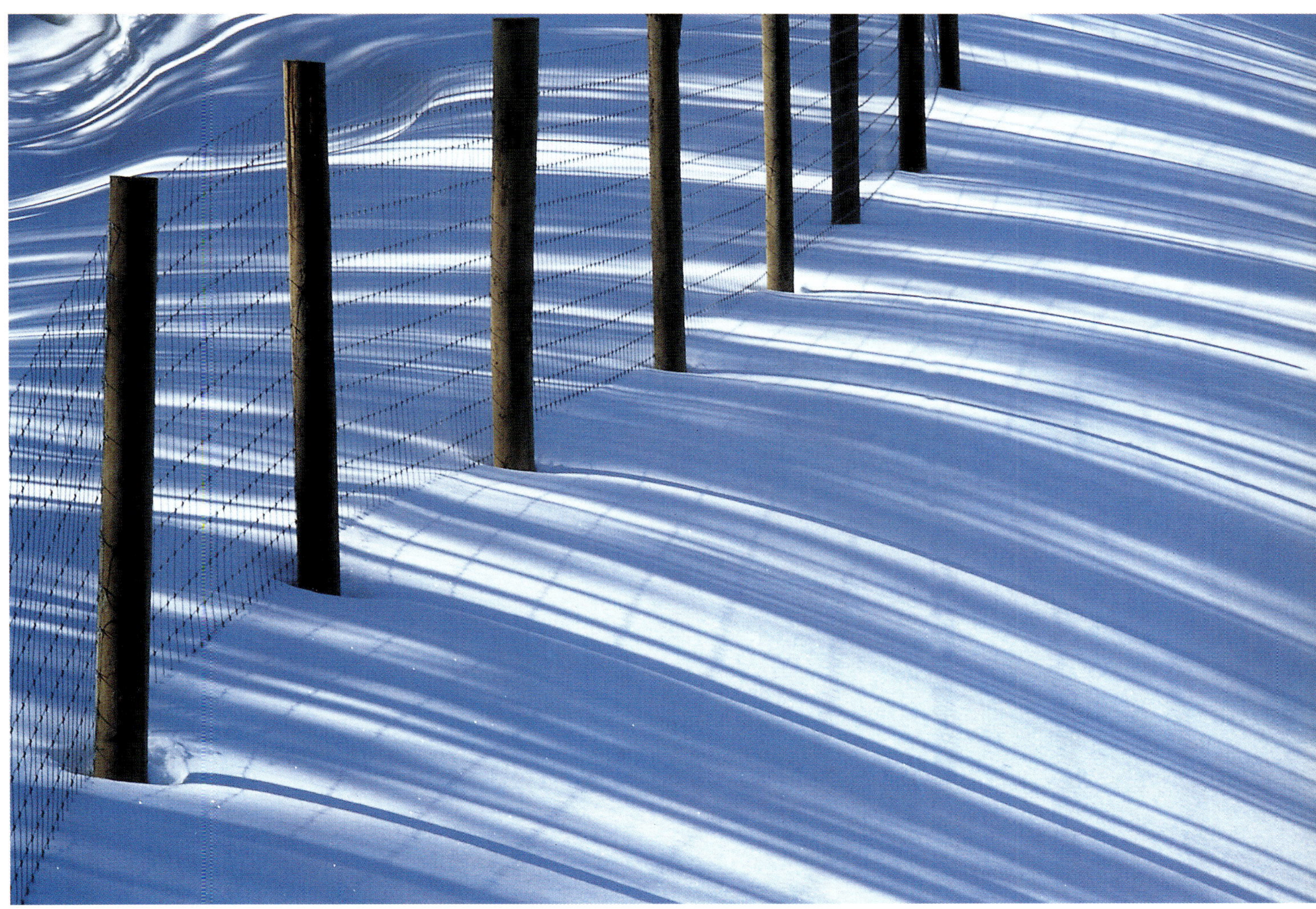

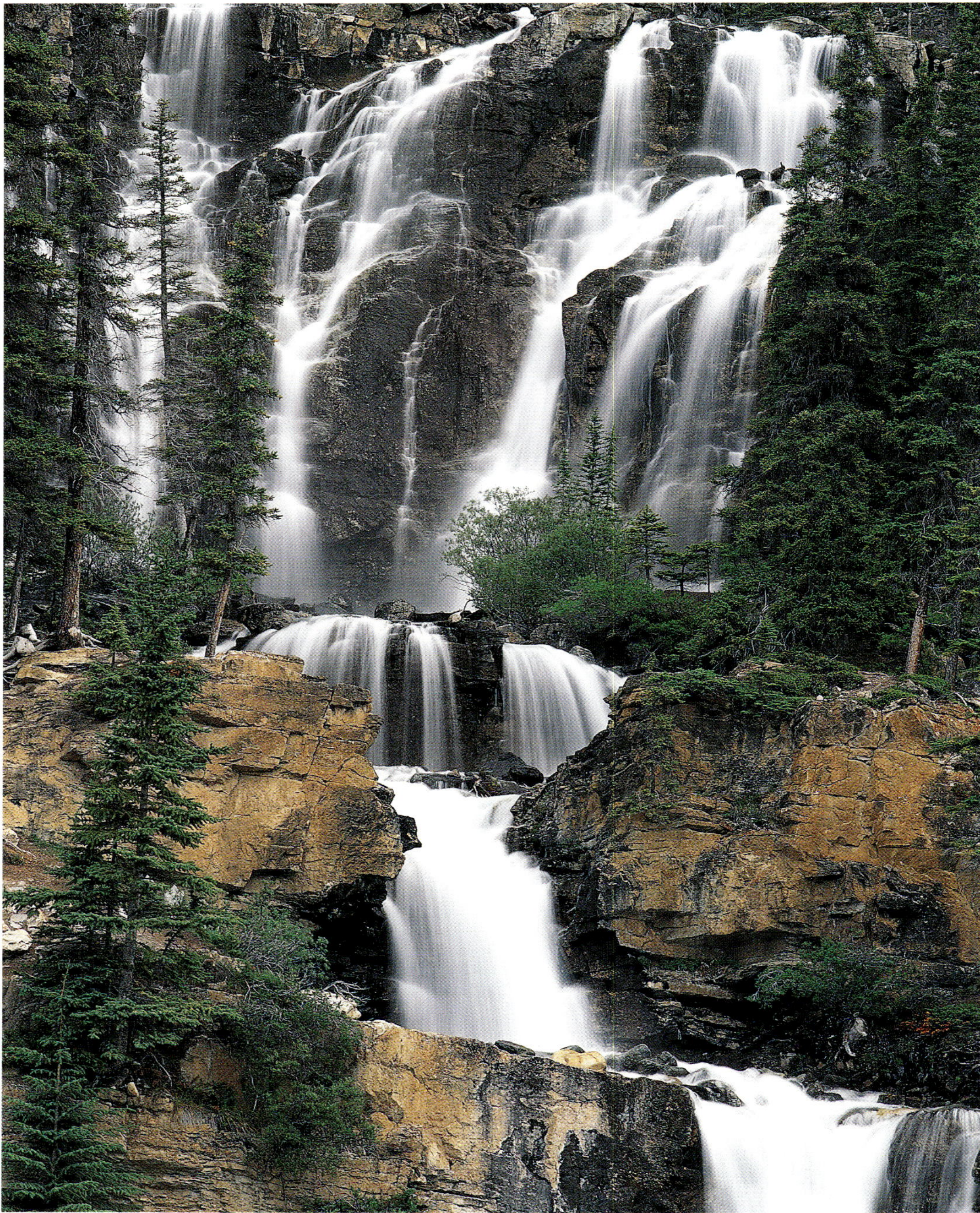

Tangle Creek Falls in Jasper National Park sits just off the road, thereby creating two problems: traffic and debris, which from both the road and from the waterfall itself. I don't like to crop the bases of waterfalls, but the alternative—cropping the upper part of the falls—wasn't any better.

table and the most crowded of landmarks in Jasper. The icefield is not very photogenic and really not worth the time unless you want a shot for stock purposes. Of the few roadside photos to be taken in Jasper, Tangle Creek Falls, just north of the Columbia Icefield, is a beautiful waterfall with several angles to shoot from or near the road. Waterfalls are common in this region of Icefields Parkway. Beyond Tangle Creek Falls, farther north is a series of waterfalls along a four-mile trail known as Stanley Falls Trail. Several of these waterfalls plunge into turquoise pools. You'll find other waterfalls on the parkway as you make your way toward the town of Jasper.

The lakes in Jasper National Park are quiet bodies of water surrounded by forests. The beauty lies in the serenity of the waters, which reflect the distant mountains. After working Banff's scenic lakes, it's natural to want to pass up Jasper's lakes. Don't. If you're a stock photographer, you'll discover these lakes are more salable because they are more versatile and aren't overdone. If you're shooting for fun, the lakes will challenge you to be more creative with more muted subjects. We all fall for the easy shots, but what separates the amateur from the professional, or the documentary photographer from the artistic one, is the desire to look past the obvious. The best locations have been worked over and over and challenge the photographer's vision. Accept the challenge at Jasper, and don't walk away without exposing some film.

Five lakes in particular near the town of Jasper have potential. You won't walk right up to any of these and just pull off a shot—you'll have to work them.

HORSESHOE LAKE is eighteen miles south of Jasper on the east side of Icefields Parkway. This beautiful lake's crystal-clear waters permit views of the rocky-strewn bottom in many areas. Mt. Kerkeslin stands to the south. Afternoon light is best for photographing Horseshoe Lake.

LAKE EDITH is generic compared with many of the lakes in Banff and Jasper but is good for reflections of the surrounding forest and distant mountains in the late-afternoon hours. From the town of Jasper, drive east to Highway 16, turn left and continue to the Maligne Lake Road turnoff. After crossing the bridge, keep right and take the next left. This side road will take you past Lake Annette and eventually put you at the south end of Lake Edith.

LAKE ANNETTE is a clear, spring-fed lake—another generic lake with good opportunities for stock images of morning reflections of the surrounding landscape. Directions are the same as for Lake Edith. You'll approach Lake Annette before Lake Edith.

PATRICIA LAKE is one of the prettiest lakes around Jasper. The warm morning light over the Trident Range reflects on its calm waters. Some shallow sections of the lake have grasses, which make nice foregrounds or simply nice patterns. Turn left on Cedar Avenue one block from the Jasper Visitor Centre. Follow Cedar, which turns into Pyramid Avenue and then into Pyramid Lake Road, for about two miles.

PYRAMID LAKE is another pretty lake laced with boulders with mirror reflections of forests and mountains. The warm afternoon light affords several good angles. The directions to Pyramid Lake are the same as for Patricia Lake: Just continue farther up the road until you come to the parking lot at the lake. Maligne Lake is the largest in the Canadian Rockies and also the toughest to shoot. To be successful on this lake, you'll need a canoe and a tent, or you'll need to take a potentially unproductive boat ride run by the park concessionaires. The above-mentioned lakes are your best bets for photography.

Yoho National Park

Yoho National Park is small compared with Banff and Jasper and doesn't have the reputation of its sister parks. There are really only a few locations you can photograph without taking on the backcountry; nevertheless, in the areas with easy access, the scenery is very dramatic. Yoho, on the western edge of the Continental Divide, gets colder temperatures and more precipitation than its eastern neighbors, and therefore has the best snow cover of anywhere in the Canadian Rockies. The park is most productive in the winter, and that's when I recommend going. The January freezes bring incredible ice and snow formations. The park limits access to a few plowed roads, but those that are open have lots of great opportunities.

Emerald Lake is Yoho's most popular location because of its setting and easy access-

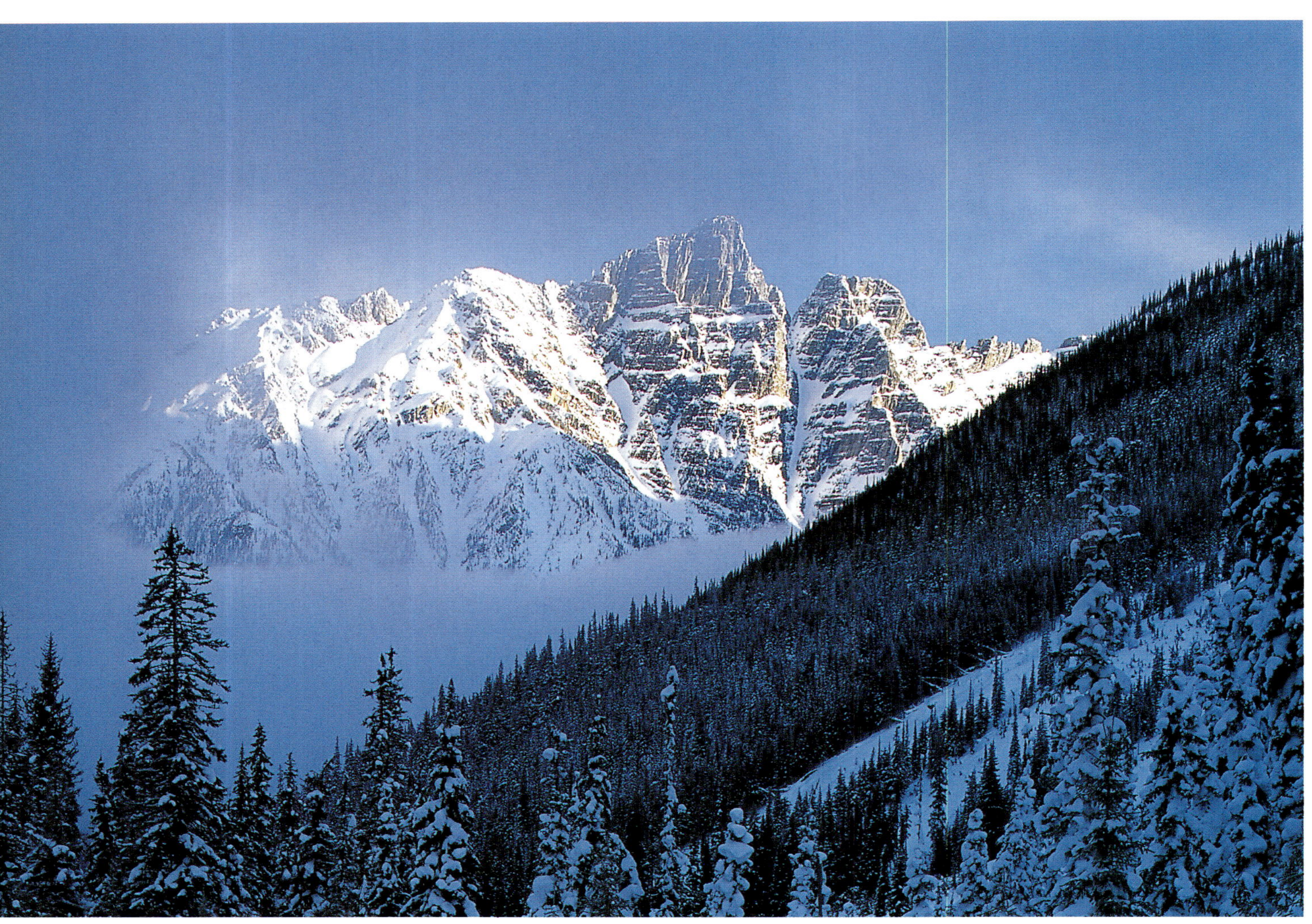

A storm had just passed when I made this image in Yoho on a bitterly cold morning. It wasn't easy pulling myself out of a cozy bed.

and possibly because of the teahouse and canoe rental. Mountain peaks surround Emerald Lake, but not as dramatically as in Banff. I have had some luck during the spring and fall at Emerald Lake but find this area to be best in winter, when the lake is frozen and surrounding trees sag with basketball-size snow piles on their branches.

Lake O'Hara is the best of the wilderness experiences in Yoho. For the best photographic opportunities, I recommend camping for a couple nights or staying at the lodge. You have two options for getting to Lake O'Hara: Take the bus, which requires a reservation, or hike eight miles. I suggest taking the bus to save your energy for the hiking once you're near Lake O'Hara. The Lake O'Hara region is closed in winter. Call the Yoho Visitor Centre at (250) 343-6783.

Kootenay National Park

Kootenay National Park is the least-traveled park in the Canadian Rockies. It is small and limited on dramatic scenery. There are several trails to backcountry locations but few roadside opportunities. Kootenay should be a last resort for photography during the spring, summer and autumn seasons because of its limited access and scenery. Winter is the best season to photograph in Kootenay. I suggest going to Kootenay before Jasper for snow scenes. You can snowshoe into the meadows a few hundred yards and find beautiful scenes along the river dotted with snow-capped rocks. In summer you can reach the Kootenay Visitor Centre at (250) 347-9505. In winter try (403) 292-4401 or (250) 347-9551.

WHEN TO GO

The Canadian Rockies have something for every season and give photographers a reason to visit these parks more than once. If you're looking for fewer crowds, new green grasses and foliage and mountains still capped with snow, then mid April through May will be best. If you're interested in photographing off the beaten path and are willing to hike on some backcountry trails, then early June through July is best. (August can be good, but I have found this to be a transition month, and things don't look fresh.) If you want to combine wildlife photography with landscapes and the changing colors, then mid September through the first week of October is good. The winter season is best from early February through mid March. (January is also a possibility but is typically the coldest month). You will need to rent snowshoes in Lake Louise

Winter shooting is nearly impossible in the Canadian Rockies without snowshoes. Even though I was only seventy-five yards from the road, I would never have captured this scene in Kootenay without snowshoes. The snow was four feet deep in the open field.

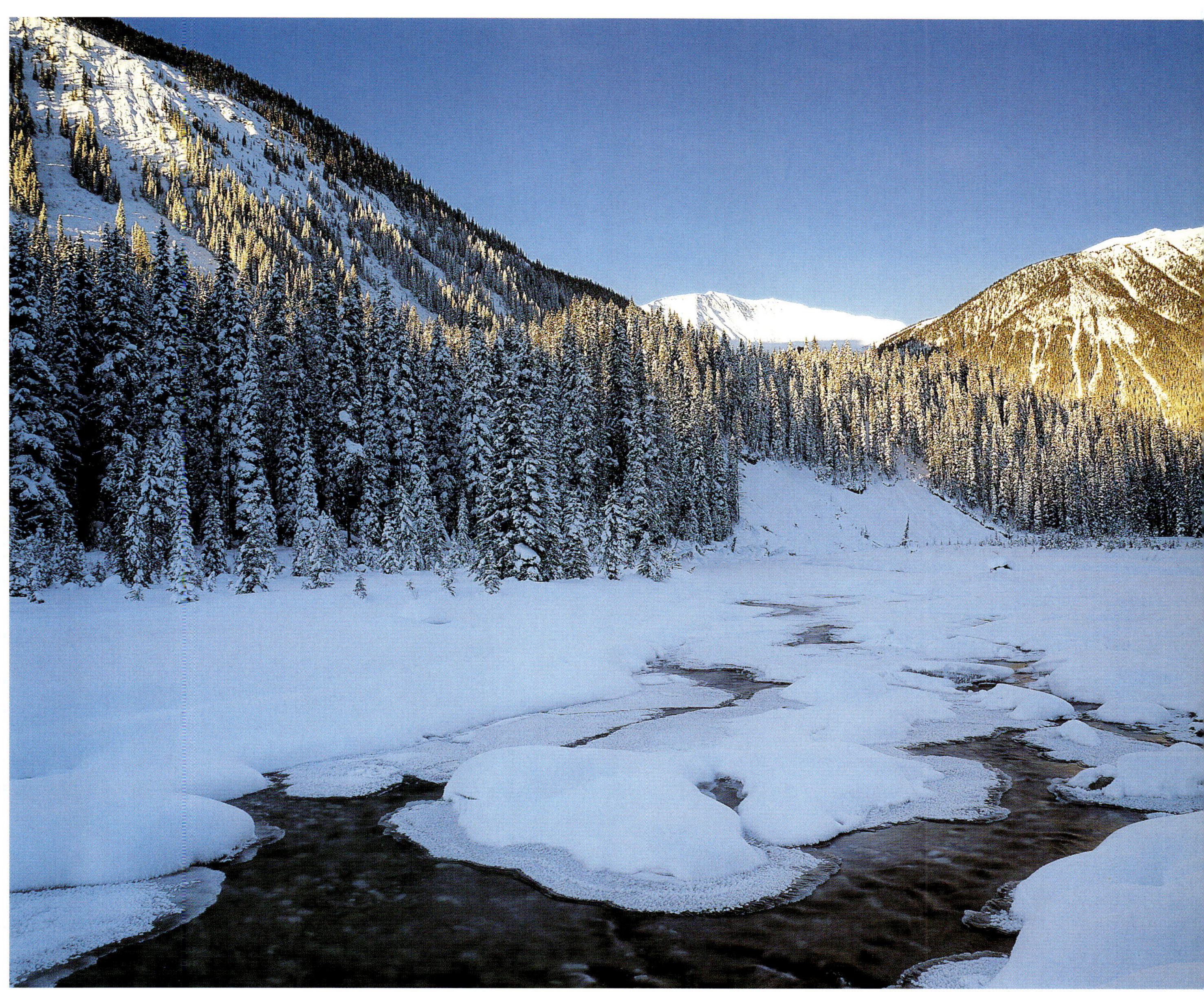

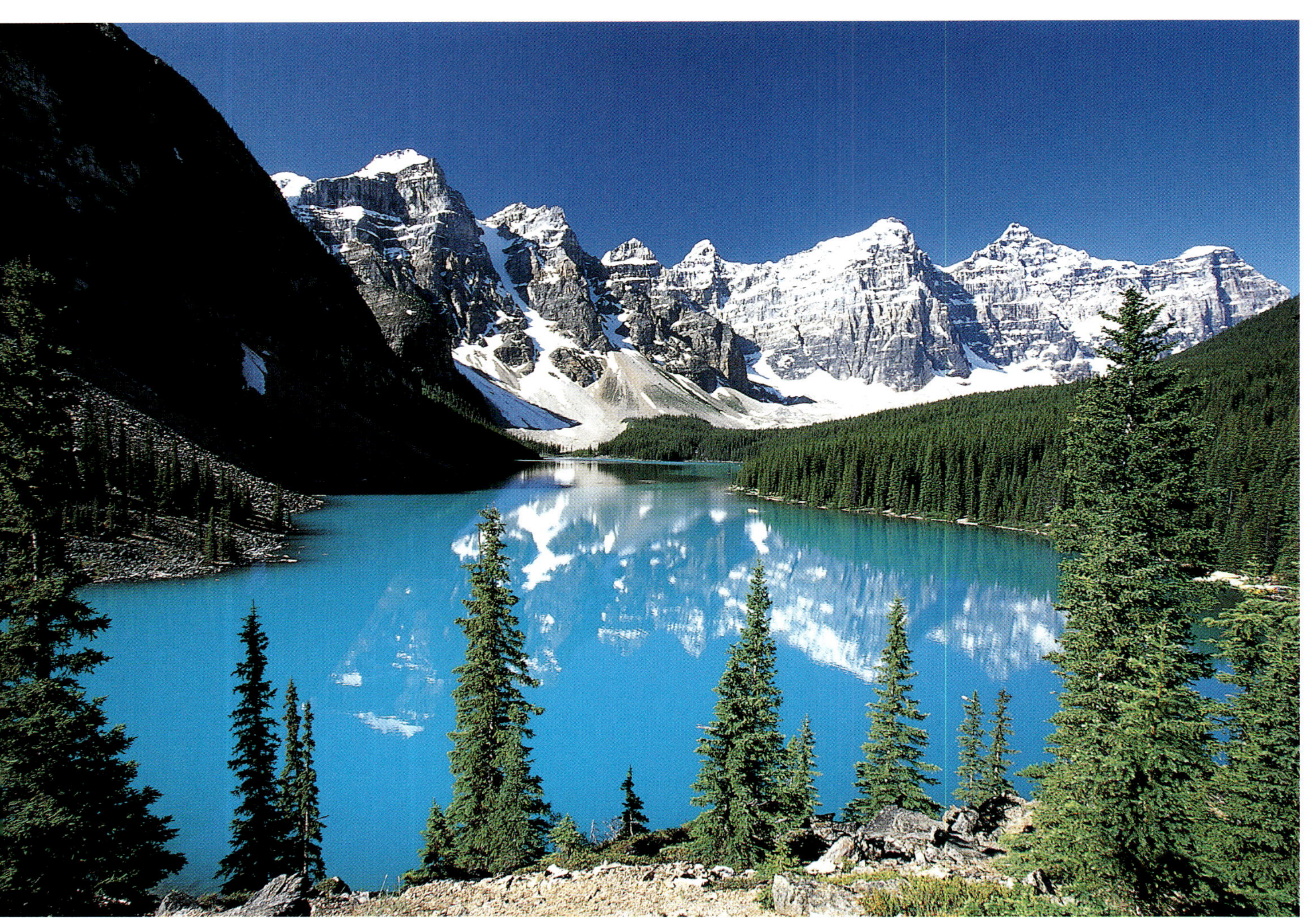

Every photographer who has ever been to Moraine Lake in Banff has probably shot this scene, but who can resist? It's okay to shoot subjects that have been done over and over as long as you don't get caught up chasing them your entire trip.

Village. This is not expensive and opens up a lot more opportunities. You will be very limited if you can't hike off the road. Don't attempt to hike across the snow without snowshoes.

TIME REQUIREMENTS

It would be impossible to photograph all four parks in one week without foregoing top locations in each. Spend less time driving, and focus on what you can reasonably cover. If you have only a week, I suggest the following: In spring and summer, spend your first night in Banff, and photograph along Icefields Parkway on your way to Jasper on the second day. Arrange for two nights in Jasper to work the area, and return to Banff for your remaining time, working both Banff and Yoho. You can cover Yoho while staying in Banff; it's a short hop and a skip from Lake Louise. Camping in Lake O'Hara during a summer trip would be the only exception to not staying in Banff. If you do want to work the Lake O'Hara area, consider adding a couple extra days.

There's little need to spend time in Kootenay unless you have an extra morning. An autumn trip should follow the spring and summer itinerary with the exception of adding an extra day in Jasper to shoot wildlife. For a winter shoot, make arrangements to stay in Banff the entire time. I suggest skipping Jasper National Park and spending your time in Banff, Yoho and Kootenay. Don't forget the snowshoes.

NEED TO KNOW

Lodging in the towns of Banff and Jasper is expensive during the height of tourist season. You can spend $150 to $180 (U.S.) per night in most hotels. In my opinion it is not worth it for the little time you'll spend in the room. Stay away from hotels in the Lake Louise area, unless it's in winter. These will be the most expensive ($150 to $200 U.S. per night). To avoid these costs, you'll have to drive a little farther. You can find a couple inexpensive and comfortable hotels in Banff, although most are expensive. Look through the listings in the AAA Tourbook. You can also stay in Canmore, but that adds another ten to fifteen miles of driving.

The best alternative to expensive hotels is camping. There are lots of campgrounds, and several with showers. Winter is the only exception to all of the above. I like to stay in the Lake Louise area, and lodging is much more reasonable during the winter season.

Jasper is expensive. You can find several nice hotels in the small town of Hinton, just outside the park boundaries. This adds an extra twenty to thirty minutes of driving, but for a $50 to $100 savings each night, it's worth it. Campsites in Jasper are also easy to find, and there are several nice campgrounds within the park.

photographer's choice

GLACIER NATIONAL PARK, in Montana, rivals the spectacular mountain scenery of its northern neighbor. You get two viewpoints in Glacier, as opposed to the one in the Canadian Parks, vistas from Going-to-the-Sun Road give a bird's-eye view of the mountains and lower elevations offer grand vistas of the distant mountains along with several beautiful lakes. GRAND TETON NATIONAL PARK in Wyoming also offers one of Americas most recognized mountain ranges. [Glacier, (406) 888-7800; www.nps.gov/glac; Grand Teton, (307) 739-3309; www.nps.gov/grte]

directions

Getting to Banff from the Calgary airport is easy. Allow one and a half to two hours for the drive. Follow Trans-Canada 1 from Calgary to Banff. It is a straight shot to all four parks.

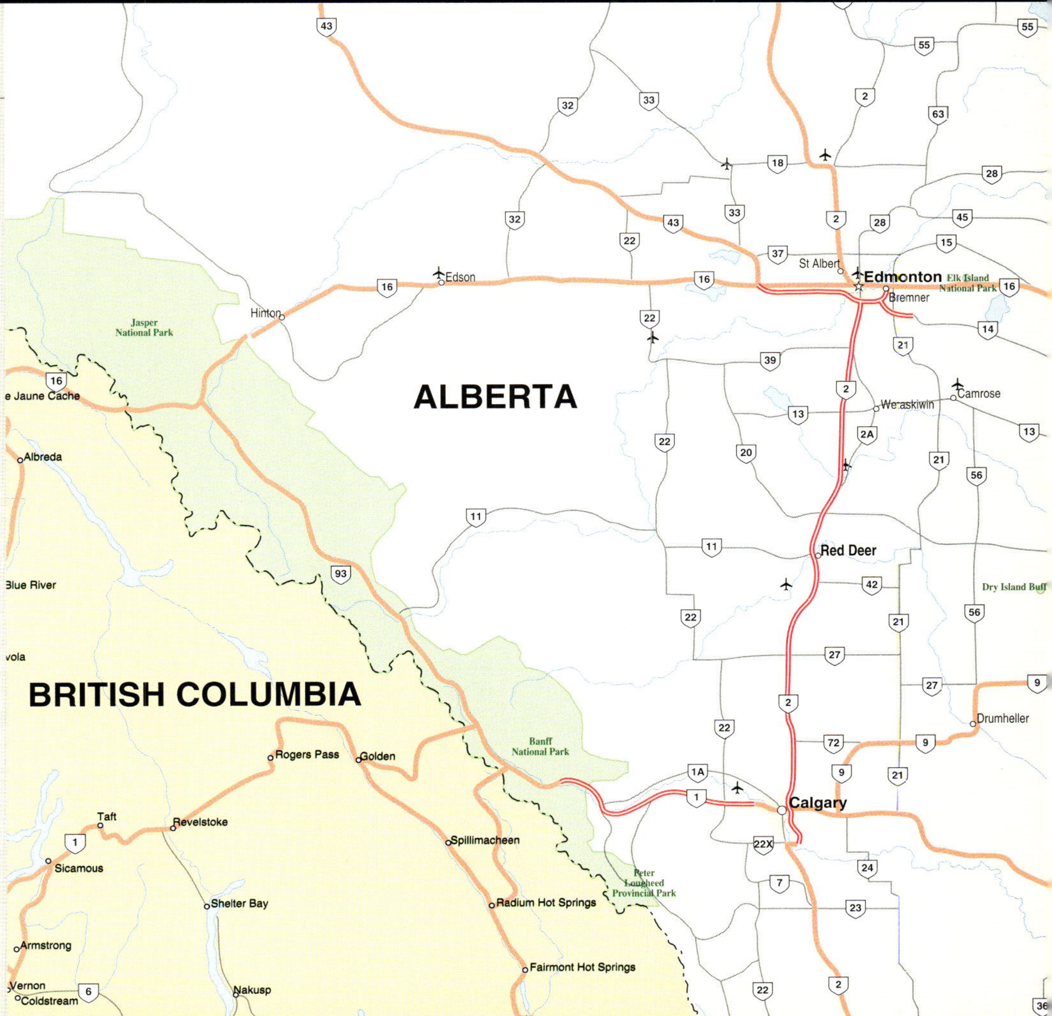

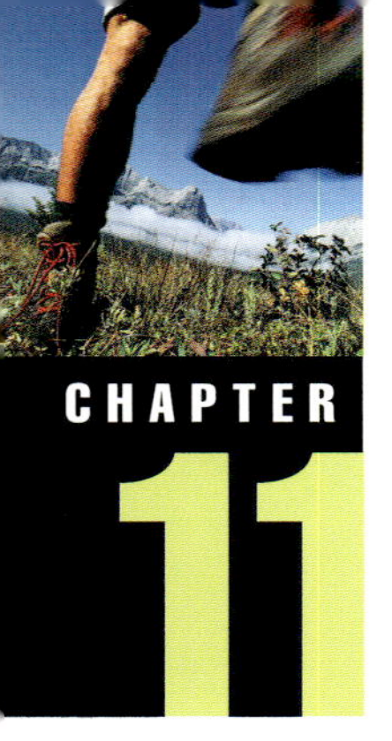

CHAPTER 11

Utah's Color Country

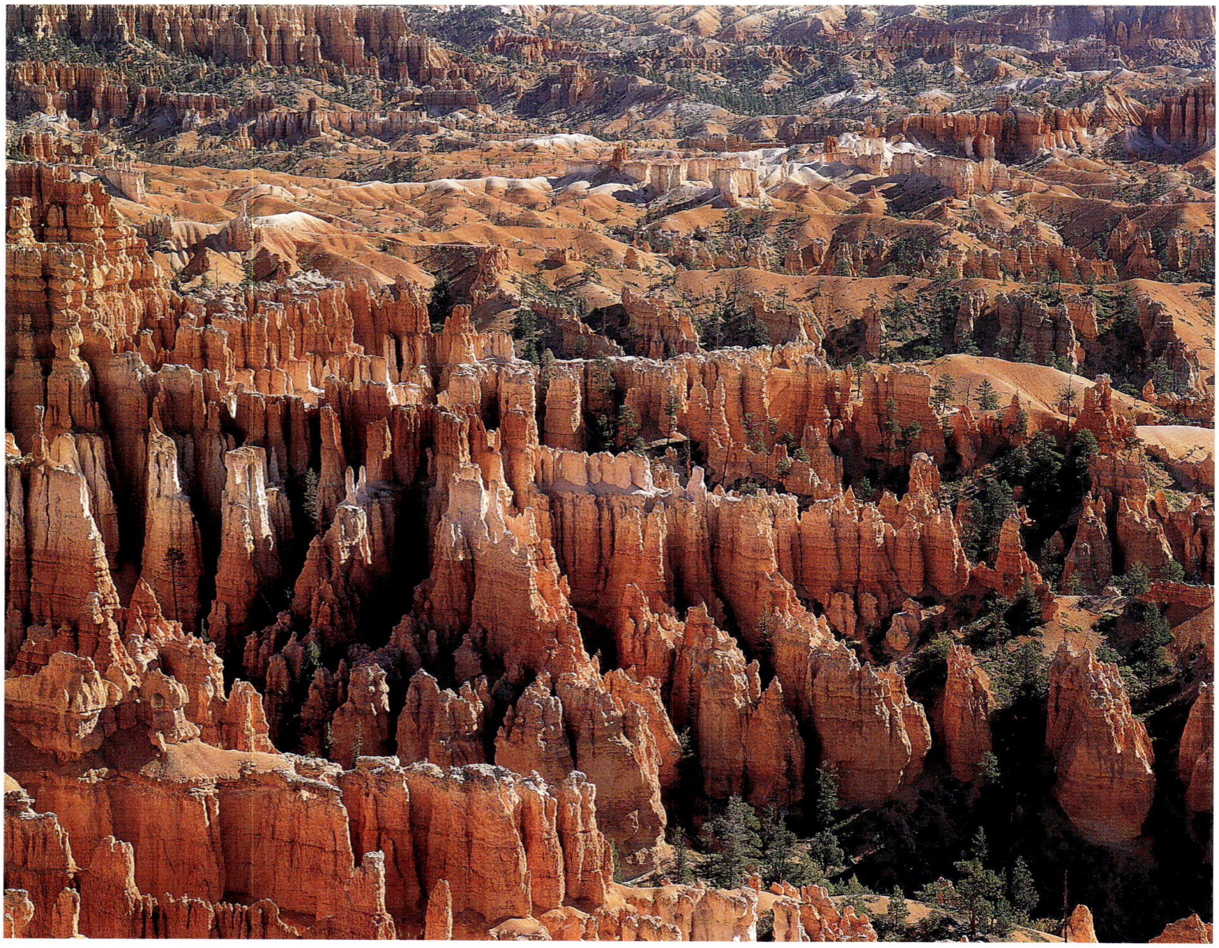

Southern Utah, "Color Country," is a natural draw for photographers where colorful canyons, sculpted rock formations and desert rivers contrast with an azure sky. Utah's own corner of the American Southwest holds several national parks, state parks, Bureau of Land Management (BLM) land and private lands, all on alienlike landscapes vastly different from one another.

This chapter covers three unique locations you can reasonably cover in seven days: Zion National Park, Bryce Canyon National Park, and the slot canyons on the Utah/Arizona border. You may choose to take a few additional days, or to combine the trip with the Grand Canyon and the Paria/Vermilion Cliffs Wilderness area, outlined in chapter twelve. See page

117 for a list of possible itineraries and trip combinations.

Several other Utah locations offer opportunities for side trips if you have an extra day: Cedar Breaks National Monument, Red Canyon, Coral Pink Sand Dunes and Kodachrome Basin. Don't leave home without some knowledge of the locations you plan to photograph and some idea of what you hope to accomplish.

Zion National Park

Zion National Park was established as Mukuntuweap National Monument in 1909 and designated Zion National Park by Congress in 1919. Hiking or horseback is the only way into most of Zion's 229 square miles (147,551 acres), but the beauty itself is evident from the moment you enter the park. Zion Canyon, the most visited area in the park, is more than two thousand feet deep. (The Grand Canyon, by comparison, is more than five thousand feet deep in places.) The often peaceful Virgin River carved this valley over 13 million years. Lined with Fremont cottonwoods, willows and velvet ash, the river is itself a destination.

High above Zion Canyon on the east side of the park is the high plateau, known as slickrock country. Checkerboard Mesa, a prominent landmark, is typical of the Zion landscape on the high plateau. The sagebrush and juniper of the plateau contrast sharply with the deciduous trees of the river valley.

PHOTOGRAPHER'S VIEW

The Zion landscape is breathtaking but offers its share of challenges for the photographer. The beauty of Zion comes in a grand package, so compositionally it is difficult to isolate elements and translate what you see and feel while standing amidst its big-picture beauty. The multiple tonalities of Zion Canyon as well as the sharp contrast between sunlit walls and those in deep shadow mean exposure often requires careful thought.

Exploration here is paramount for a successful shoot. I know few photographers who have walked away with a Zion landscape without doing their homework and working hard to get it. Zion is another park where I suggest you look for little scenes and generic shots. More so than in other parks, timing is everything here.

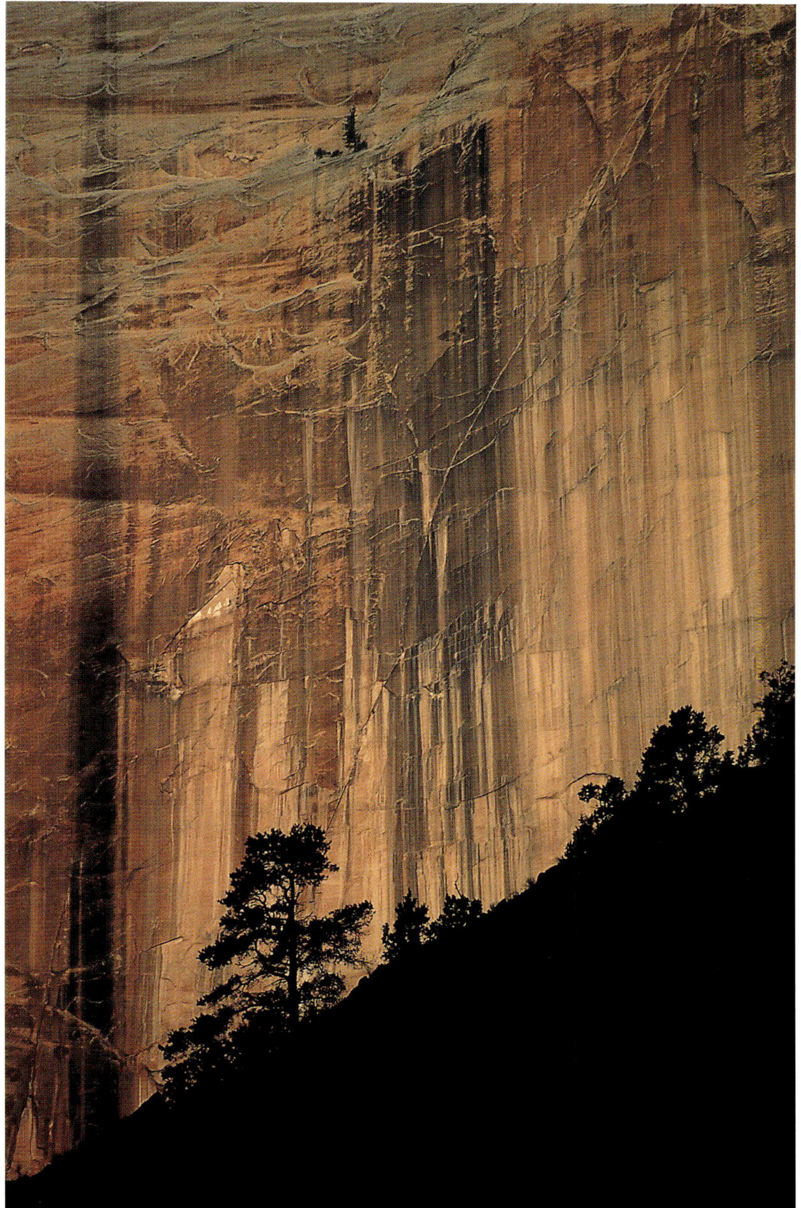

Zion National Park is a challenge to photograph. I enjoy looking for patterns and graphic elements on the towering canyon walls in Zion Canyon.

Zion Canyon

Zion Canyon is the most popular area of the park. Once you see the canyon, it is easy to see why. Throughout the morning and late afternoon, you will find that some canyon walls are warmly lit, while others sit in deep shadows. All too often the valley floor is in shadow as well. Shadowed and sunlit walls don't record well together on film since you must expose for one or the other. During these morning and late-afternoon hours, look for intimate scenes that don't require a grand view of the canyon. One can stand at many places along Zion Canyon Scenic Road and zoom in and out on sections of the canyon wall to find patterns or little scenes. An 80–200mm zoom lens is most useful for panning along the wall. I like the low-angle light because it provides the soft glow I come to think of when I'm in Red Rock Country. Therefore, I'm confined to the intimate scenes I describe. It is possible to capture the whole canyon when the sun is directly overhead, but you can forget about any red glow. This in no way should stop you from photographing, however.

Several trails in the canyon open up opportunities that are frequently overlooked. Two trails that have been good to me are Gateway to the Narrows (2 to 3.2 miles round-trip) and Emerald Pools (1.2 to 1.9 miles round-trip). These trails give a completely different perspective on the beauty of Zion. Gateway to the Narrows follows the Virgin River upstream in a narrow canyon with hanging gardens of blooming wildflowers in the spring and summer months. Emerald Pools has three waterfalls at the lower pool.

Zion-Mt. Carmel Highway leads out of the valley and starts its steep climb to the high plateau toward Checkerboard Mesa, about ten

Trees are sparse throughout the park, but individual trees, such as this ponderosa pine, can have personalities all their own. This one has that "king of the hill" look.

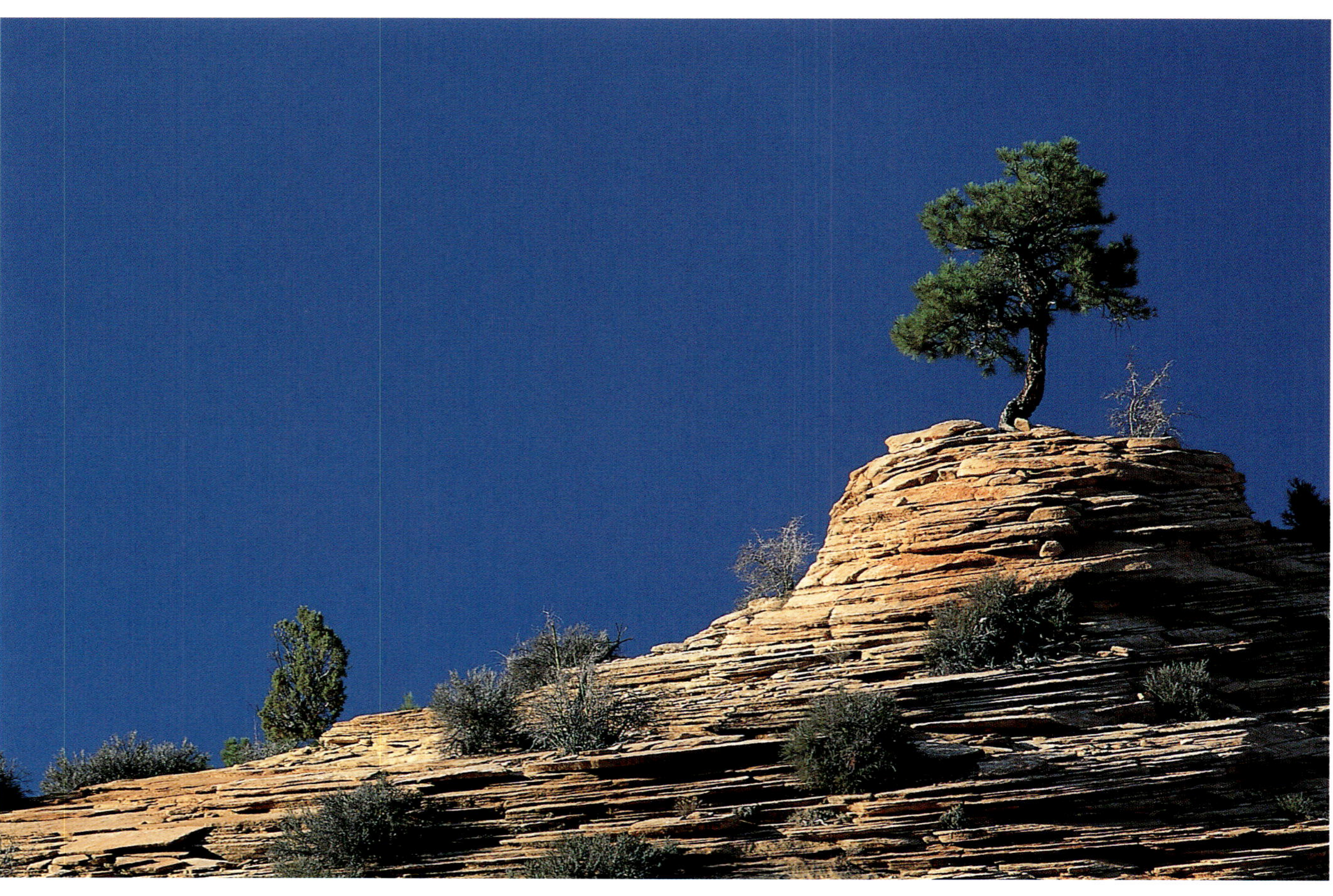

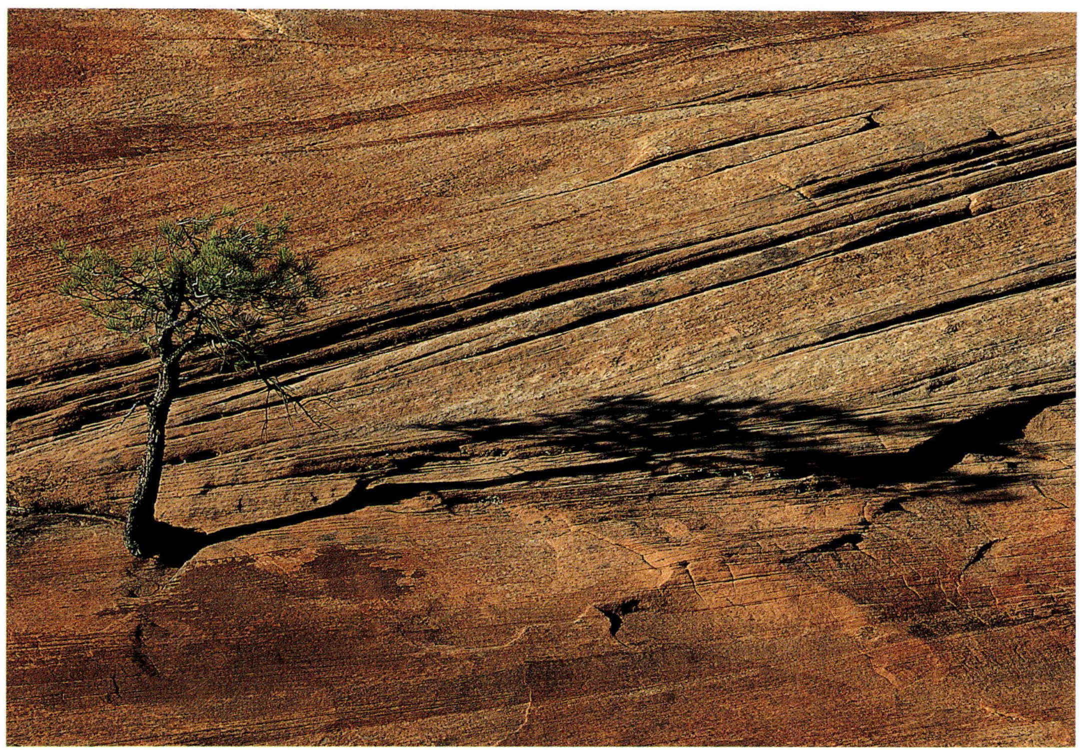

Some viewers might say the subject is the tree, and some might say it's the shadow of the tree, but I think the strong diagonal line is the subject. The important thing is that all three elements work together. If you have an element in your composition that isn't working with the others, eliminate it.

miles from the south entrance on the eastern edge of the park. There are several wonderful vistas of the canyon along this road, but none presents a great artistic opportunity unless you get a weather pattern coming through. If this is your first visit to Zion, I suggest you stop and decide for yourself whether you want to photograph. You will at least be rewarded with a wonderful view. Canyon Overlook Trail (one mile round-trip) is your best bet for viewing lower Zion Canyon and Pine Creek Canyon.

Checkerboard Mesa

Once you peak out on the incline of Zion-Mt. Carmel Highway, you have reached the Checkerboard Mesa area. This is relatively small and leads you toward the park's east entrance. As with Zion Canyon, you'll be challenged to find a composition that captures the grandness of the entire landscape, so you'll want to concentrate on small-scale subjects and intimate scenes. Wall and rock patterns are some of the best subjects to work. You'll find beautiful wildflowers such as Indian paintbrush, prickly pear, penstemon and scarlet gilia blooming through the cracks of sculpted sandstone. Incorporating sandstone patterns with blooming wildflowers makes beautiful and unique photos. A diffuser is a must for wildflower photography in Zion. You'll see little or no overcast light.

Kolob Canyons

Kolob Canyons sits in the northwestern corner of Zion National Park and is the least-visited section. You can't reach it by driving through the park. Exit the south entrance at Springdale and drive west on State Route 9 to State Route 17 north, then take Interstate 15 north. Follow signs for Zion National Park and the Kolob Canyons exit. Kolob Canyons is a series of finger canyons carved from Navajo Sandstone by the middle and south forks of Taylor Creek. As with Zion Canyon and Checkerboard Mesa, this area is colorful and offers its own spectacular scenery and notable landmarks. Kolob Arch, the world's largest free-

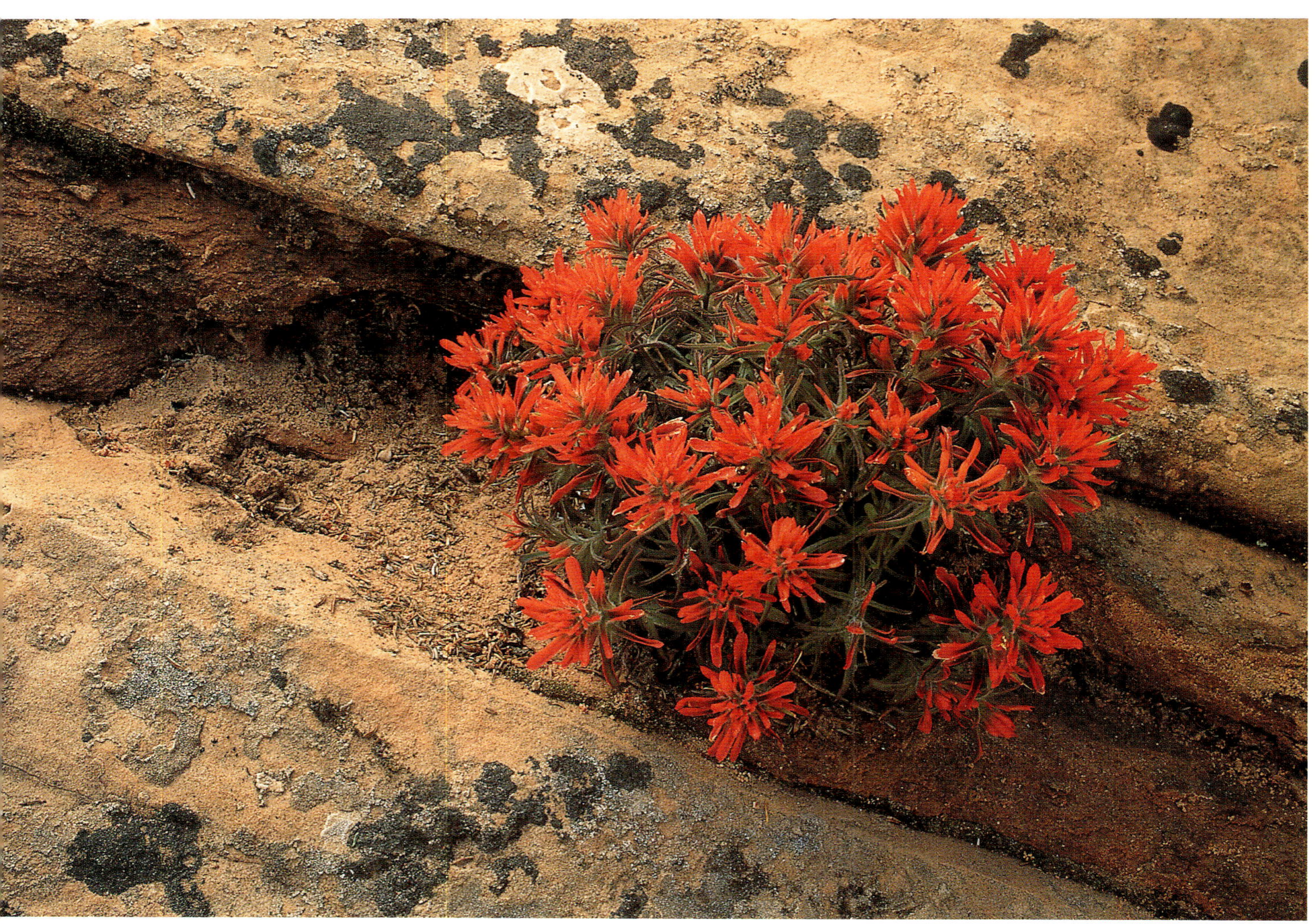

Flowers, such as this desert paintbrush, can pop up anywhere in Zion. I used a large diffuser to soften the mid-afternoon light and made it a much more pleasing image. The closer you can work with the diffuser to your subject, the better; you can make your subject appear to be almost glowing.

standing arch (spanning 310 feet), is one such landmark at the end of a long and strenuous seven-mile trail. I suggest shooting the Kolob Canyons region only if time permits and you want to spend time working rarely photographed backcountry landscapes.

WHEN TO GO

Zion National Park, like most of the American Southwest, can be photographed throughout the year, but summertime temperatures can be grueling, and winter is unpredictable. I have found March through mid May to be extremely pleasant and offer new foliage along the Virgin River and wildflowers blooming in the plateau regions. Mid October through early to mid November is another beautiful time to visit Zion. In autumn, golden cottonwoods contrast with both shadowed and glowing red canyon walls. Both spring and autumn bring more comfortable weather and fewer crowds than the summer months.

TIME REQUIREMENTS

Zion National Park is challenging, and you'll need time to research on-site, drive and hike the park, take compass readings, and visit the information center and local bookstores. Give yourself at least three full days. You won't need to cover a large area unless you enter the backcountry. Day hikes and established roads will give you plenty of park access and photo opportunities. See the end of this chapter for directions and a suggested itinerary.

NEED TO KNOW

Like most national parks, Zion has wonderful lodging. Zion Lodge [(435) 772-3213; <www.zionlodge.com>; (303) 297-2757; <www.xanterra.com/properties/zion.htm> for reservations] is open year round and offers several types of lodging, from standard motel rooms to cabins and suites. Springdale, located directly south of the park, also provides plenty of good lodging. Springdale is only minutes from the park and Zion Canyon. For more information on Zion, call (435) 772-0170, or go to <www.nps.gov/zion>].

Bryce Canyon National Park

Bryce Canyon is a fairyland of rock formations carved by wind and water over 60 million years. Hoodoos—dramatic fins, spires and pillars of rock—are what bring photographers to Bryce Canyon National Park. Few people even in Utah knew about Bryce Canyon until the 1930s, when the Union Pacific Railroad started advertising its lodges in and transportation to the area.

The park, officially created in 1924 as Utah National Park, is a relatively small fifty-six square miles (35,835 acres) ranging in elevation from 6,000 feet to more than 9,000 feet. Bryce is higher than other parks in the Colorado Plateau and so more frequently provides snow to contrast with its impressive range of colors. You can reach any canyon vista from the eighteen-mile roadway along the plateau rim.

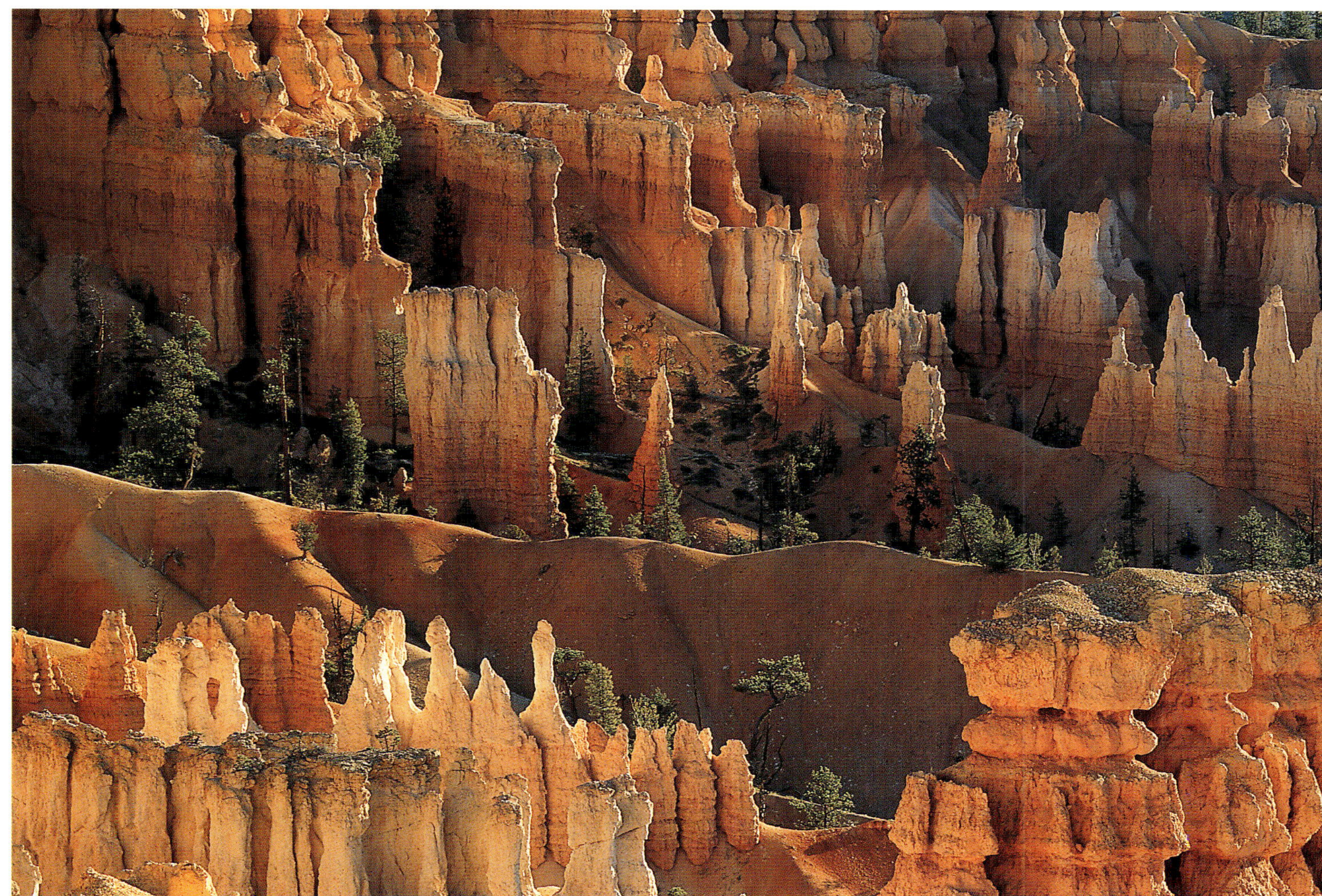

I call images like these documentary shots because they are more technically proficient than creatively exceptional. Documentary shots sell well in editorial markets.

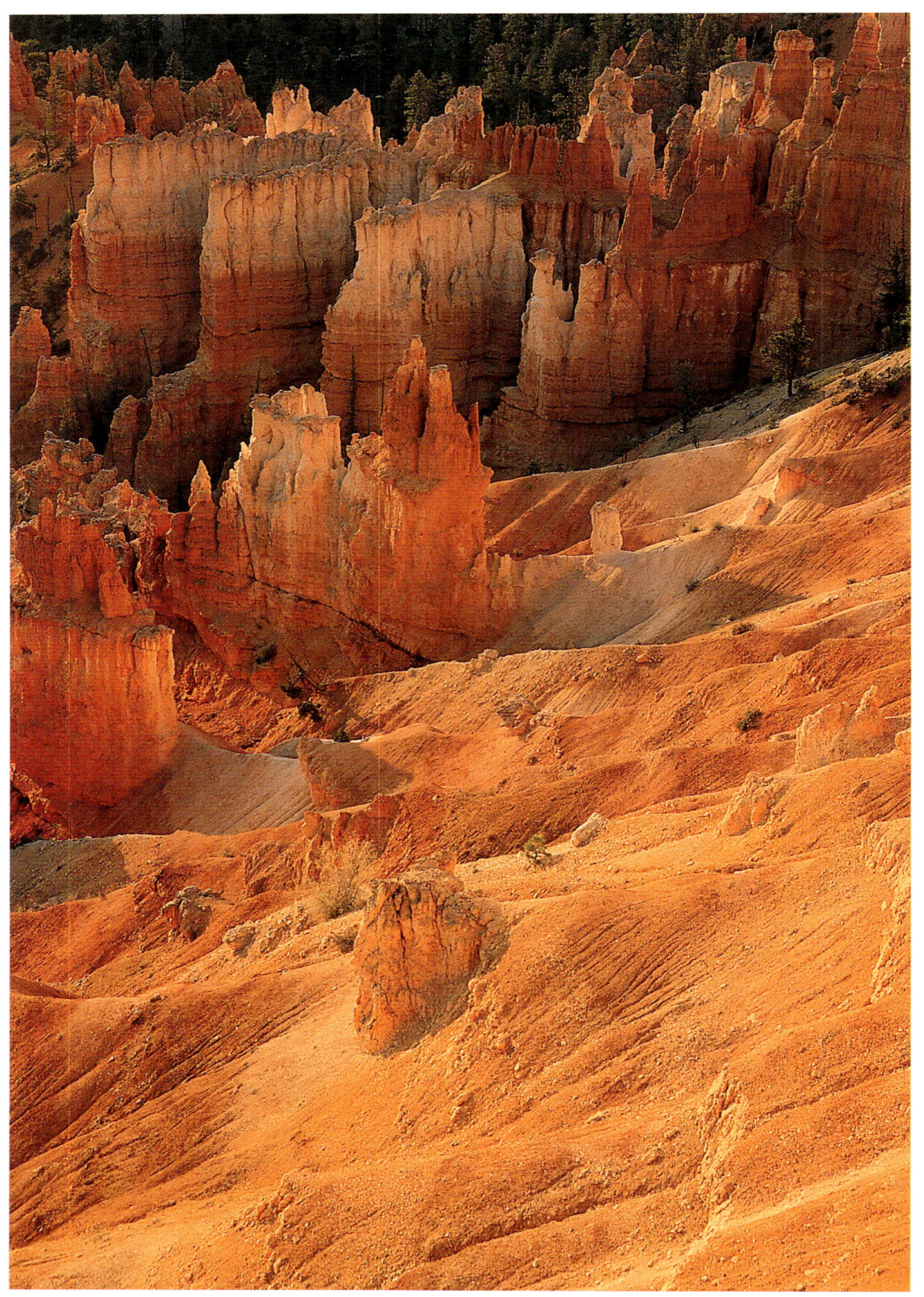

The early-morning light show in Bryce Canyon is magical. Light bounces off the canyon walls and from hoodoo to hoodoo. Be on location well before sunrise.

PHOTOGRAPHER'S VIEW

Bryce Canyon National Park could be called a "point-and-shoot park" because everywhere you look there is a potential shot. It is not difficult to walk away from a day or two of shooting in Bryce and feel well rewarded. Any of the twelve major overlooks hold opportunities, but as you drive farther south into the park, the high concentration of hoodoo formations gives way to more panoramic views of the distant landscape. The most popular and maybe the best overlooks are within an easy drive from the park entrance around the Bryce Amphitheater.

The best time for photography along the plateau rim above Bryce Canyon is in the hours before sunrise, just after sunrise and in the late afternoon before sunset. The light-colored hoodoos reflect light from one formation to another and make the whole canyon glow. This is one park where you don't want to oversleep; be out well before sunrise, and you'll walk away happy. I suggest spending an afternoon driving to every overlook, taking compass readings and making notes of what overlooks seem to present the best opportunities. After the sun rises and the light show ends, consider moving into the canyon itself. There are lots of trails that twist and turn amongst the formations with a completely different perspective. It is possible to work with the shadowed areas from below because the light-colored formations act as giant reflectors. If you are photographing from the canyon floor and have both sunlit and shadowed formations, meter for the sunlit areas. More than likely your shadowed areas will record some detail because of the reflected light.

Overlooks

Sunrise, Sunset, Inspiration and Bryce Points are all viewpoints above Bryce Amphitheater and are the four most common overlooks for visitors. You'll find something at each of these locations whether it's morning or late afternoon. These overlooks face east, and the canyon runs north and south. As its name suggests, Sunrise Point is a good location to start your morning. As the sun peeks over the horizon, watch for lens flare, caused by direct sunlight striking the front lens element. If you start to get lens flare, concentrate on shooting away from the sun to the north or south. You can also shade your front lens element with a hat or hand if you need to shoot toward the sun.

Sunset Point is equally good in both the morning and a couple hours before sunset. The sun will set behind you, so the Bryce Amphitheater will be in shadow before actual sunset. Wall Street, Cathedral and Organ are classic landmarks in Bryce Canyon and are why many people consider Sunset Point to be their favorite.

Inspiration Point is no less important or dramatic. Inspiration Point is a great location to photograph ridgelines leading out from the canyon rim into the hoodoo formations. After

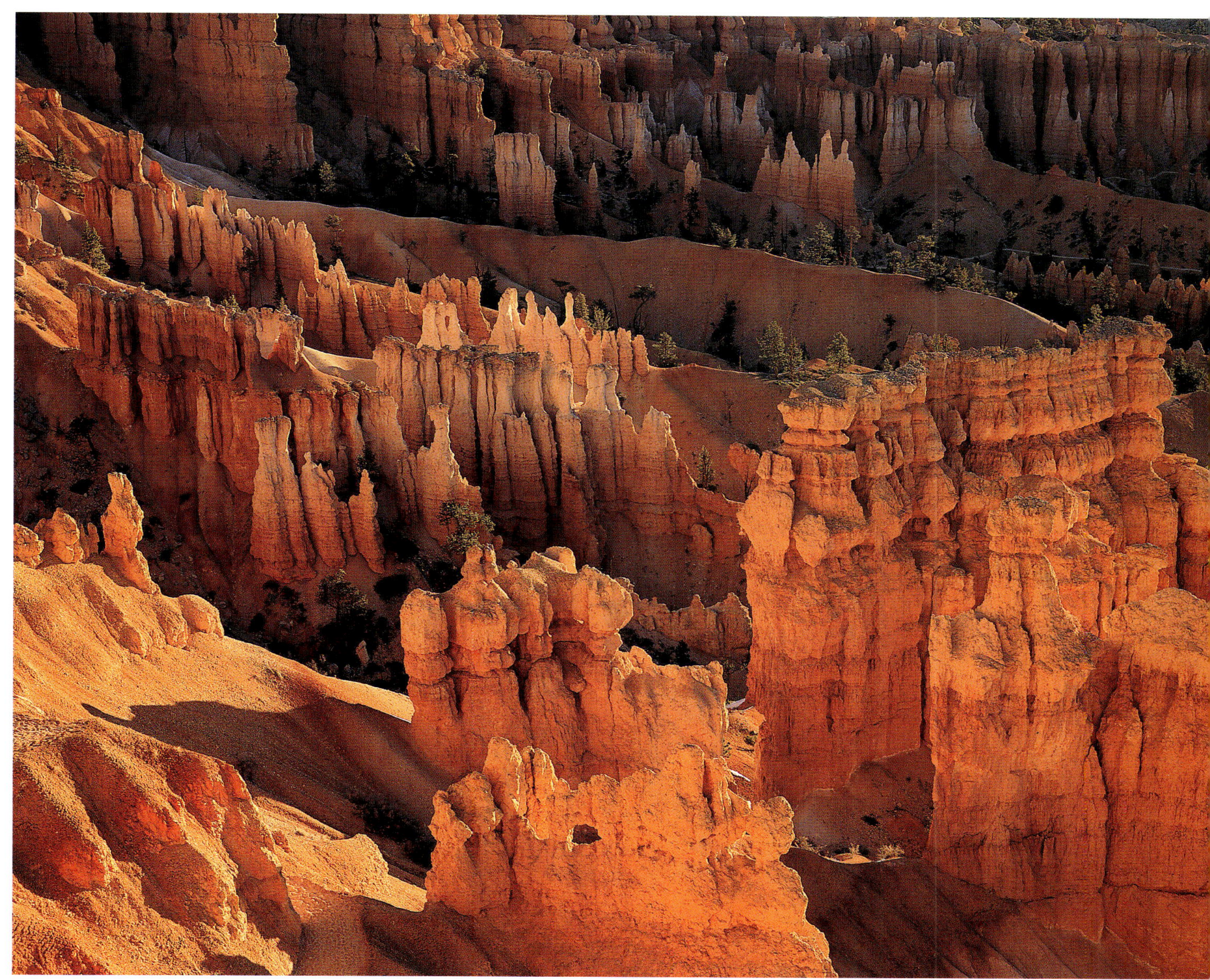

This is a classic view into Bryce Canyon and typical of what you might see from many points on the rim.

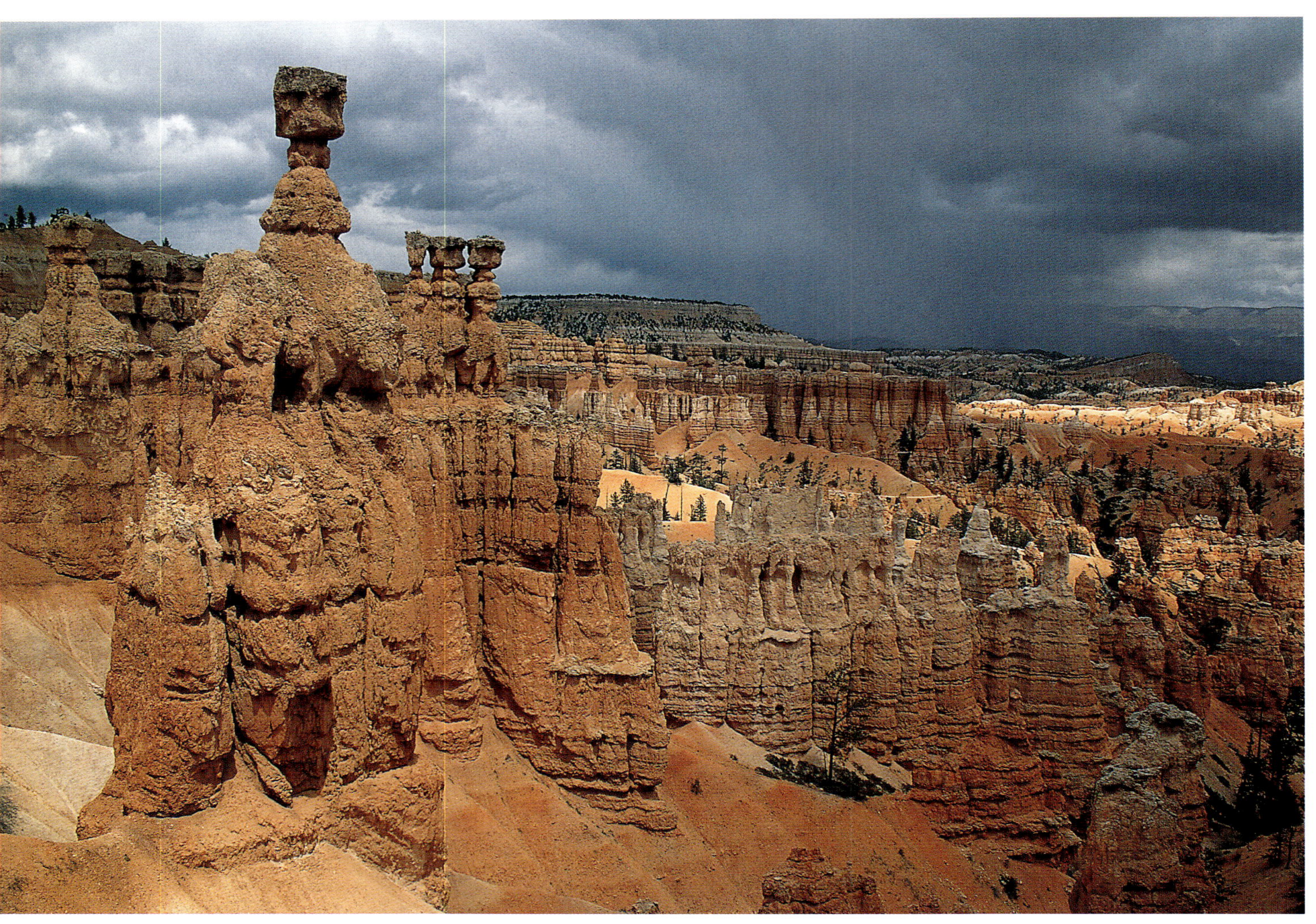

The threatening sky over Thor's Hammer makes this much less marketable than the same image with a blue sky. I like using it in my slide shows but have never sold the rights.

the sun has risen, this is also a great location to photograph Bryce Amphitheater with the surrounding landscape and a nice cobalt sky. Bryce Point is much like Inspiration Point in that it looks north and offers good sidelighting and similar views of the canyon rim after the sun has risen.

Visitors often overlook Fairyland Point because access lies just beyond the park entrance, but it's worth a visit. Fairyland Point provides the opportunity to shoot hoodoo formations at much closer range. It doesn't present the panoramic views you get from the overlooks I have covered above, but I recommend stopping here before going to other vistas beyond Bryce Amphitheater.

Other viewpoints south of Bryce Point have nice vistas but differ greatly from those I've already mentioned. I suggest these locations only if you have the time and feel the need to explore beyond the hoodoo formations. I don't want to discourage you, but photographically these are challenging. Most scenes are distant landscapes requiring incredible light.

You will find endless possibilities for photographing along the plateau rim, but they call for an observant eye and a variety of lenses. Don't make the mistake of putting on a wide-angle lens and never considering other focal lengths. I recommend using every lens you have, with a minimum range of 28mm to 200mm. Make sure you have polarizing filters to fit each of these focal lengths—you'll need them.

Below the Canyon Rim

Like other backcountry locations, hiking into Bryce Canyon presents its share of challenges:

1. the hassle of carrying heavy gear
2. selecting the trails with the best opportunities
3. selecting trails that match your physical ability

I can tell you it is much better to leave equipment behind than to completely pass up a photo opportunity. For the canyon descent, I recommend a wide-angle zoom or a fixed focal length 28mm–50mm, a polarizer and a tripod. There are many trails twisting and turning around hoodoos, but after a while they start to look alike. The Queens Garden Trail is probably one of the best in the park for color and interesting features. It is a mile and half round-trip with only 320 feet in elevation change. This should be feasible for most people, although it's still no cakewalk. You can also hike partway into the canyon on other trails and find great photos. You won't have to wander far in Bryce to find great photo opportunities.

WHEN TO GO

The timeframe for photographing in Bryce Canyon National Park is the same as in Zion. The difference between the two parks is elevation: 6,500 feet to 9,500 feet in Bryce vs. 3,600 feet to 8,700 feet in Zion. Therefore in Bryce expect colder temperatures and a little snow cover along the rim from March to early April. March through mid May and mid October through early to mid November are good windows for visiting Bryce.

TIME REQUIREMENTS

Bryce is not a difficult park to get around in and is easy to plan a photo shoot for. A couple hours driving to the overlooks and a short stop at the visitor center should net you enough information for a successful shoot. If you get one really good day, you can do a lot of shooting here. You will need a good morning shoot on the rim, a late morning for a hike into the canyon and a late-afternoon shoot once again on the rim. Two days should be more than enough time and might even provide a little downtime. If you are planning only one full day, consider spending two nights. Use the following morning (the day you plan to depart) to photograph at another location on the rim before you continue your trip.

NEED TO KNOW

There aren't a lot of hotel chains around Bryce Canyon National Park, but typically you won't have a problem finding lodging for your short stay. Bryce Canyon Lodge [(435) 834-5361, <www.brycecanyonlodge.com>; (303) 297-2757, <www.xanterra.com/properties/bryce.htm> for reservations], like most park lodging, is ideally situated within the park, but you need to make reservations a year in advance, if possible, more if you plan to stay through a weekend. The town of Bryce has few motels, but one of my favorites is an old historic hotel called Ruby's Inn. Ruby's Inn [(866) 866-6616, <www.rubysinn.com/lodging.html>] sits one mile outside the park boundary and is an easy drive into the park for your morning shoot. Restaurants are few as well; both the Bryce Canyon Lodge and Ruby's Inn have nice dining facilities.

The Slot Canyons

The Colorado Plateau's geography often is as obvious as the sky above, but hidden below narrow openings are dazzling passages carved by water in the delicate Navajo Sandstone—Arizona and Utah's slot canyons. Slot canyons are essentially dry washes but can succumb to flash floods during the summer rainy season and, periodically, at other times of the year. Some people believe there are hundreds

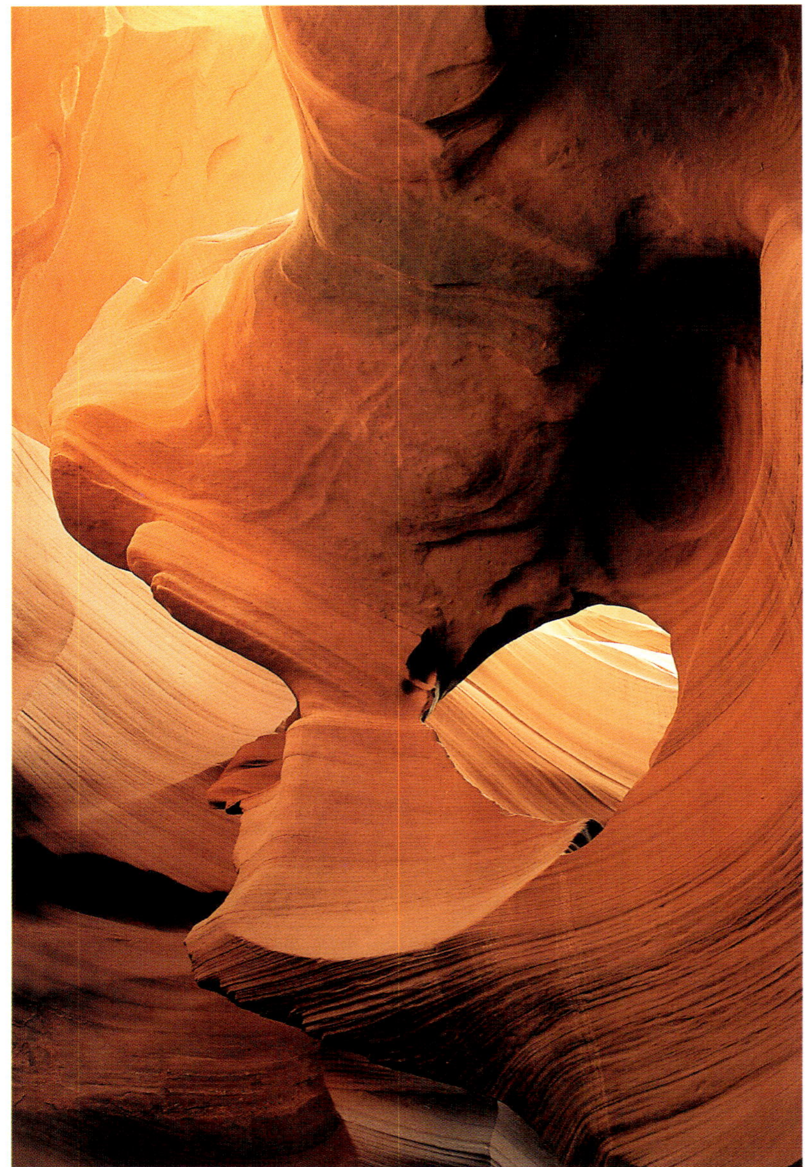

Slot canyon photography is a unique experience. Your subjects are patterns, shapes and light. Every twist and turn within these confined walls is a new image.

throughout the Colorado Plateau. Several popular and many unknown slot canyons are within a stone's throw of the road and range from a hundred feet to twelve miles in length, as at Buckskin Gulch.

PHOTOGRAPHER'S VIEW

The slot canyons' walls often reveal glowing patterns and shapes, which is why photographers come here in the first place: It is not typical of southwestern landscapes. The slot canyons I discuss are along the Utah and Arizona border near Glen Canyon National Recreation Area and Page, Arizona. I will only mention a few that are well known and also managed to some degree. Slot canyons are incredibly beautiful and photographically rewarding but also can be dangerous for the uninformed. Summer is the rainy season in the Colorado Plateau region, and thunderstorms can pop up at anytime. Storms miles away can create flash floods in the canyon you're in, even when you have blue skies directly overhead. Regardless of the time of year, be aware of the weather in the entire region. Familiarize yourself with the canyon you are photographing, and find out where you can exit the canyon.

Antelope Canyon

Antelope Canyon refers to two different slot canyons: Upper Antelope and Lower Antelope. These are by far the best-known slot canyons and are considered to be the prettiest. Both Upper and Lower Antelope canyons are on LeChee Navajo Lands and require a fee. The fee is very reasonable and includes both entry and transportation to Upper Antelope Canyon. Upper Antelope is two miles off the main road and would entail a difficult hike on the sandy surface. The fee is good for both Upper and Lower Antelope on the same day.

Upper Antelope, also called the Corkscrew, is the most-visited canyon by photographers and other tourists. This is an easy walk with little or no physical challenge. Upper Antelope Canyon boasts twisting and spiraling sandstone walls colored in shades of purple, reds, pinks, oranges and yellows. Photography is best in the late morning and early afternoon when light filters through the thin opening and bounces from wall to wall. Beautiful delicate patterns and shapes reveal themselves as the sun continues overhead and constantly changes the subtle colors and patterns glowing in the swirling, soft sandstone. Exposures are long in slot canyons and will vary from location to location within the canyon itself. Don't be surprised to have exposures of two minutes and longer.

You'll encounter lots of people in the narrow passageway, but most of the time this poses little or no problem. Most of the time you will be shooting over the heads of people walking through the canyon. The biggest problem will be your tripod in the way of people trying to get through. If you need to shoot lower than head level, let people know you are shooting. Typically they are kind enough to wait for you to finish. Photographers should understand that other visitors also have the same right to pass through and enjoy the experience.

Lower Antelope Canyon is far less visited than Upper and requires a bit more effort to enter. The entry into Lower Antelope is a mere crack in the surface with an opening just wide

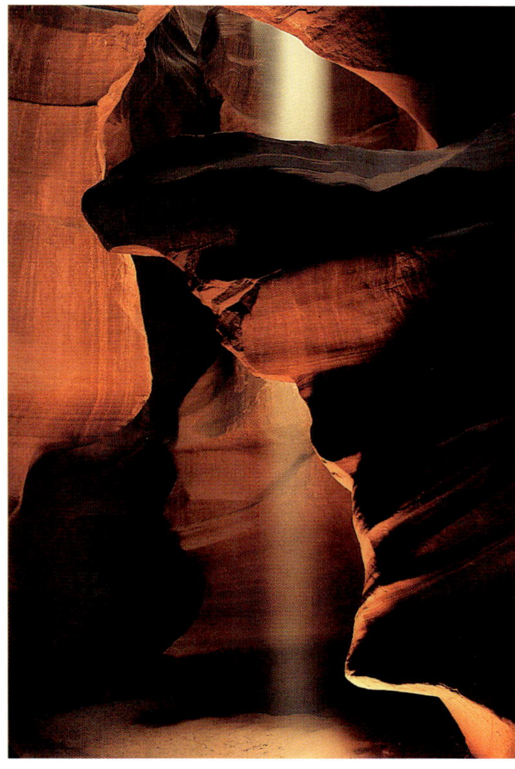

Working the slot canyons requires patience and quick reactions. The sun shone through a narrow crack in this scene, and the light lasted no more than a few minutes.

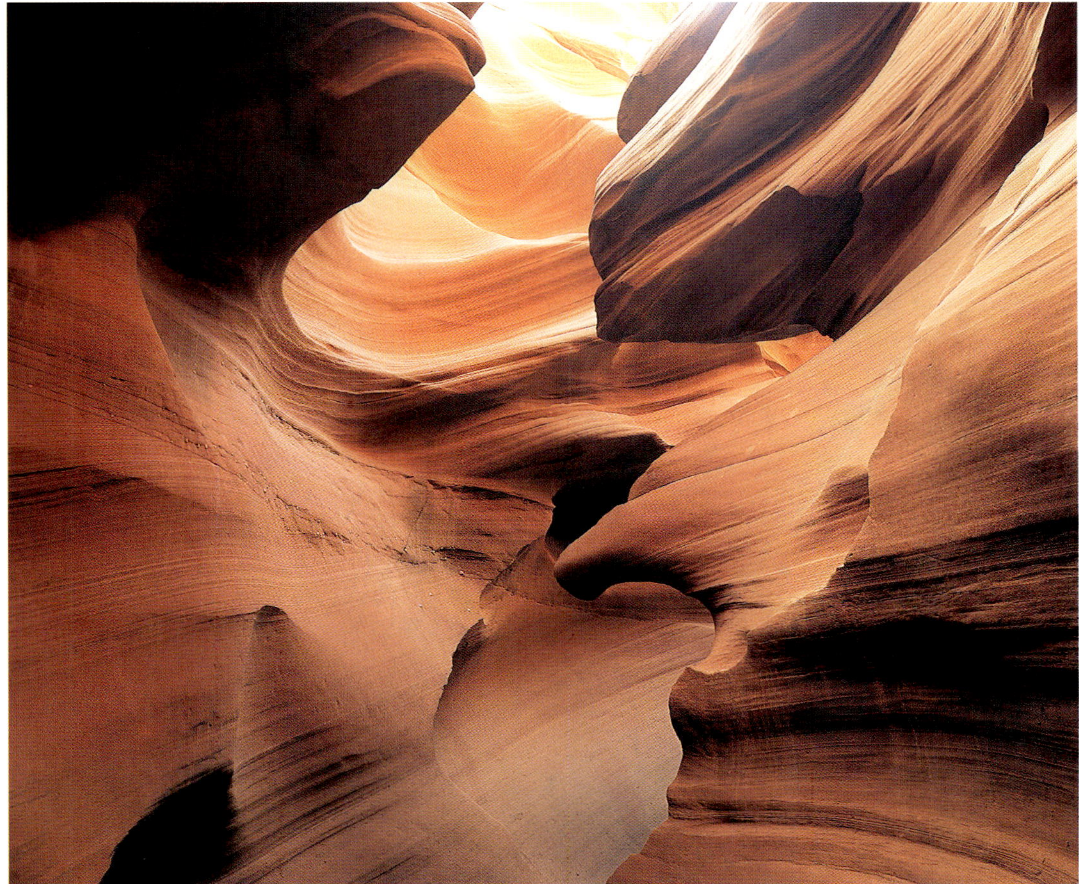

Watch out for hot spots. Take several spot meter readings from different parts of your composition and try to avoid areas more than one stop brighter than the rest of the composition. I would rather underexpose part of a frame than overexpose because hot spots distract the viewer. I was getting close to washing out the upper portion of this image.

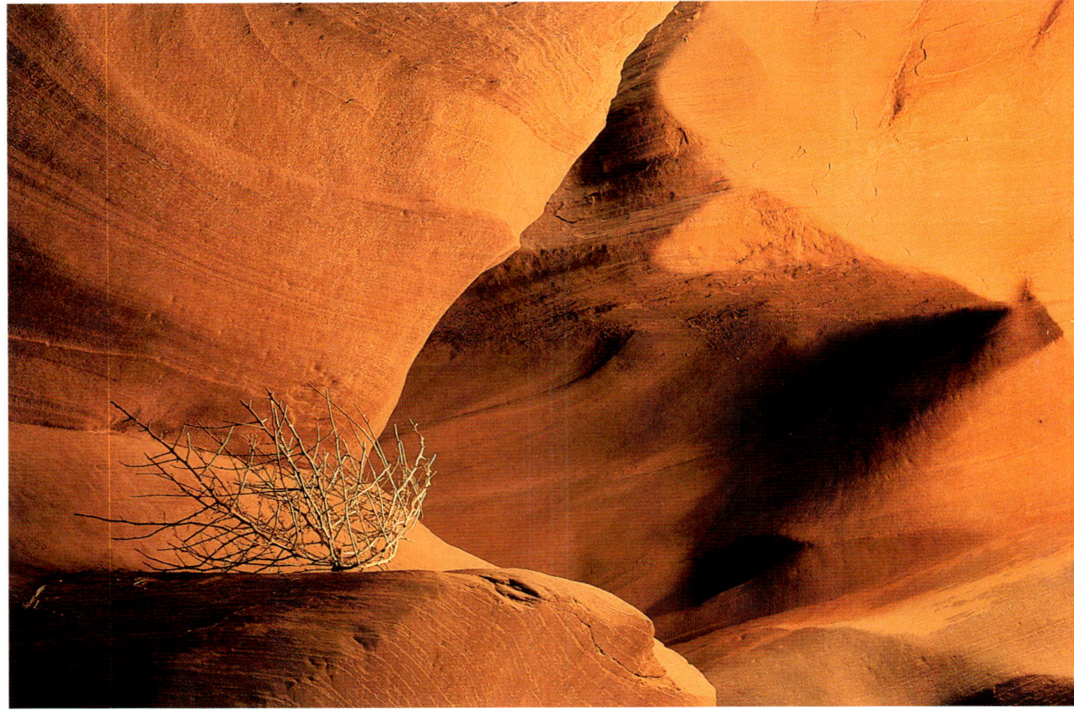

You'll see little but rock in the slot canyons. This bit of sagebrush was a welcome addition.

enough to lower a body with a camera pack. At one time this slot canyon required a rope for climbing in and out but is now equipped with steel ladders anchored into the sandstone walls. The climb isn't difficult but will require a little creative maneuvering when lowering yourself with a camera pack. Lower Antelope Canyon has shapes and patterns equally as good as Upper Antelope. You won't encounter many people in Lower Antelope, but chances are you won't be alone. The same unwritten rule I described about Upper Antelope applies here as well; communicate with other visitors, and let everyone enjoy the same rewarding experience.

Water Holes Canyon

Water Holes is another slot canyon with the same beautifully sculpted Navajo Sandstone formations as those of Antelope Canyon. Water Holes is little known and much less visited than Antelope. If you want to experience a slot canyon in solitude and have nothing but yourself and the magic of bouncing light, Water Holes is the place for you. This canyon is also on Navajo land and requires a fee, which varies depending on the services provided but ranges from $15 to $25 and is good for most canyons on the same day. Remember to let someone know where you will be if you decide to enter any slot canyons alone.

There are obviously many other slot canyons in the Colorado Plateau, but Upper and Lower Antelope are the best known and probably the safest. Unless you feel the need to shoot somewhere no one else has found or photographed, these locations will provide all the patterns and shapes you would want to shoot. Because the light and conditions change constantly in the canyons, on any given day you can walk away with pictures no one else could have taken.

WHEN TO GO

The slot canyons can be good anytime, but summer is incredibly hot (20 degrees cooler in the canyons) and also brings the possibilities of those dangerous flash floods. You will probably be combining the slot canyons with other spots in Color Country or the Grand

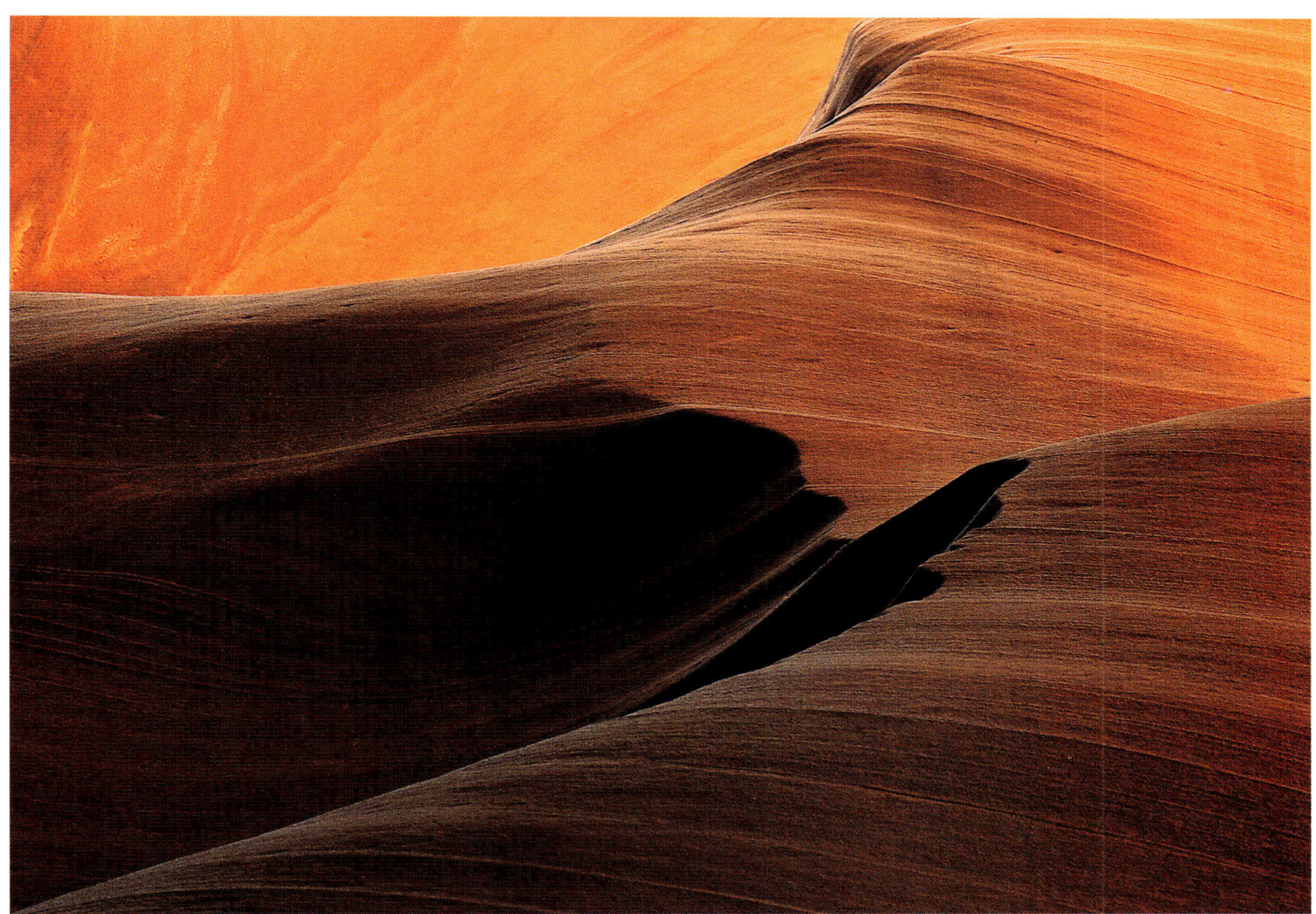

The beautiful patterns from the soft sandstone walls will make up most of your shooting. Images such as this make good background images.

Canyon region, so as with those locations, March through mid May and mid October through early to mid November are perfect.

TIME REQUIREMENTS

The slot canyons don't require a lot of time. One day is all you need; if you really like photographing here, you could pull off two days of shooting. The best light comes from mid morning to mid afternoon. There is little need to scout the slot canyons as all you need to do is show up and walk through until you find an area you want to work.

NEED TO KNOW

There are lots of hotel chains in Page, Arizona. Page is an easy drive to all of the slot canyons in the area and the only place where you'll find lodging. Spring and fall are busy; I recommend making reservations well in advance. Lake Powell brings in lots of people, and special events often fill the hotels.

Itinerary: Zion and Bryce National Parks, Antelope Canyon and Coyote Buttes

You can cover Zion, Bryce and the slot canyons in a week (two travel days and five or six shooting days). I discuss Coyote Buttes in chapter twelve. The itinerary below is based on air arrival in Las Vegas or Salt Lake City. Plan on a five- to six-hour drive from either airport to Zion National Park, your first stop. If you arrive late in the afternoon, you'll have time to drive through Zion Canyon, scout the area and stop by the visitor center or local bookstore for some last-minute research and information gathering. Spend three full days exploring Zion National Park in both the

Canyon and the Plateau area. On the evening of your third day or the morning of your fourth day, travel to Bryce Canyon National Park. The advantage to departing on the evening of your third day is you have the next morning to photograph along the plateau rim into Bryce Canyon. The downside is you won't have the opportunity to scout an overlook, but you can't go wrong at Sunrise Point. If you travel the morning of your fourth day, you'll lose that morning on the rim, but you can take a side trip to another location to explore and arrive in Bryce in the late afternoon: enough time to scout your morning shoot. Give yourself at least one full day in Bryce; a second day will allow you to enjoy more of the park. Your departure from Bryce will take you to Page, Arizona, where you choose between the slot canyons or Coyote Buttes. You need only one day in either area. Add an additional two hours of driving for your return to the airport.

photographer's choice

All of Utah's national and state parks and public lands are so unique that no other region comes close to rivaling these places. Each has its own landscape and special features. Start with ARCHES NATIONAL PARK, backdrop for Edward Abbey's *Desert Solitaire*, or check out DEVIL'S GARDEN, in the Escalante region. Outside of Utah, consider the Great Sands Dunes of Colorado or DEATH VALLEY NATIONAL PARK in California [Arches National Park, www.nps.gov/arch; Great Sands Dunes, www.nps.gov/grsa; Death Valley National Park, www.nps.gov/deva; Canyonlands National Park, www.nps.gov/cany]

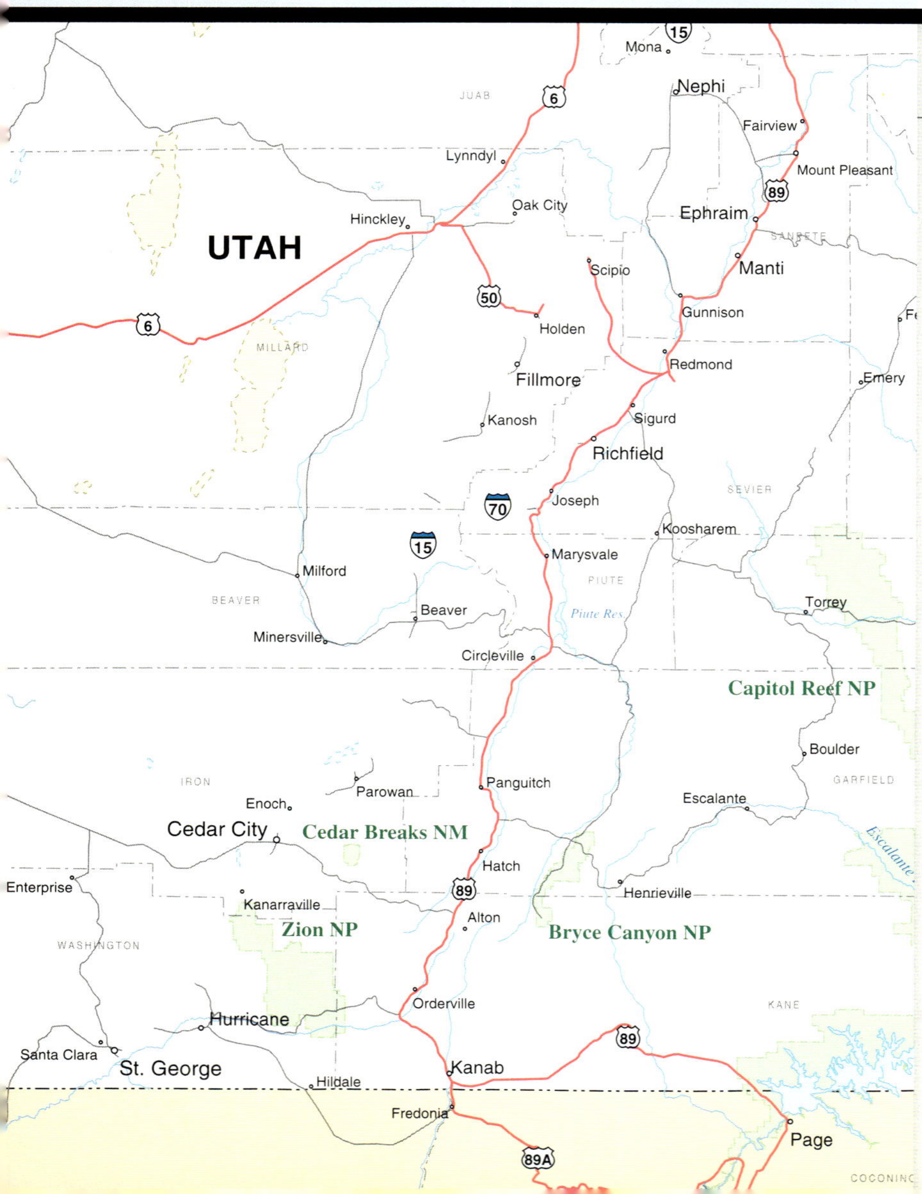

directions

ZION NATIONAL PARK:

- From Salt Lake City take I-15 south to exit 40, and follow signs to Zion; from Las Vegas take I-15 north to St. George, and follow signs to Zion.

ZION NATIONAL PARK TO BRYCE CANYON NATIONAL PARK:

- Take Highway 89 north to State Road 12 east. Follow signs to Bryce.

BRYCE CANYON NATIONAL PARK TO PAGE, ARIZONA:

- Take State Road 12 east to Cottonwood Canyon Road, just before you reach Cannonville. Cottonwood Canyon Road is a gravel road most of the way and passes Kodachrome Basin State Park. This road ends at Highway 89. Turn right and follow Highway 89 into Page.

PAGE TO UPPER ANTELOPE CANYON:

- Follow Highway 98 east approximately 3 miles. A good landmark to watch for is a large power plant with huge smoke stacks on your left. The gate into Upper Antelope Canyon is on the right-hand side.

PAGE BACK TO LAS VEGAS OR SALT LAKE CITY:

- Follow Highway 89 west to Route 9 past Springdale into St. George. Pick up I-15 south for Las Vegas or I-15 north for Salt Lake City.

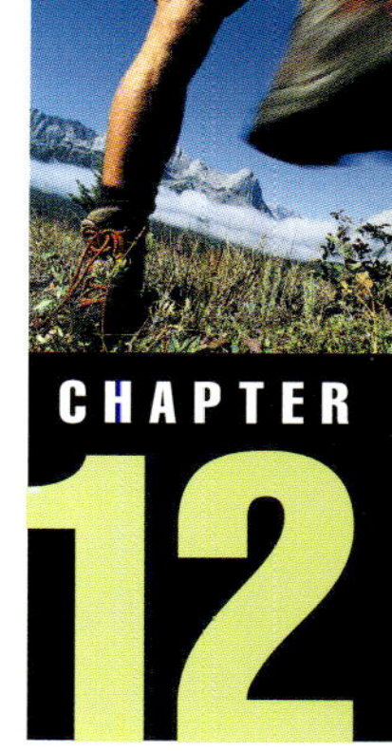

CHAPTER 12

Arizona Canyon Country

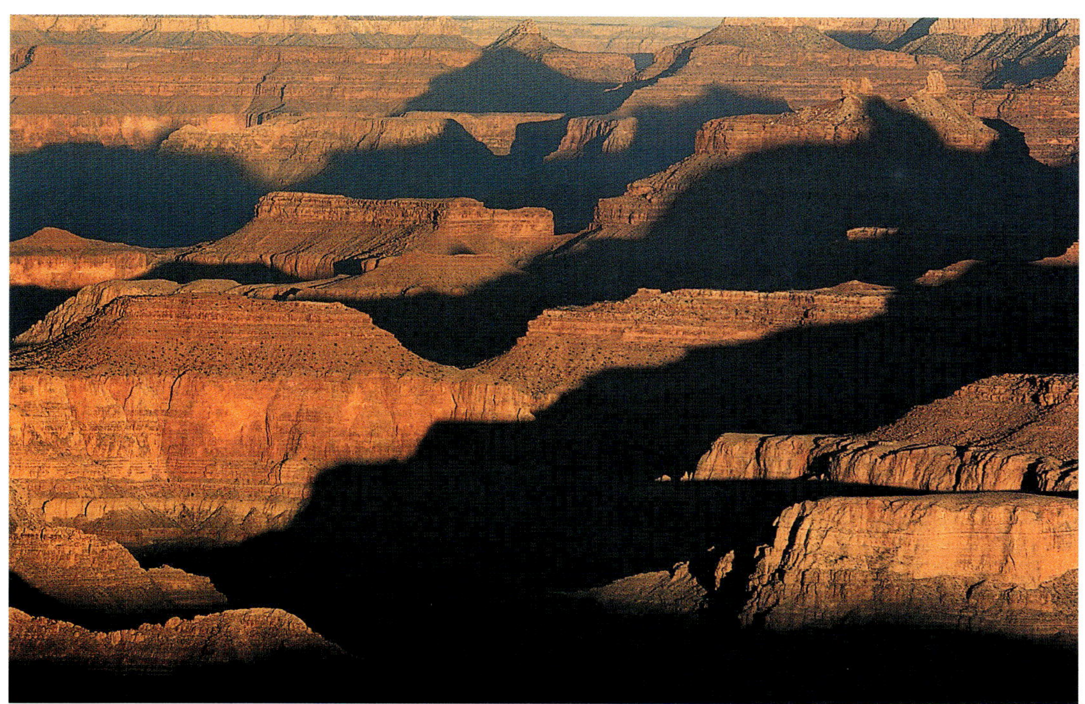

Arizona's canyon country is the geographic and emotional heart of the Colorado Plateau, and for that matter, the entire Southwest. Teddy Roosevelt declared that the Grand Canyon is "the one great sight which every American should see," and it still holds true. This chapter covers both Grand Canyon National Park and another photographer's favorite, Coyote Buttes, which is part of the Paria Canyon/Vermilion Cliffs Wilderness Area (see page 123). While the geography of both entails canyons, rivers and lots of sun-baked rock, each is unique. Combined, the two locations complement the panoramic, alienlike landscapes so abundant in southern Utah.

Grand Canyon National Park

Being one of the seven wonders of the world is reason enough to photograph in Grand Canyon National Park. The Colorado River flows 1,450 miles from the Rocky Mountains to the Gulf of California in Mexico and has

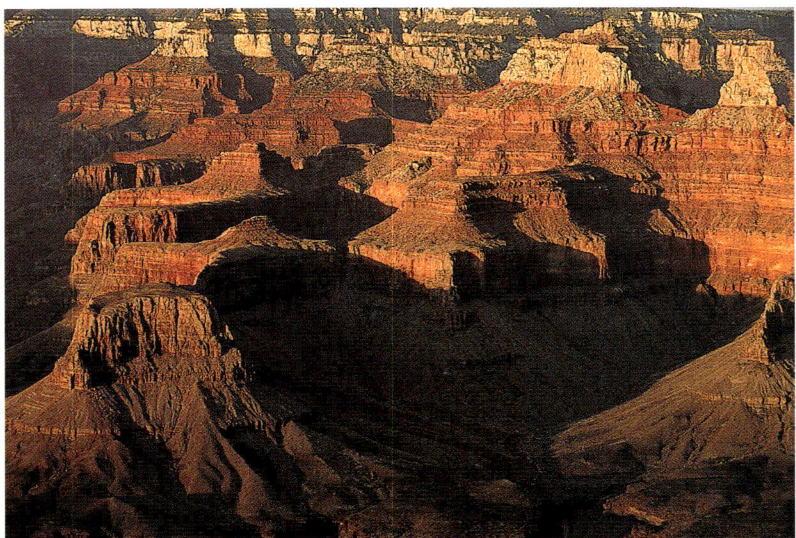

Late in the day, the sun creates beautiful patterns in the canyon. Don't overlook these opportunities. Long telephoto lenses are best for scanning inside the canyon.

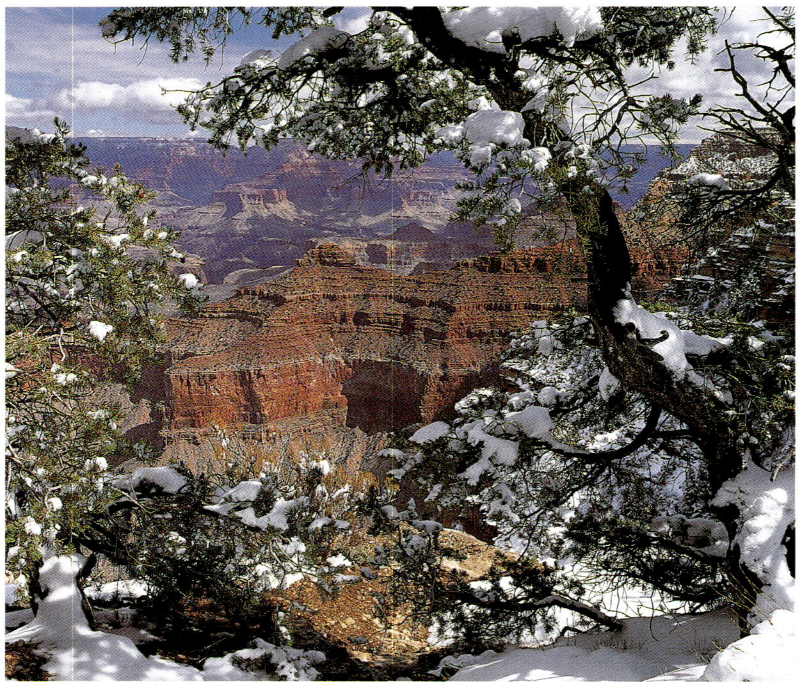

The Grand Canyon, like most other national parks, has been shot over and over. While scouting locations for the next morning's shoot, I found this spot. I felt it held promise, but after an overnight snowfall, the scene became exceptional.

carved three canyons along its route, Cataract Canyon, Glen Canyon and the Grand Canyon. The latter is the most famous and with good reason. The Grand Canyon is 1,904 square miles in size and the Colorado River flows 277 miles through its deep colorful ancient walls of rock and one of the most incredible examples of natures ability to carve and shape the earth through erosion.

The Grand Canyon was unknown by most until after the Civil War. Major John Wesley Powell, a Civil War veteran, changed all this after his exploration of the Grand Canyon by wooden boat on the Colorado River. His exploration built curiosity among mining companies to further explore the canyon for mineral resources such as copper and asbestos. As settlements began to develop along the canyon rim, settlers realized tourism would be much more profitable than the expensive explorations of mining in such a rugged environment. The Grand Canyon received its first protection status as a forest reserve, then as a national monument and by 1919 became a national park, three years after the establishment of the National Park Service.

Grand Canyon National Park is divided into three regions, the Grand Canyon North Rim, the Grand Canyon South Rim and The Grand Canyon West Rim. The South Rim is the most visited (it receives 90 percent of all visitors) of the three regions and has been developed with roads running along the rim that offer spectacular views of the canyon. The North Rim is two hundred miles away by road and attracts visitors for its remoteness and lack of development. The North Rim is closed during winter. The entrance is typically closed from mid October till mid May, but much depends on weather. The views on the North Rim are equally impressive. The West Rim is located on both the Hualapai Reservation and the Havasupai Reservation. The West Rim is very much isolated from developed roads and requires an eight-mile hike on foot or horseback.

PHOTOGRAPHER'S VIEW

Grand Canyon National Park is incredibly huge and one can easily spend a week or two exploring the grandeur and beauty of the canyon. After a couple of days photographing in Grand Canyon National Park, you might start to feel that many of your photos are starting to look alike. For this reason, I really believe your visit will be better served if you combine it with other destinations in canyon country or those discussed in chapter eleven. I'm not going to spend much time talking about the Grand Canyon because I believe it speaks for itself, and unless you decide to spend time hiking into the canyon or rafting the Colorado, you will pretty much be confined to the overlooks along the park road.

The Grand Canyon is well known for its heavy haze, which can spoil even the prettiest of photos. The Grand Canyon can be covered in haze anytime of year, but you can minimize your frustration if you are out well before sunrise and out after sunset. I find it very interesting how many people crowd the overlooks at sunrise but take off five minutes afterward. Don't be discouraged when you see so many people out as early as you. The haze is much more workable when the sun is lower in the sky and therefore providing more opportunities to shoot on a day that will be much wasted after the sun rises higher in the sky. The early and late light will also create nice shadows and patterns which should not be overlooked.

The South Rim

The South Rim of the Grand Canyon offers the best opportunities to maximize your photography time. There are many overlooks along two roads, Desert View Road and Hermit Road (formally known as East and West Rim roads, respectively). These overlooks will provide plenty of photo opportunities and should satisfy your shutter finger. Look for more than just an overall view of the canyon, as there are many possibilities beyond the grand vista. I suggest using the good morning and evening light to photograph patterns, shapes and more intimate views of the canyon. Look at your compositions both vertically and horizontally. If you vary your lenses and use every focal length you have, you'll be sure to find an image hidden within the maze of canyon walls. Exploit every avenue, and you'll walk away happy.

Constant crowds at the South Rim make shuttle service there a must. The Park Service has plans to ease congestion and improve the park experience by eliminating private vehicles around the overlooks on the South Rim. A bus-based system would transport people to these overlooks, which could inconvenience photographers hoping to hit more than one or two locations during the good light. The sys-

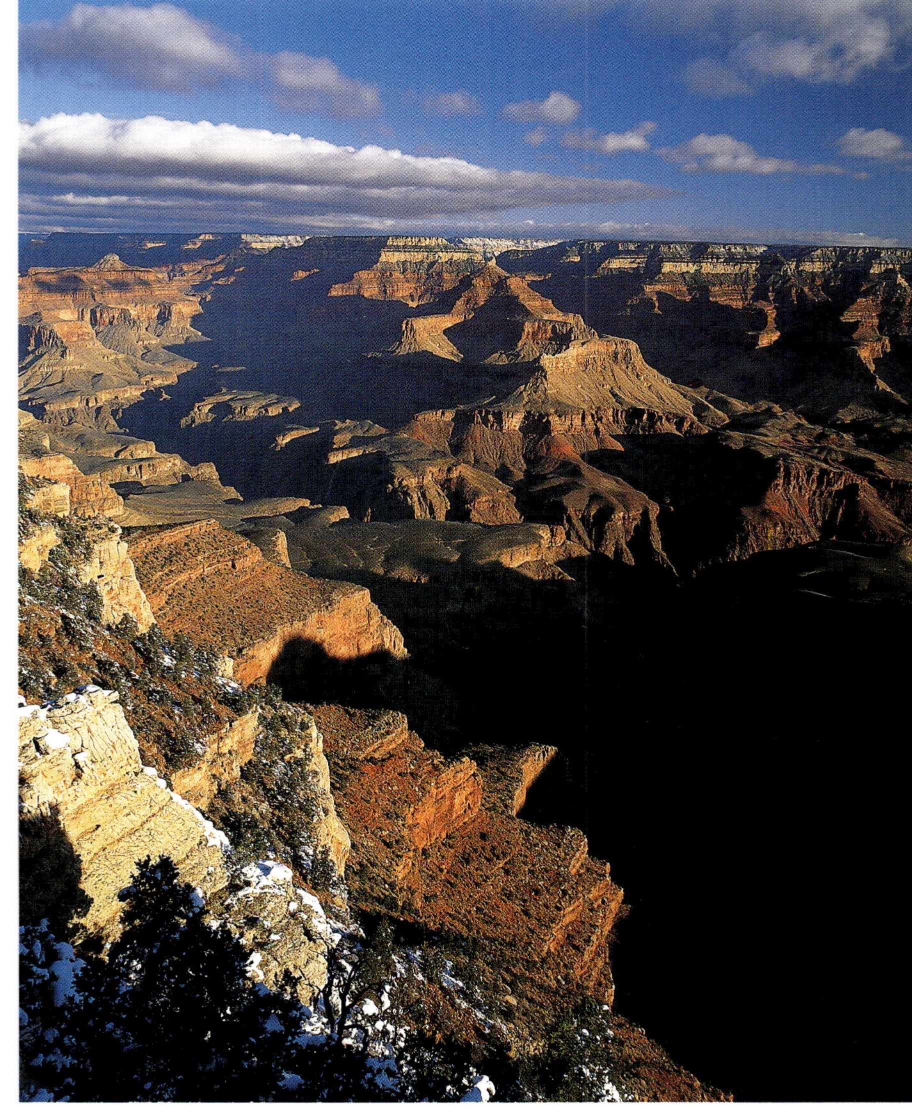

The early and late hours of the day provide the best conditions for shooting into the canyon from the rim. During the afternoon the light is flat, and you lose detail in the land formations.

tem is currently on hold as officials examine future increases in visitors. For more on the future of South Rim transit, part of the park's General Management Plan, see <www.nps.gov/grca/transit/index.htm>. For details on the current shuttle system, see <www.nps.gov/grca/grandcanyon/trip_planner/transportation.htm>.

The North Rim

There is good news and bad news about the North Rim. The good news is you can avoid public transportation and most of the crowds, and the vistas are equally impressive. The bad news is the elevation gain of one thousand feet brings colder temperatures and heavy snowfall. To get to the North Rim, follow Highway 89A or State Route 389 to Jacob Lake, then take Highway 67. The road to the North Rim is typically closed from mid October to mid May, but much depends on the weather. This time frame doesn't coincide with the window I am suggesting for Coyote Buttes and the locations in chapter eleven, so you'll likely be confined to the South Rim.

The West Rim

The West Rim of the Grand Canyon is isolated with no easy access to other vistas or other major features. You can travel to Havasu Canyon by paved road but will encounter some hiking. The main reason most photogra-

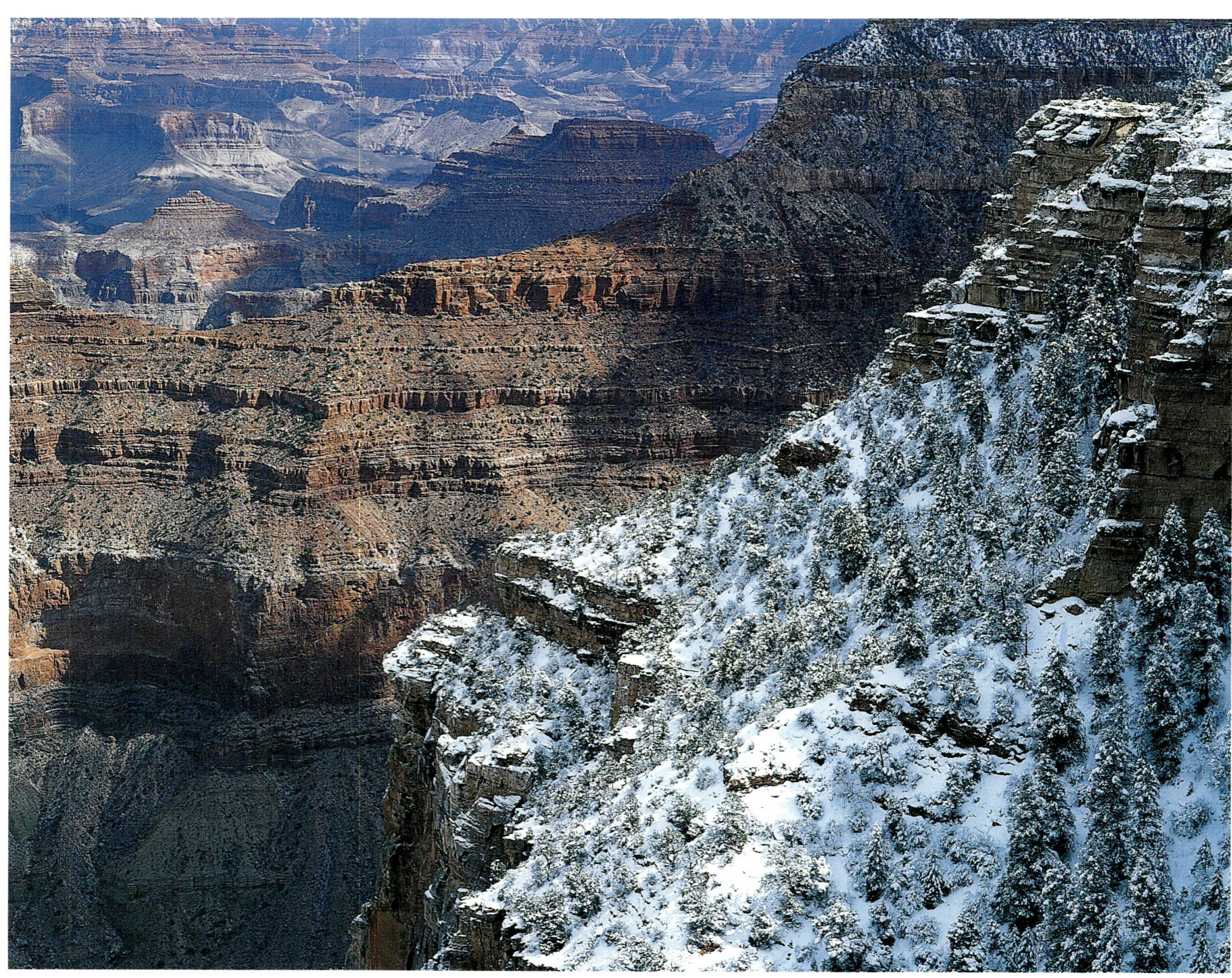

Early spring in the Grand Canyon gives you the best chance for clear skies and a fresh snowfall. Haze is much more common throughout the summer and decreases your chances of a productive shoot.

phers venture into the western region of Grand Canyon National Park is to photograph Havasu Falls and its blue-green pools. To reach this waterfall you'll hike eight miles in on foot or horseback. This area is managed by the Havasupai Indian Reservation.

WHEN TO GO

The early spring and late autumn months are much cooler and provide the best opportunity for a clear sky. March to mid May should allow you to enjoy these clear skies, but you might encounter some snow cover on the South Rim in early March and, rarely, into early April. The further you get into May, the better your chances of getting hazy skies.

TIME REQUIREMENTS

I think two full days in the Grand Canyon should allow you to spend quality time photographing along the overlooks on the South Rim. The new public transportation should not put too much of a strain on your time and creativity. You'll need to enter into the shooting situation with an open mind, accept the limitations and make the most of your time on location. If you plan on spending time hiking into the canyon, you'll need several days, as you will be spending at least one night in the canyon.

NEED TO KNOW

There are several hotels both in and outside Grand Canyon National Park at the South Rim. Don't wait until you arrive to reserve lodging. It's best to arrange lodging at least three to four months in advance if you plan to stay in Tusayan and a year in advance if you want to stay in one of the park lodges. Finding lodging a few weeks before your arrival is unlikely. Lodging on the North and the West rims is extremely scarce if not nonexistent, but camping is an option.

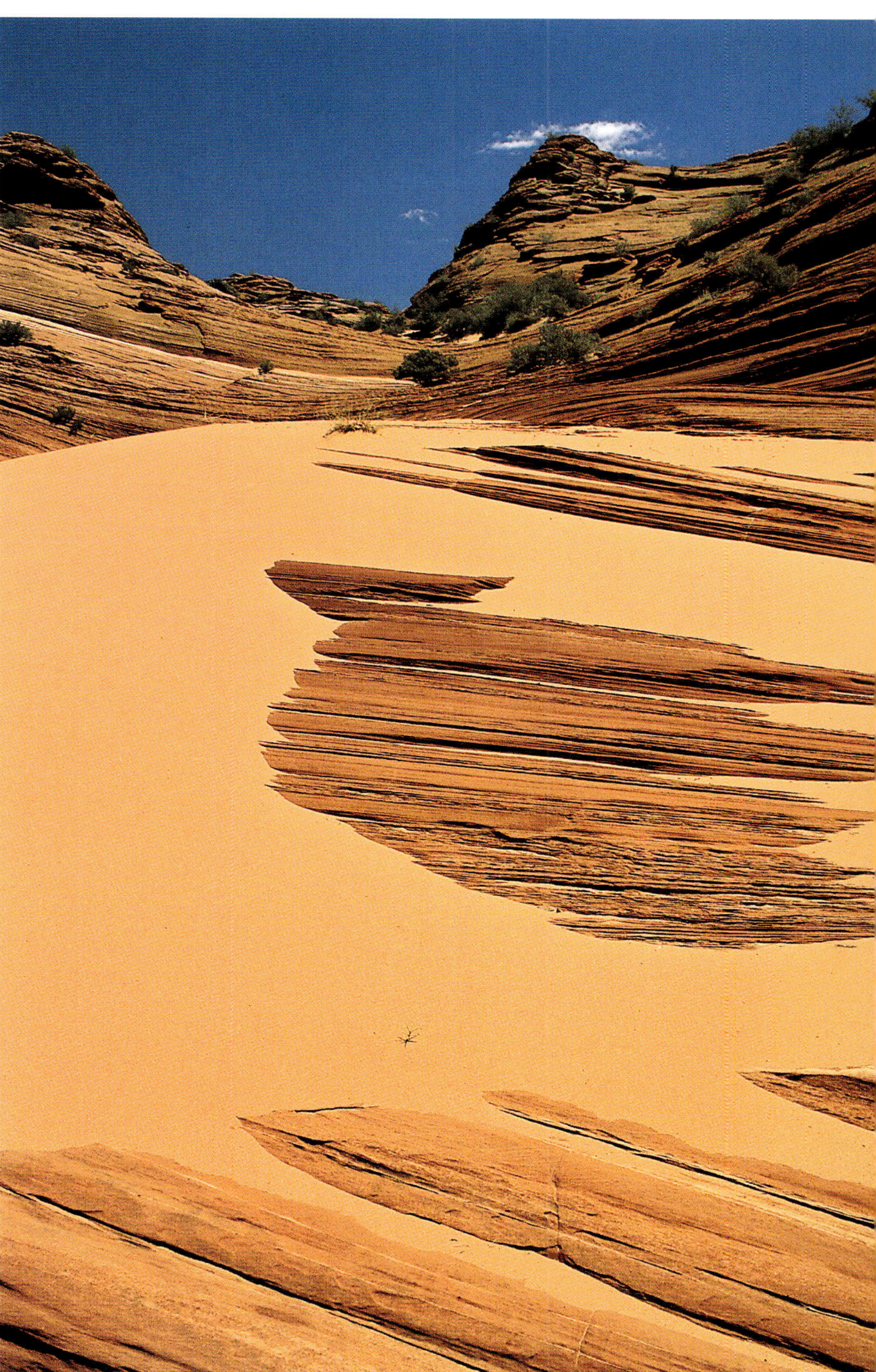

I found this scene hidden in a tight valley covered in pink sand. I liked the way the sandstone protruded in different directions, and I used its contours to lead the viewer through the composition.

Coyote Buttes

Photographers use so many names for Coyote Buttes—Paria Canyon, Vermilion Cliffs Wilderness, Vermilion Cliffs National Monument, the Wave and others—that it's easy to get confused. All of these names are correct, but the specific location most photographers

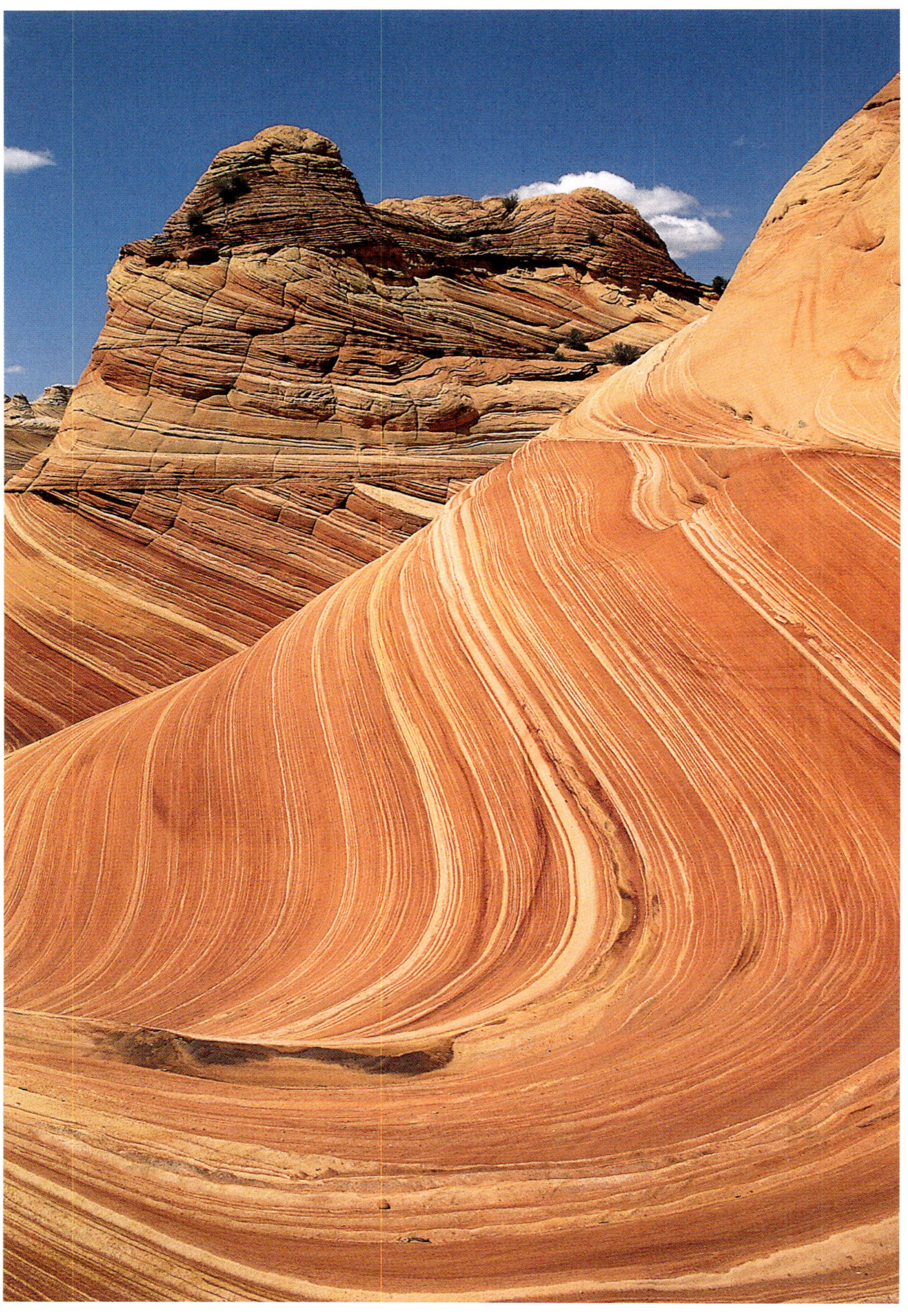

Watch for merges (two elements appearing to touch each other) in your composition. Although these two elements merge, I feel the direction change of the lines and the color change from butte to butte hold this composition together.

speak of is Coyote Buttes North, which is located in the Paria Canyon/Vermilion Cliffs Wilderness Area, part of Vermilion Cliffs National Monument. This rugged preserve consists of 90,000 acres shared by Utah (20,000 acres) and Arizona (70,000 acres). The Arizona portion of this wilderness is part of the larger 293,000-acre Vermilion Cliffs National Monument, comprising the Paria Plateau, the colorful Vermilion Cliffs and the Paria River Canyon with elevations ranging from thirty-one hundred feet to seventy-one hundred feet. Although there are many photographic opportunities within the national monument and wilderness area, I will focus on Coyote Buttes.

PHOTOGRAPHER'S VIEW

The main attraction here is the Wave, a geological formation that has made the area well known in the photo community: a landscape of swirling yellow, pink, orange and red sandstone formations caused by climatic changes. This fragile environment looks much like a candy maker's shop of taffy-shaped cones and colorful swirls twisted into beautiful shapes. Coyote Buttes consists of two regions, Coyote Buttes North and Coyote Buttes South. Coyote Buttes South is accessible only by four-wheel drive vehicles.

Coyote Buttes and the Vermilion Cliffs National Monument in general are fragile environments that need to remain controlled to some degree in order to protect this fascinating landscape. The Bureau of Land Management has limited the number of people allowed in the Coyote Buttes North area to ten people per day. I suggest registering for a permit five to six months in advance through the BLM's Web site <https://www.paria.az.blm.gov/index.html>. The site also links to the calendar of open dates and the number of slots open for each day. Of course you can't predict the weather six months in advance, and unfortunately you can't register for a permit for two consecutive days. But if you plan your visit for the spring or autumn, your chances of a clear sky are pretty good.

Getting to Coyote Buttes requires a three-mile hike with no clear trail. A worn path over the soft sandstone is becoming visible, but there is no developed trail. You can get a map from the BLM offices in St. George or Kanab, Utah. Bring plenty of water with you and enough food to help maintain your energy for the day. There are no waste facilities, so you'll need to pack out what you pack in.

Don't complicate your hike with a lot of unnecessary equipment. One or two lenses and a camera body are really all you need. Any wide-angle lens of at least 28mm will work, but a 28–70mm wide-angle zoom is ideal. A polarizer and warming filter round out the equipment you need. If you wouldn't think of going in with only one lens, then I suggest another wide-angle (wider than the 24mm).

Most photographers' goal is to make it to the Wave, but there's much more to the area. After crossing the sandy wash about three-quarters of a mile into your hike, you'll start to see swirled and sculpted sandstone. Every direction holds a photo opportunity. Since you'll want to be at the Wave in early morning or late afternoon and have a three-mile return hike, you have two less-than-ideal options:

1. Begin your hike in the dark.
2. Return to your car in the dark.

If you're not familiar with the area, I don't recommend returning in the dark.

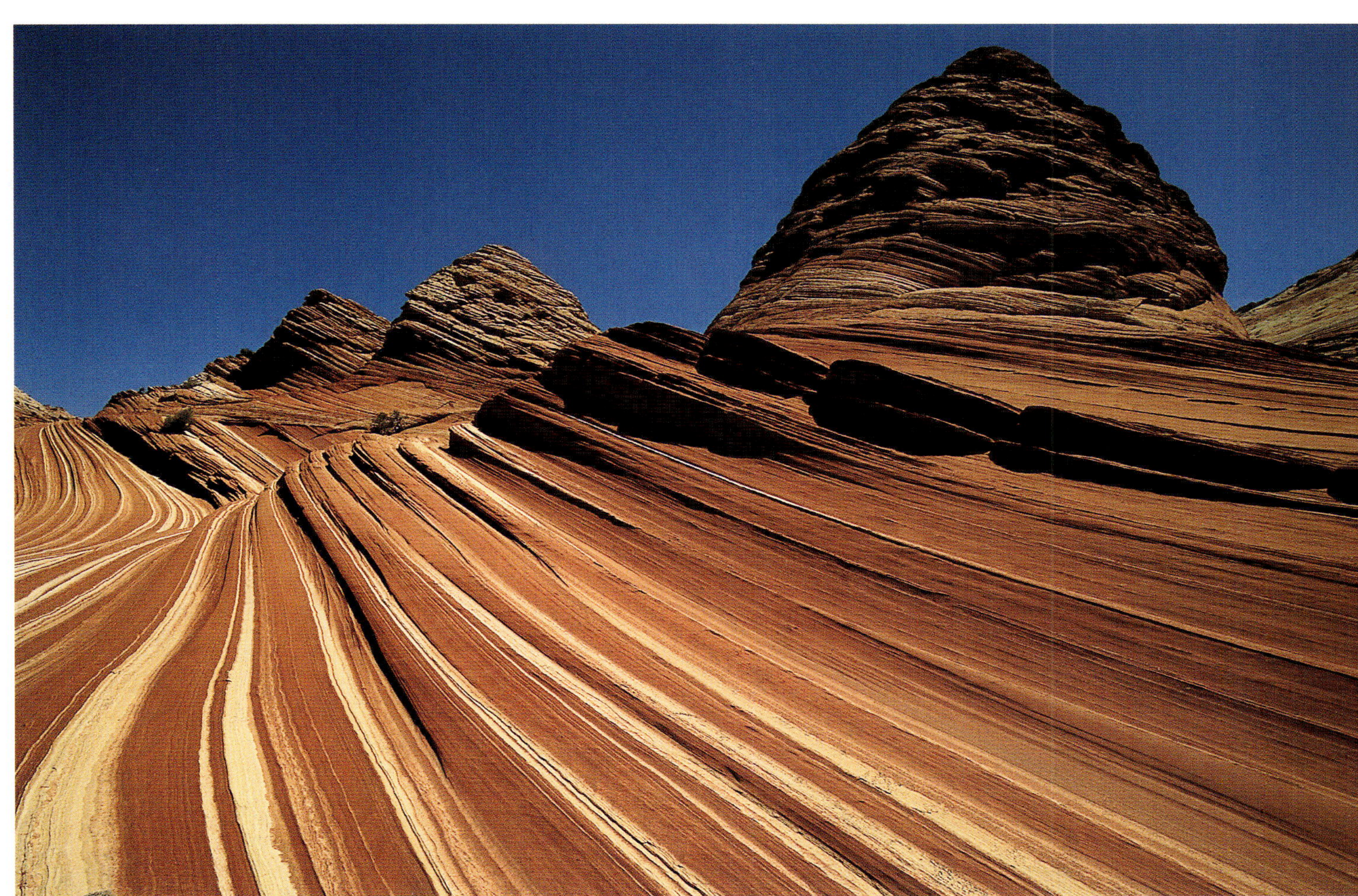

Coyote Buttes is a wonderland of multi-colored sandstone formations. These beautiful lines can be used effectively as foreground subjects to lead the viewer into the picture.

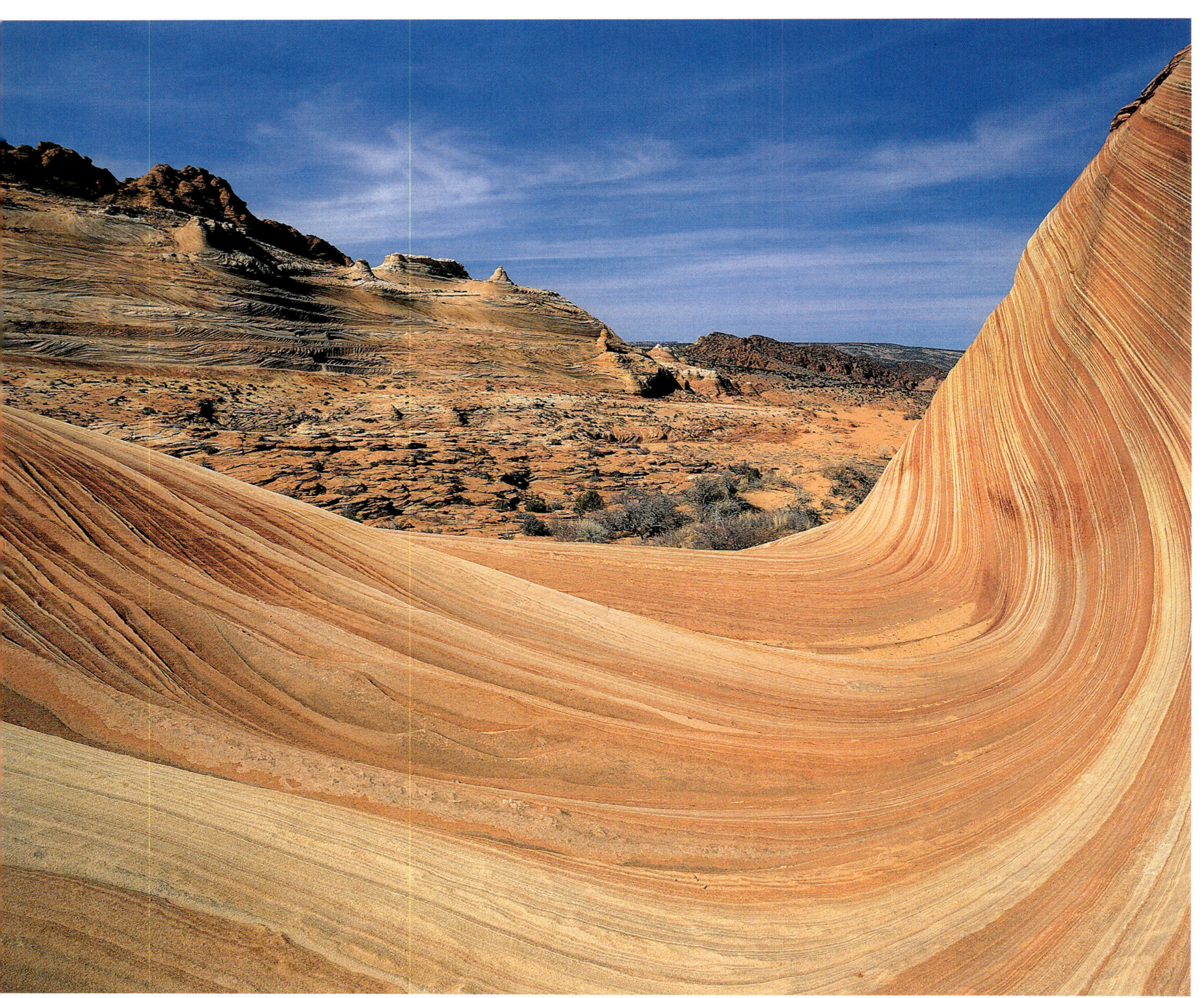

It's hard to be on location during both the morning light and late-afternoon light, but it's still doable if you start out early. Allow at least two hours to hike from the trailhead to Coyote Buttes, and another two for the return.

To maximize opportunities without jeopardizing your safety, I recommend beginning your hike just before first light. The first three-quarters of mile is on a well-defined, sandy path. The going is slow, and once you cross over the wash, you will use a firm sandstone surface for the remainder of the hike, but then the trail disappears. By the time you hit sandstone, you should have enough light to walk confidently. If you hike directly to the Wave, you'll have plenty of good morning light left to work the area.

Consider taking a break to wait out the harsh midday light before you shoot on the return trip. Begin at least three to four hours before sunset, and you'll get several hours of good late-afternoon light and still arrive back before dark.

WHEN TO GO

Spring and fall are best. As with other Southwest locations, summers are hot, and Coyote Buttes is too dangerous to attempt if you're not accustomed to hiking in this kind of climate and terrain. Try to time your trip here with the Grand Canyon and places covered in chapter eleven.

TIME REQUIREMENTS

Because of permit restrictions, you'll be limited to one day in Coyote Buttes. This should be plenty of time for most photographers. I sometimes wish I could have two days, but I've gotten plenty of good images from one-day visits. Normally I'd never tell you to pass up a photo op, but you'll be pressed for time when hiking to Coyote Buttes for the best light. If you do want to photograph on the way there, keep it to a minimum.

NEED TO KNOW

Page, Arizona, is the best location for lodging when planning a trip to Coyote Buttes. Allow at least forty-five minutes to get to the trailhead—eight miles of the drive is on a dirt road. I suggest driving to the trailhead the day before to familiarize you with the road and make finding the trailhead in the dark easier. If you're combining a Coyote Buttes photo shoot with the slot canyons, Page is an ideal location.

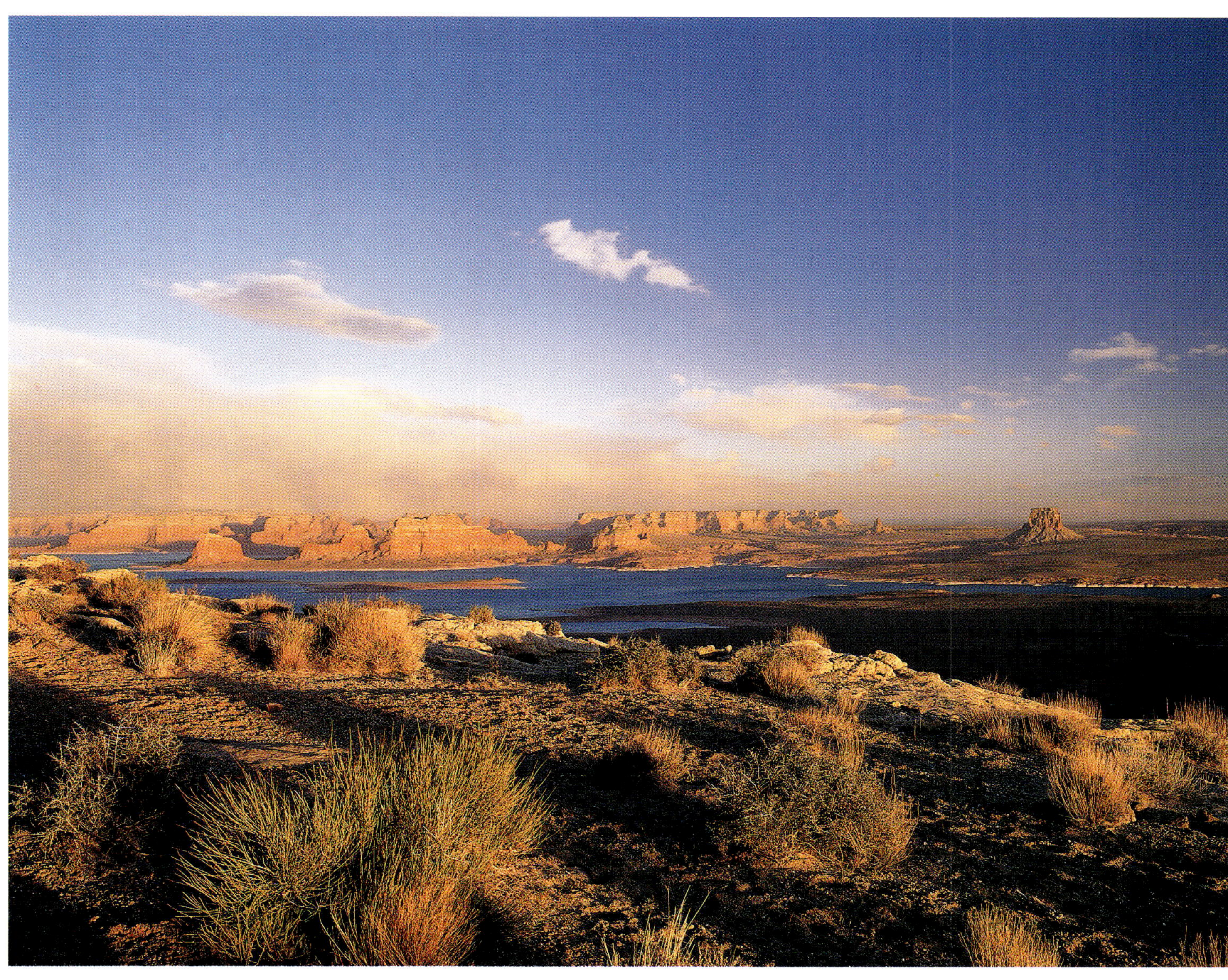

Lake Powell is just west of Page. Good research will yield opportunities others would pass up,such as this shot of Gunsight Butte. There is a lot of potential for photography around Lake Powell if you know where to go.

Itinerary: Grand Canyon National Park and Coyote Buttes

Hitting the Grand Canyon and Coyote Buttes should take you about a week (two travel days and four shooting days). You can also combine them with the locations listed in chapter eleven for a ten- to fourteen-day trip. See page 117 for a suggested itinerary for Color Country. The Grand Canyon itinerary is based on an airport arrival in Phoenix. Allow four to five hours to drive to Grand Canyon National Park. You might not have time to get any shooting in, but try to pick up some additional information at one of the visitor centers. (Canyon View Information Plaza, at Mather Point, and Desert View Information Center, near the east entrance, are both on the South Rim.) You'll want to find out how the park shuttle system works as soon as you arrive.

I recommend reserving two full days for photography on the South Rim and leaving the Grand Canyon on the third morning. You won't want to miss the wonderful evening light on the second day, and driving to Page in the dark can be dangerous. Drunken drivers are a problem on these roads at night. Arrange lodging for one or two evenings in Page. This will give you a full day in Coyote Buttes. You will need a good night's rest before hiking into Coyote Buttes and prepare for a very long day. Keep in mind you will need a permit to hike into Coyote Buttes. From Coyote Buttes allow an additional three hours to get to Phoenix.

photographer's choice

CANYONLANDS NATIONAL PARK in Utah is the closest you'll find that offers vistas of an incredible maze of canyon walls and buttes. Two smaller locations affording similar experiences are DEAD HORSE POINT STATE PARK, just a few miles outside of Canyonlands, and COLORADO NATIONAL MONUMENT, near Grand Junction, Colo. [Canyonlands National Park, www.nps.gov/cany; Dead Horse Point, http://parks.state.ut.us/parks/www1/dead.htm; Colorado National Monument, www.nps.gov/colm]

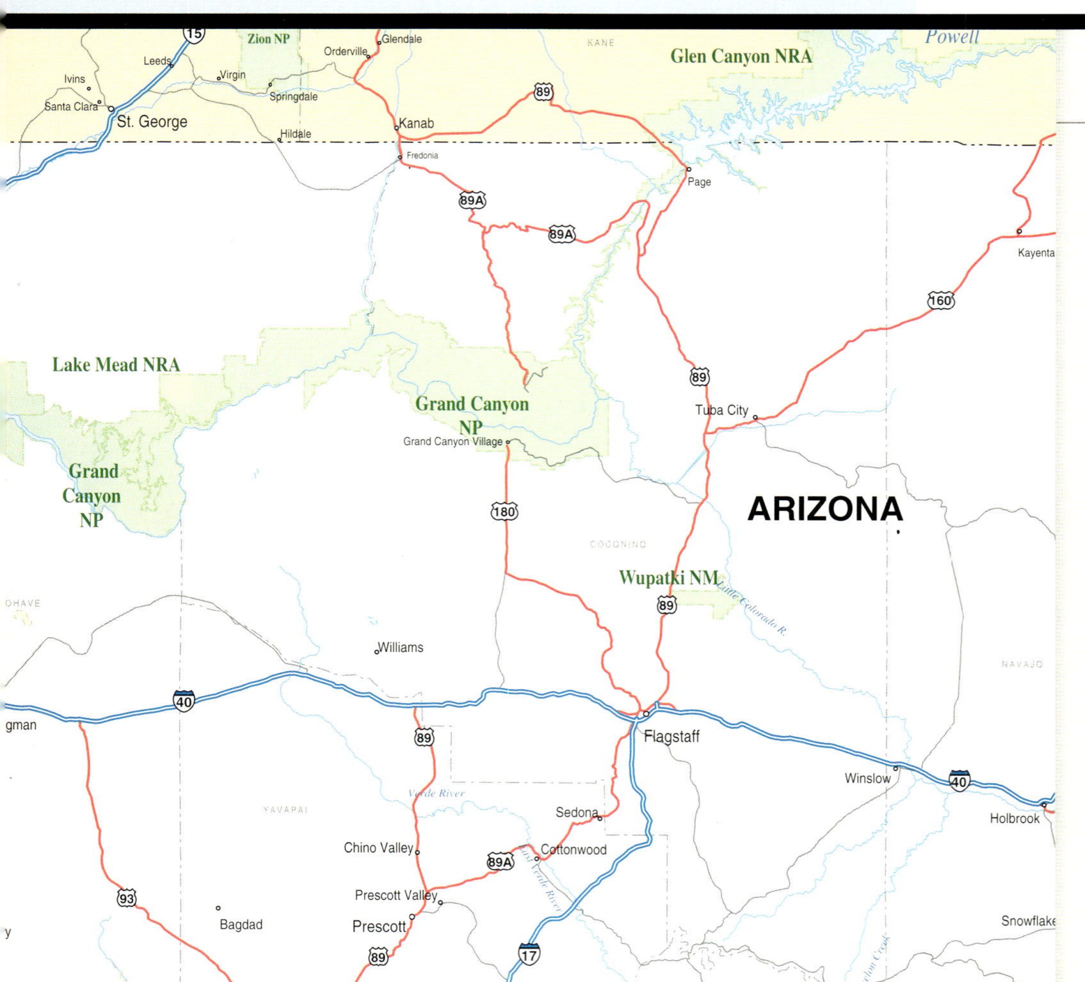

directions

FROM PHOENIX TO GRAND CANYON NATIONAL PARK:

- I-17 north to Flagstaff; take Highway 180 north to Grand Canyon National Park.

GRAND CANYON NATIONAL PARK TO PAGE:

- State Route 64 east to Highway 89 north to Page.

PAGE TO WIRE PASS TRAILHEAD (COYOTE BUTTES):

- Follow Highway 89 west toward Kanab. Turn onto House Rock Valley Road; the road is unmarked but is between mile markers 25 and 26, approximately 34 miles west of Page. Wire Pass trailhead is 7.9 miles from Highway 89.

PAGE TO PHOENIX AIRPORT:

- Highway 89 south to I-17 south.

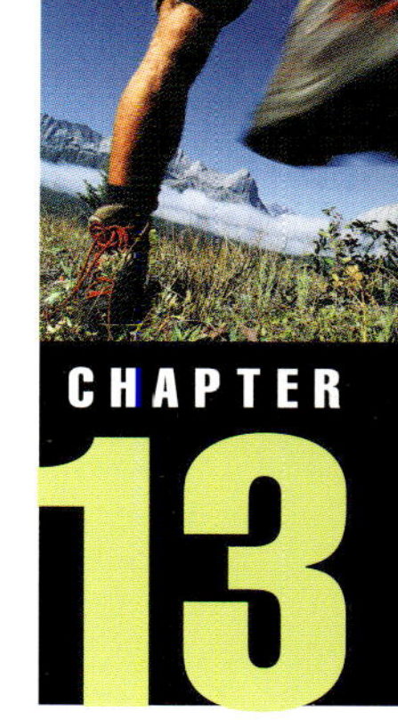

CHAPTER 13

Olympic National Park

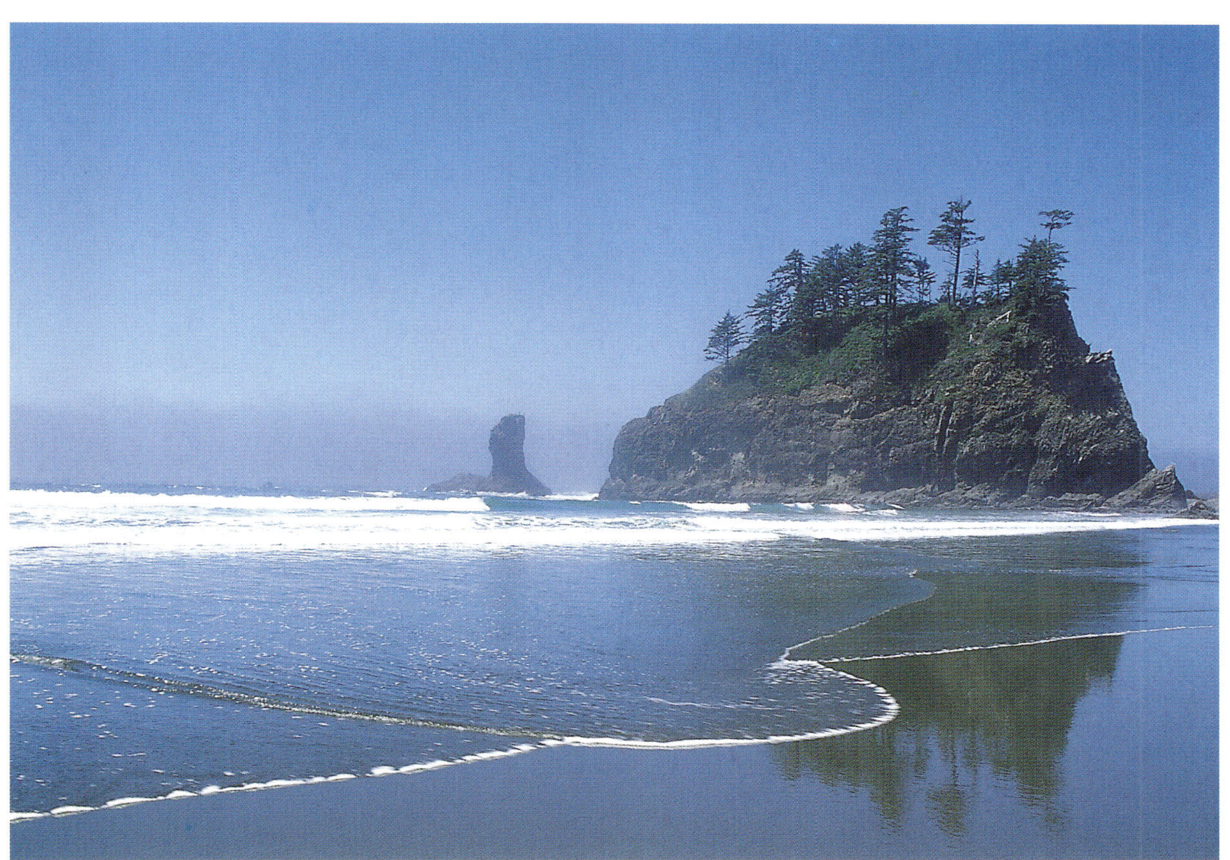

Olympic National Park sits on the rugged Pacific coast bordered by old-growth forests and also rises to the east to just under 8,000 feet at Mount Olympus. In 1938 Franklin Roosevelt signed legislation creating Olympic National Park, a true wilderness and a wonderful place to refresh the mind and soul. Olympic occupies much of the Olympic Peninsula, as well as a fifty-seven-mile strip of the peninsula's western coast. Aside from coastline, the park consists of the Olympic Mountains and four types of forest: lowland, temperate rain forest, montane and subalpine. The park's diversity can leaving you scratching your head trying to de-

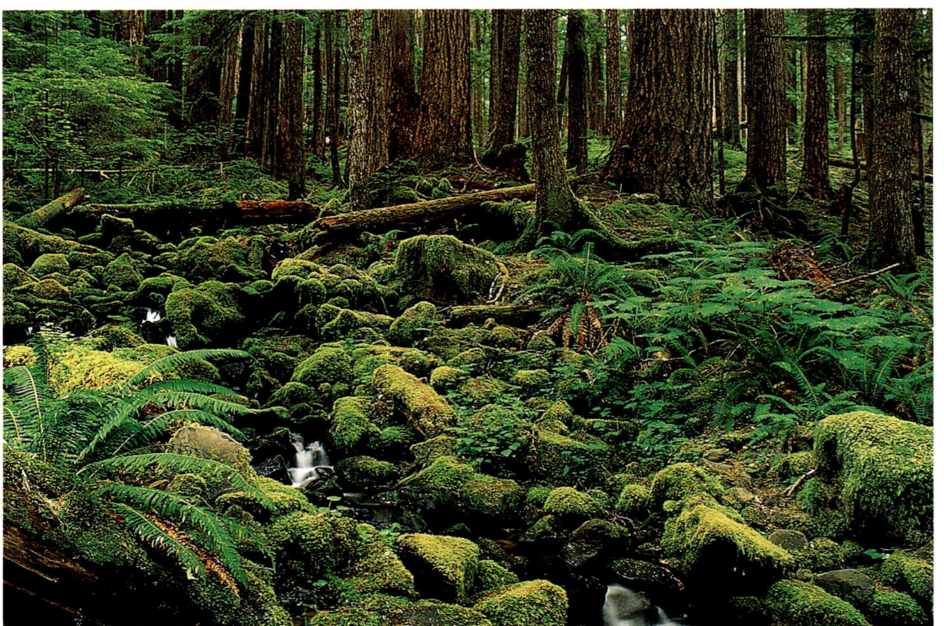

I chose an overcast day to photograph this rain forest scene in the Sol Duc region. Overcast created the soft, even lighting I needed to achieve a pleasing image. If I had chosen a sunny day to shoot this scene, I would have had an exposure nightmare. Sunny conditions (contrasty situations) would have had me exposing either for the shaded areas or the sunlit areas. Whichever I would have decided on, the other would have been grossly over- or underexposed.

cide what to shoot first.

One can experience the wealth and beauty of the sea by exploring tide pools and watch the rainbow of colors in these pools come to life. The forest zones in Olympic National Park are as lush and vibrant as any along the Pacific coast. The best known of these forests is the Hoh Rain Forest, a temperate rain forest. Temperate rain forests are found at low elevations along the Pacific coast and in western-facing valleys of the peninsula, where there is an abundance of rain, summer fogs and moderate temperatures. The Hoh Rain Forest is what most people envision when they think of the forests in Olympic National Park: mosses and ferns draped over fallen trees lying beneath the towering Sitka Spruce. The Hoh Rain Forest is truly a magical experience. Another favorite forest area of many photographers is the Sol Duc region, a lowland forest. Lowland forests lie in the rain shadow and grow at low elevations and move inland. The lowland forest eventually gives way to the montane forest, which sits farther inland and receives more rain and colder temperatures. In the higher elevations, where temperatures are colder, snowfall is common, and growing seasons are shorter, subalpine forests take over. The lower portions of the subalpine forests might be thick, but they eventually thin and open up to alpine meadows.

PHOTOGRAPHER'S VIEW

I don't like to label one location as a favorite, but if I were forced to make a decision, Olympic National Park would probably be at the top of the list. There is so much to shoot here regardless of the weather or season. Olympic is a very large park, and most of it is dense forest with no easy access. Few roads penetrate the park, making it a great getaway from the everyday gridlock of city life and well-suited to the true explorer. I recommend taking your first day to drive the few roads that do exist and hike some of the trails to get acquainted with the park and see what's happening in different areas. Take notes as you scout. This one day of familiarizing yourself with the park will pay off later when you have to decide where to go.

Most people coming to Olympic National Park will arrive in the Port Angeles area, the largest town around and most popular park entrance. There is a great visitor center in Port Angeles [(360) 565-3130] just before you start your seventeen-mile journey up to Hurricane Ridge. Park rangers should be able to give you some idea about wildflower blooms and other happenings in the park but more importantly the five-day forecast along the coast and in the mountains. Use this information to help you make decisions on where to start your shooting. Take the time to look over books, postcards and other items pertaining to the park to help give you some ideas and hopefully get that creative mind working.

Most photographers come to Olympic

National Park wanting to shoot the coast, the rain forest and the mountains. This is possible during certain times of the year if the conditions are right, but be open-minded, and do your best with whatever the conditions allow. Don't try to force something to happen, such as going into the forest on a sunny day. You'll only end up frustrated and lose valuable shooting time. It can take awhile to get to different locations in this park. The end of June through most of July is the optimal time to photograph wildflowers in the subalpine meadows of Hurricane Ridge. This time is also a good bet on the coast for colorful sunsets, and possibly foggy mornings. You might get an overcast morning, or a heavy fog bank might settle in along the coast, providing that soft, diffused light you need to shoot the rain forest successfully.

If rain forest photography is your main reason for photographing in Olympic National Park, you're better off coming in May. The mountains aren't very pretty this time of year, but you might get a few good days on the coast. May typically brings showers, which will facilitate the conditions you need in the forest. The Hoh Rain Forest is the best known of the forest areas in Olympic, but I personally find it very challenging to photograph. Don't skip the Hoh Rain Forest—it is worth the visit regardless—but it might not result in your best photography from the park. Sol Duc is a cleaner-looking forest and much easier shoot. There are also some photogenic streams in the area, and Sol Duc Falls is an absolutely beautiful waterfall. Another worthy rain forest location is the Quinault River Valley along Graves Creek, on the south side of the park.

The Pacific Coast is very nice in Olympic, but if this is your main reason for visiting the park, consider hitting the Oregon Coast instead. I always photograph along the coast in Olympic, but I consider it a side trip on my visits in the park. The most accessible and

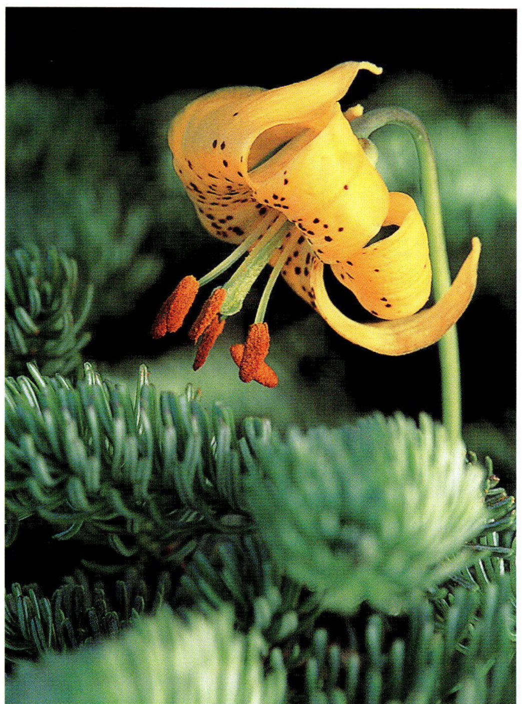

Close-up (macro) photography should be in every nature photographer's library. I shot this Columbia tiger lily with an inexpensive macro setup, an 80–200mm lens with a #25 extension tube. Extension tubes and a close-up diopter can be used together or independently to achieve different magnifications.

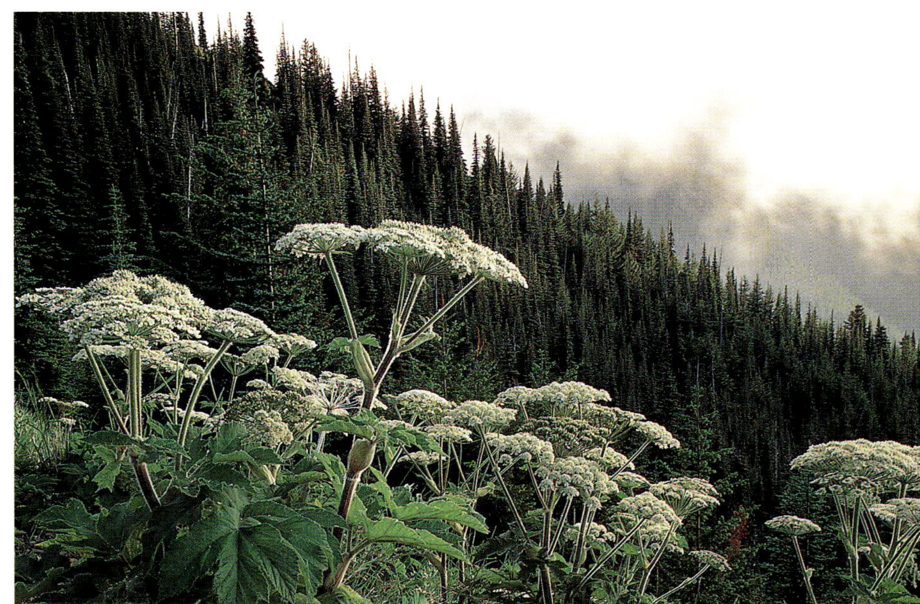

Avoid white skies when possible. White skies will typically draw the viewer's eye away from the subject. When you have no choice, try to minimize the sky or, as in this image, use an element that can balance or compete with the sky. The use of white cow parsnip here helps to hold the image together. It's also an inviting element, making it an effective foreground subject.

beautiful beaches in Olympic are Ruby Beach and Second Beach (not Beach 2, which lies much farther south). There is an easy one-mile hike into Second Beach. The most beautiful and probably most difficult beach to reach is Shi-Shi Beach, which is at the extreme northern edge of the park's coastal section, near the Makah Indian Reservation. There are some wonderful sea stacks and rock arches in the area. Any time of year when the sky looks good for a sunset, the coast is worth a visit. Morning shooting on the coast can also be good.

Most people take in the mountains in Olympic National Park at Hurricane Ridge. There is an incredible view of the surrounding Olympic range at the top of Hurricane Ridge, but there are several other wonderful vistas along the road before you reach the summit. Most visitors overlook the road out to the Obstruction Point trailhead. There are many wonderful photographic opportunities along this road and lots of wildflowers in July. The dirt road to Obstruction Point looks intimidating at the beginning, but it gets much better as it continues on. I enjoy finding areas that few visitors reach. Deer Park, on the park's east side and reachable from Port Angeles, is one such area. It holds some beautiful views of the distant mountains, and on a clear day, one can see the Strait of Juan De Fuca to the north. I wouldn't recommend driving the dirt road to Deer Park if narrow roads and heights make you nervous. This is a good place to check out after you've exhausted all the other mountain areas. George Wuerthner's book *Olympic: A Visitor's Companion* offers ideas for other places to visit.

Regardless of your photographic interests, there's something in the Pacific Northwest for you. Mt. Rainier National Park, covered in chapter fourteen, and the Columbia River

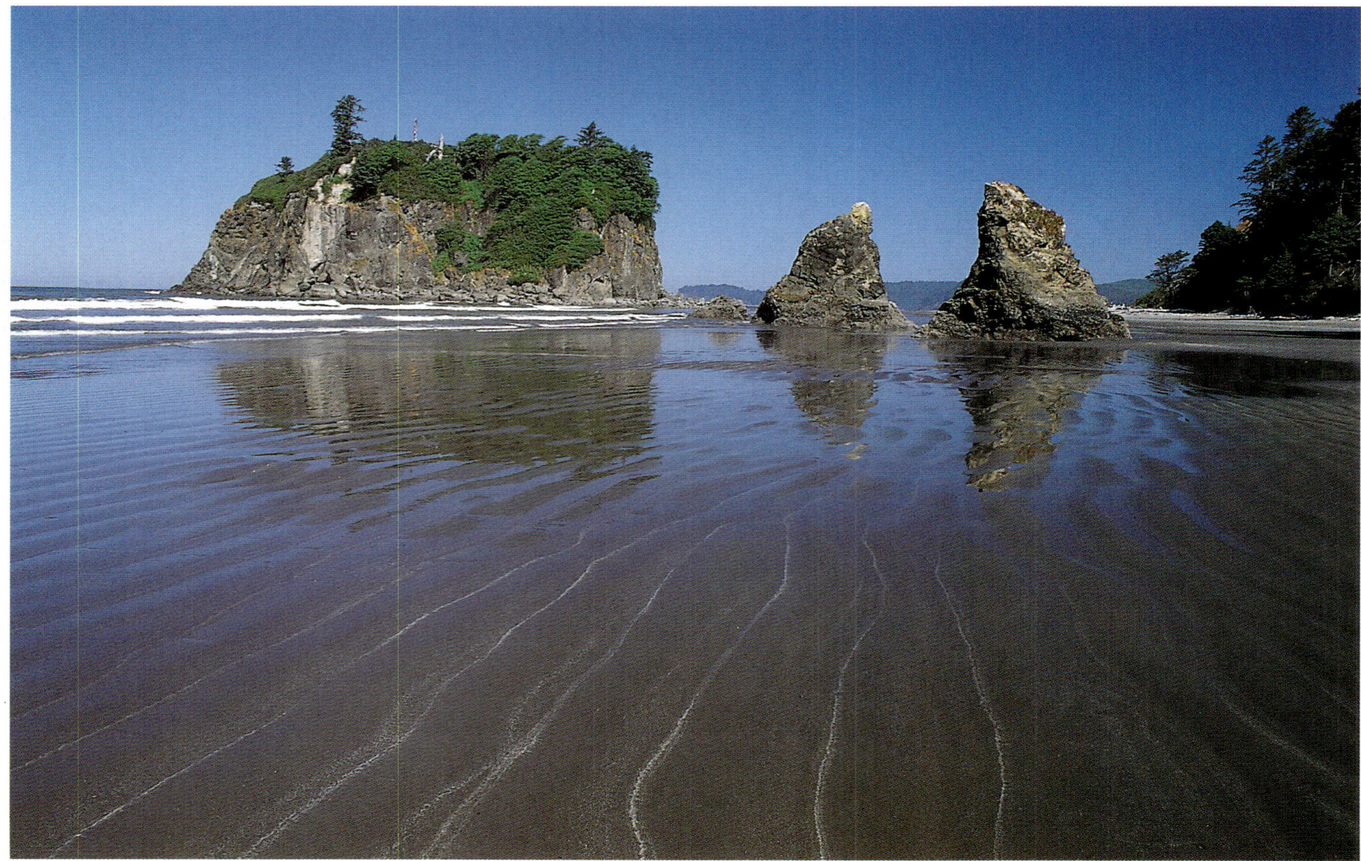

It is only natural to want to be on the western facing beaches in Olympic at sunset, but don't pass up the good light during the early morning hours. I used these subtle lines in the sand for my foreground, leading my viewer to the distant sea stacks on Second Beach. This clean simple composition opens the possibility of having text designed within and maybe used in the advertising markets.

Gorge, in chapter fifteen, are two such options. It would be impossible to cover every location in the Pacific Northwest in this book, as there are so many. With a little homework, you should have no problem finding side trips to add to your itinerary. Seattle offers some exciting urban photography opportunities and an outstanding zoo well worth a day or two of shooting. Several hours to the east of Seattle is one of my favorite agricultural regions in the country, the Poulouse, just south of Spokane. Portland, Oregon, has two absolutely wonderful gardens, The Japanese Garden and the Rhododendron Garden, if you happen to be in the area in April or May. Oregon has one of the best state park systems in the country. It would be hard to go wrong if you decide to take a side trip to one of these parks.

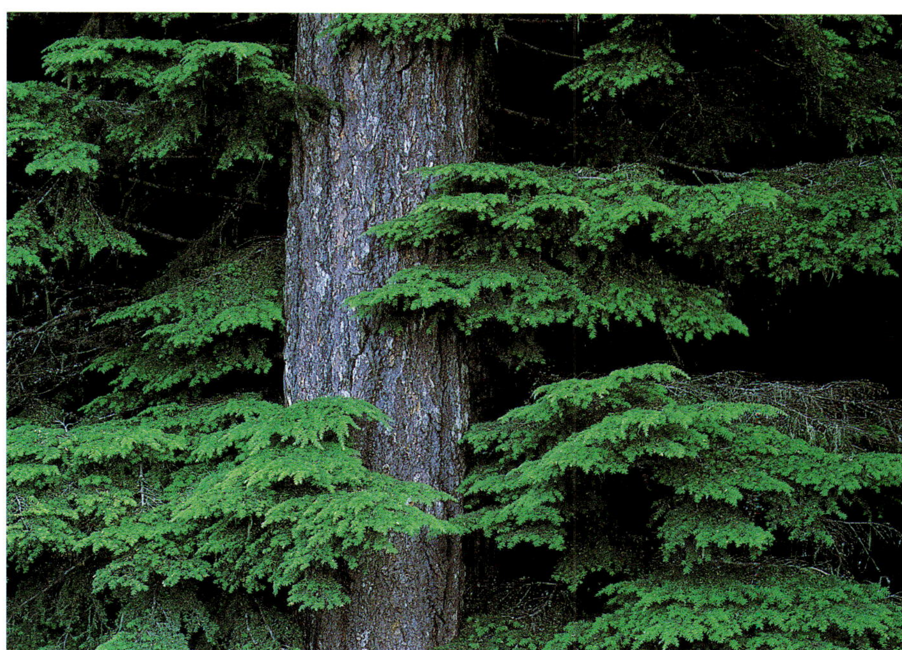

Patterns can be found almost anywhere. Look in the most ordinary of places and you'll find a unique pattern. Patterns can be repeating shapes, lines or even textures, and they open up a world often overlooked as photographic subjects, such as the branches and tree trunk of this western hemlock.

WHEN TO GO

If you're hoping to photograph the coast, the forest and the mountains, the overall best time to visit is the last week of June through the third week of July. Depending on the weather, you might have a lot of shooting time in the rain forests, but the coast and the mountains will be quite rewarding. I recommend two or three days on the western side of the park, which offers easy access to both the coast and the forests. If the forecast calls for a lot of sun during your stay and you really want to shoot the forest, start out very early in the morning, use a strong warming filter and watch out for sunlight filtering through the trees. You'll have some long exposures regardless of weather conditions, but don't be frightened of these exposures as long as foliage isn't swaying in the wind. Spend another two or three days in the mountain areas. Shooting in the mountains will be good both in the morning and late-afternoon light. On days with white skies, concentrate on little intimate scenery and wildflower photography.

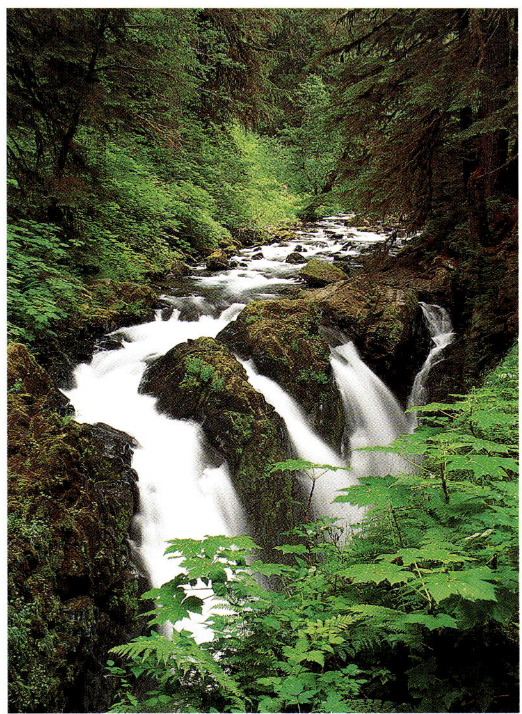

This image of Sol Duc Falls took me thirty minutes to shoot because the breeze created by the falls kept the vegetation swaying in the foreground. If you see a good shot, be patient. My patience paid off as this image sells on a regular basis.

If your interest is the rain forest, May is

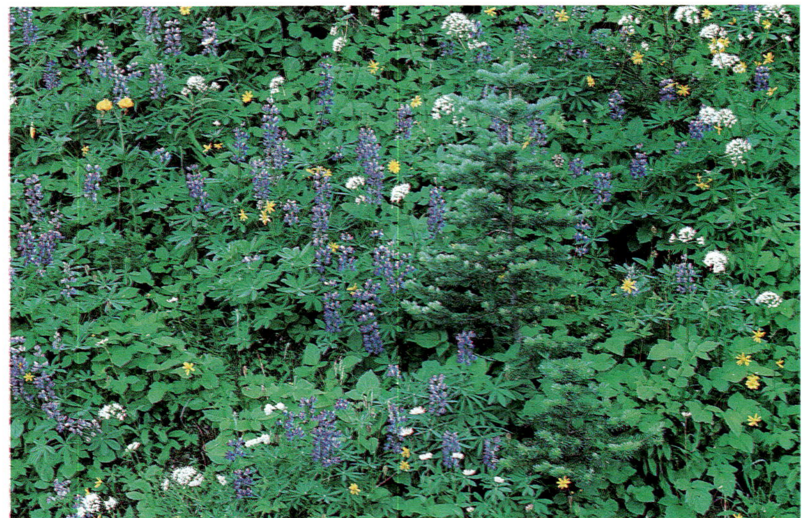

I enjoy creating visual challenges for the viewer. Subtle changes in tonalities sometimes require a second look to find the different elements that make up a composition. Here the two evergreen saplings blend in with the ground vegetation, and the lupine adds enough tonal change to draw the viewer's eye away from the trees.

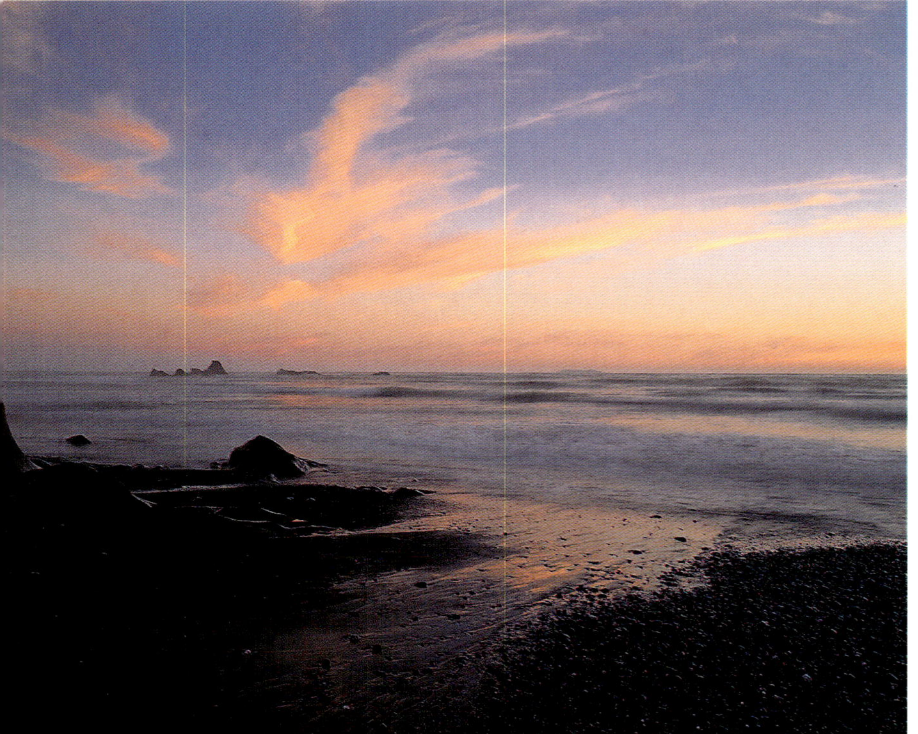

Sometimes you only need a good situation, not necessarily a good subject. The beautiful light from the setting sun became the subject.

your best bet, as the conditions are much more predictable for overcast skies. I suggest any time between the first week and the third week of May. Be prepared for anything from misty rain to downpours. You can really explore and shoot a lot of film in a four- or five-day visit. You might get a couple evenings on the coast, but I don't think a visit to the mountains is worth the trip for photography this time of year.

TIME REQUIREMENTS

Give yourself a minimum of four to six days to shoot in Olympic National Park, during the June and July window. I suggest spending two mornings in the forest and the evenings on the coast. Spend your remaining days in the mountains. Let the weather dictate where and when you shoot. Be ready to change your plans if necessary. You might also consider combining your Olympic trip with a visit to Mt. Rainier National Park. If you decide to shoot both parks, visit Olympic the third week of July, and drive to Mt. Rainier the last week of July. Don't try to shoot both parks in a one-week trip. Allow yourself a minimum of ten days. You will lose a good portion of one day driving between parks.

For rain forest photography, give yourself a minimum of four shooting days from the first week to the third week of May. This should provide you ample time to cover the Olympic's forests.

NEED TO KNOW

I recommend two towns for lodging and dining. If you're shooting along the coast or in the rain forests, you'll want to arrange lodging in Forks. There are several nice motels and a couple of nice dining locations in town. Forks's economy is split between tourism and logging, so you'll encounter a lot of big trucks while in town.

Port Angeles should be your location of

choice for mountain shooting. Port Angeles is larger than Forks with a greater variety of restaurants and lodging. There's also a nice shopping center and grocery store if you need supplies. Don't make the mistake of staying the whole time in Port Angeles if you plan to shoot the coast and forests. The drive is too long and tiring. After a long day of shooting on the western side of Olympic, it's dangerous to drive back to Port Angeles in the dark, especially while sharing the road with logging trucks.

Also, the camping in Olympic National Park is phenomenal. Olympic has some excellent developed campgrounds, or you might consider camping on Second Beach or one of the other beaches where camping is allowed—a great experience. Deer Park has some nice camping spots as well, but keep in mind that you can't get to Hurricane Ridge for a morning shoot from Deer Park. For more information on Olympic and the peninsula, go to <www.nps.gov/olym> or contact the Olympic Peninsula Visitor and Convention Bureau [(800) 942-4042; <www.olympicpeninsula.org>]. Ferries run from Seattle to the peninsula as well <www.wsdot.wa.gov/ferries>.

photographer's choice

If it's old-growth forests you're looking for, there are several great places along the Pacific coast. MUIR WOODS, just outside San Francisco, is a good place to start. Head north to REDWOOD NATIONAL PARK, then inland to SEQUOIA NATIONAL PARK. All of these California parks provide plenty of forests with huge towering trees. The OREGON COAST, especially the middle section, has some beautiful forests and is a great place to photograph the rugged Pacific coast. [Muir Woods, www.nps.gov/muwo; Redwood National Park, www.nps.gov/redw; Sequoia National Park, www.nps.gov/seki; Oregon coast, www.visittheoregoncoast.com]

directions

U.S. Highway 101 is the main road navigating around Olympic National Park. Several routes from the Seattle/Tacoma area will get you on U.S. Route 101. You can cross Puget Sound on one of several Washington State Ferries, or you can drive around Puget Sound. Travel time is approximately two and a half to three hours from Seattle/Tacoma to Port Angeles.

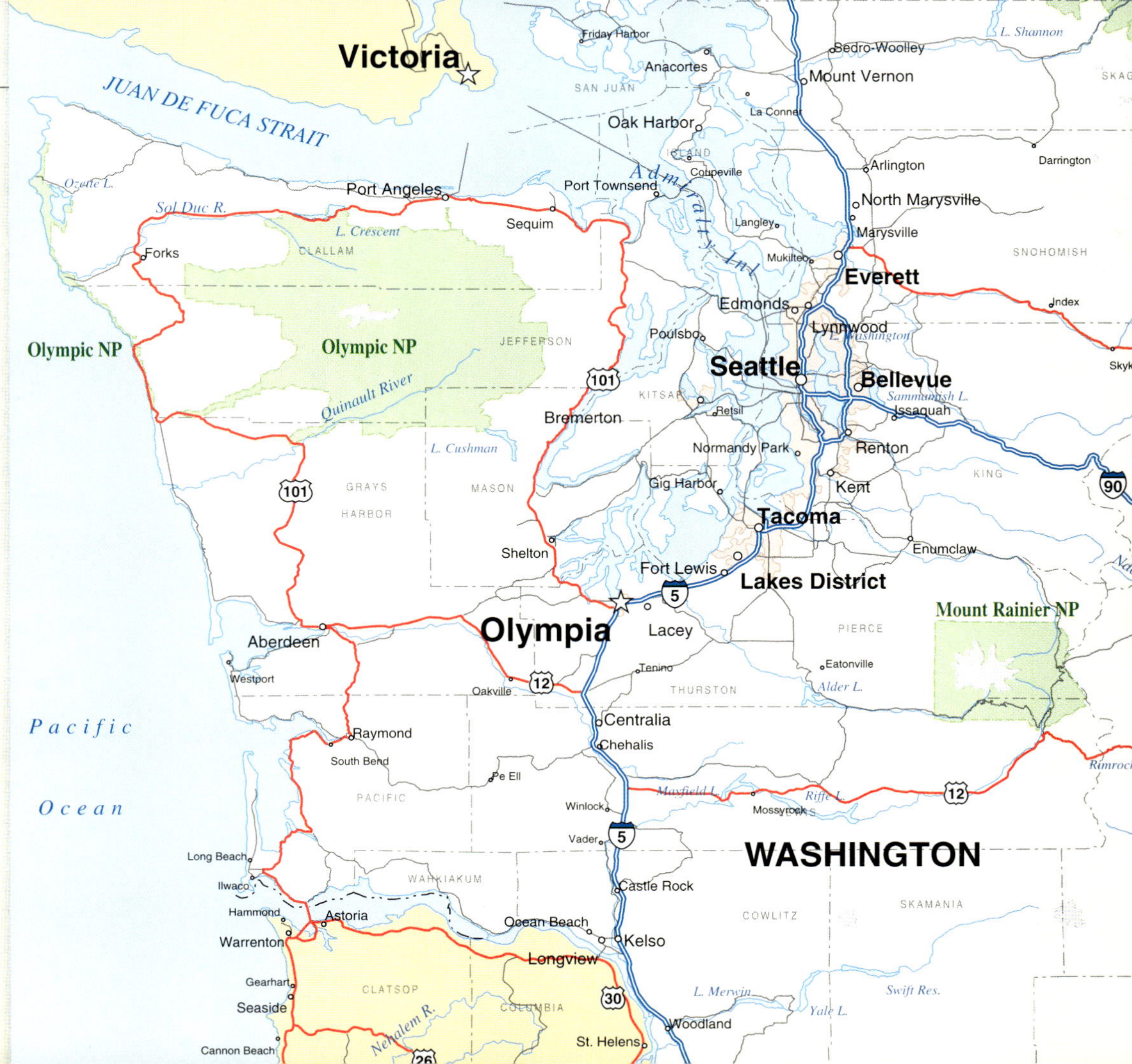

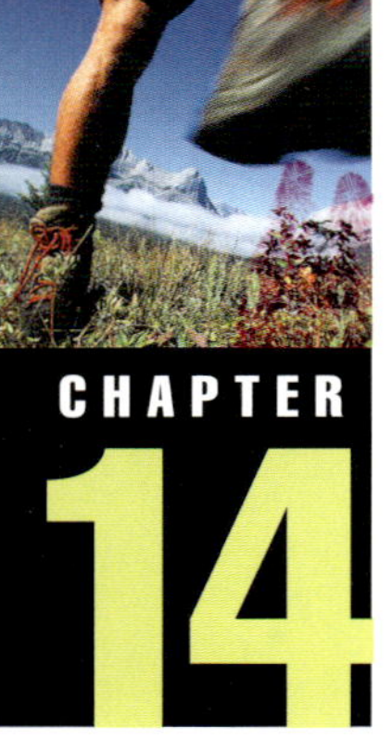

CHAPTER 14

Mt. Rainier National Park

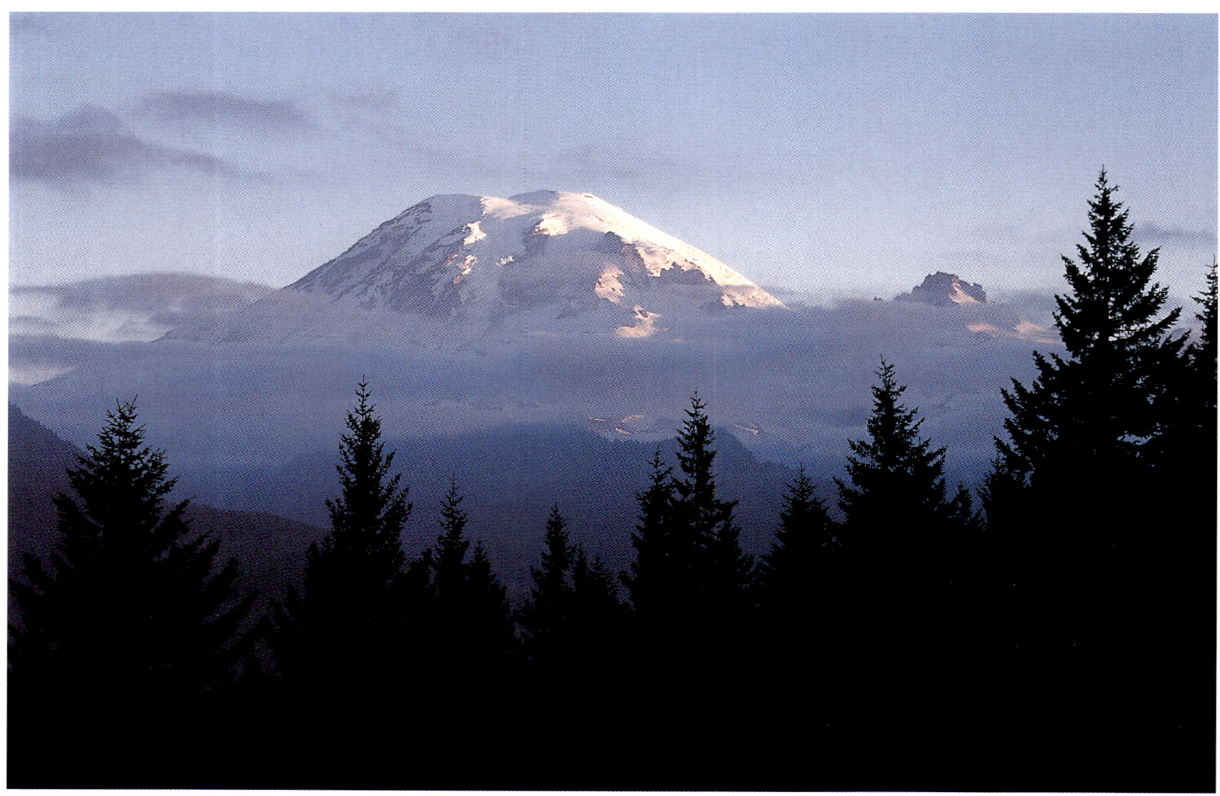

On the horizon just south of the steel and glass structures of Seattle lies the most celebrated mountain peak in the Pacific Northwest, Mt. Rainier. Mt. Rainier at 14,411 feet is the highest peak not only in the state of Washington but also in the entire Cascade Mountain Range. Mt. Rainier is an active volcano covered in perennial snowfields and glaciers. Glaciers cover nearly thirty-six square miles of the mountain's surface and help shape the geological features of Mt. Rainier. It is also the largest single-peak glacial system in the contiguous United States. The mountain is a protected landmark within the boundaries of Mt. Rainier National Park, established in 1899. Ninety-seven percent of the park's 235,000 acres is designated wilderness, made up of large expanses of pristine old-growth forest, subalpine meadows and spectacular alpine scenery.

Mt. Rainier, although part of the Cascade Mountain Range and the Ring of Fire, a volcanic range almost encircling the Pacific Ocean, looks as if it stands alone. It is a place of beauty and serenity. The forests lying beneath this massive peak are just as impressive. The old growth forest of Mt. Rainier National Park is known as a lowland forest with trees reaching up to two hundred feet in height and several hundred years old. Western hemlock is the most common tree in these forests shared with western red cedar and Douglas fir.

The forests cover the mountainside up to 5,000 feet, where they thin out and open up to subalpine meadows. These meadows become a rainbow of color as wildflowers bloom beneath the jagged and glaciated peak of Mt. Rainier. Many trails twisting and turning throughout the meadows allow visitors to enjoy and experience firsthand this fragile but lively environment.

PHOTOGRAPHER'S VIEW

Mt. Rainier National Park, although photographically very different from Olympic National Park but equally beautiful, has much to offer the photographer. One can leisurely pass through the park and pick up the icon (obvious) shots of Mt. Rainier and probably go home happy with the results, but chances are good that you're passing up many other great opportunities. I think we're all guilty at times of photographing places and things the way we have seen them in calendars, postcards and guidebooks. Look for a new approach to those shots you have seen over and over. Photography in Mt. Rainier National Park doesn't have to say Mt. Rainier, and that goes for any location. Look for generic, eye-catching shots. For example, a cool evening around Reflection

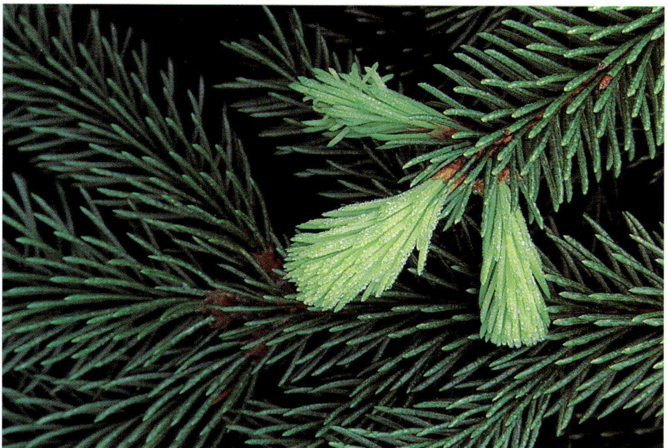

Careful observation of the surrounding environment opens up many possibilities. Make a habit of exploring the elements that make up the environment. I used my simple but effective macro setup to get this image of new growth on a Norway spruce. I attached an extension tube to an 80–200mm lens to get this image.

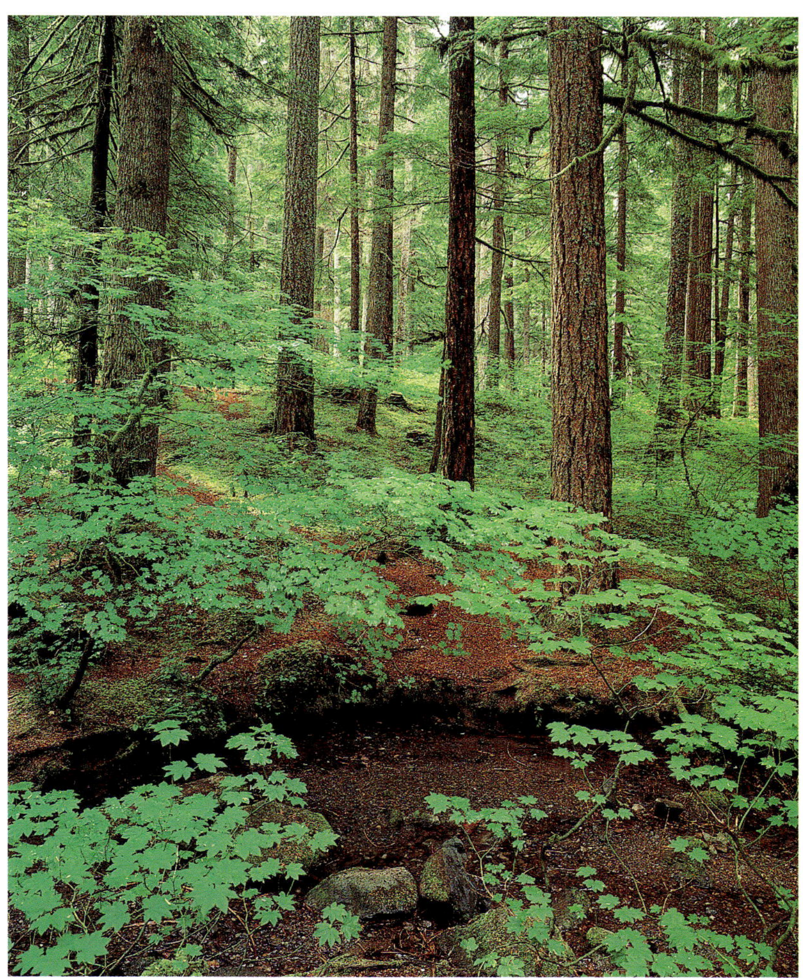

Good images can be found anywhere. I shot this image from my campsite at the Ohanapecosh campground.

I make a habit of listening to the weather report in the evening when I'm photographing on the road . By anticipating the weather conditions, I'm better prepared for my morning shoots.

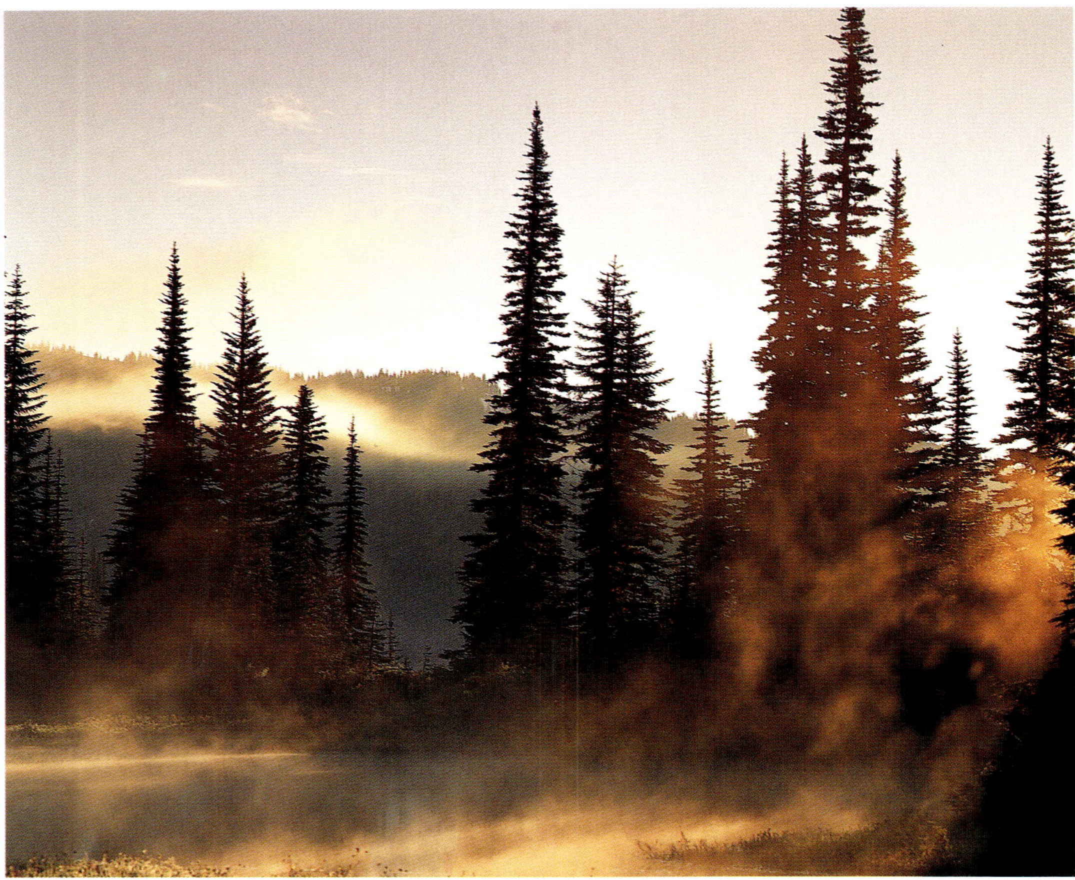

Lakes during the warmer months of July and August might create a light fog on the water at first light, while anticipating sunny conditions the following morning, you may catch rays of light beaming through trees or the fog itself. I hope that as a photographer, you can envision the possibilities.

Photographers typically come to shoot at Mt. Rainier National Park for two reasons: the mountain itself and the wildflowers. The good news is both subjects are best photographed in the same window of opportunity, the end of July through the middle of August. Mt. Rainier sees lots of rain, and the mountain itself creates its own weather pattern. Therefore, you can go days or even weeks without seeing the mountain break through the clouds. July and August are the driest months of the year and improve your chances for blue skies immensely.

Wildflowers

The first-time visitor to Mt. Rainier National Park typically begins exploring at the base of Mt. Rainier at Paradise, one of the best locations for wildflower photography. This is where you can see the glory of this mountain as it rises above the meadows in which you stand. Here at Paradise is probably the best of the three visitor centers, Jackson Visitor Center. As I always suggest, start your "on-location" information gathering here, and begin making adjustments or changing your plans if necessary. If you plan your journey around the wildflower season, you can see for yourself from the visitor center at what stage or condition the wildflowers are in. From here you can decide when you want to spend your time working the meadows. Keep in mind that you'll find flowers in other areas away from Paradise. You may find flowers at the meadows around Sunrise as well as near the Reflection Lakes.

Glacier lilies, plumed bear grass, magenta paintbrush, purple lupine, yellow marsh marigolds and white avalanche lilies are all common during the short growing season from the end of July into August. If you plan to shoot macro photography, remember that flower movement becomes a persistent problem as the sun rises higher, and there is very little, if any, protection from the wind. Diffusers will be very helpful on those sunny mornings, as light will hit the meadows very early. Consider shooting more intimate scenes with wildflowers later in the morning. These shots are bit more forgiving when there is movement.

Be aware that visitors venturing off the path in meadows will quickly be greeted by a park ranger. Sometimes it's difficult to get the right position for the shot you want without getting off the path, but the park rangers are adamant about protecting these fragile meadows.

Mt. Rainier

There are several wonderful places to photograph the mountain. Keep in mind that the park's size makes it impossible to shoot each location on the same day during the best hours of light. In the northeastern portion of the park is an area called Sunrise, a beautiful meadow area with an incredible view of Mt. Rainier. As its name implies, sunrise is the best time to shoot here. There are several great locations along the winding road to Sunrise to

Sunrise at Sunrise Point in Mt. Rainier can be absolutely magical. It pays to be on location at first light. If I had arrived five minutes later, I would have missed this shot.

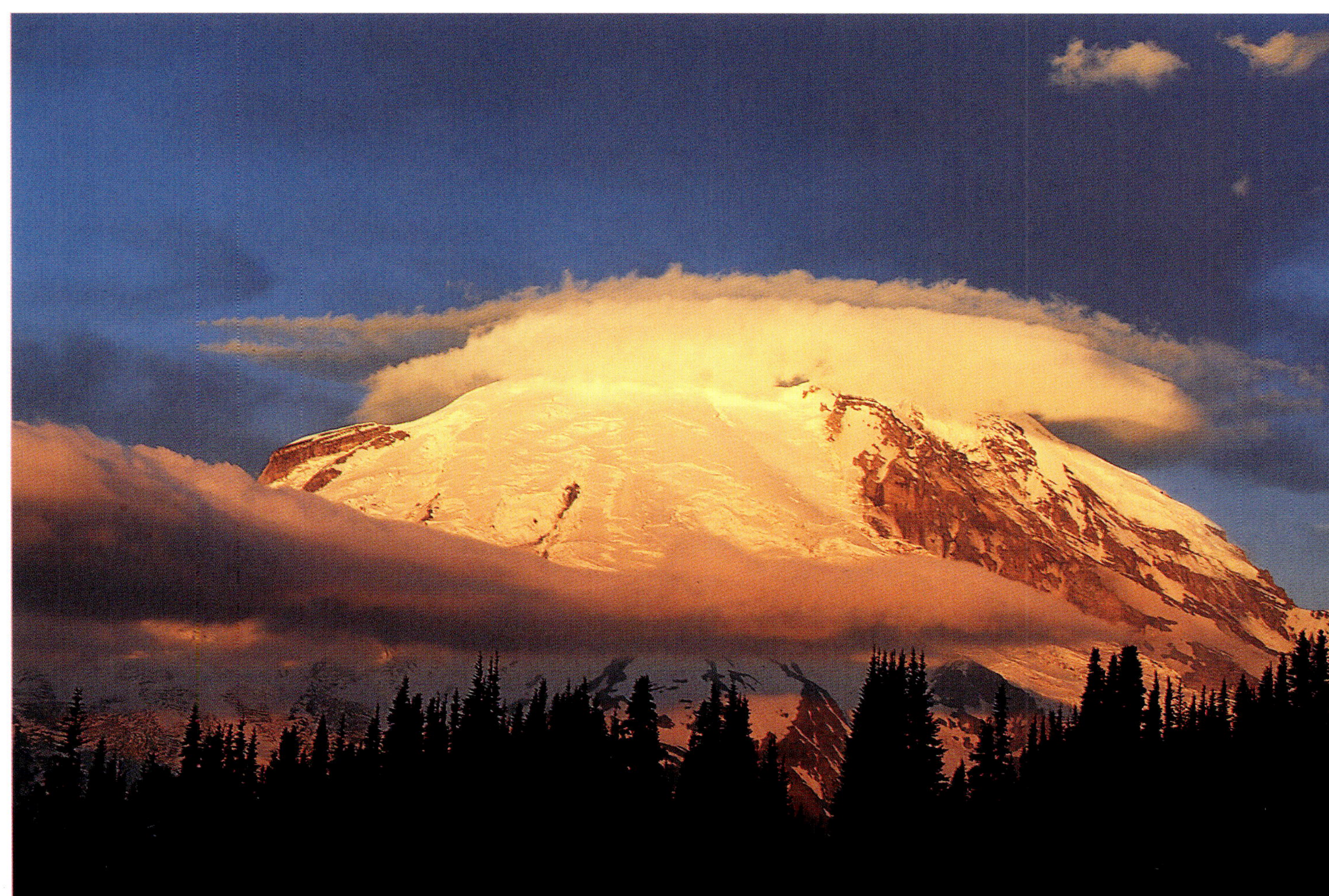

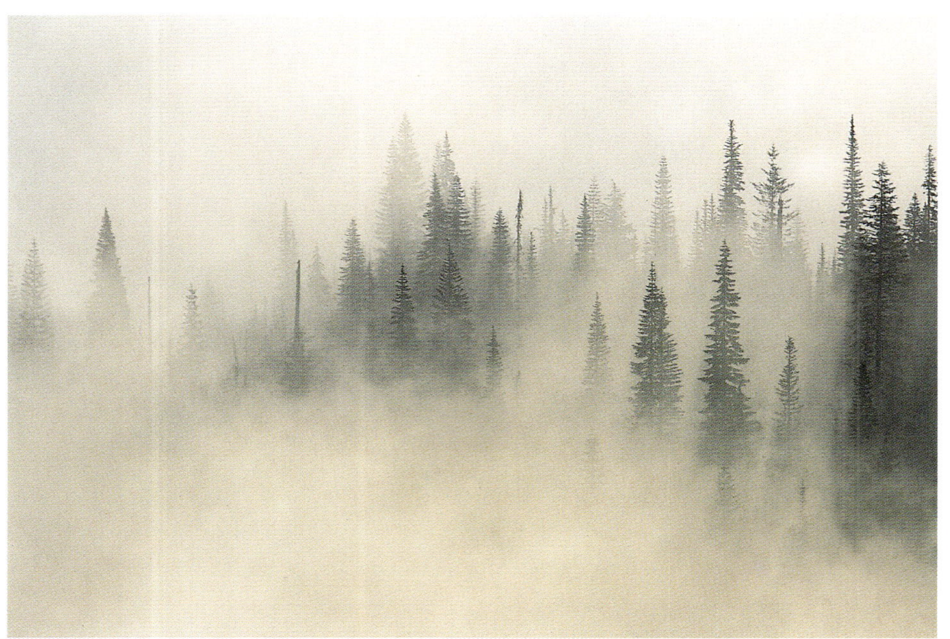

This is a good example of a generic image. It can be interpreted and used for many different situations and purposes.

catch the morning light as it touches the peak and moves down into the valleys. I suggest you scout the location the night before to see where you want to be for the first rays of light. I also suggest you time your drive to see how long it takes to get here from your campsite or hotel. Nothing is very close to Sunrise; you might expect at least an hour drive. Another nice morning shoot is Tipsoo Lake, a small reflection pond about halfway in between Sunrise and Ohanapecosh on Route 410 just before you exit the park. Tipsoo Lake is best at sunrise or just as the morning light starts to reach into the meadow surrounding the lake. The Paradise region is of course always a great location to capture the morning light on the mountain. I am including Reflection Lakes and the surrounding areas as part of Paradise. One could spend an entire morning just on Reflection Lakes photographing the mountain, reflections of the mountain and little intimate scenes around the lakes.

The best location to catch the warm evening glow on Mt. Rainier is in the Mowich Lake region—on the far west side, a long way from the common areas of the park. Unfortunately, there is no easy way to get to the Mowich Lake area. You will need to exit the park from either Route 706 on the southwestern side or exit from the northeastern side on Route 410 and reenter the park from Route 165 in the far northwestern corner. There are no facilities in the area, but you will find a ranger station and a campground.

Forests and Streams

The old-growth forests in Mt. Rainier are a delight to visit and a great getaway from the crowds in other areas of the park. These forests will challenge even the most seasoned of photographers. Olympic National Park is the better park to shoot forests. If you do want to shoot forests in Mt. Rainier, the best place to witness these forest treasures is in the Grove of the Patriarchs, which rival any along the Pacific coast.

But working these forests will present some challenges. If you are visiting during the July/August window, you will probably encounter clear, sunny skies giving you a contrasty situation. You will be better served if you look for smaller scenes within the grandness of these forests. Don't pass up the campgrounds for good forest photography. I have shot some of my favorite forest scenes of Mt. Rainier in the Ohanapecosh campground. This is also an excellent place to set a tent up for the night. There are not as many waterfalls and streams with easy acccess as one might expect in Mt. Rainier, but one waterfall worthy of a visit is Narada Falls, just off the road between Longmire and Paradise. You will find a couple streams near roads in the Paradise area. You may find some of the smaller streams lined with wildflowers, regardless, water always seems to provide something for the photographer. There is one waterfall worthy of a visit if you're up for a long hour of hiking: Comet Falls is situated with a beautiful meadow at its base. The hike to Comet Falls is a long winding uphill trail. The good news of course is you get a pretty waterfall, and the hike back is all downhill. There is also a nice stream to work near Ohanapecosh.

WHEN TO GO

The best time to photograph in Mt. Rainier National Park with some predictability is the last week of July through the first week of August. This time period should be peak wildflower bloom and is also one of the best chances to catch the right skies for photographing Mt. Rainier. I think you'll find the most opportunities for variety in this time frame. The time frame I'm suggesting is traditional, but, as always, Mother Nature has her own ways. I don't want to discourage photographers from visiting Mt. Rainier in other times of the year, but be prepared to make alternate plans if your purpose is to shoot Mt. Rainier as bad skies are more common than good skies.

TIME REQUIREMENTS

Give yourself a minimum of three full days to shoot in Mt. Rainier, and this is if the conditions are just right each day. Three days will also eliminate the get acquainted with the park day that I believe is so important. I recommend four to six days as optimum, preferably six days. This should give you the time you need to capture the best of the park. Mt. Rainier is a big park and you really need quality time in each location. Go after a fresh new approach and stay away from too many of those "been there, done that" shots as Mt. Rainier has been shot millions of times from the same tripod holes. Look for those generic shots or another approach to shooting a subject that has already been well documented. In other words, develop a new set of tripods

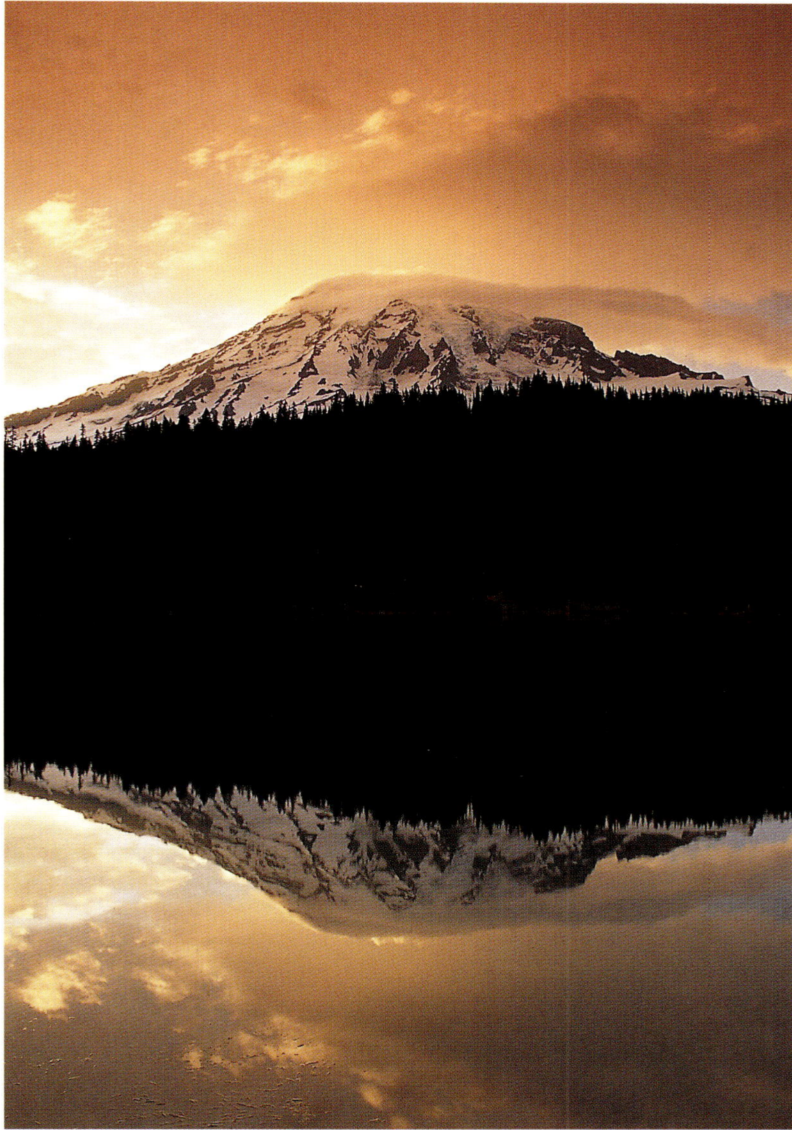

Mt. Rainier is difficult to catch in good evening light unless you travel well beyond the major roadways in the park. I photographed this image from Reflection Lakes. The subtle colors in the sky mirrored in the calm water make this a pleasing image.

holes. I mentioned in the Olympic National Park section of this chapter you could combine Olympic and Mt. Rainier for an extended trip. Give yourself at least ten days for the two parks. I suggest four or five days in Olympic. One whole afternoon will be lost for travel. Spend your remaining days in Mt. Rainier. It's a toss-up as to which one you give five days. If the forecast calls for sun, I would opt for five days in Mt. Rainier. Photograph Olympic the third week of July and the fourth week or the week overlapping July and August in Mt. Rainier.

Another travel possibility is combining

Mt. Rainier National Park along with the Oregon coast for a ten- to fourteen-day trip. Don't even consider trying to cover Olympic, Mt. Rainier and the Oregon coast unless you have three weeks and a lot of energy.

NEED TO KNOW

There are only two places I would consider for lodging in Mt. Rainier National Park. The first without question would be at the Paradise Inn at Paradise. Mount Rainier Guest Services operates this inn [(360) 569-2275; <www.guestservices.com/rainier>]. I would choose this location only because of its beauty. The better location for a more reasonable drive to Sunrise for morning shoots is Packwood. But the downside is you still will have a long drive to Paradise. Lodging in Paradise will almost double your drive for morning shoots at Sunrise. You can also stay at the National Park Inn at Longmire [(360) 569-2275; <www.guestservices.com/rainier>]. This adds even more driving time, but it's a good alternative if you insist on lodging in the park and can't get in at Paradise. For more information about the park, visit <www.nps.gov/mora>. For camping inquiries or reservations, call (800) 365-2267.

photographer's choice

MT. SHUKSAN and MT. HOOD offer photographic experiences similar to Mt. Rainier, but with fewer people. Mt. Shuksan is in North Cascades National Park just north of Seattle, although it's better photographed from Mt. Baker National Forest on State Highway 542. Mt. Hood, near Hood River, Oregon, is beautifully situated and very close to the Columbia River Gorge area. [Mt. Hood, www.fs.fed.us/r6/mthood, www.mthood.org]

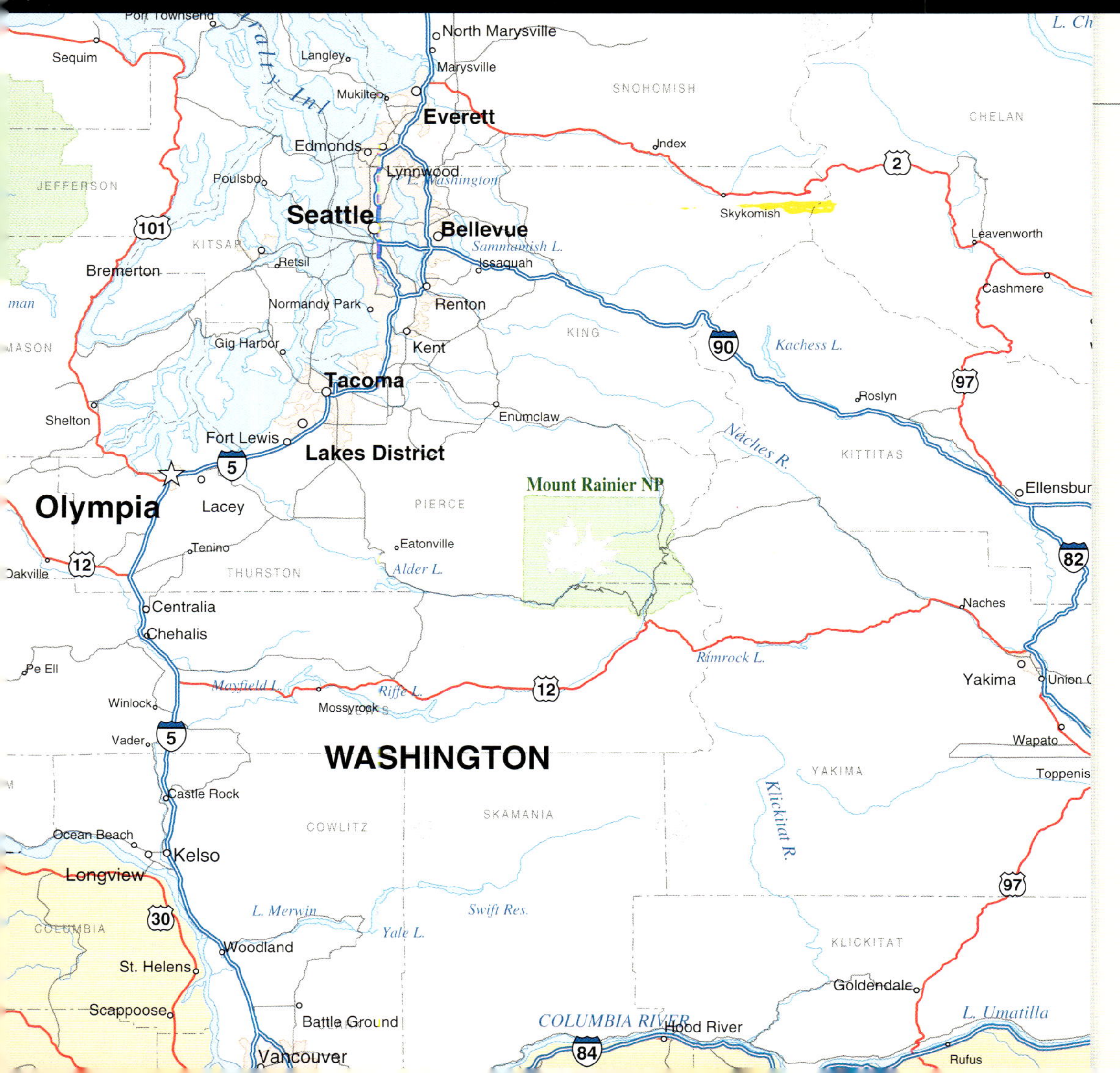

directions

FROM SEATTLE TO MT. RAINIER NATIONAL PARK AT PARADISE:

- Take I-5 south to SR 7 then east on SR 706 through Elbe and Ashford to the Nisqually entrance.

FROM PORTLAND, OREGON TO MT. RAINIER NATIONAL PARK AT PARADISE:

- Take I-5 north, east on U.S. 12, north on SR 7 then east on SR 706 to the Nisqually entrance.

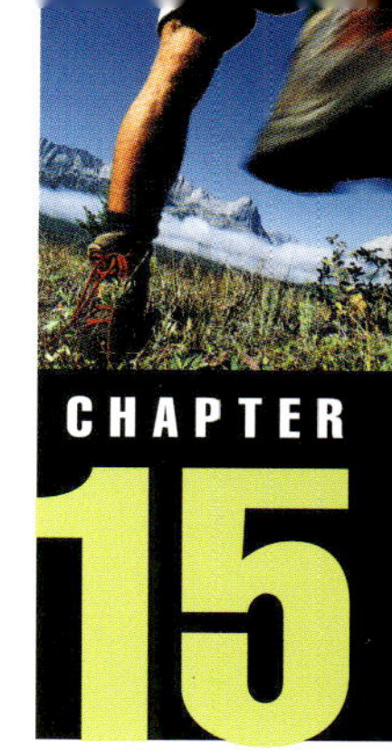

CHAPTER 15

Columbia River Gorge, Oregon

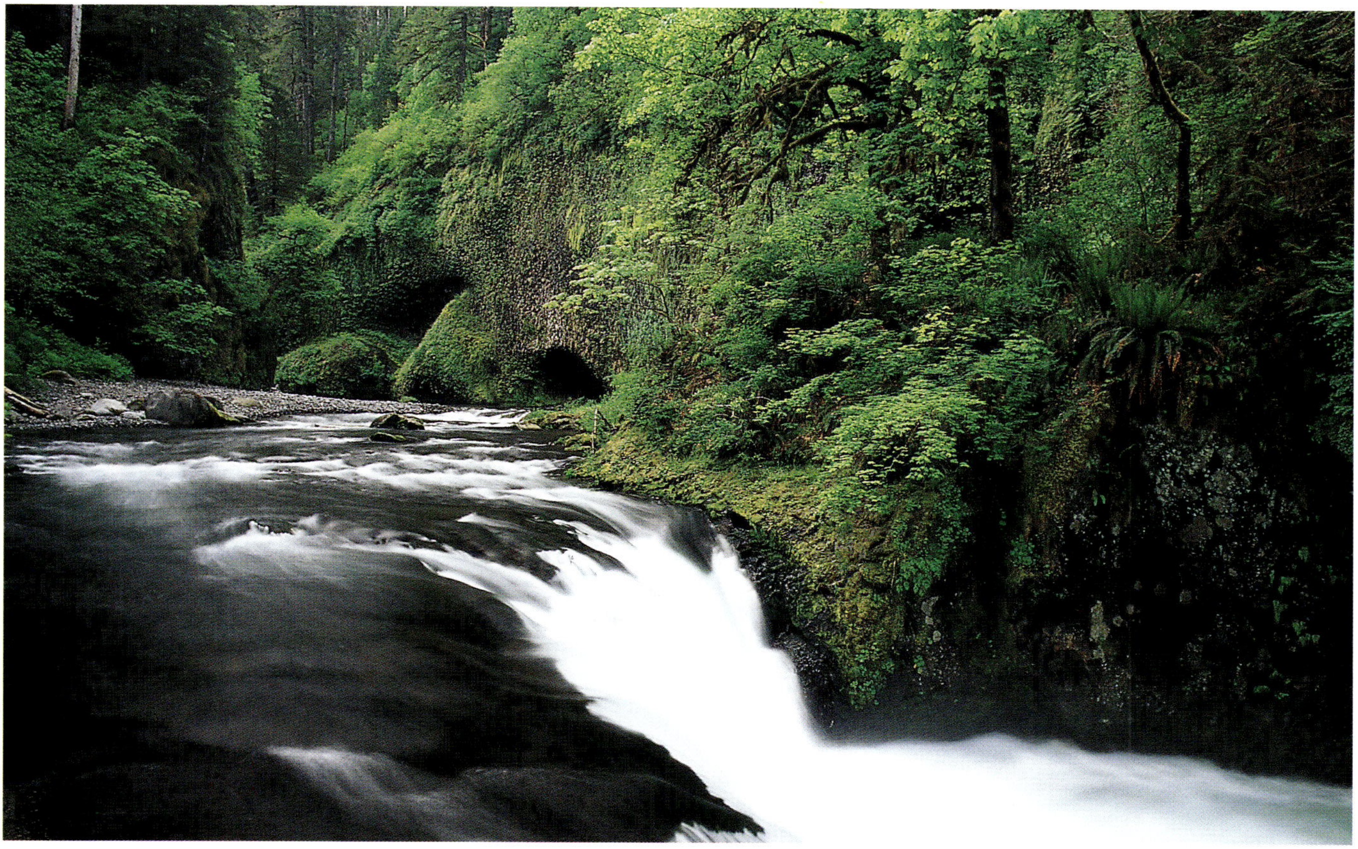

Columbia River Gorge divides Washington and Oregon and cuts deep into the Cascade Range. The gorge runs for eighty miles along the Columbia River with canyon walls at times reaching 4,000 feet above the river and covered in pristine rain forests. This description alone allows people to build a visual picture of the area without ever seeing it with their own eyes. The Columbia River Gorge was designated the first National Scenic Area in 1986 by Congress and signed into law by President Reagan. The pure natural beauty of the gorge is reason enough

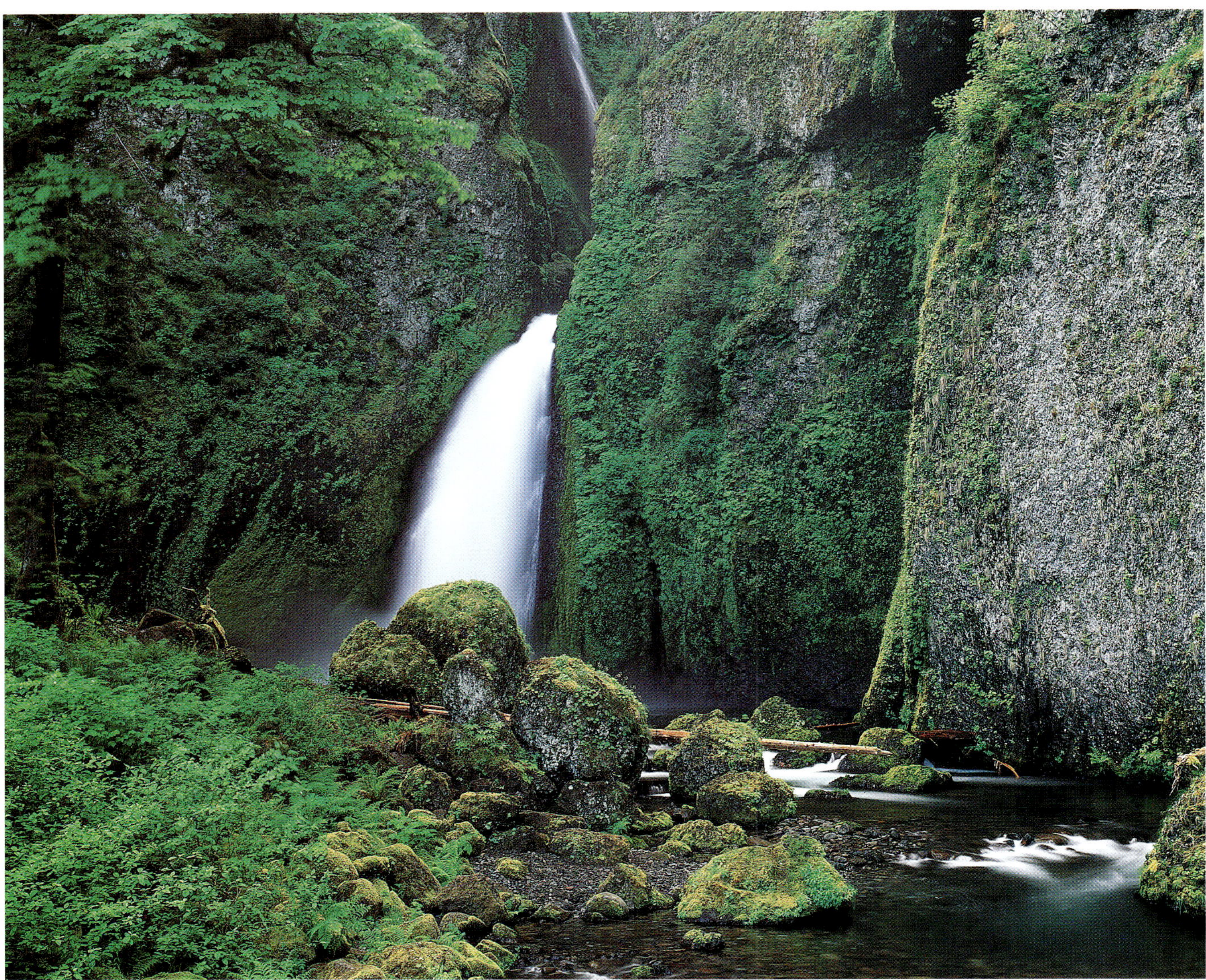

Wahclella Falls is a classic waterfall in the Columbia River Gorge. There are numerous angles to work this waterfall. I walked away with four very different shots of which all have sold. Waterfalls are very salable and have a wide range of uses.

to visit, but it offers so much more to the outdoor enthusiast, from hundreds of miles of hiking trails to world-class boardsailing (also some great photo opportunities) on the Columbia River. As a matter of fact, the Columbia River Gorge is considered to be the best boardsailing in the world. The gorge is also a thirty-minute drive from Portland.

Photographers are attracted to the Columbia River Gorge for its abundance of waterfalls: seventy-seven waterfalls on the Oregon side. For our purposes, I will talk only about the Oregon side of the gorge. The area receives more than one hundred inches of rain in most years and that—combined with the snowmelt from Mt. Hood that cascades down the slopes to the Columbia River—results in the proliferation of waterfalls that have made the area famous. The abundance of rainfall and snowmelt in the area is also responsible for the area's incredible rain forests.

PHOTOGRAPHER'S VIEW

Compared with other western parks and natural areas, the Columbia River Gorge is relatively small (292,000 acres including both the Oregon and Washington side) but has a high density of waterfalls. The waterfalls of the Columbia River Gorge are not the riffles or modest cascades some people label waterfalls. They commonly range from a hundred feet to several hundred feet. In Oregon, there are officially seventy-seven waterfalls, but not all are accessible, and many are not really worth photographing. Some falls start to look alike after a while. As with any other location, a little research will improve your chances immensely for productive photography. I'll talk about several waterfalls that are worth photographing based on the surroundings of the waterfall and its "personality."

Waterfalls are best shot in overcast light. Sunlight creates too much contrast in a forest setting. With overcast skies, there is a chance of rain. Don't let a light rain drive you indoors. Misty rain provides nice saturated color in the foliage and surrounding landscape. When I don't get the wet scene I want, on many occasions I have splashed water on dry rocks along a streambed to improve the image. Dry, light-colored rocks can be distracting. A polarizer is incredibly helpful in both overcast light and misty rain. It helps reduce or eliminate glare on foliage, rocks and water. The downside is that you lose two stops of light with a polarizer; therefore, you might have some long shutter speeds. As long as there isn't any other major movement in the vegetation, long shutter speeds won't be a problem. The only solution for movement is to compromise and forget the polarizer or use a faster film, which isn't much of an option for professionals. If the conditions are good and shutter speeds aren't a problem, consider adding a warming filter along with your polarizer. Don't overdo it—an 81A filter should be fine. (See page 20 for an overview of polarizers and warming filters.) Shoot with and without the warmer, and decide for yourself on your light table which image you like best.

Many of the waterfalls in the Columbia River Gorge require some hiking. Most of the

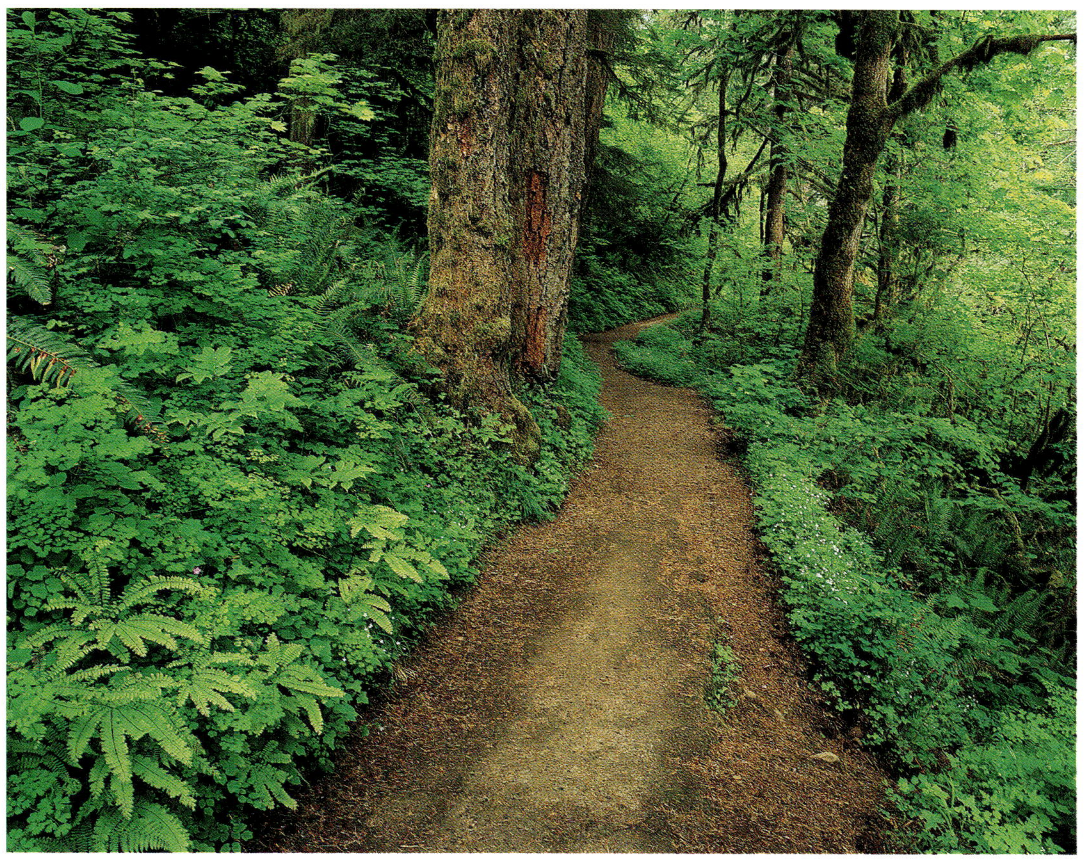

Paths through a forest convey a pleasant or peaceful message and are very sellable in the market place. Regardless if you sell your work or not, don't pass up an opportunity to shoot images like this, they can be nice fillers in a slide show.

hiking is along well-maintained trails that often climb upward, but they are very beautiful hikes through rain forests. There are also several waterfalls just a hop and skip from parking lots. Stop at each of these to see for yourself if you want to photograph them; you won't lose much time.

The following waterfalls are only a few of many I believe are worth a visit. If you have a limited amount of time, these are good bets for classic waterfall images.

WAHCLELLA FALLS (also known as Tanner Falls) is a classic waterfall. Wahclella plunges fifty to seventy feet between two canyon walls covered in vibrant green mosses and into a beautiful pool. Tanner Creek sits below this waterfall and is surrounded by foliage and moss-covered rocks. Wahclella Falls is an easy half-mile hike from the Tanner Creek Trailhead parking lot. This waterfall provides several angles to work. You should have no problem walking away with at least three or four good shots.

EAGLE CREEK has twelve waterfalls along a six-mile trail. Three very nice waterfalls (Metlako Falls, Lower Punch Bowl Falls and Punch Bowl Falls) are within the first two miles. On a good overcast day, you can spend the entire day working along this beautiful trail on both forest scenes and waterfalls. You can work all three waterfalls from the creek bed if you don't mind getting a little wet and taking a short, steep climb down into the canyon on established trails. Metlako Falls and Punch Bowl Falls can both be photographed from the trail along the canyon rim and are classic waterfalls cascading down canyon walls, while Lower Punch Bowl has a short drop of fifteen feet. The attraction to Lower Punch Bowl Falls is the angle and the beautiful moss-covered walls running beside Eagle Creek. With so many waterfalls in the Columbia River Gorge, I'm not sure the entire hike is worth doing unless you really feel the need to hike twelve miles round-trip.

PONYTAIL FALLS is part of the Oneonta Gorge, a half-mile hike from the Columbia Gorge Scenic Highway. Ponytail Falls drops 125 feet into an open pool surrounded by forest. There are only a couple angles to photograph this waterfall from, but one is from behind the waterfall itself with the forest as your backdrop. This is a nice waterfall with a short hike and few people.

MULTNOMAH FALLS is probably the best-known waterfall in the gorge for two reasons: It's the fourth-highest waterfall in the United States (611 feet), and it has a visitors center, souvenir shop and

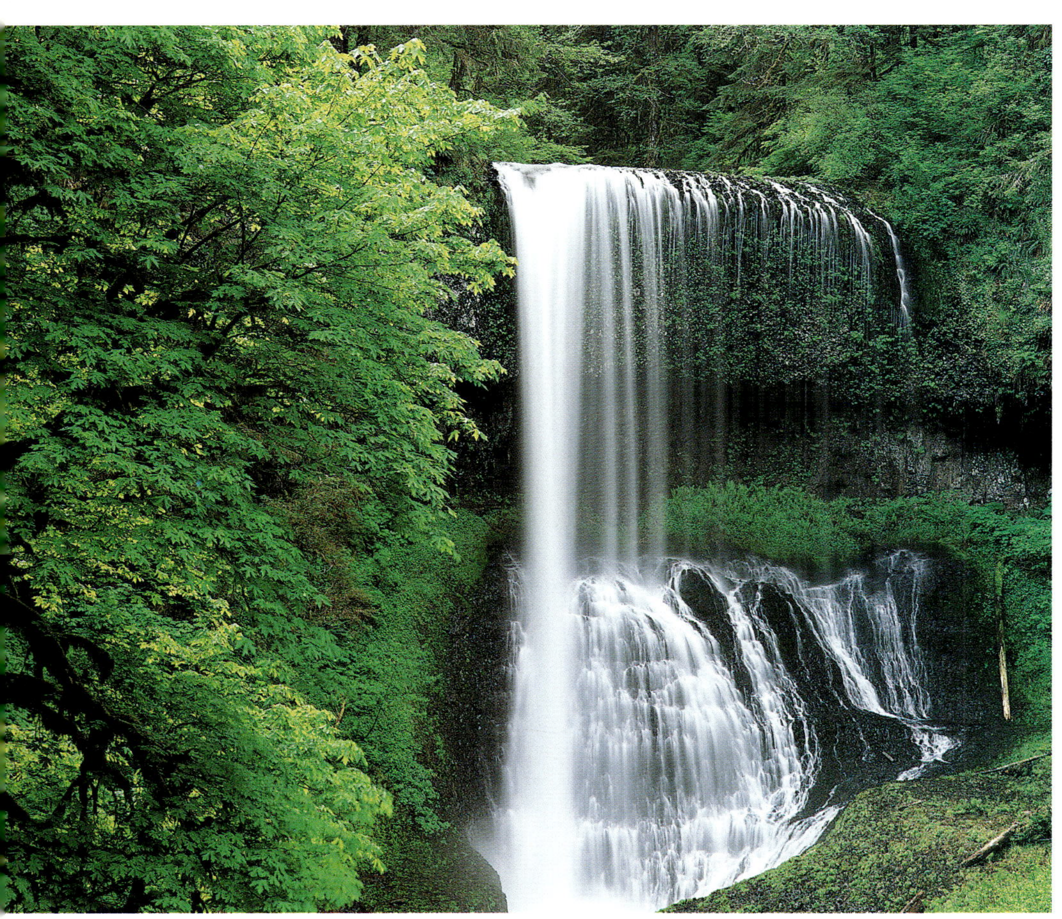

Middle North Falls in Silver Falls State Park is one of the prettiest falls in the park. I shot this image from a distance. This allowed me to isolate the distracting elements I encountered when approaching the falls up close.

snack bar on site. In other words, there will be lots of people. The reason I mention this waterfall is because it is incredibly beautiful and very well known. If you're a stock photographer, this is a good image to have in your travel files; someday you'll find a photo buyer needing this waterfall. This is a tough shoot if you're trying to avoid getting people in your photo. You might want to try an early-morning shoot before the crowd arrives.

Oregon has no shortage of beautiful streams, cascades and waterfalls. One location well worth mentioning is Silver Falls State Park. An easy three-hour drive from Columbia River Gorge, the park has ten waterfalls, six of which are more than one hundred feet high. Silver Falls State Park sits in a beautiful old-growth forest surrounded by farmland. Not all the waterfalls are photogenic. South Falls, Lower South Falls, Middle North Falls, North Falls and Upper North Falls are the most photographic of the ten. The most photogenic in my opinion is Middle North Falls from an overlook along the trail away from the falls.

There are several locations within or near the Columbia River Gorge that offer opportunities other than forests and waterfalls. One location is an incredible overlook into the gorge itself at Crown Point State Park at the western end of the gorge looking east. An evening shoot is best here at Crown Point. Another location is the back roads between the town of Hood River and Mt. Hood. You should have no problem finding some wonderful agricultural areas with Mt. Hood in the background. Mt. Hood itself isn't worth visiting unless you're there in the middle of June or later, because dirty snow piles still lie along roads, trails and throughout the forests. Unfortunately, June is not a good time to be in the Columbia River Gorge because it's too sunny. The Tom McCall Preserve is another excellent location for something different. The preserve is a cliff-edged grassland among rolling hills filled with wildflowers in April and May. The land is owned by the Nature Conservancy and is located east of Hood River. (Take I-84 to the Mosier exit, exit 69, follow scenic loop for 6.6 miles to the Rowena Crest parking lot.)

These next two locations are in Portland, and I recommend them highly if you're in the

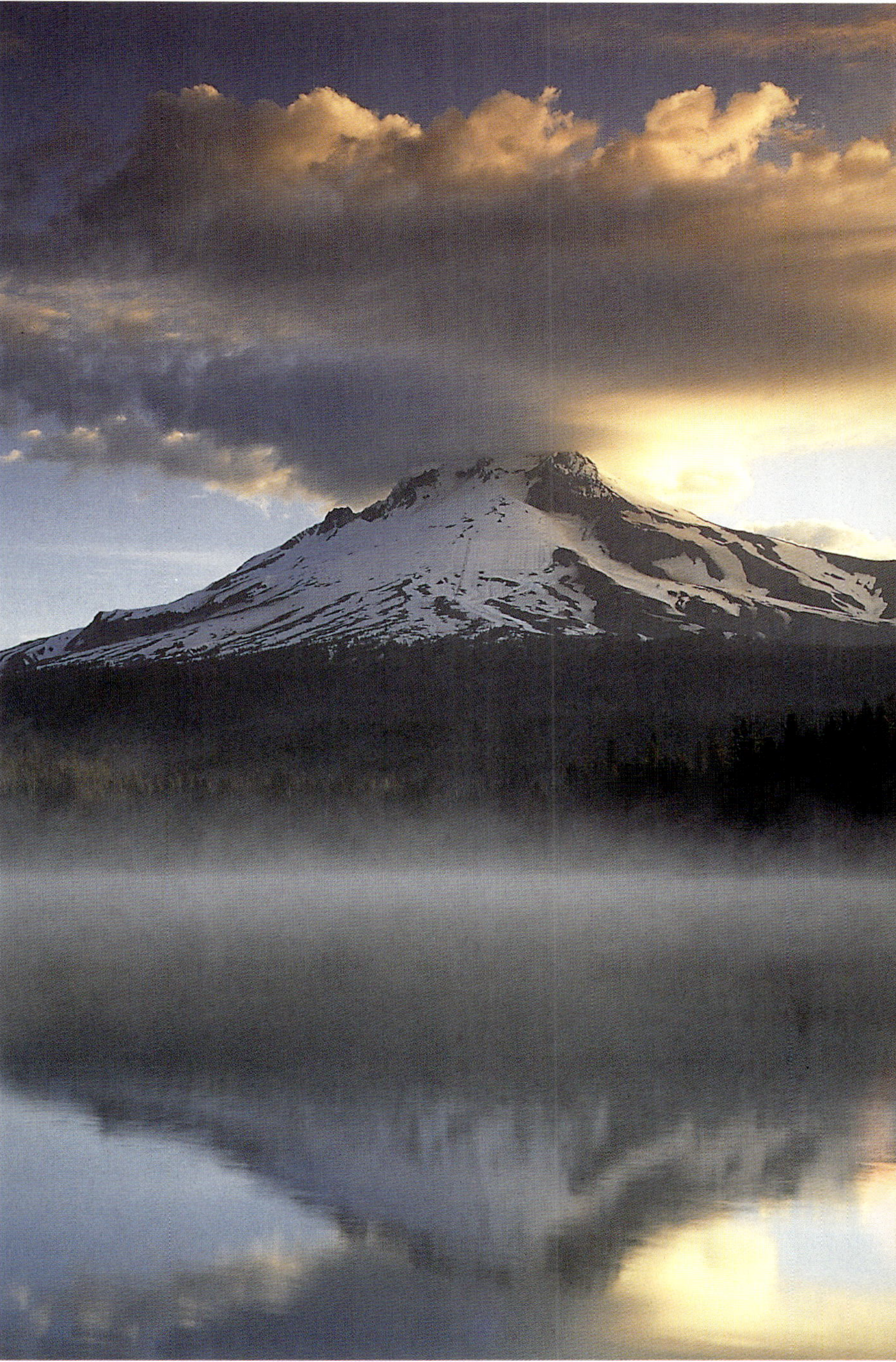

Much of the landscape surrounding Mt. Hood isn't attractive in the spring. Dirty snow rings the mountain and ruins otherwise pristine frames. I take advantage of the early and late light to hide the surrounding areas in dark shadows.

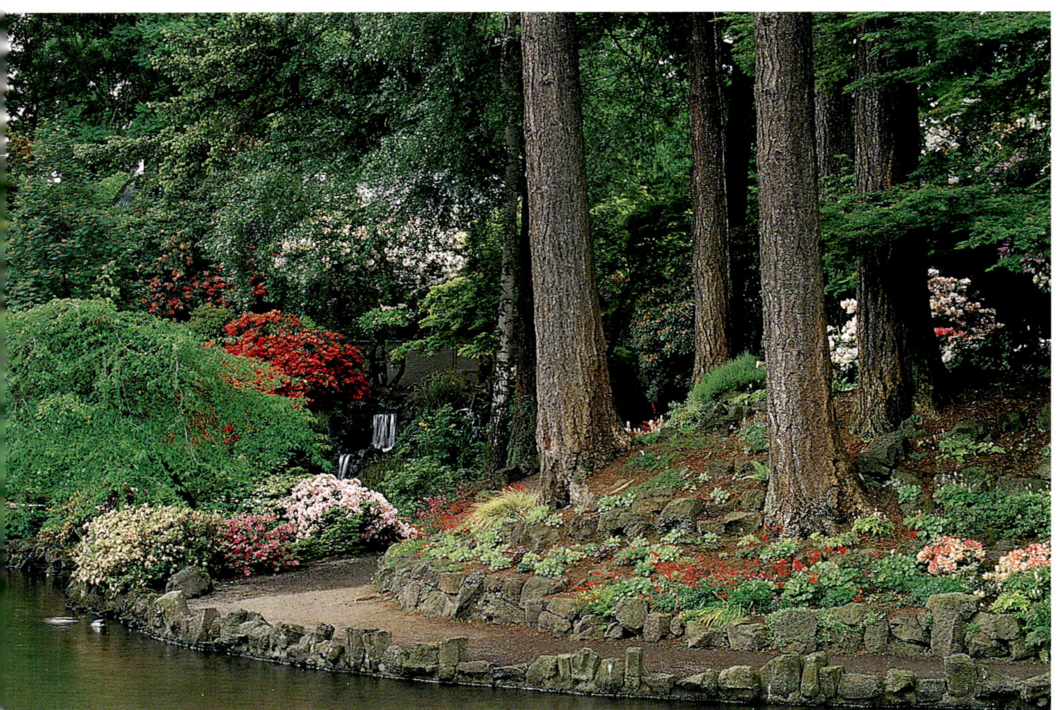

The Rhododendron Garden of Portland is one of those locations I discovered from my research prior to my trip to the Columbia River Gorge. It sounded like there might be a lot of potential here for photography, so I decided to place this high on my priority list—a good choice.

area in late April through May. The Rhododendron Garden of Portland and the Japanese Garden are colorful and offer lots of shooting possibilities. I suggest making the effort to photograph at one or both of these places—as long as you don't mind photographing beautiful, colorful gardens.

It's impossible for the purposes of this book to name every waterfall in the area, and even more so on how to get to each of the waterfalls. For details, look at *A Waterfall Lover's Guide to the Pacific Northwest*, by Gregory A. Plumb. This is the best book I have found and names many of the waterfalls, with directions to each.

WHEN TO GO

The most predictable time in the Columbia River Gorge for waterfalls and forests is the end of April through most of May. Spring showers are common. The foliage should be in full bloom, the green mosses glowing and the waterfalls flowing quite well. It's possible you'll find clear days in this window, but rain is predictable. If you find yourself fighting clear skies, you'll need to be on location early and late before and after the sun leaves the forest. In the shadowed forest with clear blue skies overhead, you'll encounter lots of blue light. Your eyes adjust to this blue light, but your film won't unless you use a warming filter. At minimum, you'll need an 81B warming filter or, better yet, a filter made by B+W, the KR6. This is a very warm filter best suited for shadowy areas when you have a clear blue sky overhead.

The winter is unpredictable for snow, but if you have the opportunity to photograph here after a snowfall, you should be regaled by a winter wonderland of snow-draped trees surrounding the waterfalls. Your best and most predictable window is the April and May time I mentioned before. This is the time you'll find new growth in the forest, when everything looks fresh.

TIME REQUIREMENTS

The Columbia River Gorge isn't a big area, and the main reason to photograph here is the waterfalls. Unless you absolutely love waterfalls and can't get enough of them, you only need three to four days if the conditions are just right. If you combine the Columbia River Gorge with Silver Falls State Park, consider this a five-day trip, as you'll need a full day in Silver Falls. There really is little need to spend more than a day in Silver Falls. If you encounter a lot of sun, Silver Falls is a wash. Give yourself about three hours to drive from Columbia River Gorge to Silver Falls. Consider shooting in the morning in the gorge and driving in the afternoon to Silver Falls State Park to shoot.

The April and May window I mentioned

is also a very good time to shoot in the Rhododendron Garden and the Japanese Garden in Portland. The middle of May is best. Give yourself half a day in each garden.

NEED TO KNOW

Lodging in the Columbia River Gorge is best in one of two locations: Troutdale is on the western side of the Columbia River Gorge, and Hood River is on the eastern side. Both locations have several hotels and motels. Troutdale will put you much closer to Portland as it sits on the edge of the city. You'll find that this area is much more congested than Hood River but very convenient for access to the city. I like Hood River better because it's farther away from the heavy traffic and closer to both the river and the agricultural area around Mt. Hood. Both locations require driving between waterfalls, so the locations don't make much difference in terms of logistics.

Lodging for Silver Falls State Park is located in the city of Salem. There are lots of motels situated off I-5 in Salem. The drive to Silver Falls State Park is an easy twenty-five to thirty minutes from Salem.

photographer's choice

GREAT SMOKY MOUNTAINS NATIONAL PARK has smaller but equally beautiful waterfalls and cascades. The mountains of NORTH CAROLINA also have some spectacular falls worth photographing. *North Carolina Waterfalls*, by Kevin Adams, will guide you to all the waterfalls on the North Carolina side. [Great Smoky Mountains National Park, www.nps.gov/grsm; North Carolina, www.visitnc.com]

directions

From Portland head east on Interstate 84. This will take you into the heart of the Columbia River Gorge. The drive from the airport to the westernmost part of the gorge will take about 30 to 45 minutes depending on traffic.

To drive from the Columbia River Gorge to Silver Falls State Park, you'll need to backtrack to Portland on I-84, pick up I-205 south to I-5 south, and continue on toward Salem. Exit on Highway 22 (exit 253 from I-5) and drive east to SR 214. Follow signs to Silver Falls State Park.

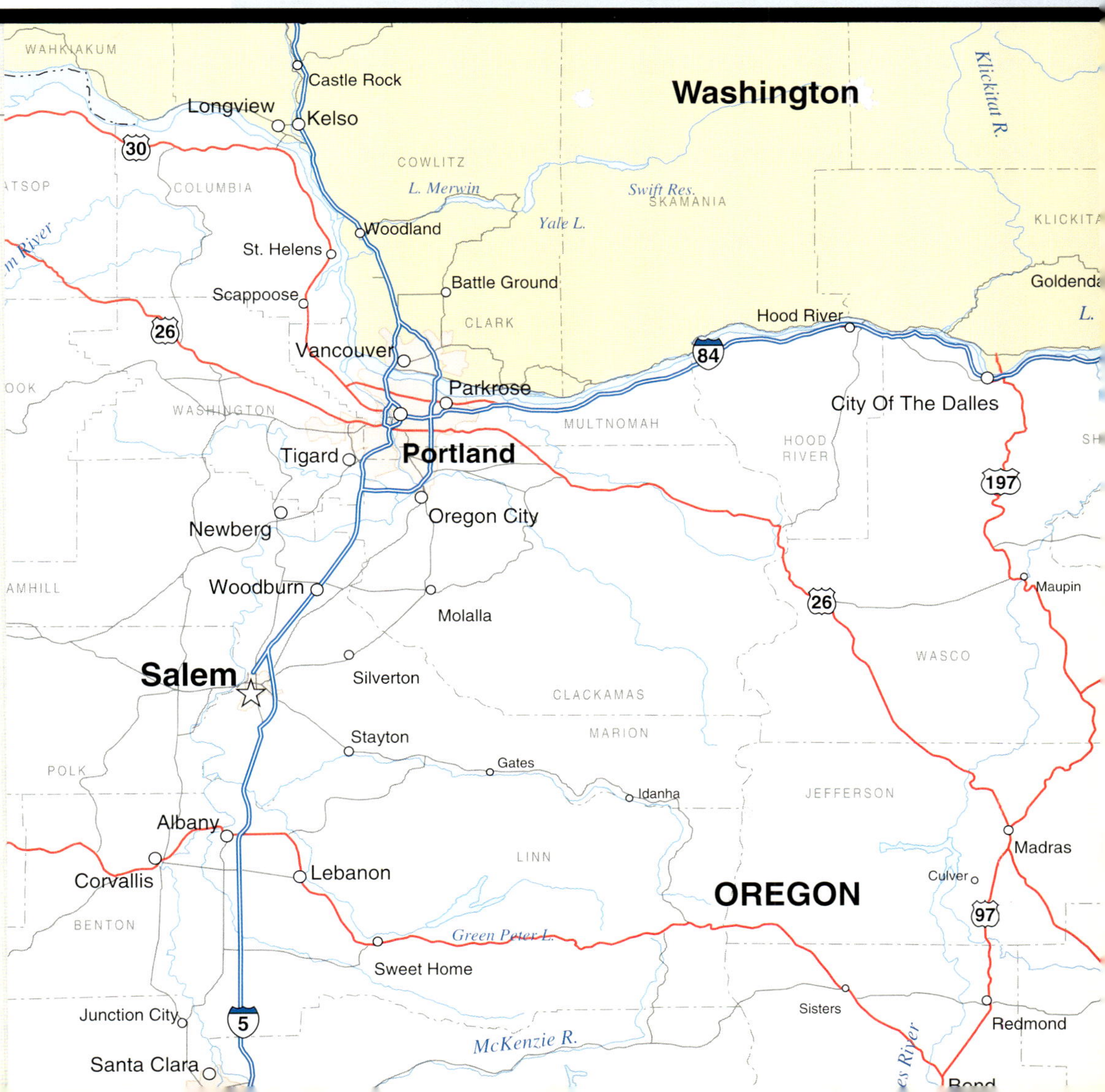

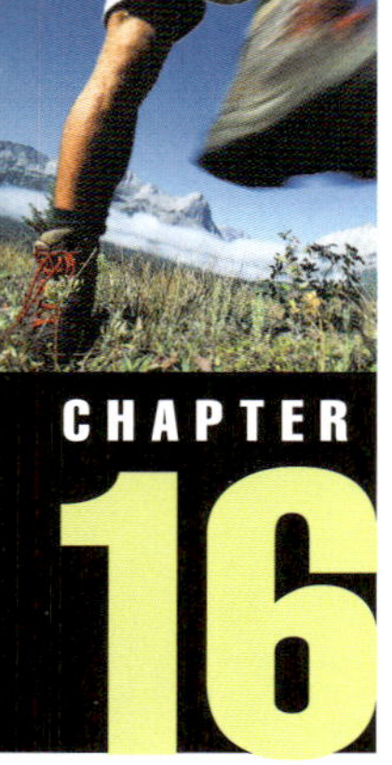

CHAPTER 16

Coup de 'graph: Editing, Organizing and Marketing Your Photos

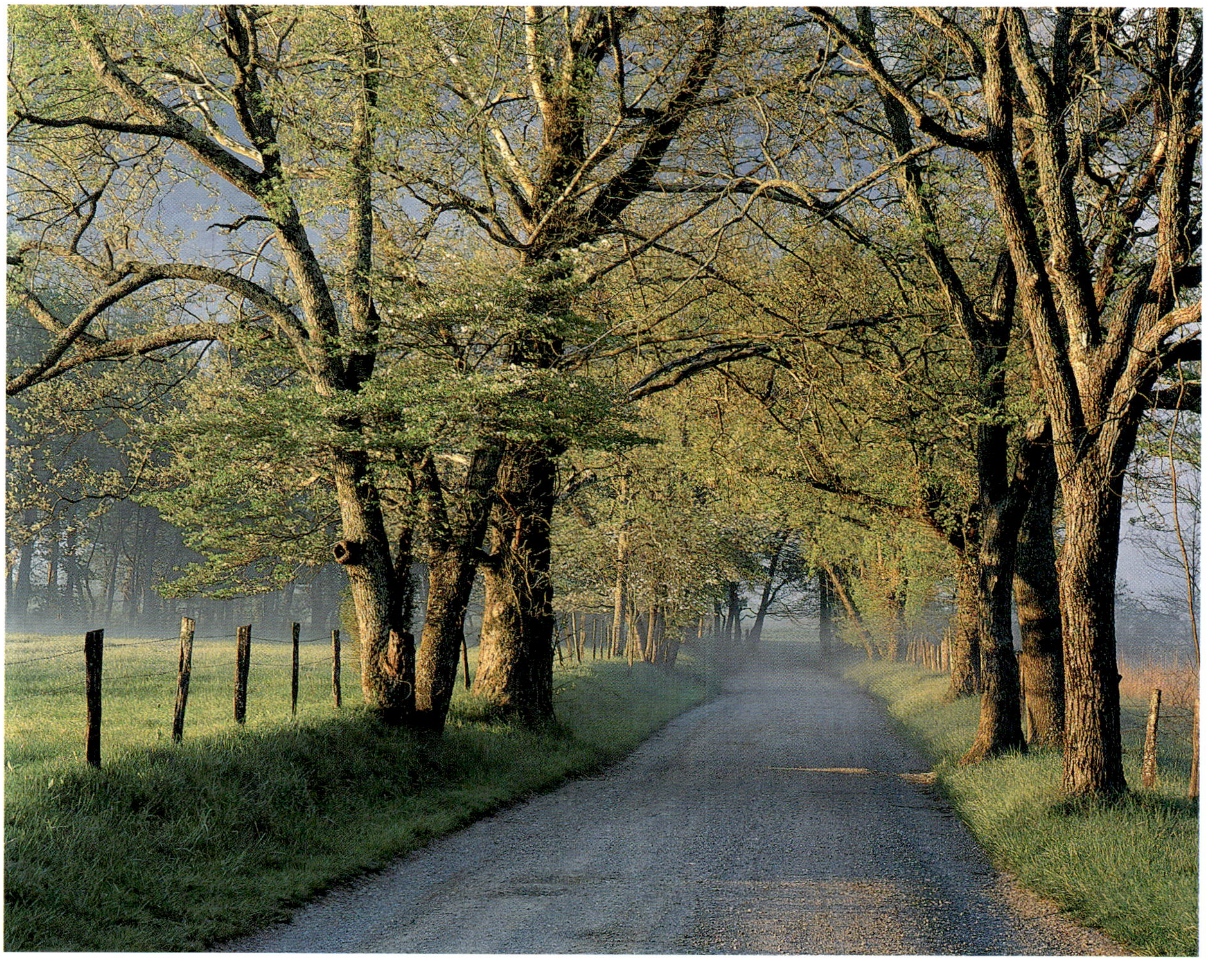

EDITING YOUR IMAGES

Editing requires a sharp eye and dispassionate analysis. To realize the fruits of your labor, you'll need four important tools:

1. A GOOD COMMERCIALLY MANUFACTURED LIGHT TABLE, OR WELL-BUILT HOMEMADE TABLE. A light table is a simple shallow box with color corrected lights. This can set you back a couple hundred dollars (depending on the size), or you can build your own at a fraction of the cost. The best source I have found for building your own light table is *Build Your Own Home Darkroom*, by Lista Duren and Will McDonald. If you prefer to buy, check out stores with large inventories such as B&H Photo <www.bhphotovideo.com> or Dick Blick Art Materials <www.dickblick.com>.

2. A GOOD 4X POWER MAGNIFYING LOUPE. A loupe in the eighty to hundred dollar range will do fine. Stay away from plastic loupes under ten dollars. A good loupe is a one-time purchase, so don't go cheap. Save your money on the light table and spend it here.

3. A GOOD SET OF EYES. Watch for both technical and compositional problems.

4. A DISCRIMINATING ATTITUDE. Don't be afraid to get ruthless. If an image is not sharp, not exposed properly or has a distracting element, cut it. Don't keep something just because you waited two hours or hiked ten miles to get the picture.

I edit all my work twice. The first time around, I look for obvious problems such as exposure and sharpness. I typically do this edit when I remove the images from the box and put them in a slide page. On the second edit, I look for composition problems: a horizon line running up and down or a dead petal on what I thought was a perfect rose. Don't attached to an image. If you're not sure whether to keep it, let someone who isn't afraid to tell you the truth look it over. If you don't like what you hear, bite your tongue, throw the slide away, and thank the person for helping you.

Good light is as important as the subject itself. I photographed this hillside on a day when heavy cloud cover kept moving in and out.

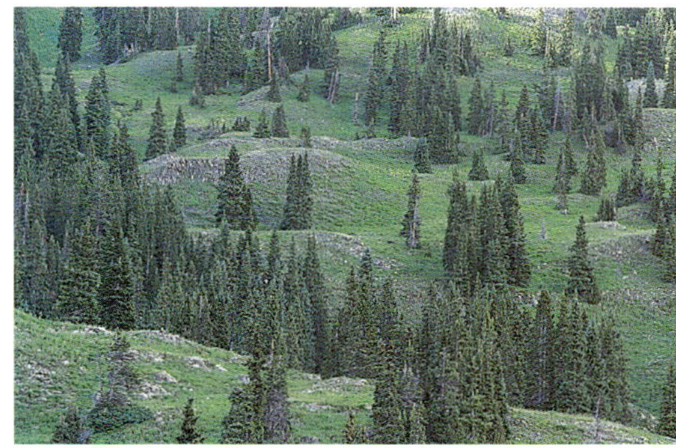

As you can see at left, I shot under heavy cloud cover and created a dull, flat image—one I'd throw away.

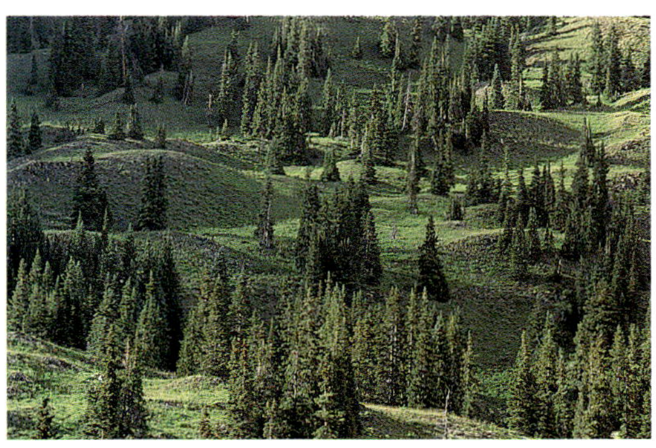

Once a pocket opened up in the clouds, the sun mottled the hillside with light. This image is much more appealing and a took a spot in my files.

EDIT RUTHLESSLY

When editing your work, look very closely at the finer details as the following images of the Ruppell's Vulture illustrates.

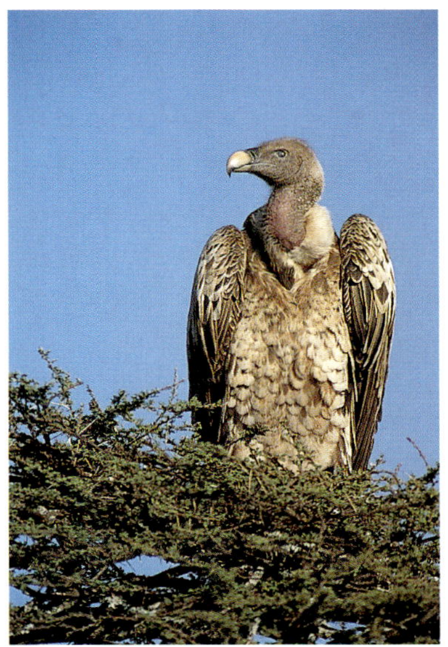

If you look carefully at the photo above using a loupe, you can see the vulture's nictitating membrane, which cleans and protects the eye.

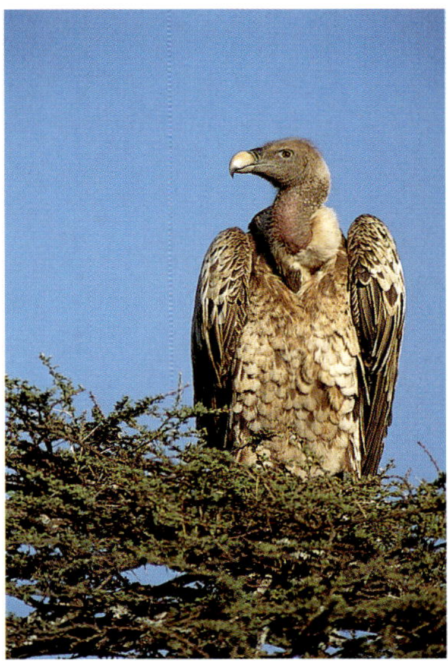

This image is a keeper because the eye is much more visible.

THE MANNING SYSTEM FOR CATEGORIZING AND LABELING IMAGES

It takes only a few good trips before images are scattered and piled all over the place. A well-organized system for categorizing, labeling and storing photos is crucial to maintaining and selling your collection. I have spoken to dozens of photographers over the years about categorizing and labeling their libraries, and each photographer has a different system. There is no wrong way to set up your library, but keep in mind that your image library will grow, and your system needs to grow with it. After several years of shooting, it becomes nearly impossible to reorganize.

I call my system the Manning System. This set-up makes access a snap and helps me keep track of many copies of the same image. Once you have edited your slides and decided what to keep, begin breaking down your collection into general categories with little chance for overlap or confusion. As a nature and travel photographer, I place my images into categories like landscapes, close-ups, wildlife, and cities. (See the chart on page 153.) When you go to store your slides, each of these categories will be a separate folder (or in a larger collection, a separate file drawer). I subdivide these categories into simple, clearly delineated topic areas and assign each an intuitive two- or three-letter code. For example, within the landscapes file, I might have categories for Kentucky (KY), Italy (ITY) and/or Washington, DC (WDC).

These letters will be the first part of a three-part ID code. How you categorize your images and what you place under each category depends on what you shoot. If you shoot a lot of one particular subject (say, birds), you may want to further divide your categories (robins, cardinals, cedar waxwings and so on). In these cases you'll add another letter or two at the end of this first string of initials. I divide my mammal subcategory into African wildlife (AWL), North American wildlife (NAW), zoo animals (ZOO) and many others. It can help to have a reference sheet listing your abbreviations for each category, especially for a large collection.

If I label an image of a grizzly bear, the first part of my three-part code is "NAW." The second part of the code is a slide page number. If my grizzly bear slide is filed in slide page thirteen, the code becomes NAW-13. Any slide I remove will always return to the same archival plastic slide sheet, no matter how many images I add to a given category. This is why it's so important to begin an organizational system early and stick with it. If you visit a location often, you could end up with several hundred pages in a category.

For sales purposes I have as many as ten copies of each image (labeled 1/10, 2/10, 3/10, etc.). Several potential buyers may ask for the same or similar images at any time, and I don't want to lose a sale by not having extra copies. A client can hold an image for several months and decide he isn't interested. This numbering of slide copies is the third and last part of the ID code. In my grizzly bear example, the fourth slide of eight duplicates would be NAW-13-4/8. To avoid confusion, all copies go into the same archival plastic sheet.

The advantage to the Manning ID code is that you can retrieve and replace any image quickly. If a photo buyer calls me and says she wants to purchase LKY-21-7/10, I know to go to my "Landscapes" file and pull page number twenty-one from the Kentucky category. When a submission comes back to the office, it takes only a moment to refile it.

DETAILS, DETAILS: LABELING SLIDES

It's not enough to code your slides for reference. Each label you place on an image should be as detailed as possible. The more information you have, the more you'll be able to jog your memory when giving a slide show several

labeling at a glance

KY-67-3/10 = A landscape image of Kentucky, found on the 67th page of that file folder, the third image of 10

FILE GROUPING	CATEGORY		PAGE NO.*	COPY NO.**
LANDSCAPES	*KY*	Kentucky	67	3/10
	OH	Ohio	198	6/8
	BD	Bermuda	17	2/3
CLOSE-UPS	*WF*	Wildflowers	137	1/7
	PT	Patterns	84	2/10
	IS	Insects	113	7/10
WILDLIFE	*NAW*	North American wildlife	13	2/10
	AW	African wildlife	122	4/9
	ZO	Zoos	200	6/10
CITIES	*NY*	New York	35	3/8
	DT	Detroit	22	4/5
	WDC	Washington, DC	120	7/10

*The page number helps me locate the correct slide page within a certain category. All duplicates of a picture share that number and go in the same slide page.

**The copy number tells me how many duplicates I have of one image. Each receives a unique number followed by a slash and the total number of duplicates: 1/10, 7/12, 4/15, etc.

years down the road or, more important, when selling your work. Your description might say something like "United States Capitol in Evening Light, Washington, DC" or "Female Cheetah with Young Cubs in the Masai Mara, Kenya."

Typically I don't put dates on labels. I have heard that some editors will nix an image because a 1991 lion is not as good as a 2002 lion. If you don't have aspirations of selling your work and want dates on your images for the sake of memories, then by all means put them on. (Alternatively, you can put dates on the slide sheet, which only you will see.) The last line on your label should be your name with a copyright symbol. Every image you shoot is copyrighted the moment you take it, and I recommend you include this copyright notice to remind buyers you own the work.

A completed label will look something like this:

> NAW-73-2/10 *(North American Wildlife, slide page number 73, the second image of ten)*
> Elk Crossing River in Early Morning Light
> Yellowstone National Park, Wyoming
> © William Manning

STORING IMAGES

Image storage is important and very easy. Most photographers find storing color transparencies in a hanging slide page to be the easiest and most convenient storage system. A slide page is an eight and a half by eleven archival plastic page, which holds twenty images per page. A plastic or metal rod can be slid into the top of the page and hung in a filing cabinet. In the first year or two a two-drawer filing cabinet will suffice but as your image library increases so will the number of cabinets you need. I use the 32" lateral files and if you have the space and feel confident you'll be adding a lot of images over the next several years you might consider one of these cabinets. There are several vendors who supply pages and hangers and all are pretty good. I use both Pro-Line [(800) 677-3686; <www.filmguard.com> and Franklin Distributors at [(888) 249-4870; <www.franklindistribcorp.com>.

TAKING YOUR PICS TO MARKET

Making a living in photography takes years of shooting and a large library of images, but you must also be familiar with a commercial audience's preferences. Even if your first sale is years away, following these guidelines will enhance your work's marketability when the time comes.

Photo editors have specific needs. Regardless of how beautiful, how colorful or how well executed an image is, if the subject doesn't meet the editor's needs, you don't have a sale. I can't stress enough how important it is to submit only images that fit the guidelines outlined by the client. You're probably asking yourself, "How do I know what to shoot?' There is no easy answer to this question. As I have said elsewhere in this book, as long as an image is technically correct (focused, properly exposed and reasonably well composed), there is a market for it. From textbooks to advertisements, magazines to corporate brochures, outdoor photography can be sold for just about any purpose.

As you gain more experience, you will learn where your work fits in. I personally keep a vigilant eye on what is being published from one market to another and from client to client within that market. I then create for that niche and hope my work catches the eye of the editors. I select my travel and my subjects based on my past sales history, but, more important, on the most requested locations and subjects. How do you know what these are? Let's take the calendar market as an example. Every calendar publisher releases a want list during its submission period each year. Most of these publishers publish the same titles every year. Therefore, if you want to sell to these publishers, you travel and shoot the subjects on their want list. If you belong to a stock photography agency, ask what its most frequently requested subjects are. It takes time to learn what is needed and to obtain the images to meet these needs. Stock photography is a slow process, but once you get the ball rolling, it builds, and in time you will be able to fulfill the many needs.

When you do find the niche you want to fill, follow some simple rules. The following is true for the majority of clients, but there might be exceptions.

1. Photograph in the best light you can for the subjects you work.
2. Produce good, clean, appealing images.
3. The simpler the composition, the better.
4. Photograph most of your subjects during the friendly seasons (spring and summer) when appropriate as these appeal to a broad audience (autumn symbolizes the end of a life cycle, and winter is thought of as bitter and cold). There are exceptions to this rule.
5. The environment plays an important role in salable images. Deserts, for example, might be interpreted as a hostile environment; the ocean might be thought of as refreshing and peaceful; a lush green forest might be interpreted as tranquil and friendly.

PHOTOGRAPHIC PRINTS

Photographers with limited experience and a smaller library can still sell their work. Perhaps the easiest option is selling photographic prints. Try marketing your work at summer art fairs and community galleries willing to give you a chance. Community and entertainment papers often list these events in their arts calendars, or you can contact sponsoring local arts guilds or museum societies to get dates in advance. Many restaurants offer artists the opportunity to hang art work on their walls for sale. This is a wonderful outlet for exposure in a casual setting. Office buildings and offices will sometimes have open wall space they are willing to have regional artists display their work. Before you commit to such an agreement, you want to make sure there is good traffic flow in the area where your work will be displayed

One major consideration in marketing your prints is pricing. Regardless of how good we think our work is, customers who want prints buy photography because it reminds them of a vacation or complements their decor. The cold hard fact is that most people don't think of photography as art. A gallery owner once said to me, "People will spend two hundred dollars on a matte and frame, but they want something under twenty dollars to put in the middle of it." The secret to getting around this is to sell your images already matted and framed and mark these items up accordingly. Pricing your art work will require a little leg work. You will need to find out who is successful at selling their photographic prints in the same region you plan on selling. Keep in mind, just because photographers have their work displayed for sale doesn't mean they are selling, this is why I say find out who is successfully selling. Once you find this out, you should have some idea of what the market will bare as for pricing. You should also consider the quality of your work and the frames you chose with that of the other successful photographers selling prints. It is difficult for me to state specific prices because every region throughout the country is different. I live in Cincinnati, and I'm lucky if I can get twenty-five dollars for a print, but a good friend of mine in Baltimore successfully sells his unframed prints for $150.

Most people buy an image because it goes with their sofa or complements the color of their walls or drapes. When you're selecting photos to sell, pick colorful, versatile images—ones that could have been taken almost anywhere. Sentimental attachments generally limit your market. Your potential buyer may be reluctant to purchase a print of Venice if she has never been there, regardless of how beautiful the picture is.

I see beautiful photos displayed at art fairs and local galleries, but the print sizes are often large and require a large wall area to hang. Bigger isn't necessarily better. The bigger your image, the fewer your sales, in most cases. It took me a long time to figure this out, but most homes don't have huge wall space. People want artwork they can hang between two windows or in other confined spaces. I suggest displaying smaller prints ranging from 5" × 7" to 11" × 14", and let your potential buyers know you can make larger prints if they wish. Your profit margin is also greater with smaller print sizes. Consider the Epson printers, such as the Stylus 1280, to produce these images. You can print as large as 11" × 13" on this printer with archival papers. These prints are often better than those you'll get at a photo lab, at a fraction of the cost.

THE CALENDAR MARKET

Another good option for photographers just getting into the commercial market is calendar publishers. The best way to find them is to visit book and calendar stores toward the end of the year. Look over the available calendars and find a publisher(s) who produce a calendar containing the subject matter you can contribute to. Write down each publisher's phone number and address and write for submission guidelines. Time frames for submitting work vary widely between publishers, and many work several years in advance. This means it may take up to a year before you see your images again (remember the in-camera duplicates I spoke about), and it can be a couple years before you get paid if they select one of your images for a calendar. Most publishers are not committed to a particular photographer, their commitment is their calendar and finding new work every year to fit that calendar.

Publishing is highly competitive, so rejection is inevitable. Stay tough and continue submitting. Once you're established, you'll be invited to submit year after year. For additional tips on submitting work to the publishing market, check out books such as Jim Zuckerman's *The Professional Photographer's Guide to Shooting & Selling Nature & Wildlife Photos* and *John Shaw's Business of Nature Photography*.

I wish you the very best of luck in your travels and growth in your photography. Photography is a pursuit that compels you to chase that one special moment. My hope is that your moment comes many miles down the road. This is, after all, what keeps that creative fire burning and the pleasure and joy in exploring.

reference calendar*

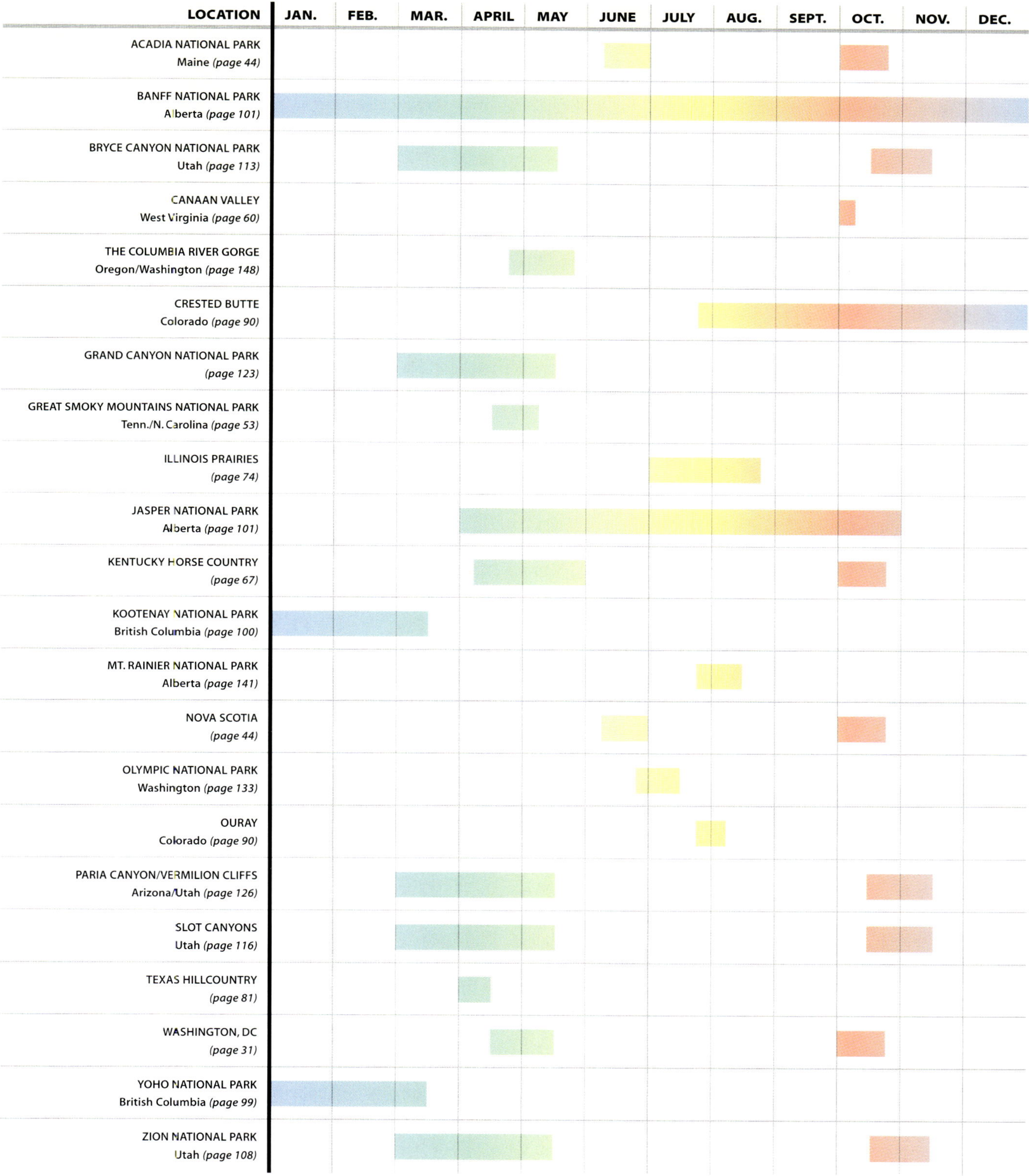

*This calendar illustrates the *ideal* time to be on location. For details on when to go, see the page listed after each destination.

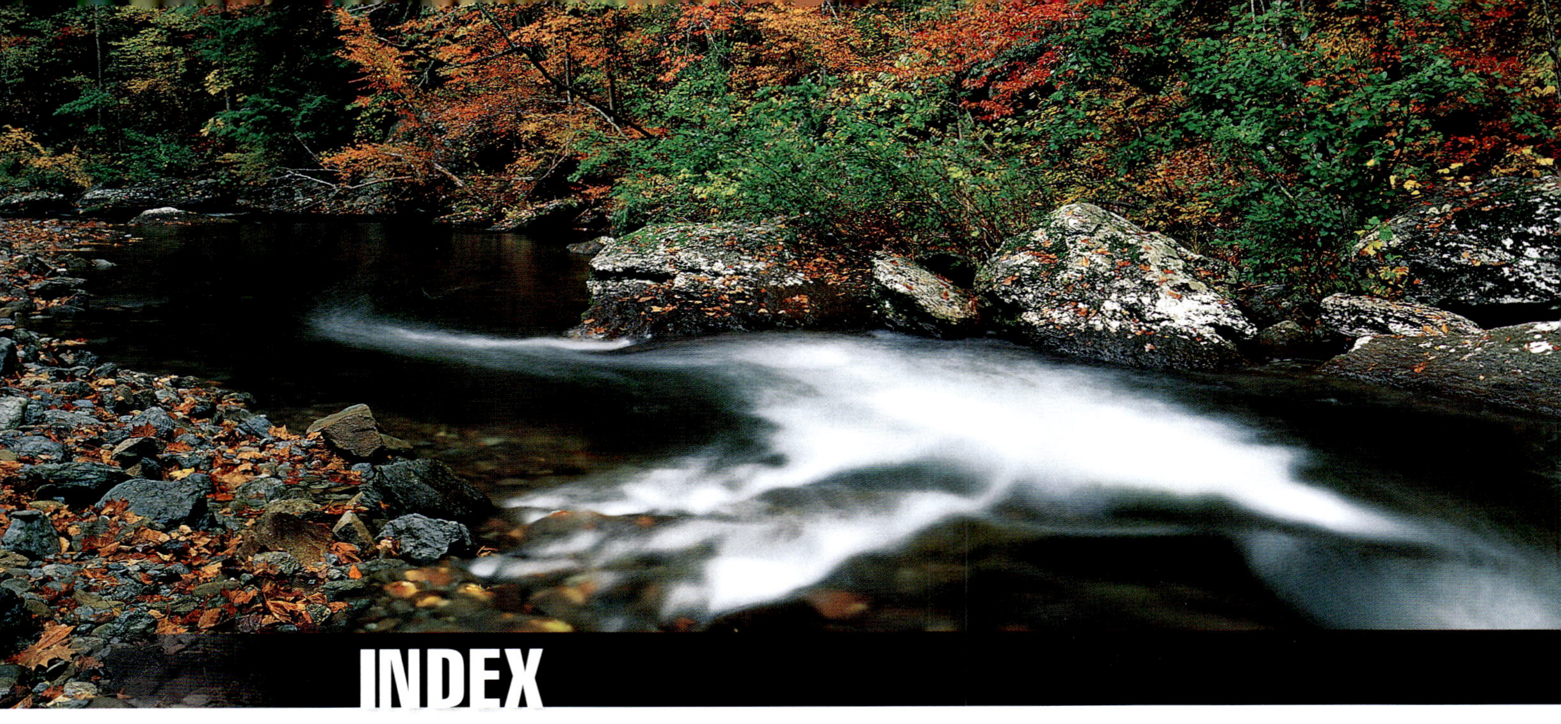

INDEX

A

AAA, 15, 16, 30, 103
Acadia National Park, 34-41, 44-45
  Acadia Revealed, 45
  Cadillac Mountain, 40-41
  coast, 38
  development, 34-36
  getting from Acadia to Nova Scotia, 41
  interior, 39-41
  lighthouses on the Maine coast, 43-44
  Mt. Desert Island, 36, 38, 39
  Web sites, 41
Accessories. *See* Equipment
Airline tickets, 16
Alberta. *See* Banff National Park and Jasper National Park
Antelope Valley California Poppy Reserve, 82
Anza-Borrego Desert State Park, 82
Arches National Park, 118
Arizonacanyon country, 119-128.
  Lake Powell, 127
  See also Coyote Buttes; Grand Canyon; Slot canyons
Assateague/Chincoteague islands, 68

B

Banff National Park, 92, 94-97, 102, 103
  Icefields Parkway, 93, 94, 95-96
  Lake Louise, 94, 102
  Moraine Lake, 94, 102
  Peyto Lake, 93, 94-95
  Vermilion Lakes, 95
  wildlife, 93
Big Sur, 44
British Columbia. *See* Kootenay National Park and Yoho National Park
Bryce Canyon National Park, 109-113, 117, 118
  Inspiration Point, 1110, 111-112
  light, 110, 111
  lodging, 113
  overlooks, 110-111
  Queens Garden Trail, 113
  Sunrise Point, 110, 111
Web sites, 113
Build Your Own Home Darkroom, 151

C

Camera gear. *See* Equipment
Canaan Valley, W.V., 55-61
  autumn color, 56, 58, 59, 60
  Blackwater Falls State Park, 55, 58, 59
  Canaan Valley State Park, 57, 59
  Cheat River, 59
  Dolly Sods Wilderness Area, 55, 56, 58-9
  lodging, 61
  Monongahela National Forest, 55, 56, 59, 60
Canadian Rockies, 92-103. *See also* Banff; Jasper; Kootenay; and Yoho
  Calgary, 97, 103
  Canadian Rockies Access Guide, 96
Canyonlands National Park, 128
Charleston, S.C., 33
Colorado. *See* Rocky Mountain National Park; San Juan Mountains
Colorado National Monument, 128
Columbia River Gorge, 143-149
  Crown Point State Park, 147
  Eagle Creek, 146
  Japanese Garden, 147
  Multnomah Falls, 146-147
  Ponytail Falls, 146
  Rhododendron Garden of Portland, 147, 148
  Silver Falls State Park, 146, 147, 148, 149
  Wahclella Falls, 144, 146
  A Waterfall Lover's Guide to the Pacific Northwest, 148
Coyote Buttes, 117-118, 123-128
  merges, 124
  the Wave, 123, 124, 125, 126
  Web site, 124
Creative considerations, 21-25
Crested Butte, Colo. *See* San Juan Mountains

D

Dead Horse Point State Park, 128
Death Valley National Park, 118
DeLorme Atlas and Gazetteer, 15, 44, 60, 64, 68, 75, 79, 80
Devil's Garden, 118

E

Eagle Creek, 16
Editing photos, 151
  Build Your Own Home Darkroom, 151
Equipment, 16-21
  accessories, 18
  camera manufacturers, 18
  diffusers, 21
  lenses, tilt/shift, 28

macro setup,18, 19
polarizers, 20
Really Right Stuff, 19
specialty filters, 20-21
telephoto lenses, 20
traveling with, 19
warming filters, 20
wide-angle lenses, 19
See also equipment under individual locations
Explore and exploit, 23-25, 121
shown, 22, 23, 24, 25

F

Film
storing, 19
X-ray machines and, 19
Flint Hills Drive, Manhattan, Kans., 74

G

Glacier National Park, 103
Grand Canyon National Park, 119-123, 128
haze, 121, 123
North Rim, 120, 122
South Rim, 120, 121-122
transportation, 121-122
Web sites, 122
West Rim, 120, 122-123
Grand Teton National Park, 103
Great Smoky Mountains National Park, 13, 46-54, 149
autumn color, 48, 53, 54
Cades Cove, 47, 52-53, 54
forests, 47,·48, 50, 53
Gatlinburg, 48, 49, 50, 54
mountain ridges, 50
North Carolina Waterfalls, 52
Pigeon Forge, 52, 54
snow, 49-50, 53
streams and waterfalls, 49, 50-51
Web site, 54
wildflowers, 49
Green Mountains, Vt., 54

H

Horses
Assateague/Chincoteague islands, 68
Baltimore County horse country, 68
Kentucky horse country, 62-68

I

Illinois prairies, 69-75
butterfly photography, 72, 73, 74
coneflowers, 70
flower groupings, 71
goldenrod, 71, 72
Goose Lake Prairie Nature Preserve, 72
Indian Boundary Prairies, 72-74
Iroquois County Conservation Area, 71
prairie blazing star, 71, 72
rattlesnake master, 71
Tallgrass Prairie, 70
Web sites, 74
Internet, online photography and travel discussion groups, 14

J

Japanese Garden, 147
Jasper National Park, 92, 93, 97-99, 103
Columbia Icefield, 97-98
Horseshoe Lake, 99
Icefields Parkway, 97
Jasper Visitor Centre, 99
Lake Annette, 99
Lake Edith, 99
Patricia Lake, 99
Pyramid Lake, 99
Tangle Creek Falls, 98

K

Kancamagus Scenic Highway, 61
Kentucky horse country, 62-68
back roads, 64-65
Bluegrass Country Driving Tour, 64
equipment, 64
Insider's Guide to Greater Lexington and the Bluegrass, 63
Kentucky Horse Park, 65, 66, 68
legalities of photographing horses, 63-64, 64-65
racetracks, 63, 65-67
Web sites, 65, 66, 68
Konza Prairie, Manhattan, Kans., 74
Kootenay National Park, 92, 100-101, 102
Kootenay Visitor Centre, 101
snowshoes, 100, 102
winter photography, 100-101

L

Labeling slides, 152-153. *See also* Organizing; Storing
Landscape photography, 21
Lenses. *See* Equipment
Lodging. *See* lodging under individual locations

M

Magnification with 80-200mm zoom, shown, 21
Maine coast. *See* Acadia National Park
Marketing photos, 154
calendar market, 155-156
photographic prints, 155
pricing your work, 155
Michigan's Upper Peninsula, 61
Mountains
Canaan Valley, W.V., 55-61
Canadian Rockies, 92-103
Great Smoky Mountains National Park, 46-54
Mt. Hood, 142, 147
Mt. Rainier National Park, 136-142
Olympic National Park, 129-135
Rocky Mountain National Park, 91
San Juan Mountains. 82-91
Mt. Hood, 142, 147
Mt. Rainier National Park, 136-142
lodging, 142
Mt. Rainier, 136, 137, 138, 139-140, 141
Narada Falls, 140
Paradise, 138, 140, 142
Sunrise, 139, 140
Web sites, 142
wildflowers, 138-139
Mt. Shuksan, 142
Muir Woods, 135

N

Networking, 14-15, 80
Newsletters, 15
North Carolina. *See* Great Smoky Mountains National Park
Nova Scotia, 41-45
Blue Rocks, 41
Cape Breton Island, 42
Discover Nova Scotia, 43
getting from Acadia to Nova Scotia, 41
Indian Harbor, 41
lodging, 45
Peggy's Cove, 41, 42, 45
Web sites, 41
Yarmouth, 41, 45

O

Olympic National Park, 129-135
Hoh Rain Forest, 130, 131
Hurricane Ridge, 130, 131, 132, 135
Olympic: A Visitor's Companion, 132
Pacific coast, 131-132, 134
Sol Duc region, 130, 131
Web sites, 135
Oregon. *See* Columbia River Gorge; Oregon coast
Oregon coast, 44, 135
Organizing slides, 152-153. *See also* Labeling; Storing
Ouray, Colo. *See* San Juan Mountains

P

Packing lists, 17
Paria/Vermilion Cliffs Wilderness Area. *See* Coyote Buttes

Photo Traveler newsletter, 15
Photograph America Newsletter, 15
Prairie State Park, Mo., 74
Pricing your work, 155

R

Research, on-location, 15-16, 94, 138
Reservations
  airline, 16
  lodging, 16
  See also lodging under individual locations
Rhododendron Garden of Portland, 147, 148
Rocky Mountain National Park, 91

S

San Juan Mountains, Colo., 82-91
  American Basin, 89-90
  Crested Butte, 86-87, 89, 90-91
  equipment, 86
  4WD Adventures Colorado, 85
  Imogene Pass, 84, 88-89
  lodging, 91
  off-road driving, 84, 90
  Ouray, 85, 87
  Web site, 91
  Yankee Boy Basin, 86, 87-88, 89, 90, 91
Savannah, Ga., 33
Sequoia National Park, 135
Slot canyons, 113-117
  Antelope Canyon, 114-116
  entrance fees, 114, 116
  etiquette, 115
  Water Holes Canyon, 116
Storing slides, 153-154

T

Tallgrass Prairie, Okla., 74
Tennessee. *See* Great Smoky Mountains National Park
Texas hill country, 76-82
  depth of field, 80
  driving routes, 79-80
  equipment, 78
  Lady Bird Johnson Wildflower Center, 77
  Marble Falls, 78, 79-80, 81, 82
  Texas Wildflower Hotline, 77, 80
  Web sites, 77, 79, 81, 82
  wind, 78
Tour companies, information from, 13
Tour companies, photographic, 16
Traveling with equipment, 19
Trip planning, 12-17
  helpful Web sites, 15
  pre-trip, 13-16, 17
  tour companies, photographic,16
  See also Packing lists
Tucson, Ariz., flower blooms, 82
Utah's Color Country, 104-118
  itinerary, 117-118
  See also Bryce Canyon; Slot canyons; Zion

V

Visual references, 10, 12

W

The Wave. *See* Coyote Buttes
West Virginia. *See* Canaan Valley, W.V.
Washington State. *See* Mt. Rainier National Park; Olympic National Park
Washington, DC
  Arlington National Cemetery, 27, 30-31
  cherry blossoms, 31-32
  equipment, 28
  Marine Corp Memorial, 27, 30-31
  photographing around people, 27, 29
  Tidal Basin, 27, 28-29
  tripods, legal use of, 29, 30
  U.S. Capitol, 27
  Web sites, 33
  White House, 30
Waterfalls
  Columbia River Gorge, 144-148
  Grand Canyon National Park, 123
  Great Smoky Mountains National Park, 50-51, 149
  Jasper National Park, 98
  Mt. Rainier, 140
  Olympic, 131, 133
  San Juan Mountains, Colo., 88, 89
Wildflower hotlines, 15, 77, 80
Wildflowers, 15
  Great Smoky Mountains National Park, 49
  Illinois prairies, 69-75
  Mt. Rainier National Park, 138-139
  Nova Scotia, 42, 44
  San Juan Mountains, Colorado, 83-91
  Texas hill country, 76-82
  Zion National Park, 108

X

X-ray machines, 19

Y

Yoho National Park, 92, 95, 99-100
  Emerald Lake, 96, 99-100
  Lake O'Hara, 100, 102
  snow, 99
  Yoho Visitor Centre, 100

Z

Zion National Park, 104, 105-109
  Checkerboard Mesa, 105, 107
  desert paintbrush, 108
  Kolob Canyons, 107-108
  Virgin River, 105
  Web sites, 109
  Zion Canyon, 105, 106-107
  Zion Lodge, 109